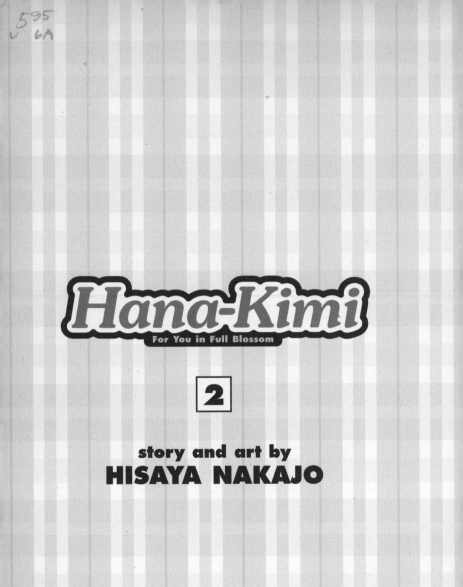

Hana-Kimi

For You in Full Blossom

2

story and art by
HISAYA NAKAJO

HANA-KIMI
For You In Full Blossom
VOLUME 2

STORY & ART BY HISAYA NAKAJO

Translation/David Ury
English Adaptation/Gerard Jones
Touch-Up Art & Lettering/Gabe Crate
Design/Izumi Evers & Judi Roubideaux
Senior Editor/Jason Thompson

Managing Editor/Annette Roman
Editor in Chief/Bill Flanagan
Production Manager/Noboru Watanabe
Sr. Director of Licensing and Acquisitions/Rika Inouye
VP of Marketing/Liza Coppola
Sr. VP of Editorial/Hyoe Narita
Publisher/Seiji Horibuchi

Printed in Canada

Published by VIZ, LLC, P.O. Box 77010, San Francisco, CA 94107

Shôjo Edition
10 9 8 7 6 5 4 3 2 1

First printing, May 2004

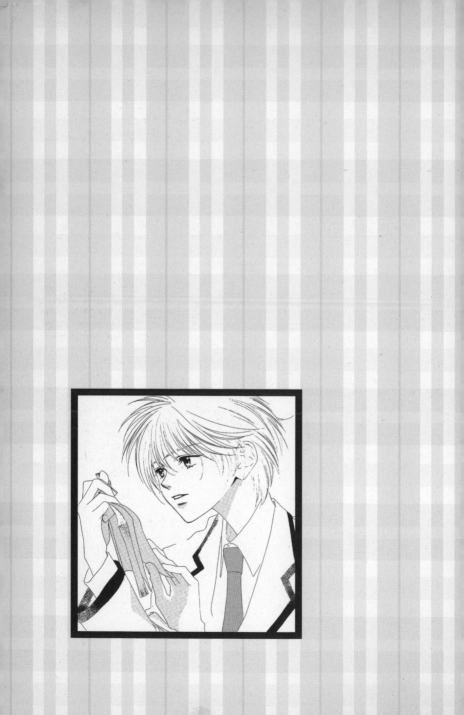

CONTENTS

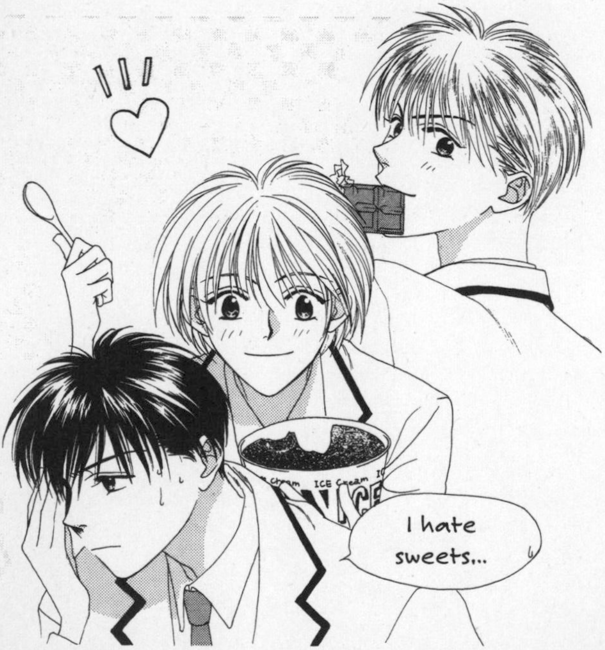
ICE Cream ICE Cream
I hate sweets...

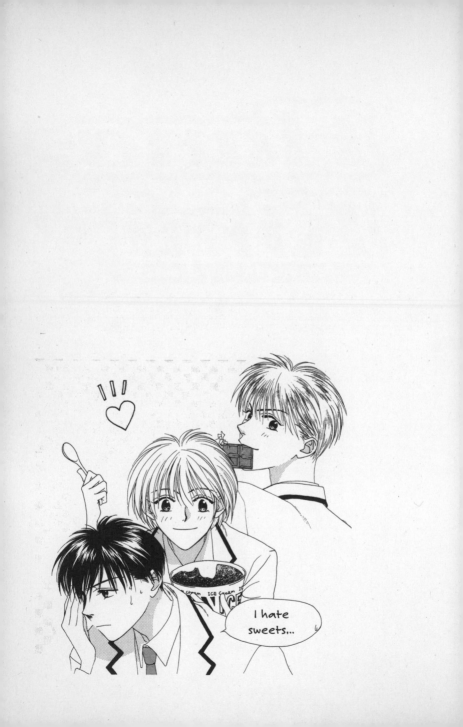

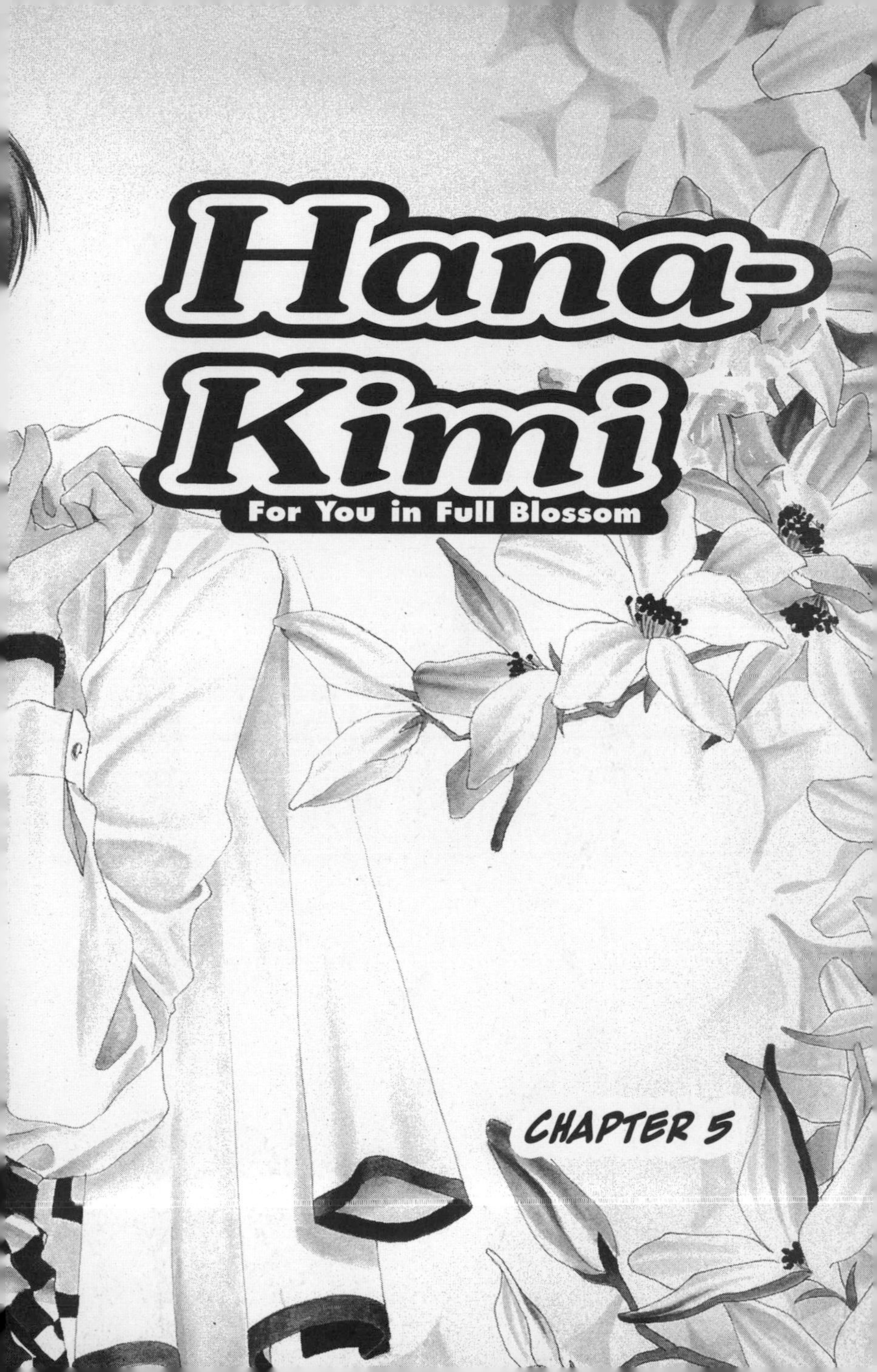
Hana-Kimi
For You in Full Blossom
CHAPTER 5

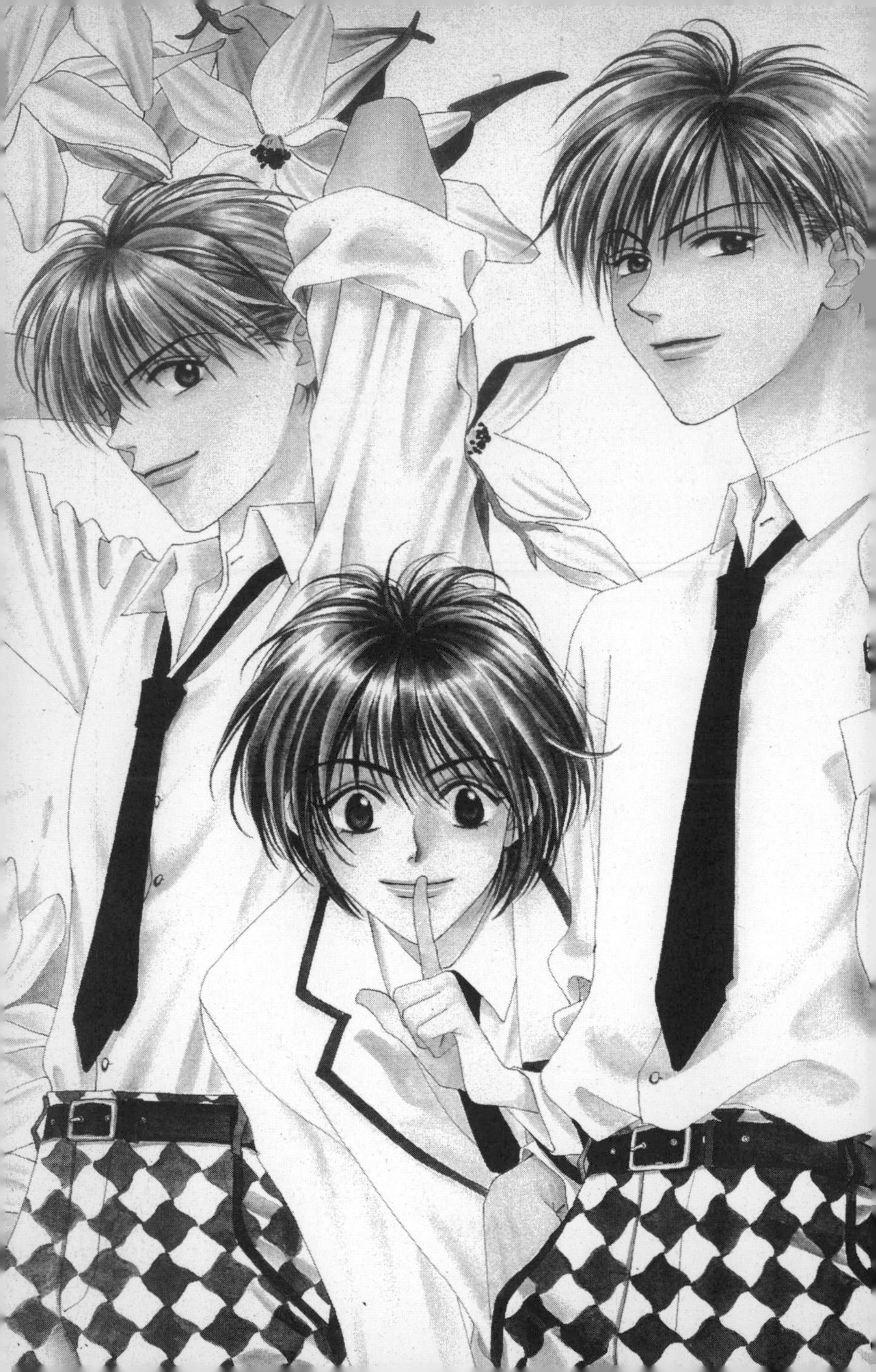

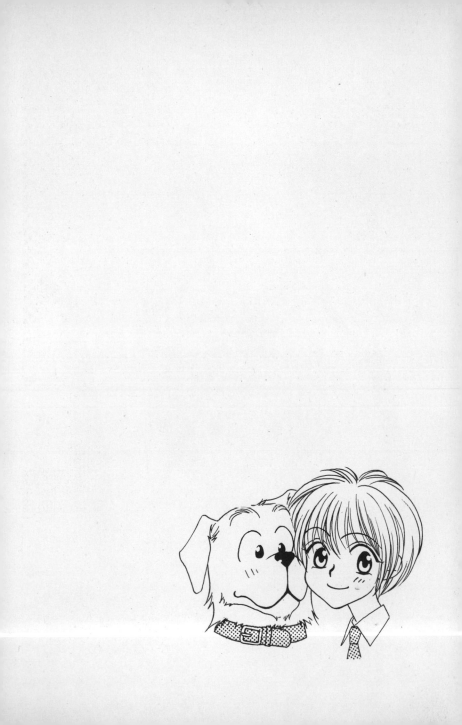

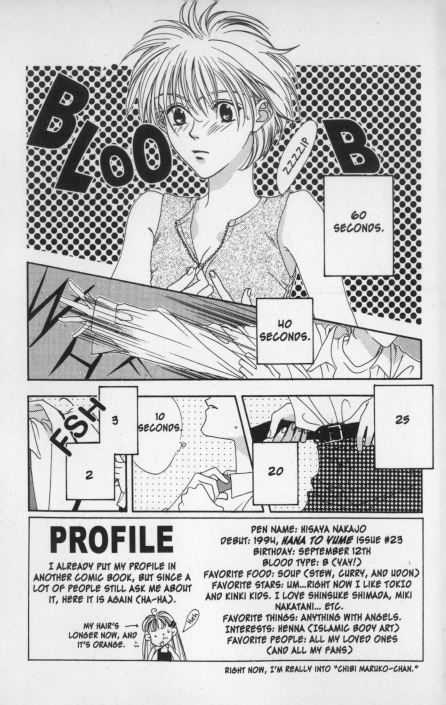

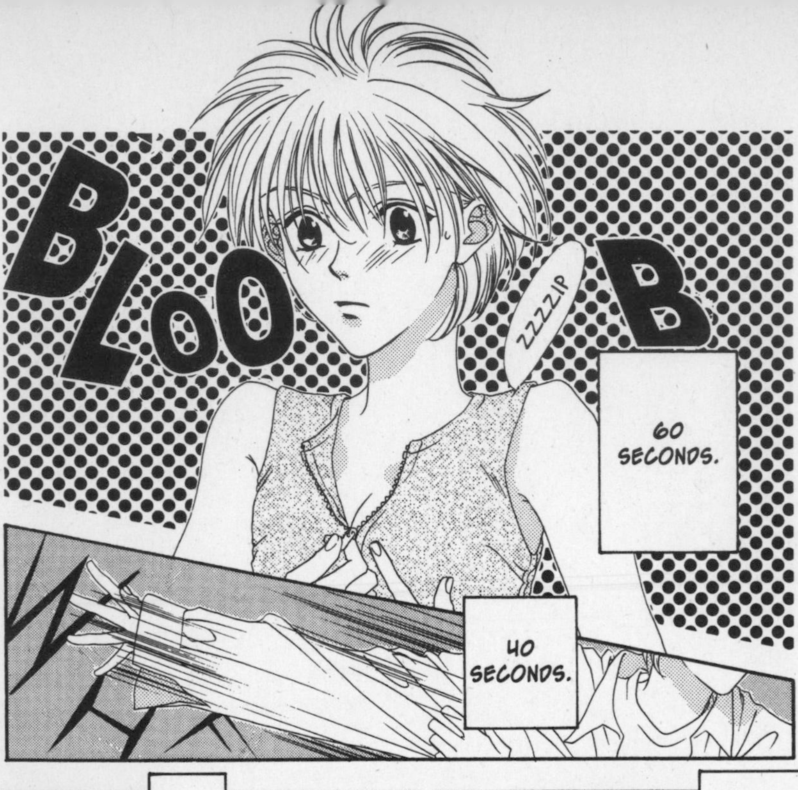
BLOOOB
ZZZZZIP
60 SECONDS.
40 SECONDS.
25
20
10 SECONDS.
FSH
3
2

PROFILE

I ALREADY PUT MY PROFILE IN ANOTHER COMIC BOOK, BUT SINCE A LOT OF PEOPLE STILL ASK ME ABOUT IT, HERE IT IS AGAIN (HA-HA).

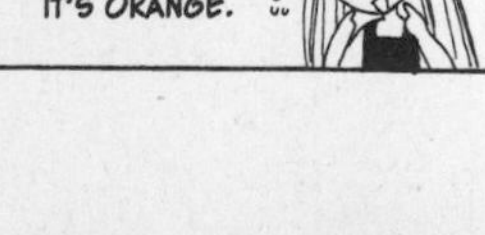
MY HAIR'S LONGER NOW, AND IT'S ORANGE.
Heh

PEN NAME: HISAYA NAKAJO
DEBUT: 1994, ***HANA TO YUME*** ISSUE #23
BIRTHDAY: SEPTEMBER 12TH
BLOOD TYPE: B (YAY!)
FAVORITE FOOD: SOUP (STEW, CURRY, AND UDON)
FAVORITE STARS: UM...RIGHT NOW I LIKE TOKIO AND KINKI KIDS. I LOVE SHINSUKE SHIMADA, MIKI NAKATANI... ETC.
FAVORITE THINGS: ANYTHING WITH ANGELS.
INTERESTS: HENNA (ISLAMIC BODY ART)
FAVORITE PEOPLE: ALL MY LOVED ONES (AND ALL MY FANS)

RIGHT NOW, I'M REALLY INTO "CHIBI MARUKO-CHAN."

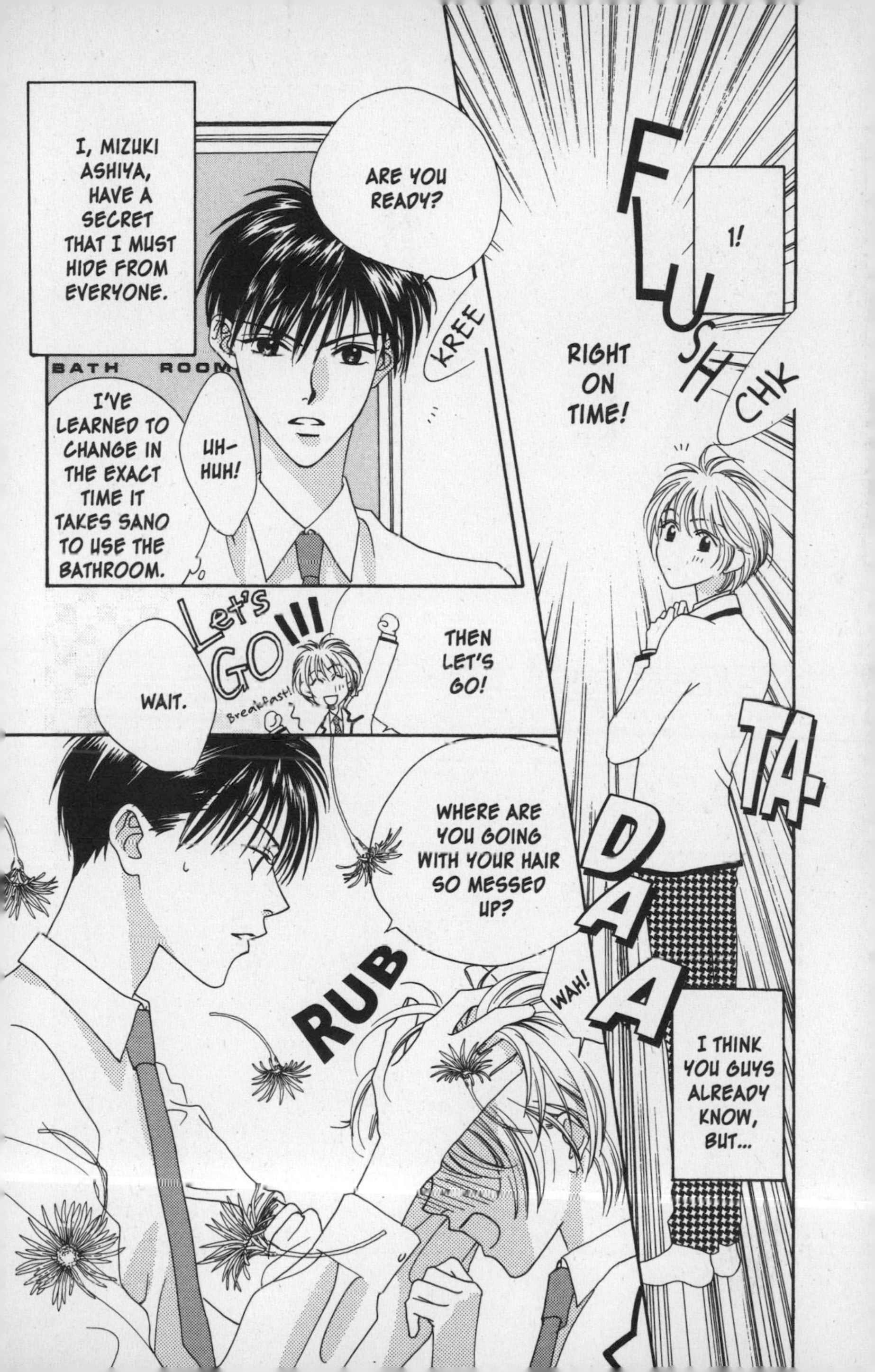
1!
FLUSH
CHK
RIGHT ON TIME!
TA-DAA
I THINK YOU GUYS ALREADY KNOW, BUT...
I, MIZUKI ASHIYA, HAVE A SECRET THAT I MUST HIDE FROM EVERYONE.
ARE YOU READY?
KREE
BATH ROOM
UH-HUH!
I'VE LEARNED TO CHANGE IN THE EXACT TIME IT TAKES SANO TO USE THE BATHROOM.
THEN LET'S GO!
Let's GO!!!
Breakfast!
WAIT.
WHERE ARE YOU GOING WITH YOUR HAIR SO MESSED UP?
WAH!
RUB

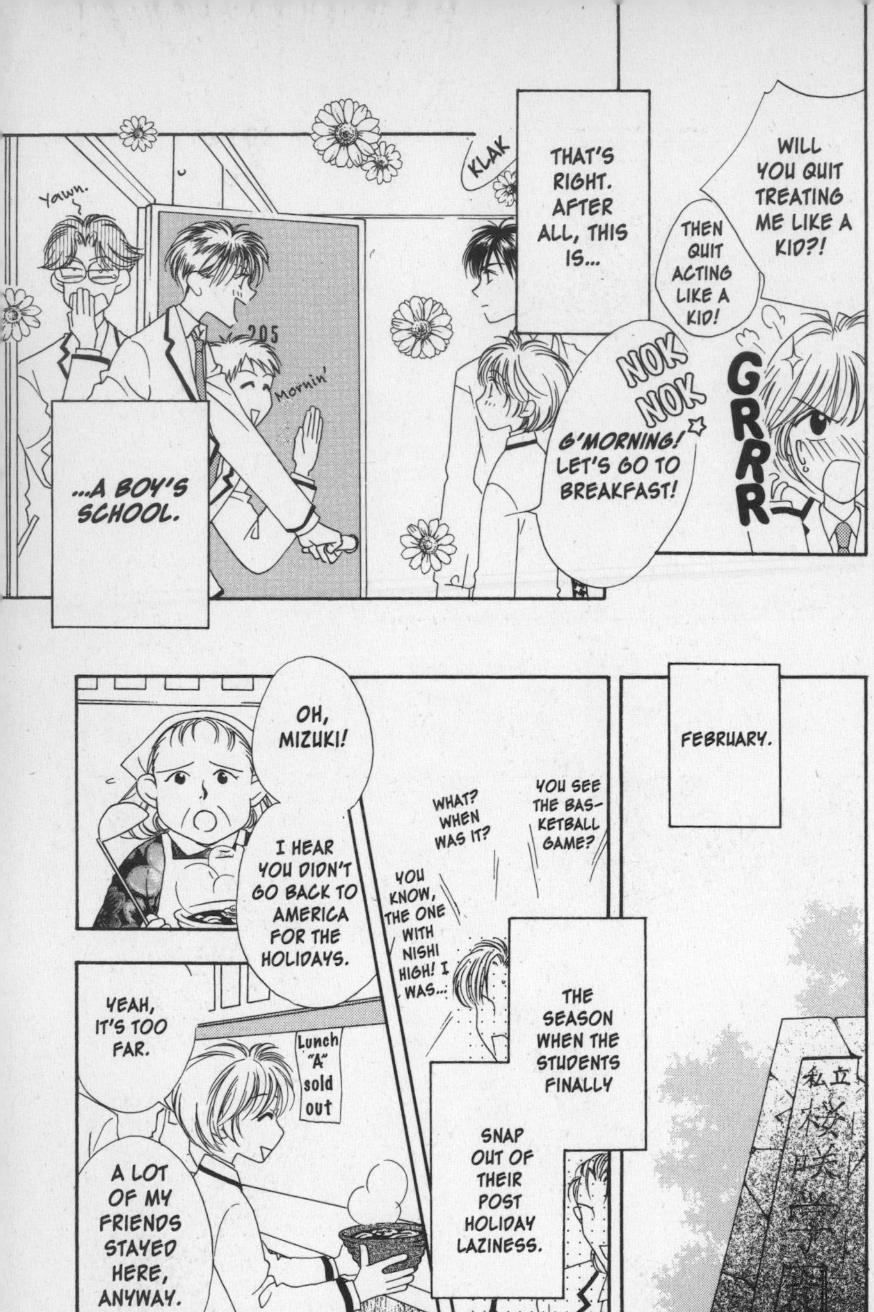
WILL YOU QUIT TREATING ME LIKE A KID?!
THEN QUIT ACTING LIKE A KID!
GRRR
KLAK
THAT'S RIGHT. AFTER ALL, THIS IS...
NOK NOK
G'MORNING! LET'S GO TO BREAKFAST!
Yawn.
205
Mornin'
...A BOY'S SCHOOL.
FEBRUARY.
私立
桜咲学園
THE SEASON WHEN THE STUDENTS FINALLY
SNAP OUT OF THEIR POST HOLIDAY LAZINESS.
YOU SEE THE BAS-KETBALL GAME?
WHAT? WHEN WAS IT?
YOU KNOW, THE ONE WITH NISHI HIGH! I WAS...
OH, MIZUKI!
I HEAR YOU DIDN'T GO BACK TO AMERICA FOR THE HOLIDAYS.
YEAH, IT'S TOO FAR.
Lunch "A" sold out
A LOT OF MY FRIENDS STAYED HERE, ANYWAY.

*Osaka High School

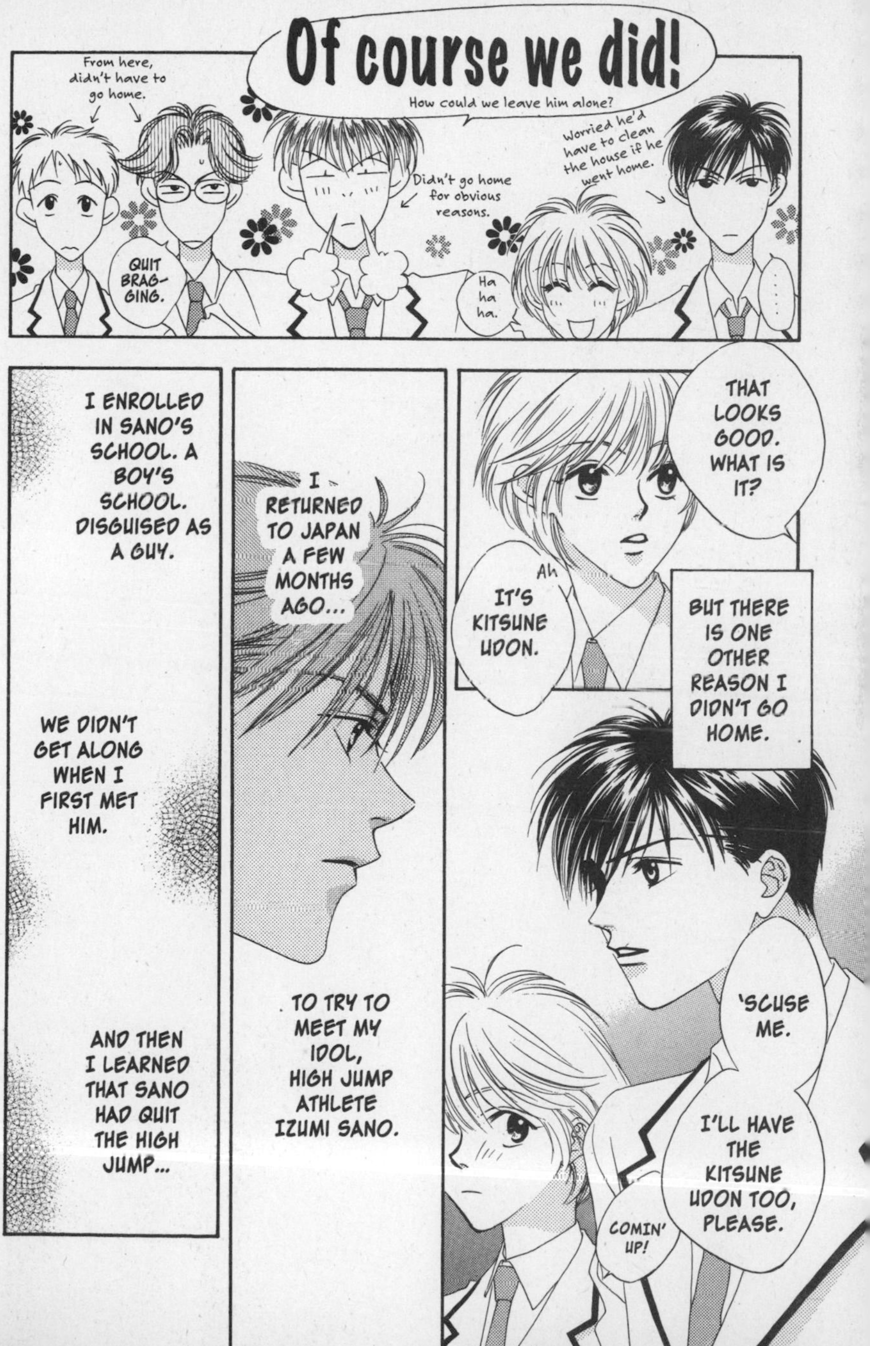
Of course we did!
How could we leave him alone?
Worried he'd have to clean the house if he went home.
......
Didn't go home for obvious reasons.
Ha ha ha.
From here, didn't have to go home.
QUIT BRAGGING.
THAT LOOKS GOOD. WHAT IS IT?
Ah
IT'S KITSUNE UDON.
BUT THERE IS ONE OTHER REASON I DIDN'T GO HOME.
'SCUSE ME.
I'LL HAVE THE KITSUNE UDON TOO, PLEASE.
COMIN' UP!
I RETURNED TO JAPAN A FEW MONTHS AGO...
TO TRY TO MEET MY IDOL, HIGH JUMP ATHLETE IZUMI SANO.
I ENROLLED IN SANO'S SCHOOL. A BOY'S SCHOOL. DISGUISED AS A GUY.
WE DIDN'T GET ALONG WHEN I FIRST MET HIM.
AND THEN I LEARNED THAT SANO HAD QUIT THE HIGH JUMP...

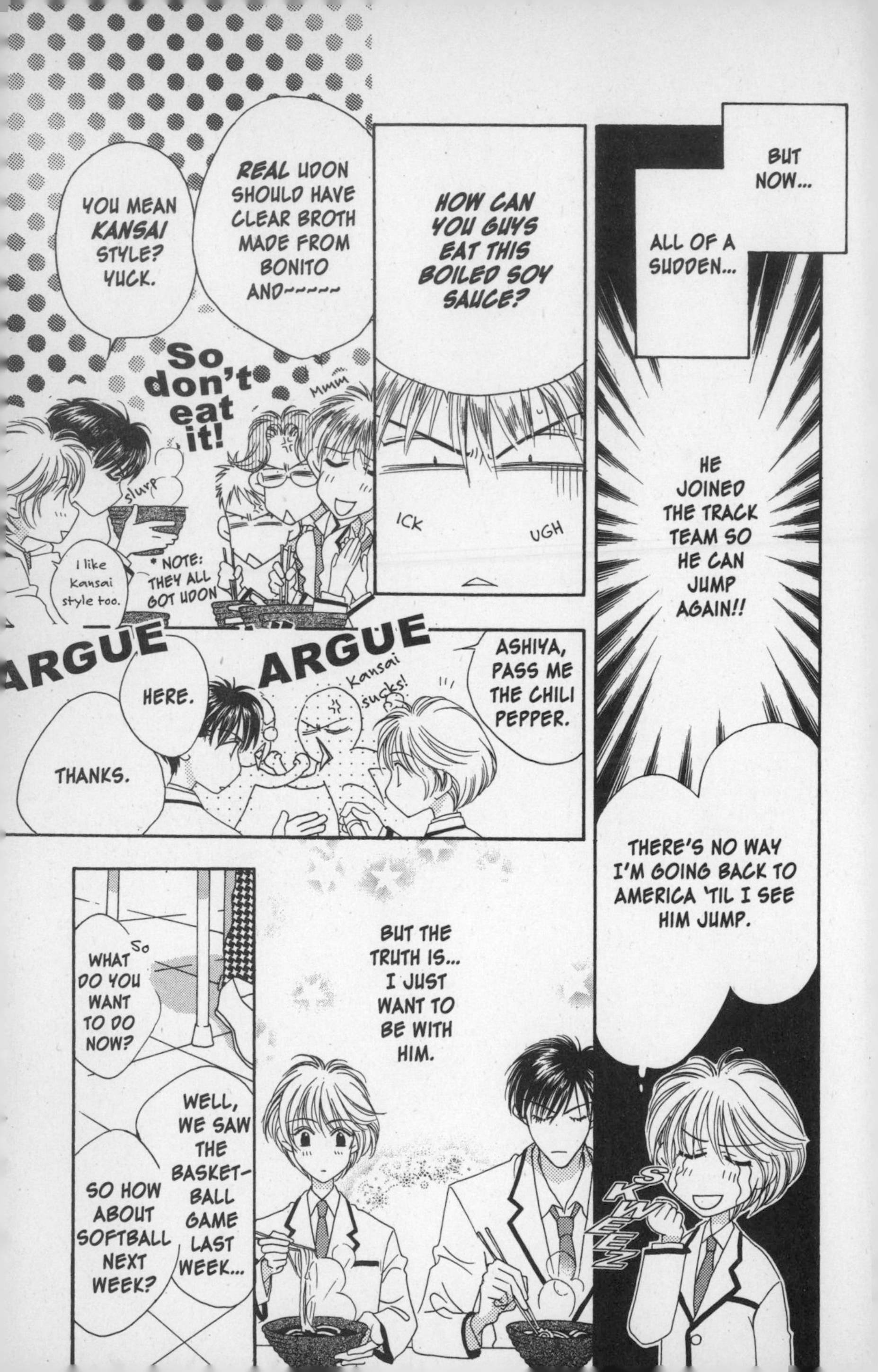
BUT NOW...
ALL OF A SUDDEN...
HE JOINED THE TRACK TEAM SO HE CAN JUMP AGAIN!!
THERE'S NO WAY I'M GOING BACK TO AMERICA 'TIL I SEE HIM JUMP.
SKWEEZ
HOW CAN YOU GUYS EAT THIS BOILED SOY SAUCE?
UGH
ICK
REAL UDON SHOULD HAVE CLEAR BROTH MADE FROM BONITO AND~~~~~
YOU MEAN KANSAI STYLE? YUCK.
Mmm
So don't eat it!
slurp
* NOTE: THEY ALL GOT UDON
I like Kansai style too.
ASHIYA, PASS ME THE CHILI PEPPER.
ARGUE
Kansai sucks!
ARGUE
HERE.
THANKS.
BUT THE TRUTH IS... I JUST WANT TO BE WITH HIM.
So WHAT DO YOU WANT TO DO NOW?
WELL, WE SAW THE BASKETBALL GAME LAST WEEK...
SO HOW ABOUT SOFTBALL NEXT WEEK?

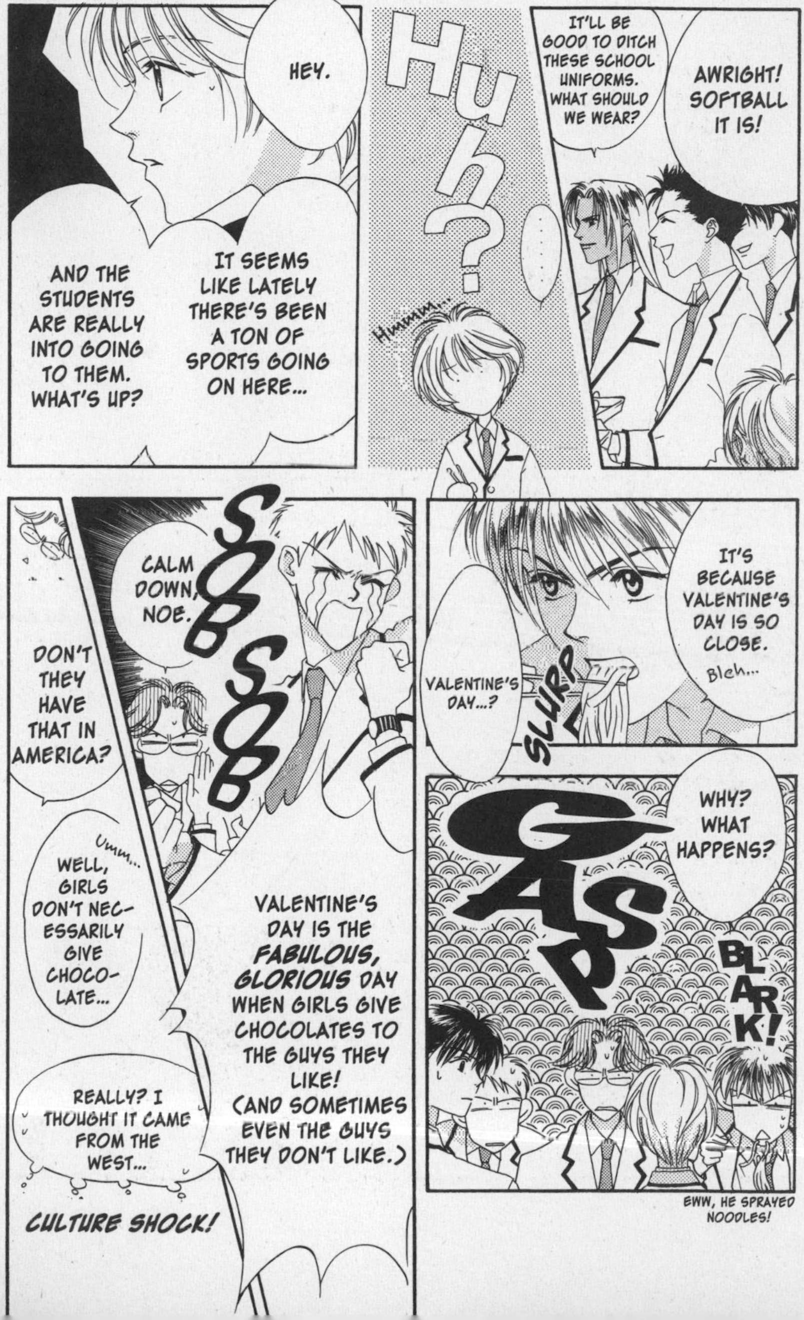
AWRIGHT! SOFTBALL IT IS!
IT'LL BE GOOD TO DITCH THESE SCHOOL UNIFORMS. WHAT SHOULD WE WEAR?
Huh?
...
Hmmm...
HEY.
IT SEEMS LIKE LATELY THERE'S BEEN A TON OF SPORTS GOING ON HERE...
AND THE STUDENTS ARE REALLY INTO GOING TO THEM. WHAT'S UP?
IT'S BECAUSE VALENTINE'S DAY IS SO CLOSE.
Blch...
SLURP
VALENTINE'S DAY...?
WHY? WHAT HAPPENS?
GASP
BLARK!
EWW, HE SPRAYED NOODLES!
SOB SOB
CALM DOWN, NOE.
DON'T THEY HAVE THAT IN AMERICA?
VALENTINE'S DAY IS THE FABULOUS, GLORIOUS DAY WHEN GIRLS GIVE CHOCOLATES TO THE GUYS THEY LIKE! (AND SOMETIMES EVEN THE GUYS THEY DON'T LIKE.)
Umm...
WELL, GIRLS DON'T NECESSARILY GIVE CHOCOLATE...
REALLY? I THOUGHT IT CAME FROM THE WEST...
CULTURE SHOCK!

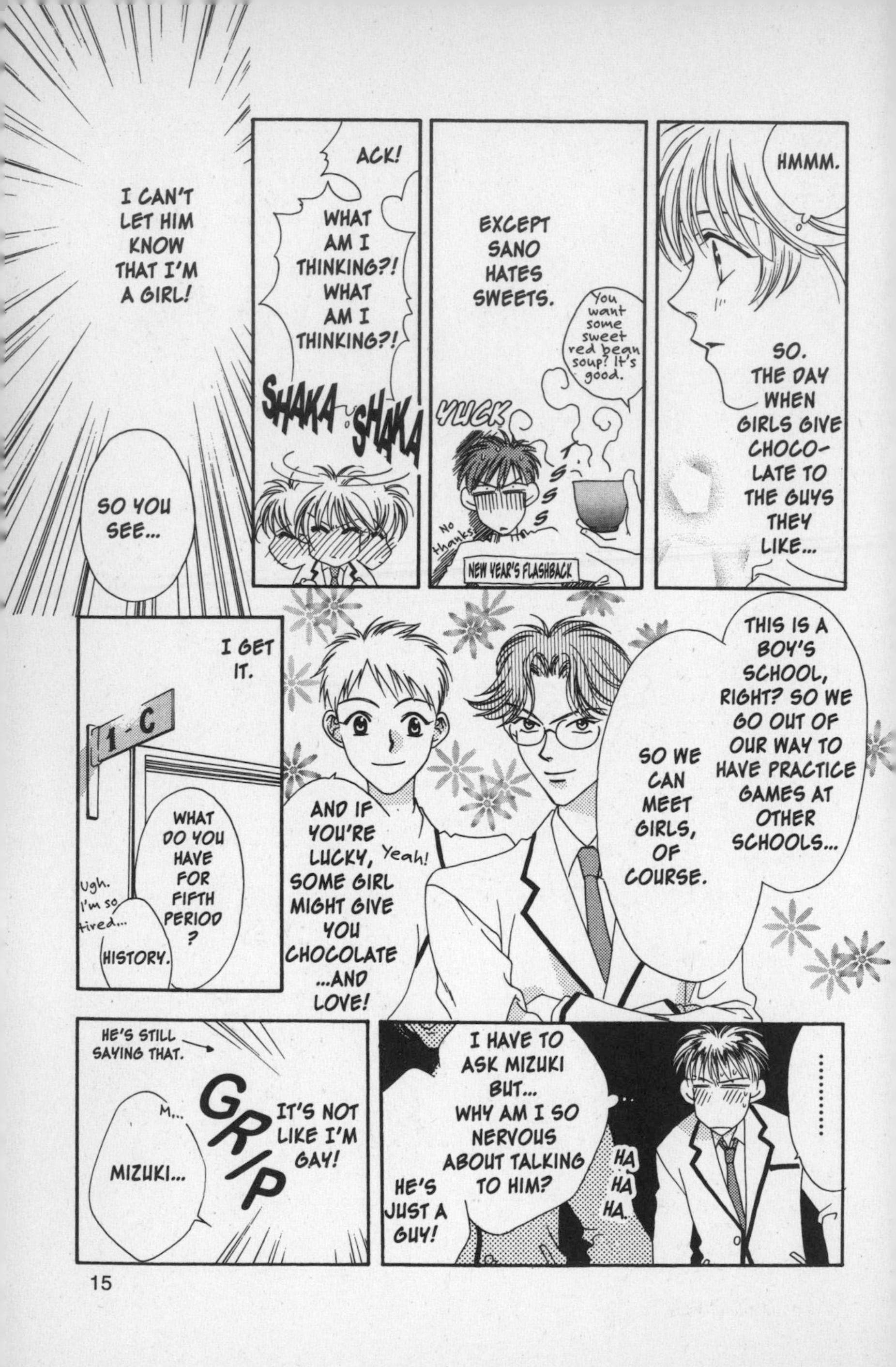
HMMM.
SO. THE DAY WHEN GIRLS GIVE CHOCOLATE TO THE GUYS THEY LIKE...
EXCEPT SANO HATES SWEETS.
You want some sweet red bean soup? It's good.
YUCK
TSSS
No thanks.
NEW YEAR'S FLASHBACK
ACK!
WHAT AM I THINKING?! WHAT AM I THINKING?!
SHAKA SHAKA
I CAN'T LET HIM KNOW THAT I'M A GIRL!
SO YOU SEE...
THIS IS A BOY'S SCHOOL, RIGHT? SO WE GO OUT OF OUR WAY TO HAVE PRACTICE GAMES AT OTHER SCHOOLS...
SO WE CAN MEET GIRLS, OF COURSE.
AND IF YOU'RE LUCKY, SOME GIRL MIGHT GIVE YOU CHOCOLATE ...AND LOVE!
Yeah!
I GET IT.
1-C
WHAT DO YOU HAVE FOR FIFTH PERIOD?
Ugh. I'm so tired...
HISTORY.
....
I HAVE TO ASK MIZUKI BUT... WHY AM I SO NERVOUS ABOUT TALKING TO HIM?
HA HA HA.
HE'S JUST A GUY!
HE'S STILL SAYING THAT.
IT'S NOT LIKE I'M GAY!
GRIP
M...
MIZUKI...

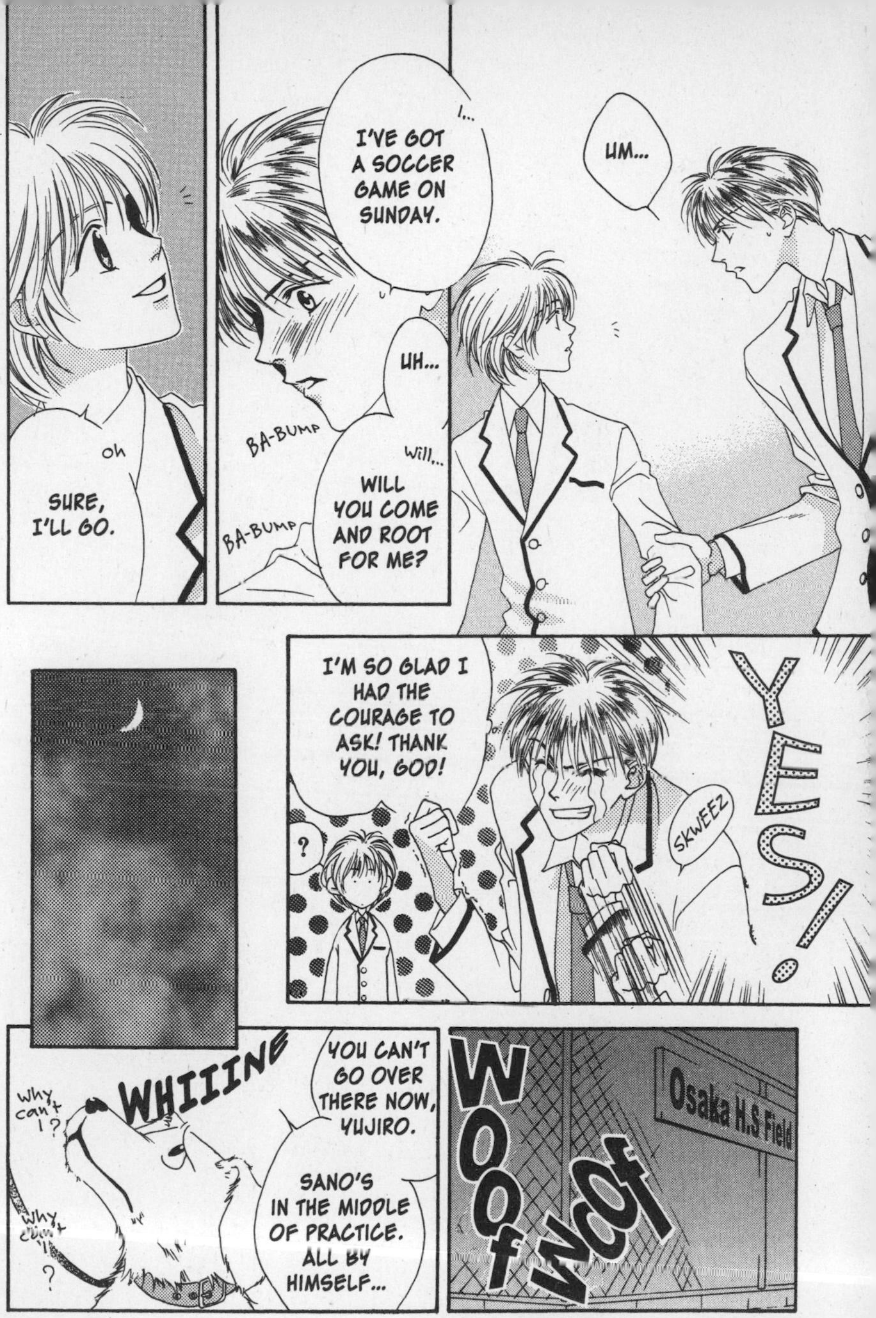
UM...
I...
I'VE GOT A SOCCER GAME ON SUNDAY.
UH...
BA-BUMP
WILL...
WILL YOU COME AND ROOT FOR ME?
BA-BUMP
oh
SURE, I'LL GO.
YES!
SKWEEZ
I'M SO GLAD I HAD THE COURAGE TO ASK! THANK YOU, GOD!
?
Osaka H.S Field
WOOf WOOf
YOU CAN'T GO OVER THERE NOW, YUJIRO.
WHIIINE
why can't I?
why can't I?
SANO'S IN THE MIDDLE OF PRACTICE. ALL BY HIMSELF...

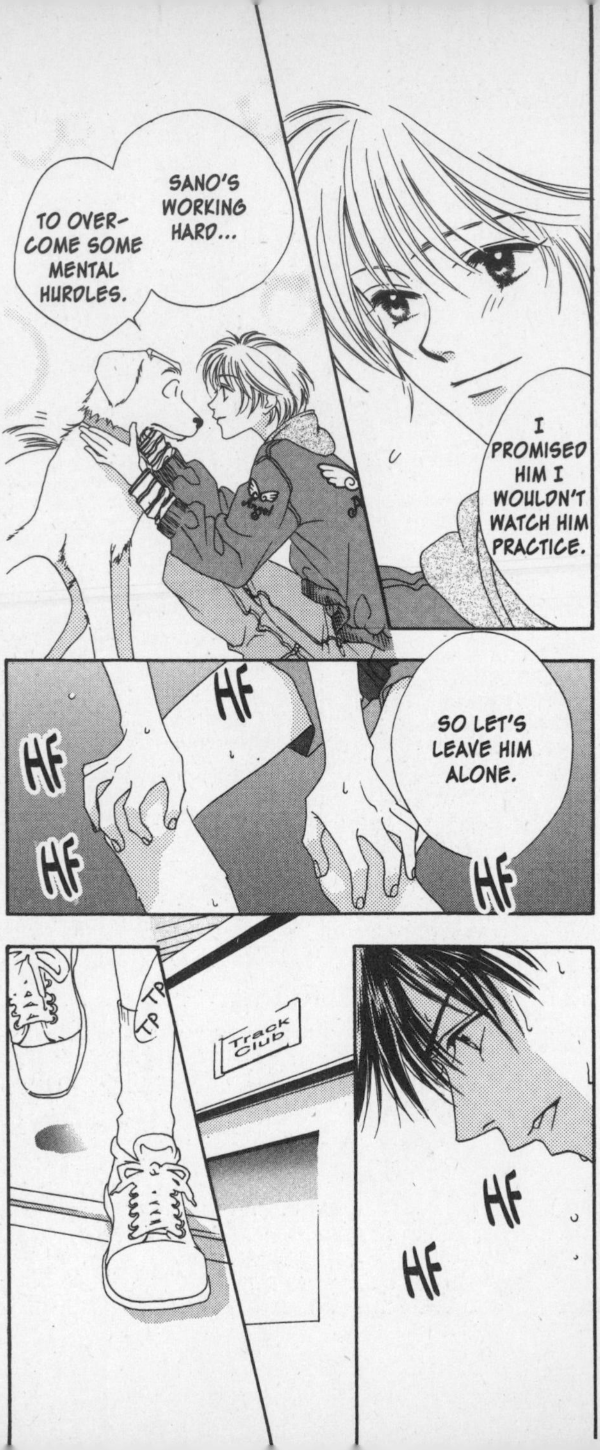
I PROMISED HIM I WOULDN'T WATCH HIM PRACTICE.
SANO'S WORKING HARD...
TO OVER-COME SOME MENTAL HURDLES.
HF
SO LET'S LEAVE HIM ALONE.
HF
HF
HF
HF
HF
TP TP
Track Club

Greetings!

WELCOME TO HANA-KIMI BOOK 2. YAY! A LOT OF PEOPLE HAVE SAID THEY CAN'T FIND BOOK 1 IN STORES. APPARENTLY, IT'S RARE! (HA HA!) INSTEAD OF TELLING ME ABOUT IT, YOU SHOULD TELL THE EDITORS AND BOOK STORES! THAT WOULD BE MORE EFFECTIVE. BUT I'M HAPPY TO HEAR THAT A LOT OF PEOPLE ARE BUYING IT. THANKS EVERYBODY! KEEP READING!!

My deadline's so close, I'm in tears!

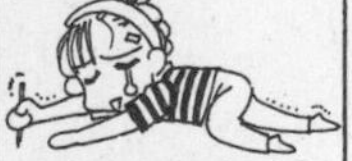

AAAUGH!

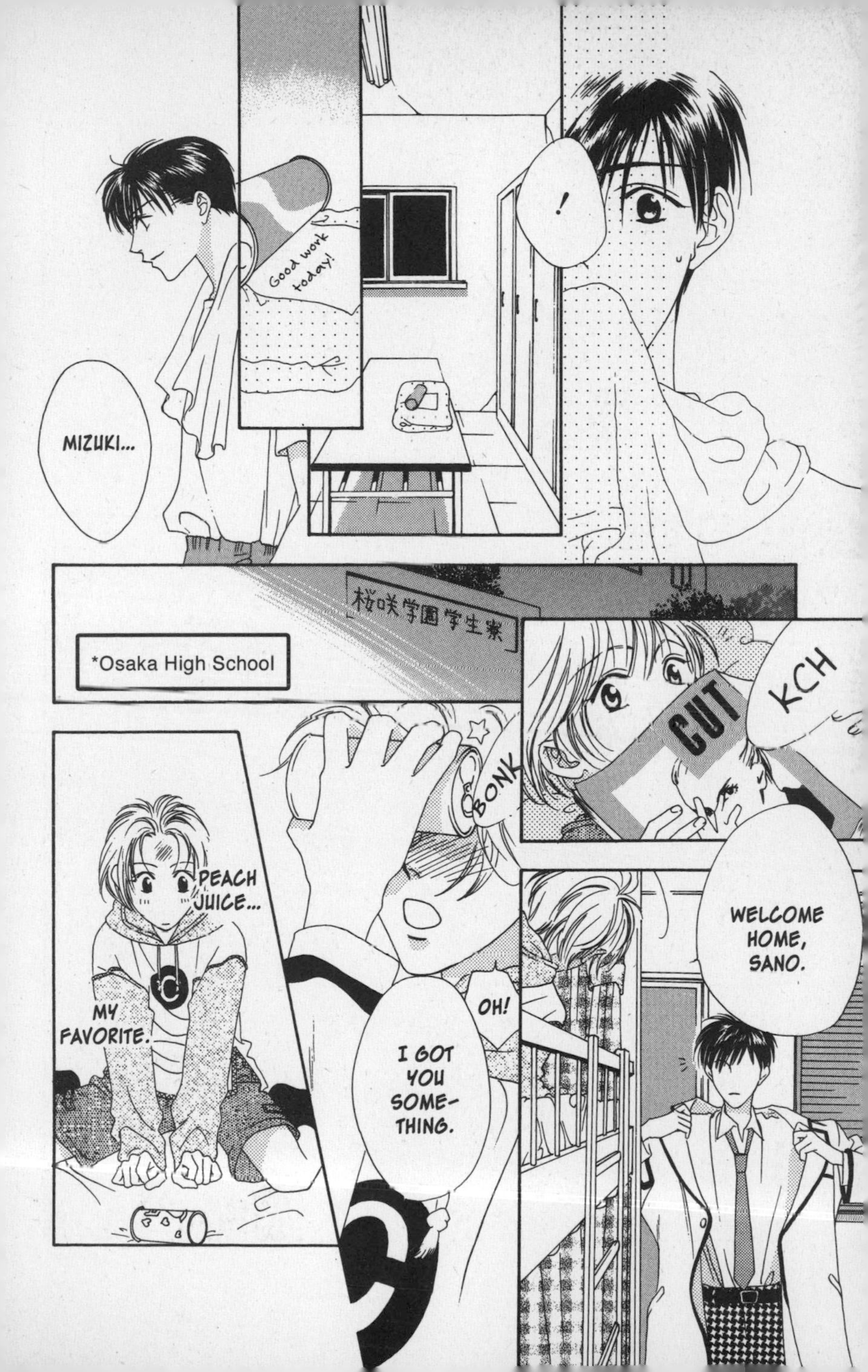
!
Good work today!
MIZUKI...
桜咲学園学生寮
*Osaka High School
KCH
CUT
WELCOME HOME, SANO.
BONK
OH!
I GOT YOU SOMETHING.
PEACH JUICE...
MY FAVORITE.

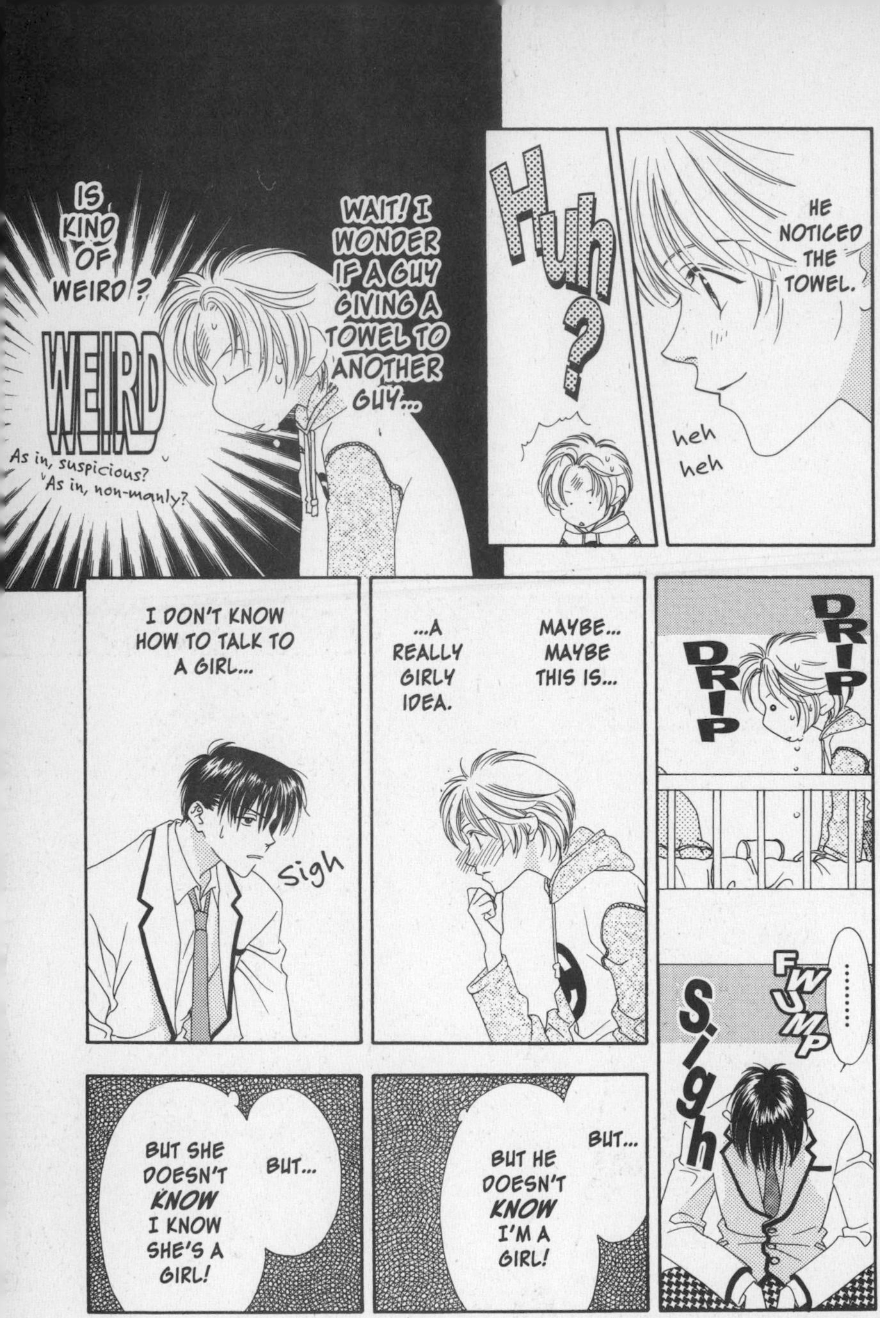
HE NOTICED THE TOWEL.
heh heh
Huh?
WAIT! I WONDER IF A GUY GIVING A TOWEL TO ANOTHER GUY...
IS KIND OF WEIRD?
WEIRD
As in, suspicious?
As in, non-manly?
DRIP DRIP
MAYBE... MAYBE THIS IS...
...A REALLY GIRLY IDEA.
I DON'T KNOW HOW TO TALK TO A GIRL...
Sigh
......
FWUMP
Sigh
BUT...
BUT HE DOESN'T KNOW I'M A GIRL!
BUT...
BUT SHE DOESN'T KNOW I KNOW SHE'S A GIRL!

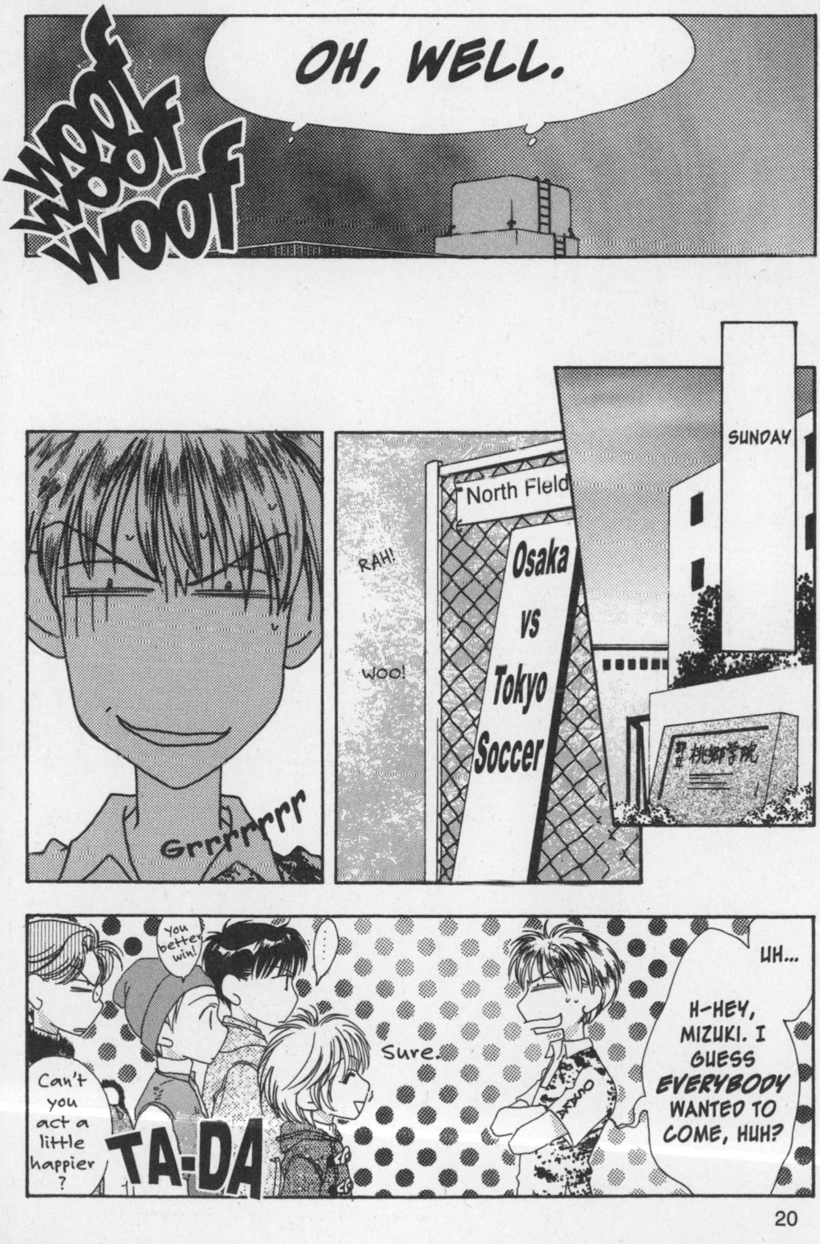
OH, WELL.
woof woof woof
SUNDAY
桃郷学院
North Fleld
Osaka vs Tokyo Soccer
RAH!
WOO!
Grrrrrrr
UH...
H-HEY, MIZUKI. I GUESS *EVERYBODY* WANTED TO COME, HUH?
Sure.
...
You better win!
Can't you act a little happier?
TA-DA

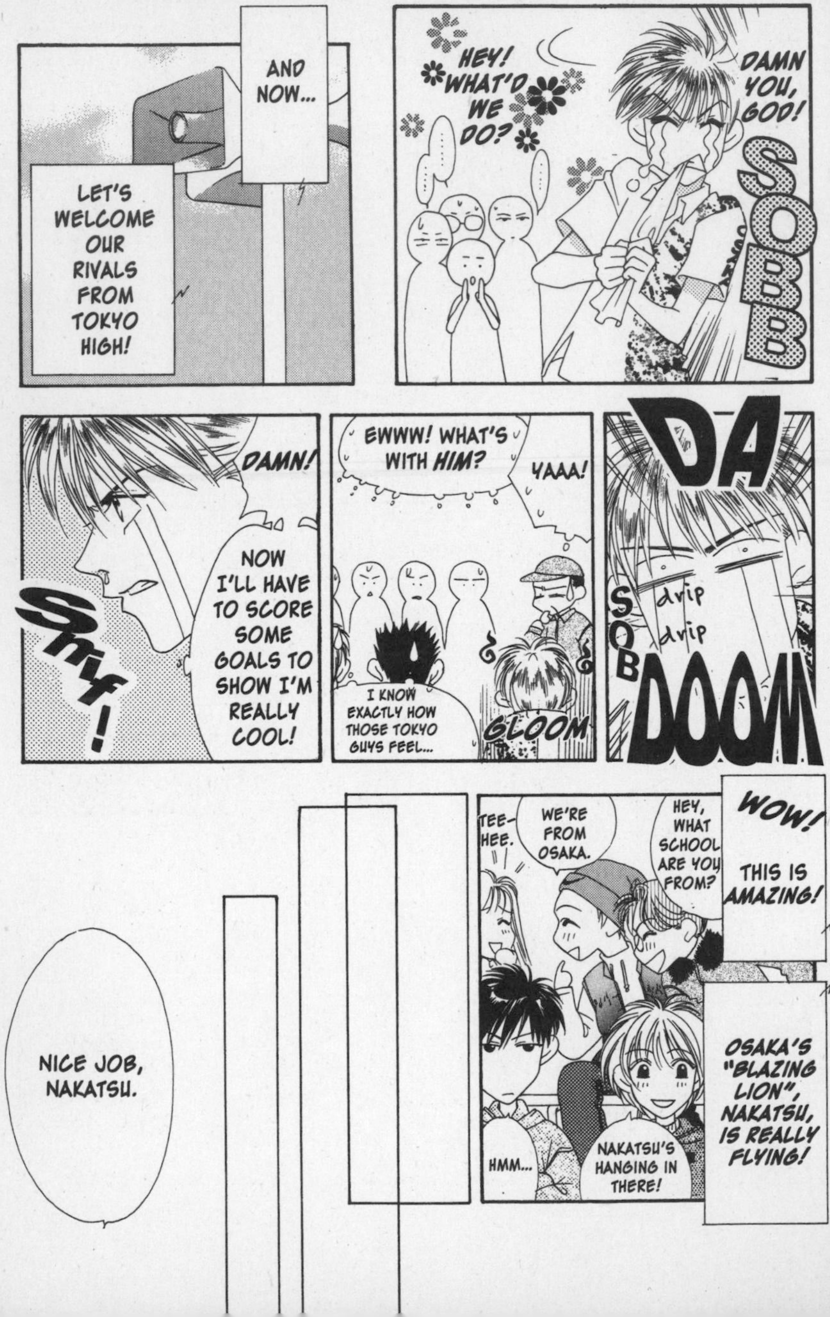
DAMN YOU, GOD!
SOBB
HEY! WHAT'D WE DO?
AND NOW...
LET'S WELCOME OUR RIVALS FROM TOKYO HIGH!
DA
SOB
drip drip
DOOM
EWWW! WHAT'S WITH HIM?
YAAA!
GLOOM
I KNOW EXACTLY HOW THOSE TOKYO GUYS FEEL...
DAMN!
NOW I'LL HAVE TO SCORE SOME GOALS TO SHOW I'M REALLY COOL!
SNIF!
WOW!
THIS IS AMAZING!
HEY, WHAT SCHOOL ARE YOU FROM?
WE'RE FROM OSAKA.
TEE-HEE.
OSAKA'S "BLAZING LION", NAKATSU, IS REALLY FLYING!
NAKATSU'S HANGING IN THERE!
HMM...
NICE JOB, NAKATSU.

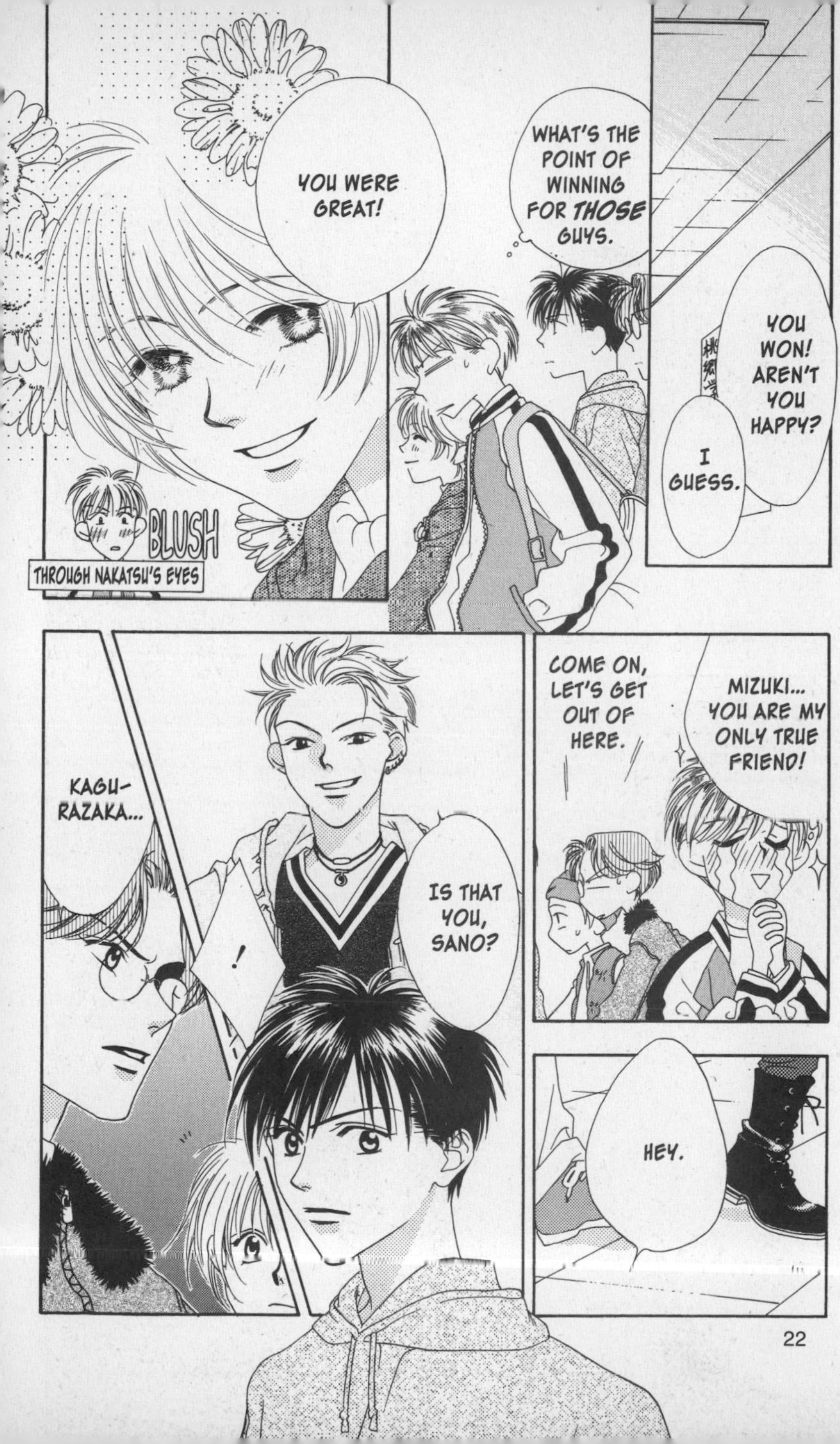
YOU WON! AREN'T YOU HAPPY?
I GUESS.
WHAT'S THE POINT OF WINNING FOR *THOSE* GUYS.
YOU WERE GREAT!
BLUSH
THROUGH NAKATSU'S EYES
MIZUKI... YOU ARE MY ONLY TRUE FRIEND!
COME ON, LET'S GET OUT OF HERE.
HEY.
KAGU-RAZAKA...
IS THAT YOU, SANO?
!

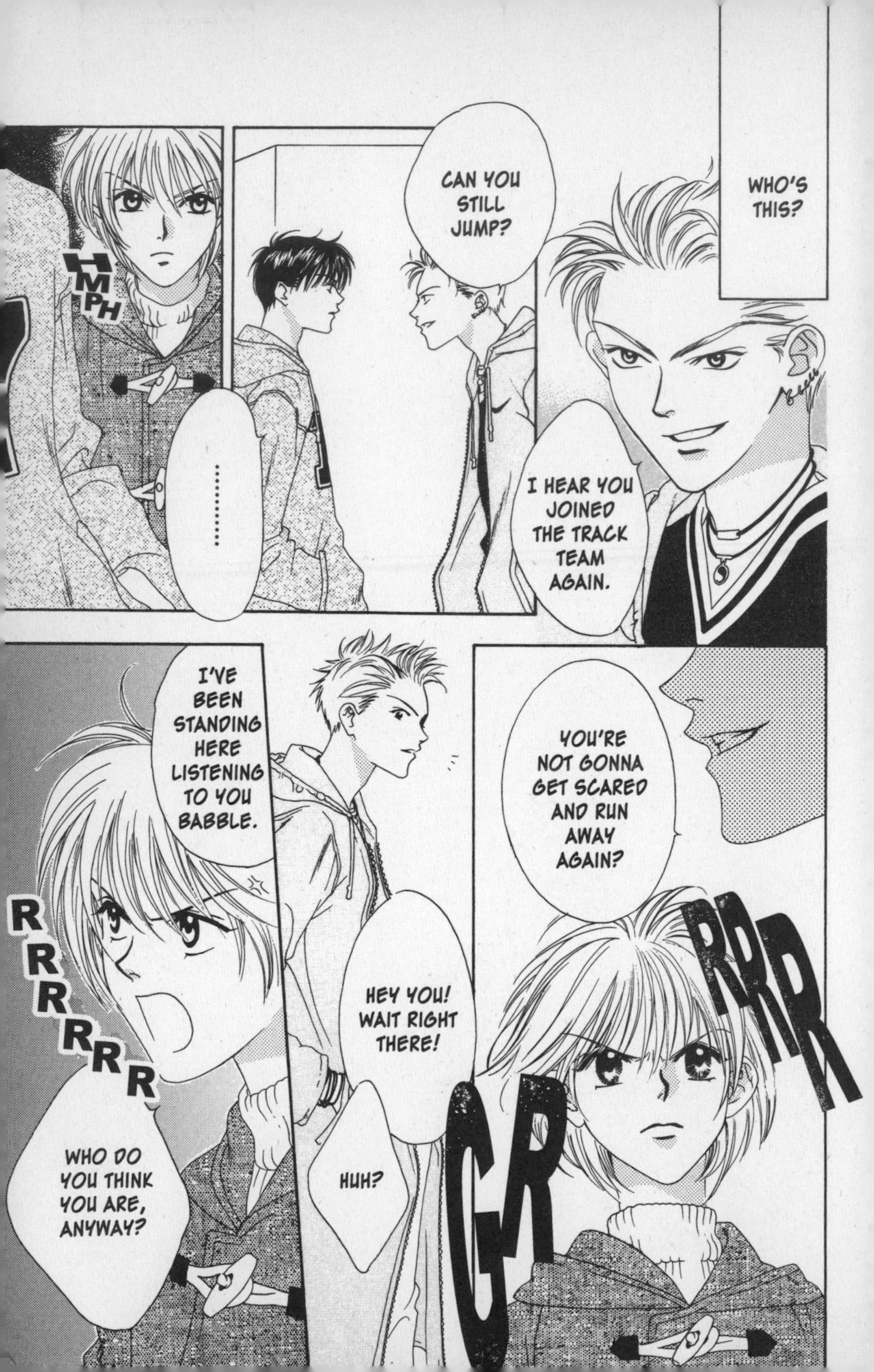
WHO'S THIS?
I HEAR YOU JOINED THE TRACK TEAM AGAIN.
CAN YOU STILL JUMP?
HMPH
......
YOU'RE NOT GONNA GET SCARED AND RUN AWAY AGAIN?
GRRRR
HEY YOU! WAIT RIGHT THERE!
HUH?
I'VE BEEN STANDING HERE LISTENING TO YOU BABBLE.
RRRRRR
WHO DO YOU THINK YOU ARE, ANYWAY?

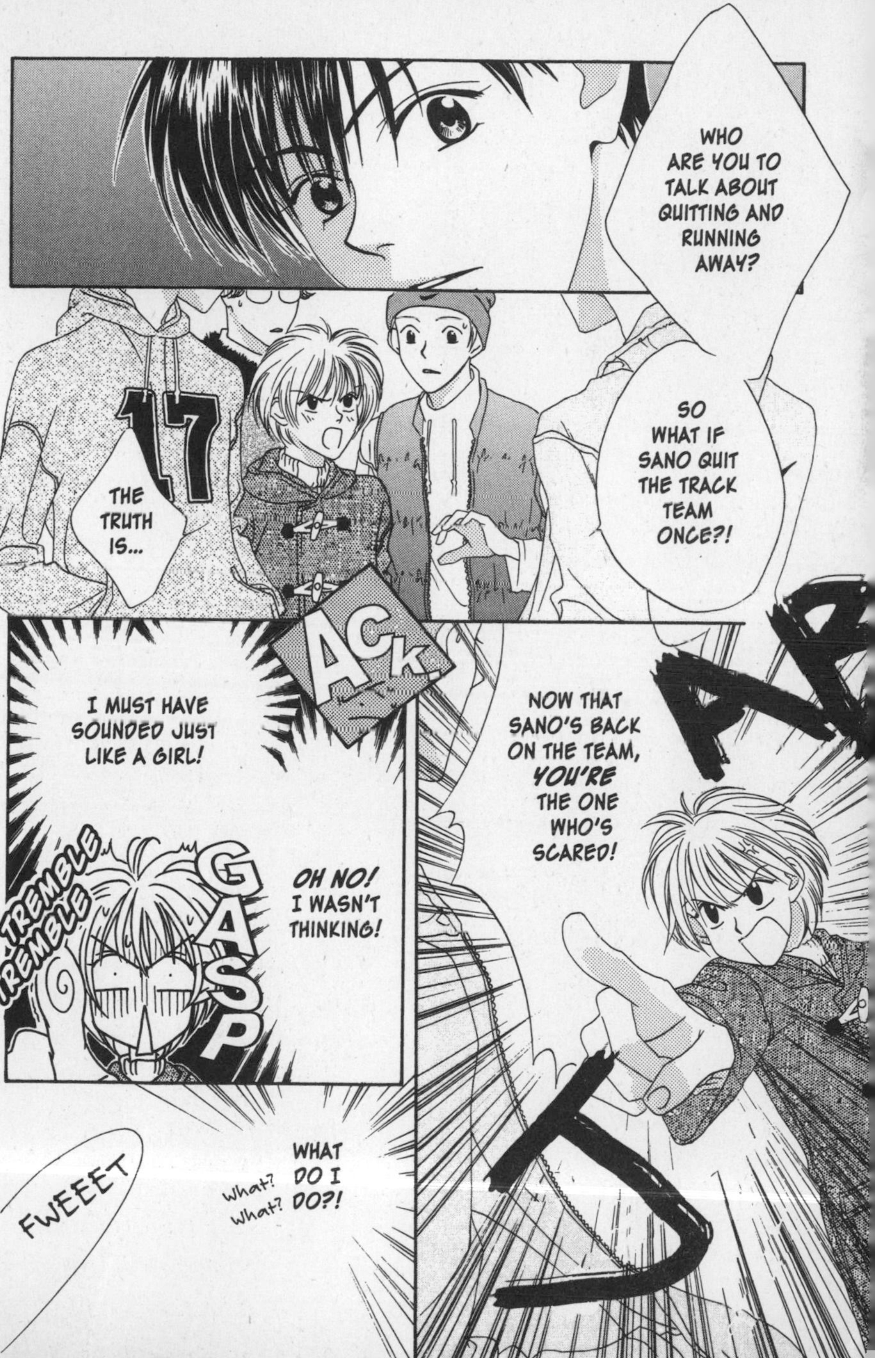
WHO ARE YOU TO TALK ABOUT QUITTING AND RUNNING AWAY?
SO WHAT IF SANO QUIT THE TRACK TEAM ONCE?!
THE TRUTH IS...
NOW THAT SANO'S BACK ON THE TEAM, *YOU'RE* THE ONE WHO'S SCARED!
ACK
I MUST HAVE SOUNDED JUST LIKE A GIRL!
GASP
OH NO! I WASN'T THINKING!
TREMBLE TREMBLE
WHAT DO I DO?!
What? What?
FWEEET

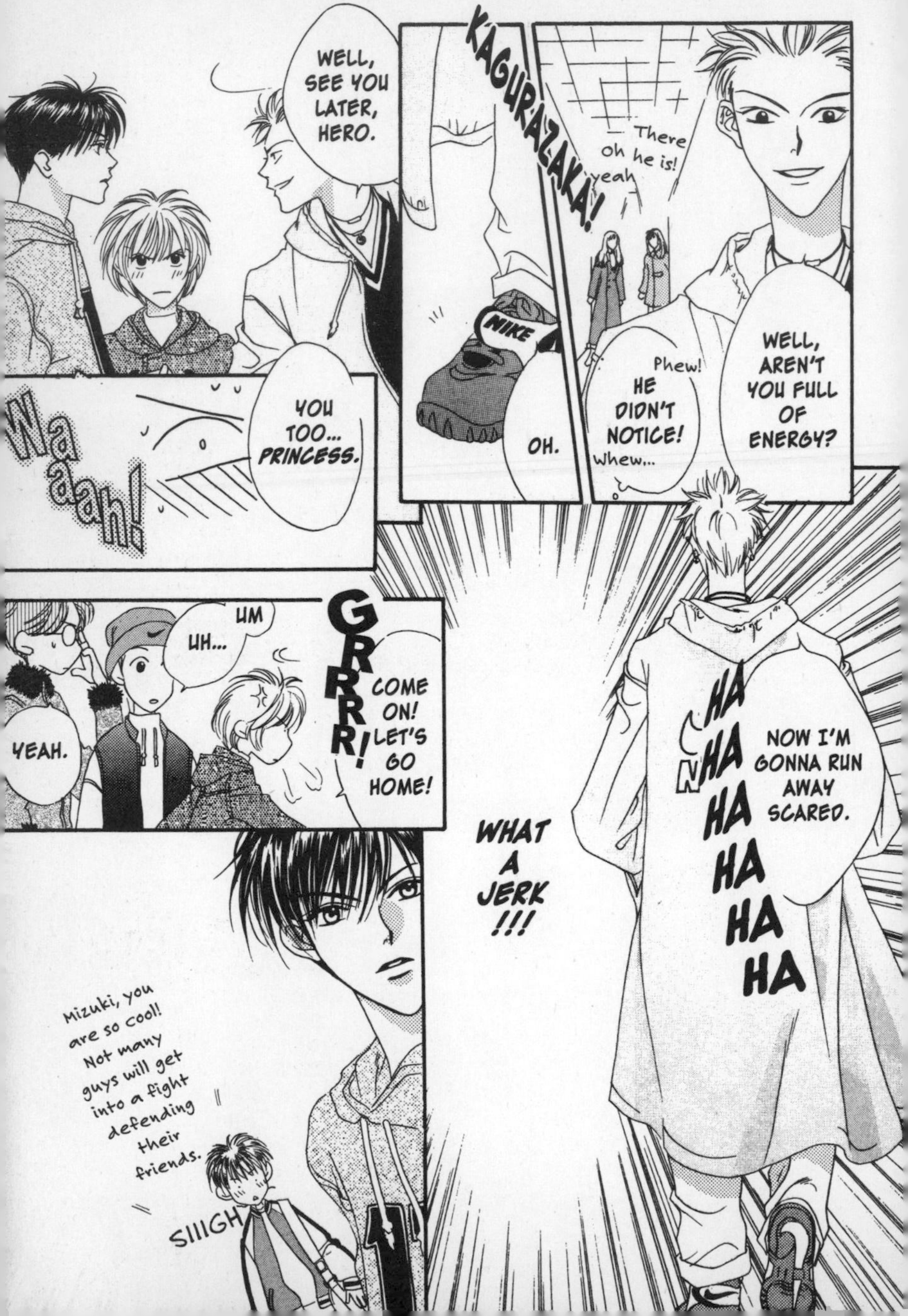
There he is!
oh yeah
WELL, AREN'T YOU FULL OF ENERGY?
Phew! HE DIDN'T NOTICE! Whew...
KAGURAZAKA!
OH.
WELL, SEE YOU LATER, HERO.
YOU TOO... PRINCESS.
Waaah!
NOW I'M GONNA RUN AWAY SCARED.
HA HA HA HA HA HA HA HA
WHAT A JERK!!!
UM
UH...
YEAH.
GRRRR!
COME ON! LET'S GO HOME!
Mizuki, you are so cool! Not many guys will get into a fight defending their friends.
SIIIGH

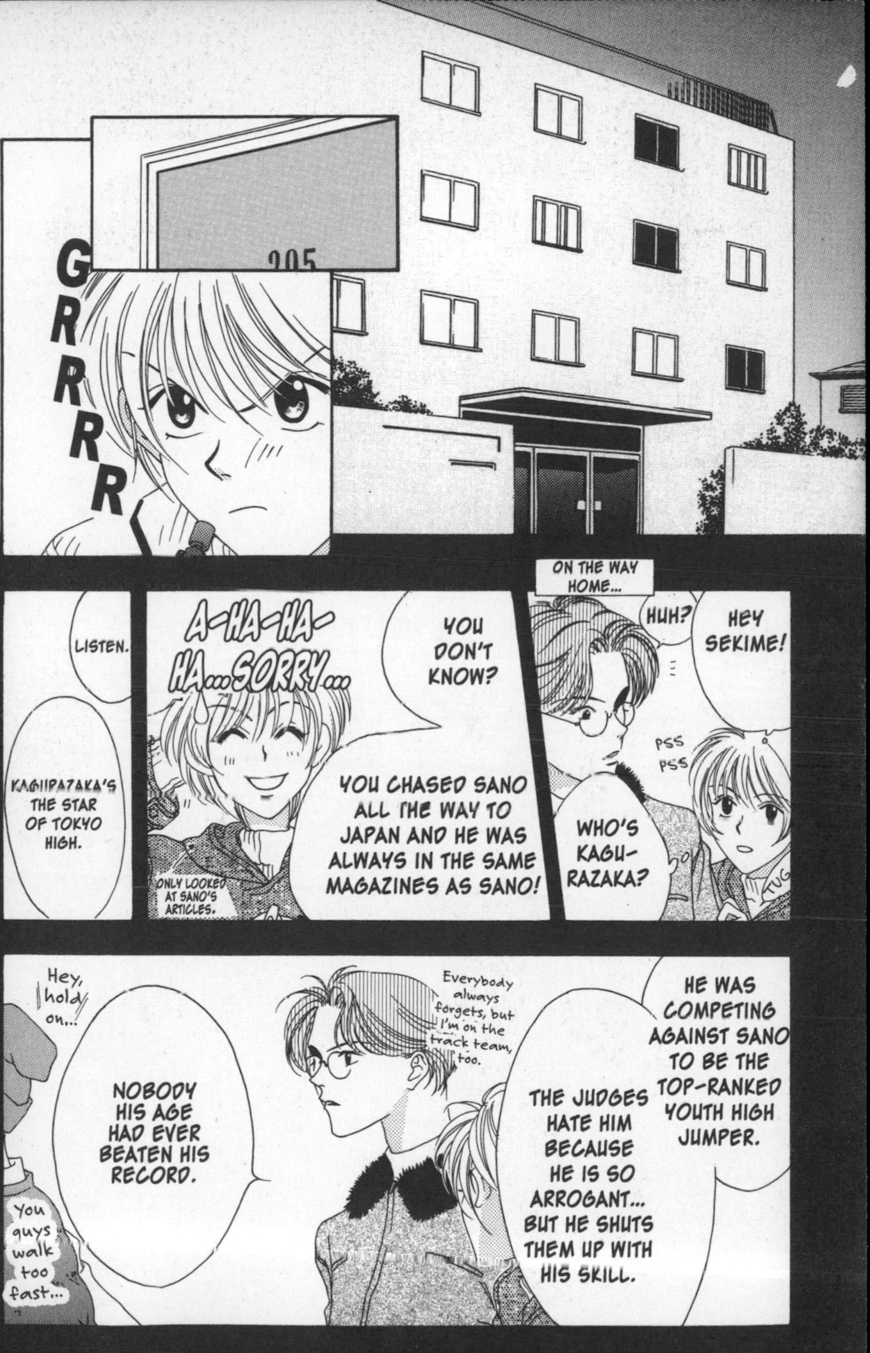
205
GRRRR
ON THE WAY HOME...
HEY SEKIME!
HUH?
PSS PSS
TUG
WHO'S KAGU-RAZAKA?
YOU DON'T KNOW?
A-HA-HA-HA...SORRY...
YOU CHASED SANO ALL THE WAY TO JAPAN AND HE WAS ALWAYS IN THE SAME MAGAZINES AS SANO!
ONLY LOOKED AT SANO'S ARTICLES.
LISTEN.
KAGURAZAKA'S THE STAR OF TOKYO HIGH.
HE WAS COMPETING AGAINST SANO TO BE THE TOP-RANKED YOUTH HIGH JUMPER.
THE JUDGES HATE HIM BECAUSE HE IS SO ARROGANT... BUT HE SHUTS THEM UP WITH HIS SKILL.
Everybody always forgets, but I'm on the track team, too.
NOBODY HIS AGE HAD EVER BEATEN HIS RECORD.
Hey, hold on...
You guys walk too fast...

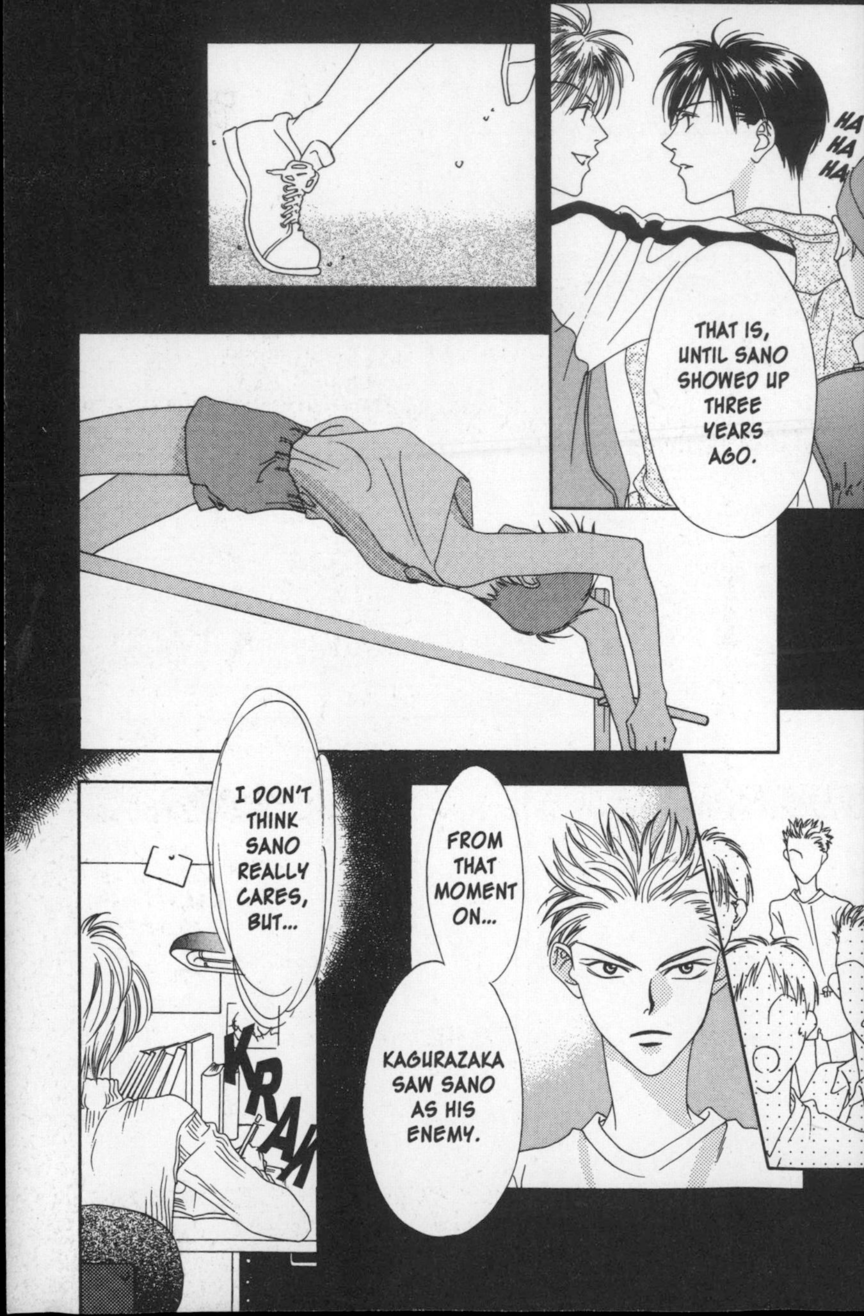
HA HA HA HA
THAT IS, UNTIL SANO SHOWED UP THREE YEARS AGO.
FROM THAT MOMENT ON...
KAGURAZAKA SAW SANO AS HIS ENEMY.
I DON'T THINK SANO REALLY CARES, BUT...
KRAK

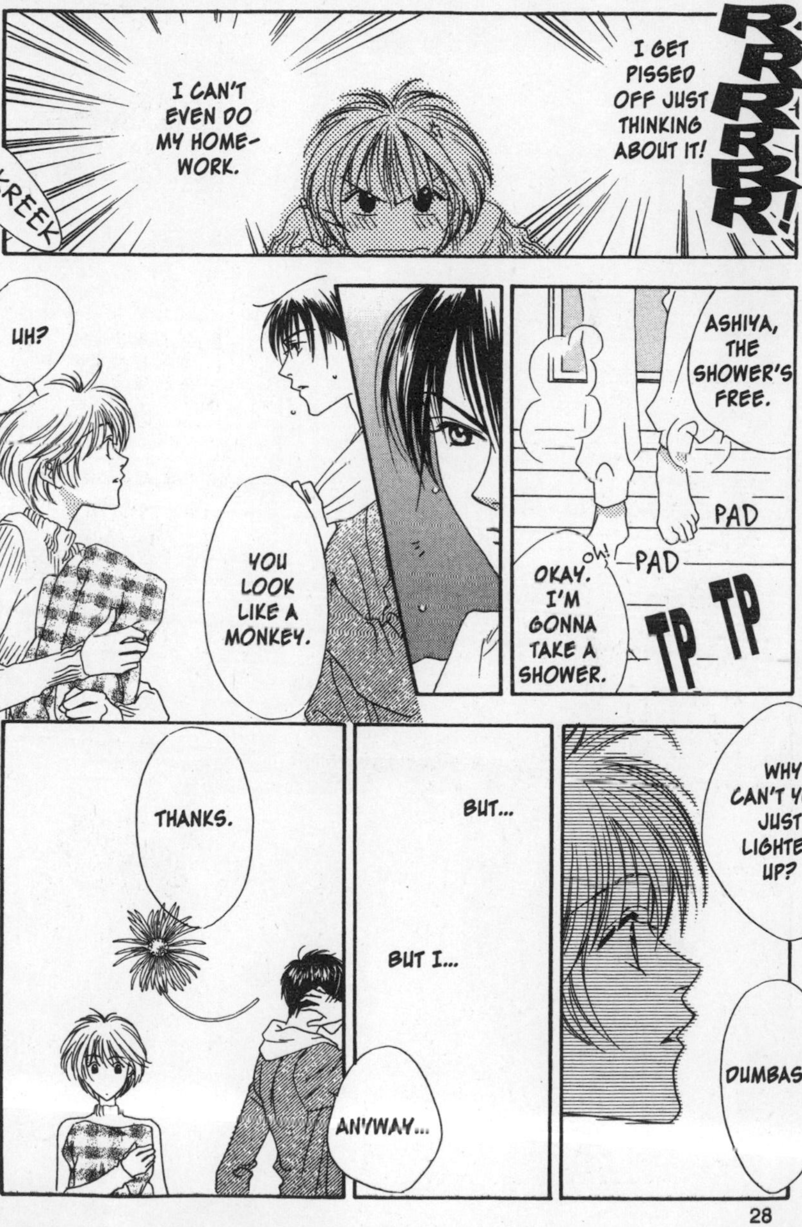
RRRRR!
I GET PISSED OFF JUST THINKING ABOUT IT!
I CAN'T EVEN DO MY HOME-WORK.
KREEK
ASHIYA, THE SHOWER'S FREE.
PAD
PAD
OH!
OKAY. I'M GONNA TAKE A SHOWER.
TP TP
UH?
YOU LOOK LIKE A MONKEY.
WHY CAN'T YOU JUST LIGHTEN UP?
DUMBASS.
BUT...
BUT I...
ANYWAY...
THANKS.

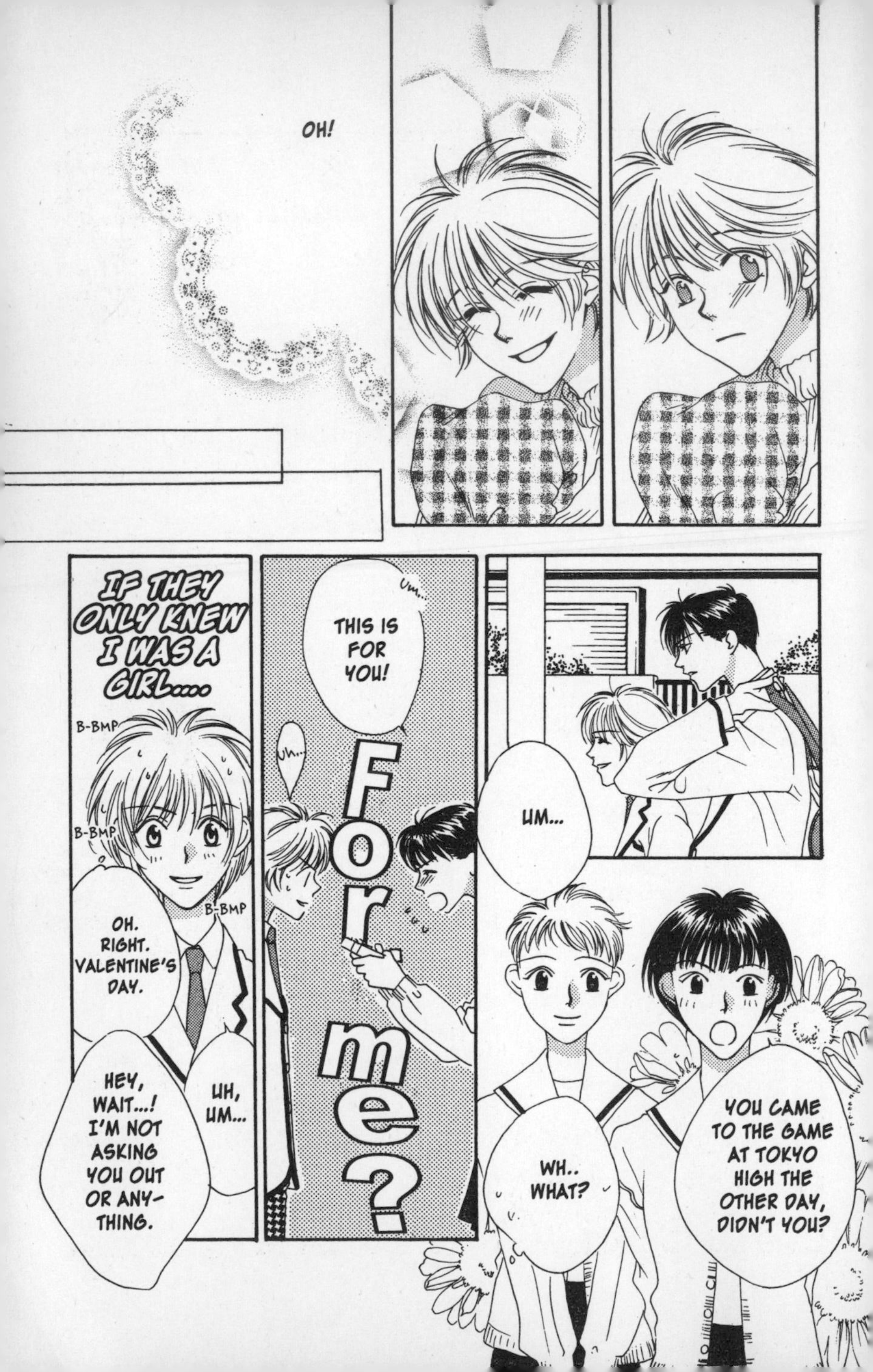
OH!
UM...
YOU CAME TO THE GAME AT TOKYO HIGH THE OTHER DAY, DIDN'T YOU?
WH.. WHAT?
Um...
THIS IS FOR YOU!
Uh...
For me?
IF THEY ONLY KNEW I WAS A GIRL....
B-BMP
B-BMP
B-BMP
OH. RIGHT. VALENTINE'S DAY.
UH, UM...
HEY, WAIT...! I'M NOT ASKING YOU OUT OR ANY-THING.

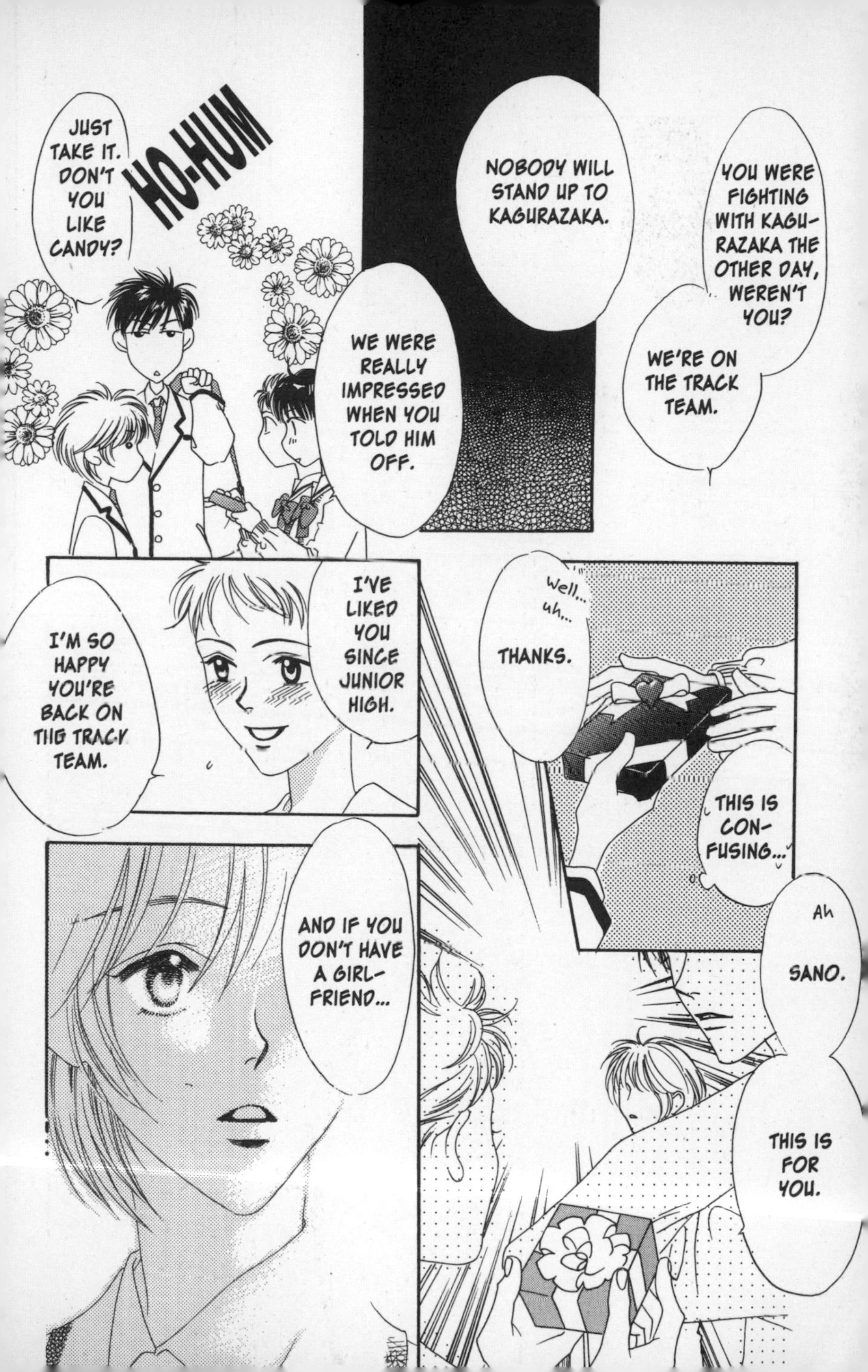
YOU WERE FIGHTING WITH KAGU-RAZAKA THE OTHER DAY, WEREN'T YOU?
WE'RE ON THE TRACK TEAM.
NOBODY WILL STAND UP TO KAGURAZAKA.
WE WERE REALLY IMPRESSED WHEN YOU TOLD HIM OFF.
HO-HUM
JUST TAKE IT. DON'T YOU LIKE CANDY?
Well... uh...
THANKS.
THIS IS CON-FUSING...
I'VE LIKED YOU SINCE JUNIOR HIGH.
I'M SO HAPPY YOU'RE BACK ON THE TRACK TEAM.
Ah
SANO.
THIS IS FOR YOU.
AND IF YOU DON'T HAVE A GIRL-FRIEND...

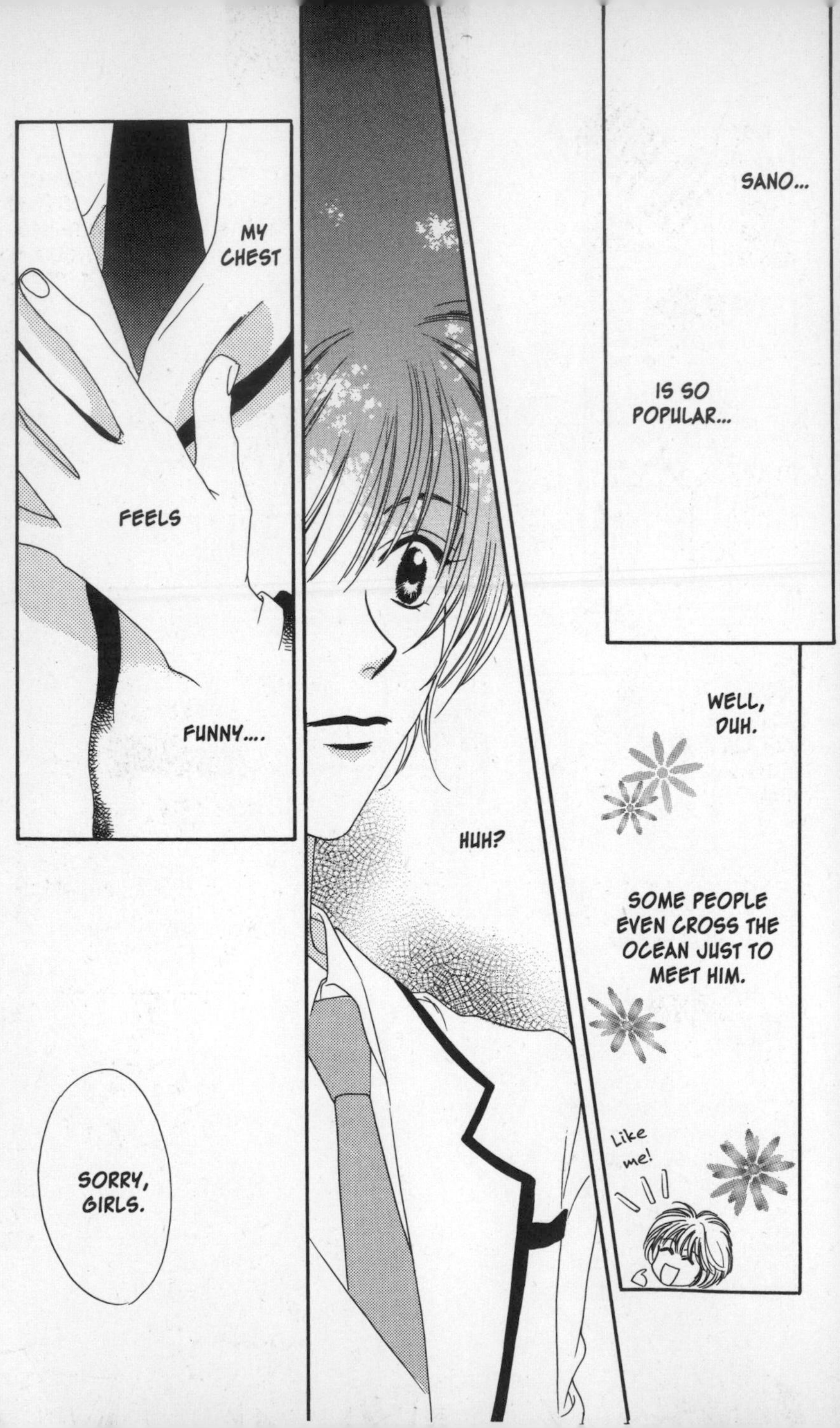
SANO...
IS SO POPULAR...
WELL, DUH.
SOME PEOPLE EVEN CROSS THE OCEAN JUST TO MEET HIM.
Like me!
HUH?
MY CHEST
FEELS
FUNNY....
SORRY, GIRLS.

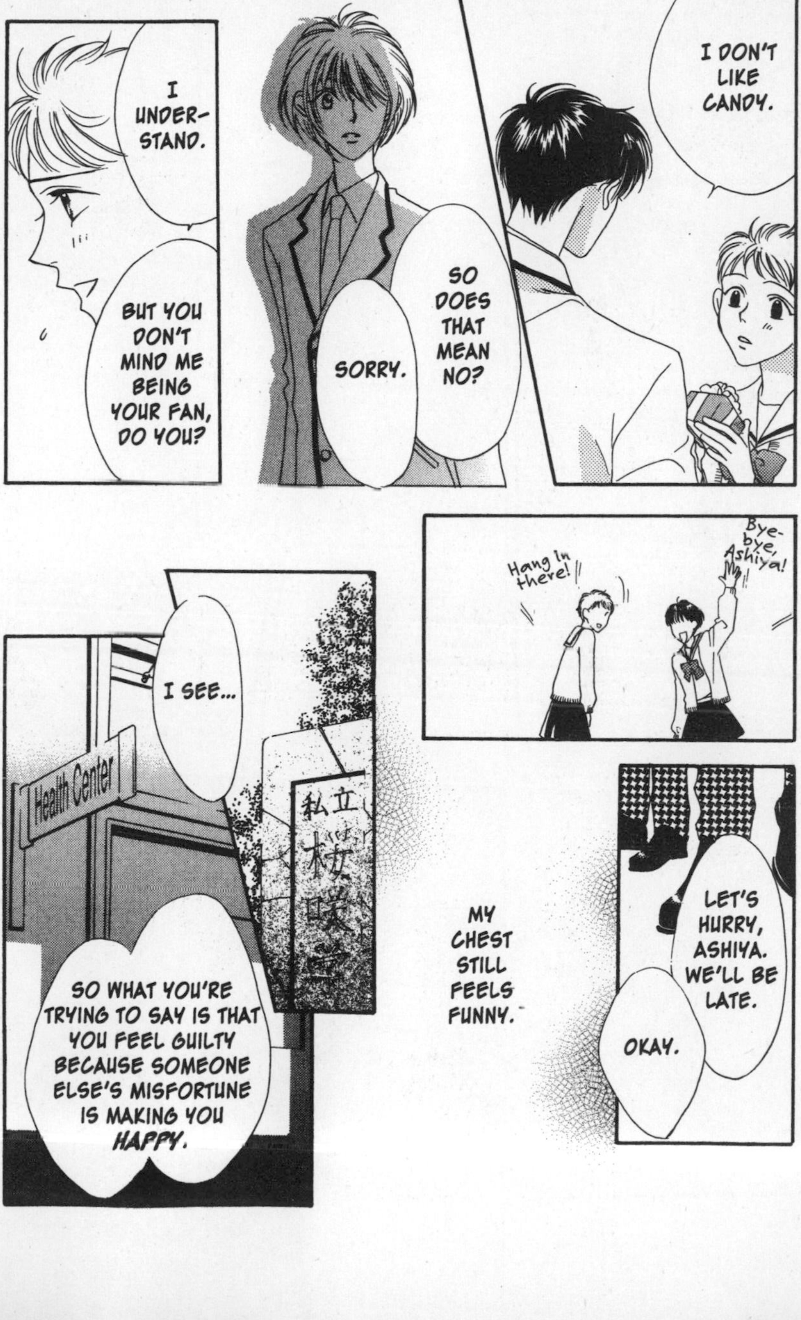
I DON'T LIKE CANDY.
SO DOES THAT MEAN NO?
SORRY.
I UNDER-STAND.
BUT YOU DON'T MIND ME BEING YOUR FAN, DO YOU?
Bye-bye, Ashiya!
Hang in there!
LET'S HURRY, ASHIYA. WE'LL BE LATE.
OKAY.
MY CHEST STILL FEELS FUNNY.
I SEE...
Health Center
私立
桜咲学
SO WHAT YOU'RE TRYING TO SAY IS THAT YOU FEEL GUILTY BECAUSE SOMEONE ELSE'S MISFORTUNE IS MAKING YOU HAPPY.

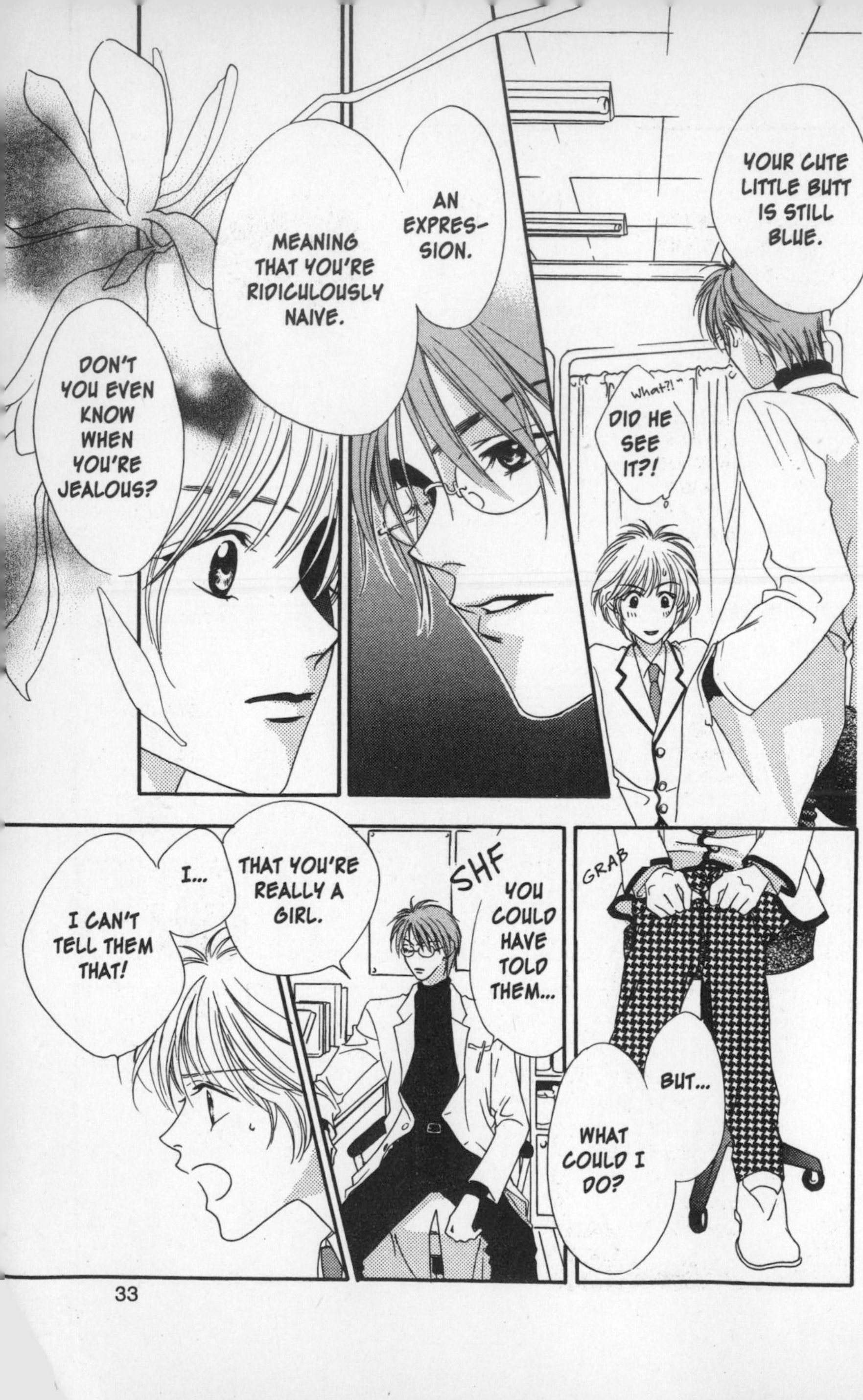
YOUR CUTE LITTLE BUTT IS STILL BLUE.
what?!
DID HE SEE IT?!
AN EXPRESSION.
MEANING THAT YOU'RE RIDICULOUSLY NAIVE.
DON'T YOU EVEN KNOW WHEN YOU'RE JEALOUS?
GRAB
BUT...
WHAT COULD I DO?
SHF
YOU COULD HAVE TOLD THEM...
THAT YOU'RE REALLY A GIRL.
I...
I CAN'T TELL THEM THAT!

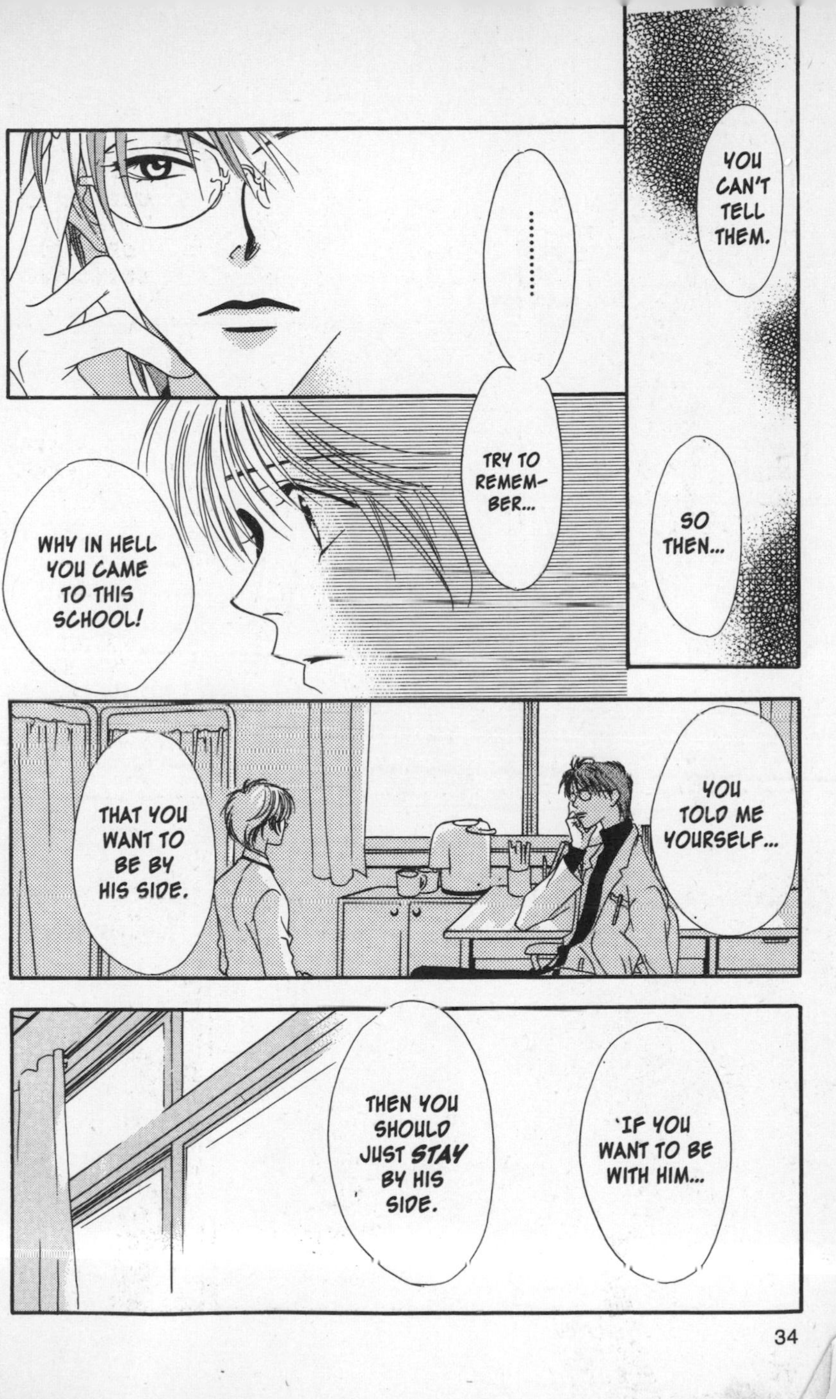
YOU CAN'T TELL THEM.
SO THEN...
......
TRY TO REMEM-BER...
WHY IN HELL YOU CAME TO THIS SCHOOL!
YOU TOLD ME YOURSELF...
THAT YOU WANT TO BE BY HIS SIDE.
'IF YOU WANT TO BE WITH HIM...
THEN YOU SHOULD JUST *STAY* BY HIS SIDE.

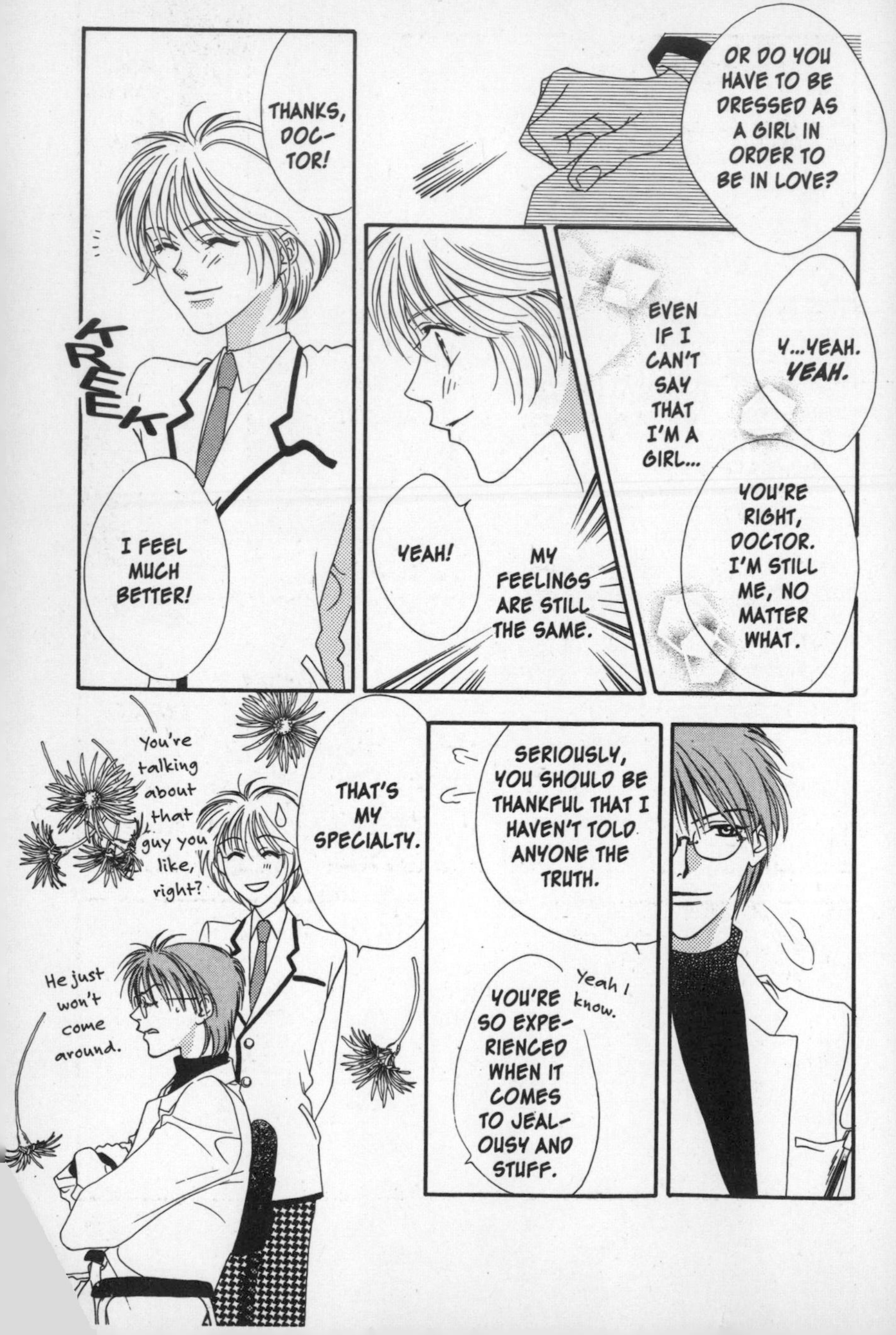
OR DO YOU HAVE TO BE DRESSED AS A GIRL IN ORDER TO BE IN LOVE?
Y...YEAH. YEAH.
EVEN IF I CAN'T SAY THAT I'M A GIRL...
YOU'RE RIGHT, DOCTOR. I'M STILL ME, NO MATTER WHAT.
MY FEELINGS ARE STILL THE SAME.
YEAH!
THANKS, DOC-TOR!
KREEK
I FEEL MUCH BETTER!
SERIOUSLY, YOU SHOULD BE THANKFUL THAT I HAVEN'T TOLD ANYONE THE TRUTH.
YOU'RE SO EXPE-RIENCED WHEN IT COMES TO JEAL-OUSY AND STUFF.
Yeah I know.
THAT'S MY SPECIALTY.
You're talking about that guy you like, right?
He just won't come around.

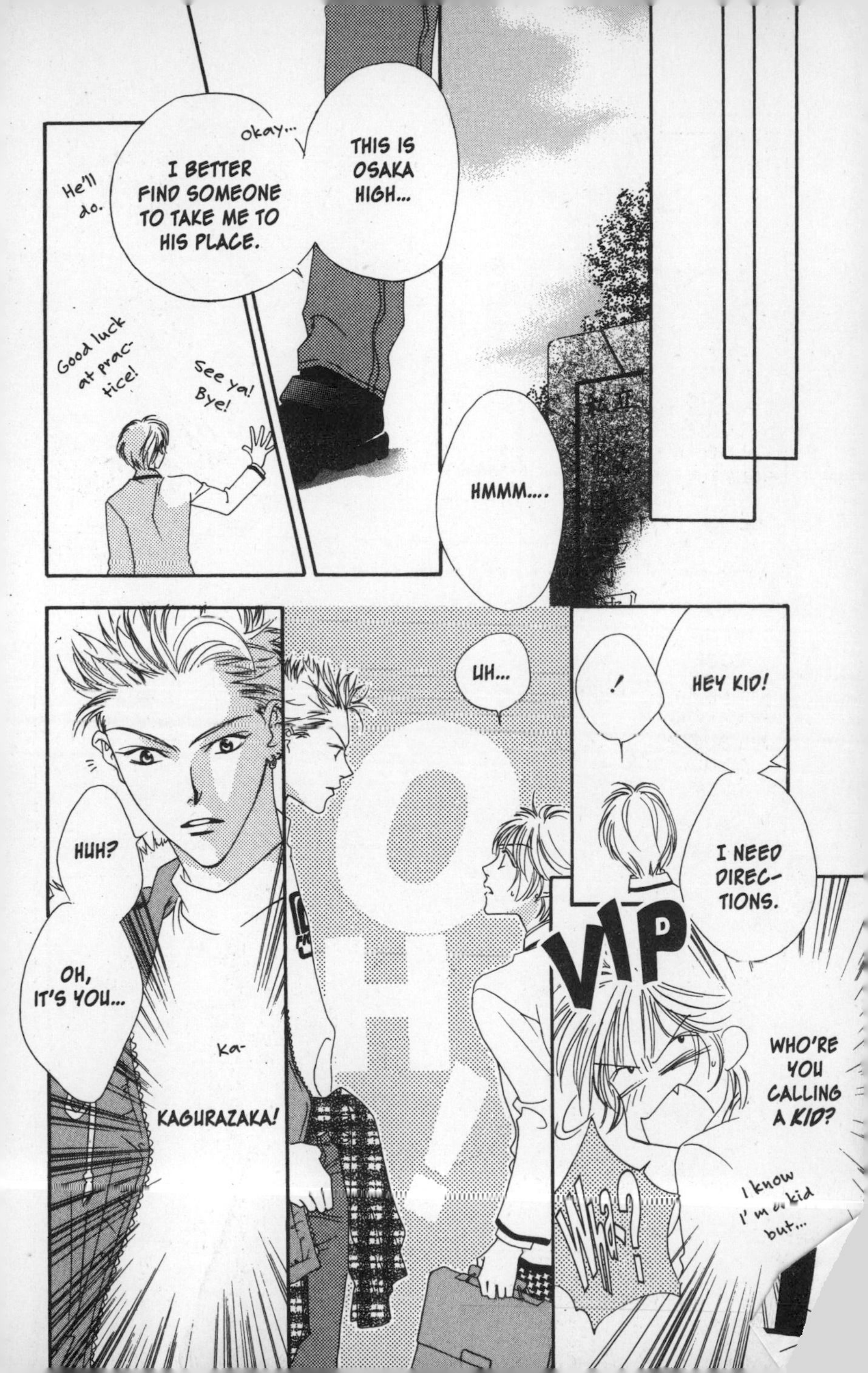
HMMM....
THIS IS OSAKA HIGH...
Okay...
I BETTER FIND SOMEONE TO TAKE ME TO HIS PLACE.
He'll do.
See ya! Bye!
Good luck at practice!
HEY KID!
!
I NEED DIRECTIONS.
VIP
WHO'RE YOU CALLING A KID?
Wha?
I know I'm a kid but...
UH...
OH!
HUH?
OH, IT'S YOU...
Ka-
KAGURAZAKA!

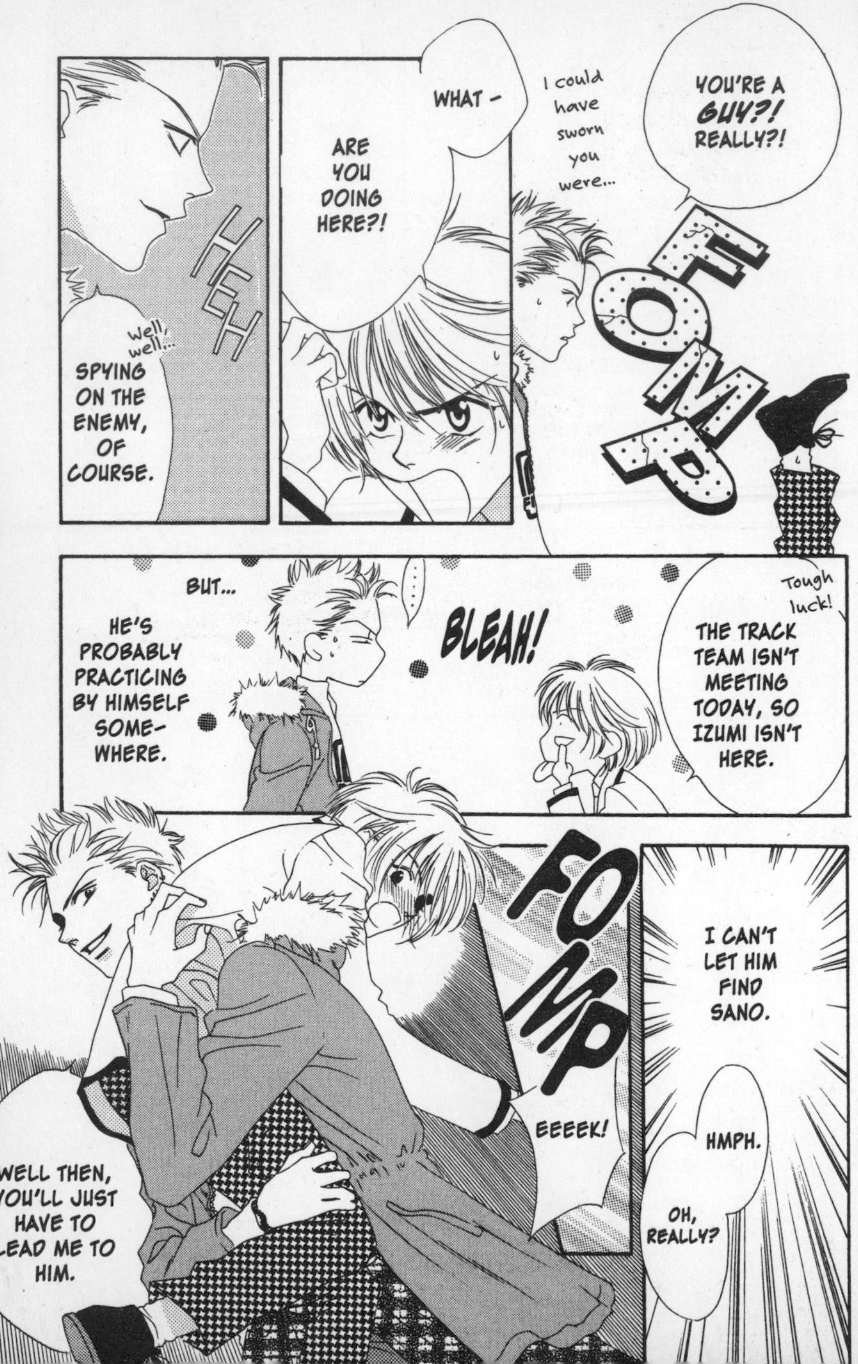
YOU'RE A GUY?! REALLY?!
I could have sworn you were...
FLOMP
WHAT -
ARE YOU DOING HERE?!
HEH
well, well...
SPYING ON THE ENEMY, OF COURSE.
Tough luck!
THE TRACK TEAM ISN'T MEETING TODAY, SO IZUMI ISN'T HERE.
BLEAH!
BUT...
HE'S PROBABLY PRACTICING BY HIMSELF SOME-WHERE.
I CAN'T LET HIM FIND SANO.
HMPH.
OH, REALLY?
FOMP
EEEEK!
WELL THEN, YOU'LL JUST HAVE TO LEAD ME TO HIM.

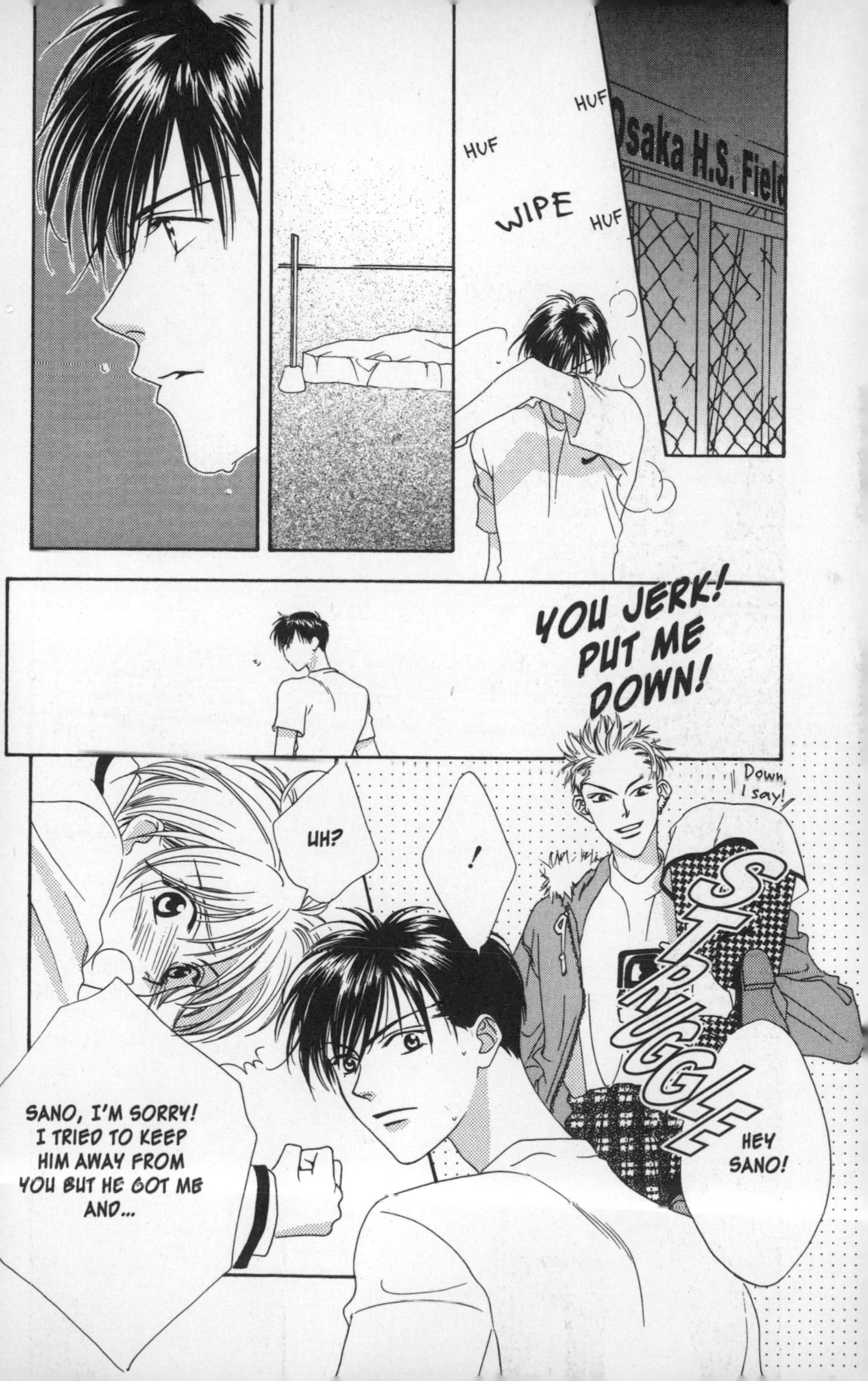
Osaka H.S. Field
HUF
HUF
HUF
WIPE
YOU JERK! PUT ME DOWN!
Down, I say!
STRUGGLE
HEY SANO!
!
UH?
SANO, I'M SORRY! I TRIED TO KEEP HIM AWAY FROM YOU BUT HE GOT ME AND...

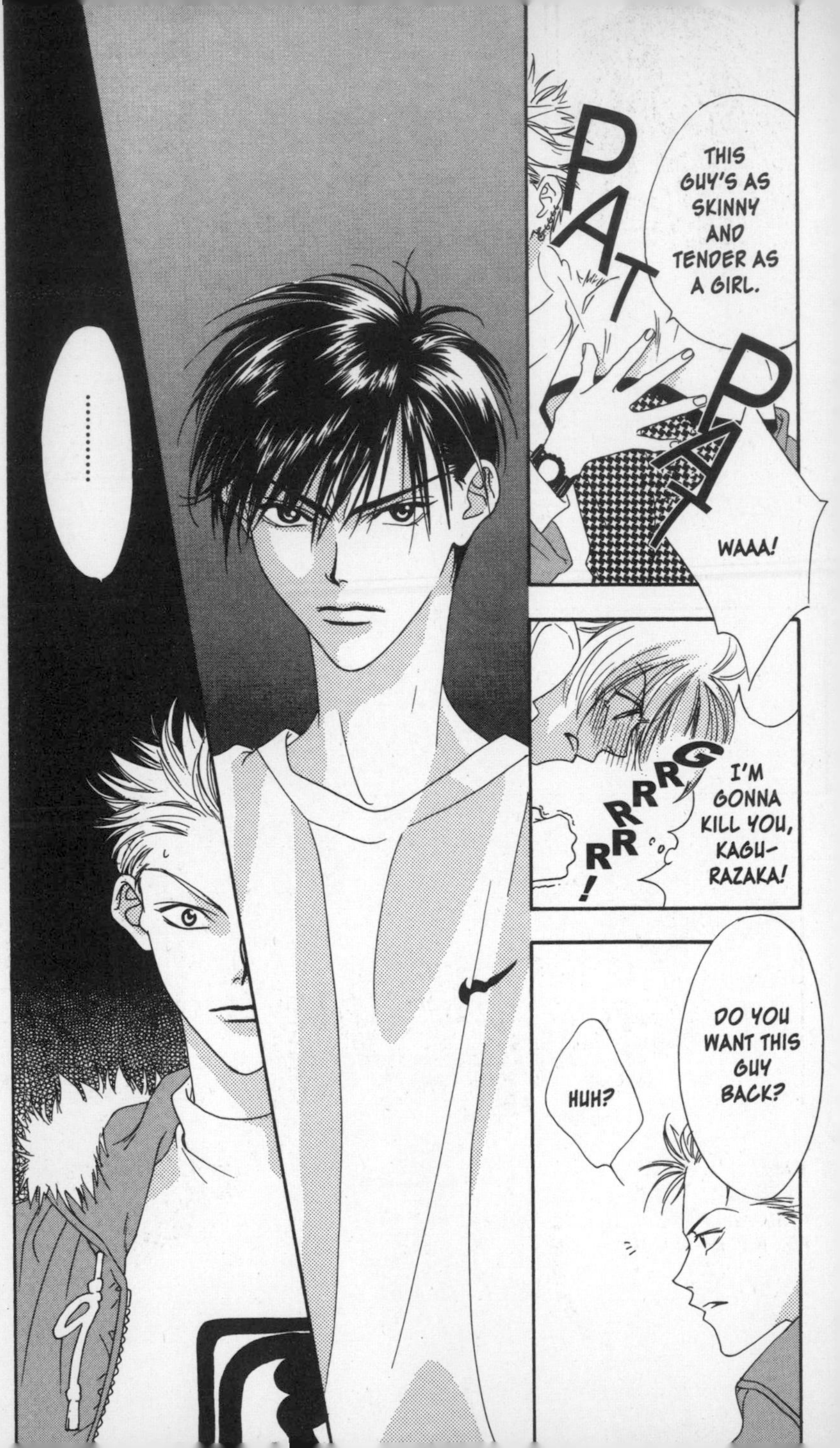
THIS GUY'S AS SKINNY AND TENDER AS A GIRL.
PAT PAT
WAAA!
I'M GONNA KILL YOU, KAGU-RAZAKA!
RRRRRRG!
DO YOU WANT THIS GUY BACK?
HUH?
......

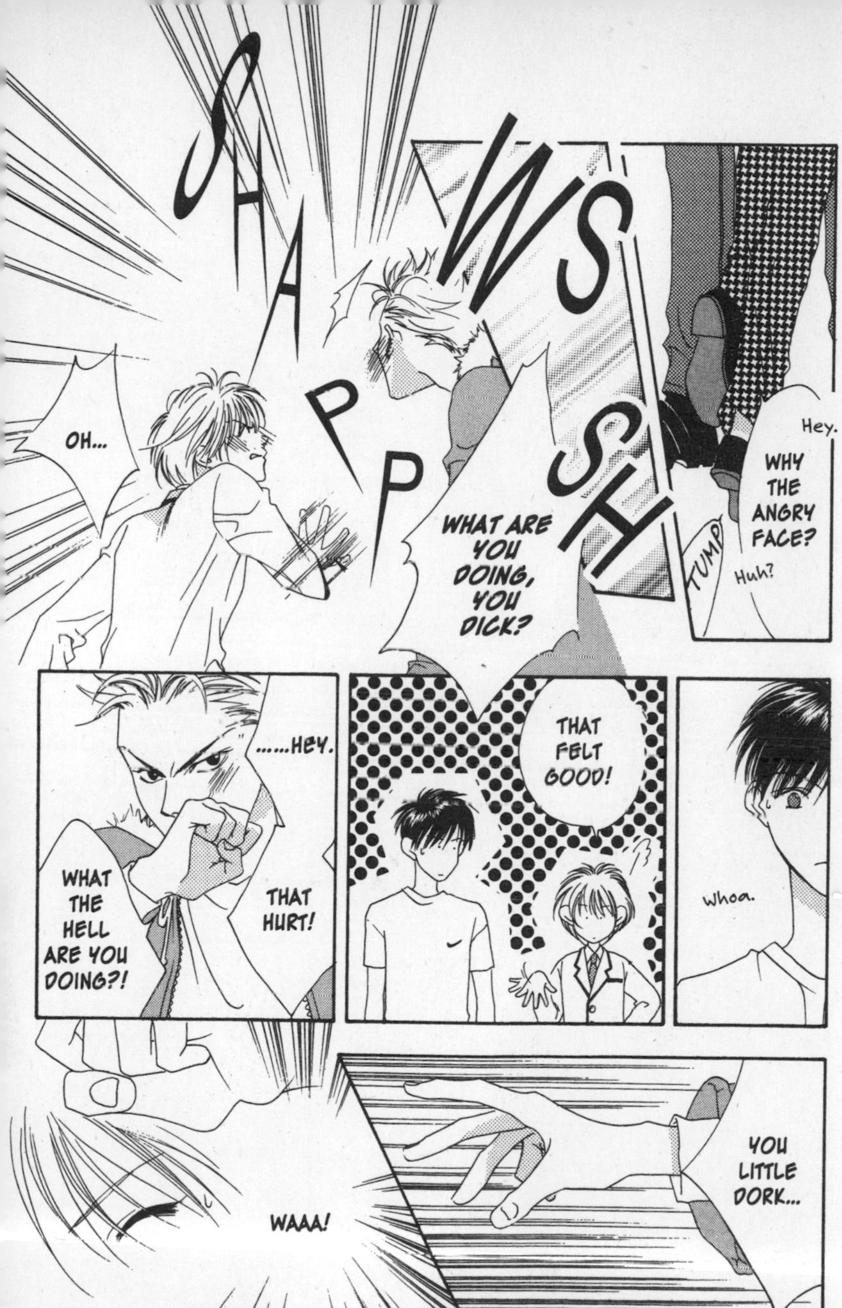

Hey.
WHY THE ANGRY FACE?
Huh?
TUMP
SWISH
WHAT ARE YOU DOING, YOU DICK?
SHAPP
OH...
Whoa.
THAT FELT GOOD!
......HEY.
THAT HURT!
WHAT THE HELL ARE YOU DOING?!
YOU LITTLE DORK...
WAAA!

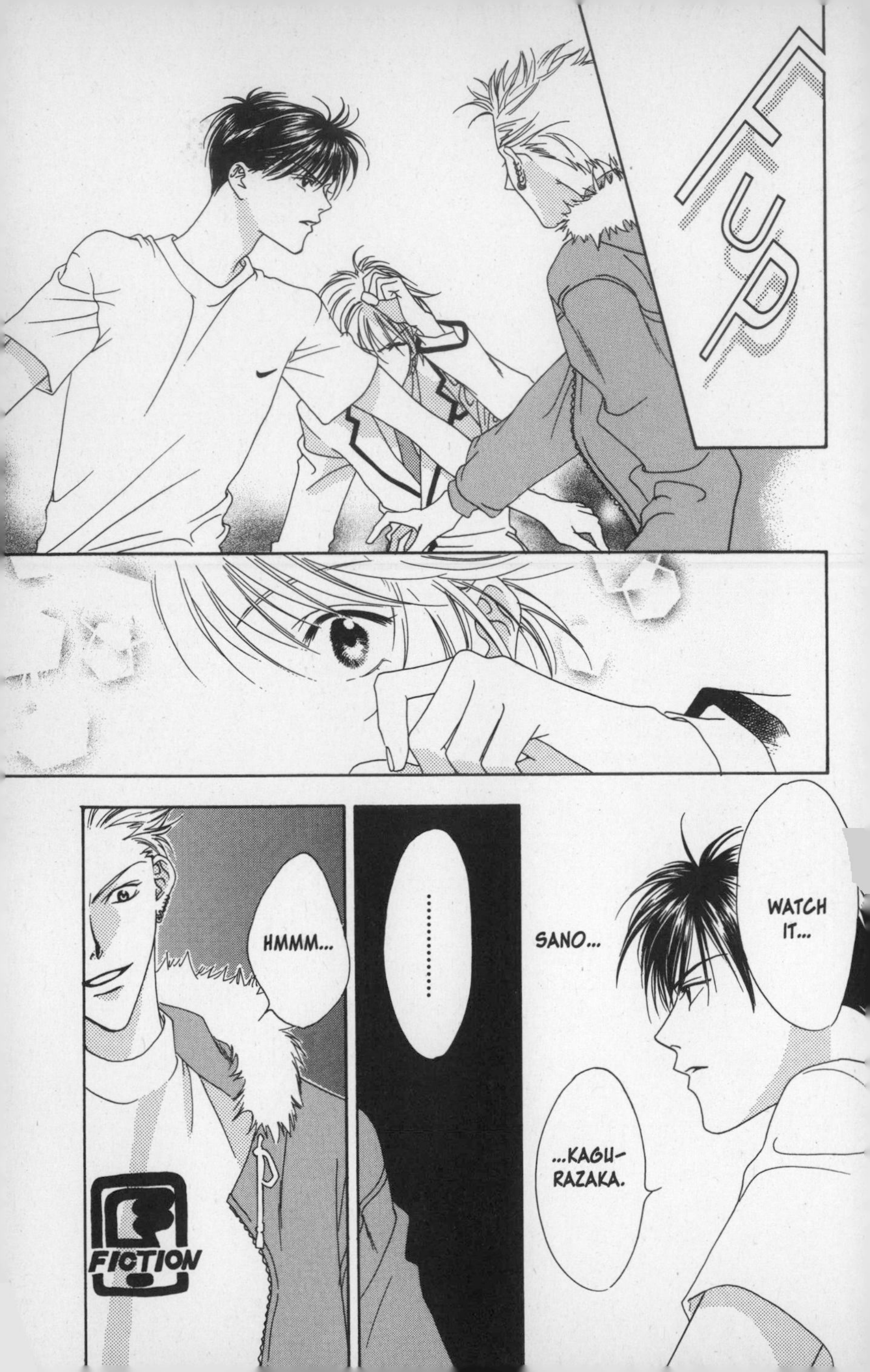
FUP
WATCH IT...
SANO...
...KAGU-
RAZAKA.
......
HMMM...

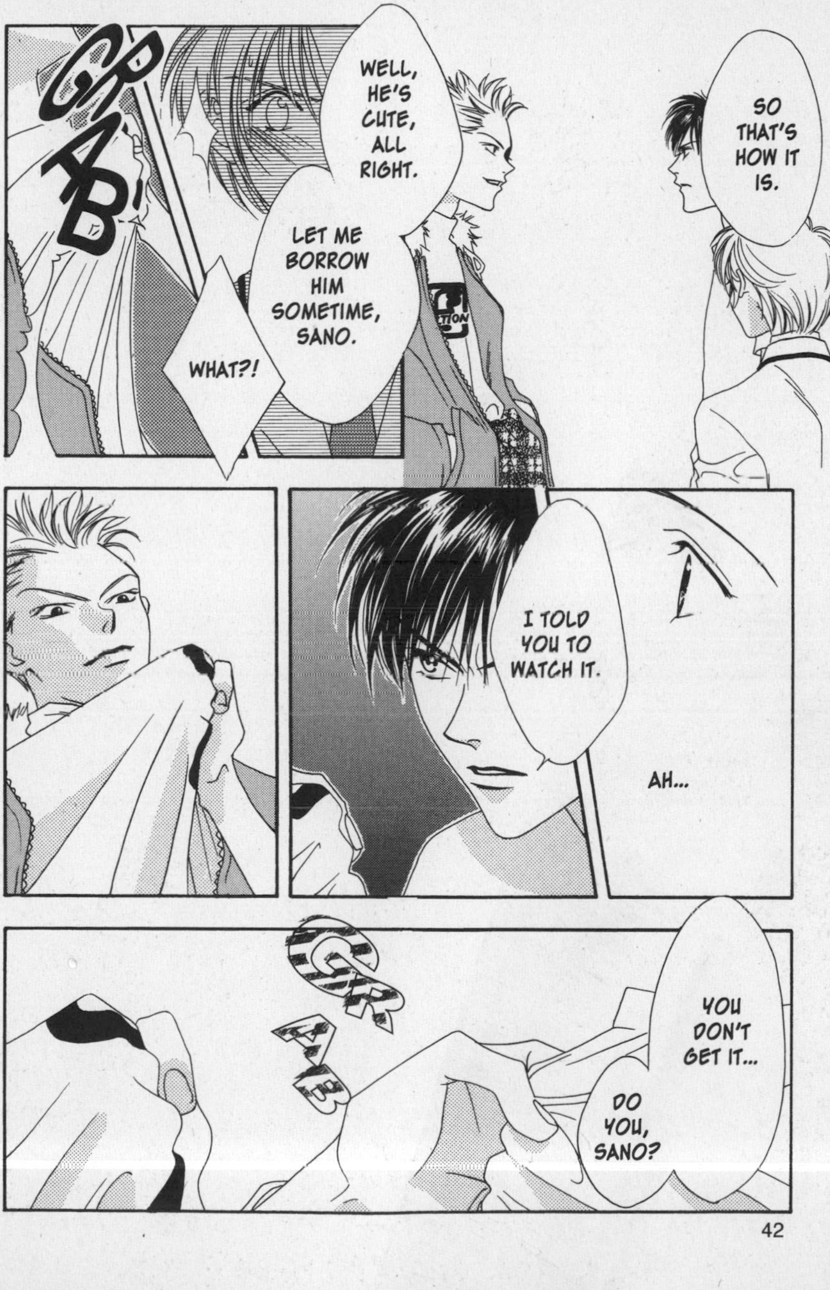
SO THAT'S HOW IT IS.
WELL, HE'S CUTE, ALL RIGHT.
LET ME BORROW HIM SOMETIME, SANO.
WHAT?!
GRAB
AH...
I TOLD YOU TO WATCH IT.
YOU DON'T GET IT...
DO YOU, SANO?
GRAB

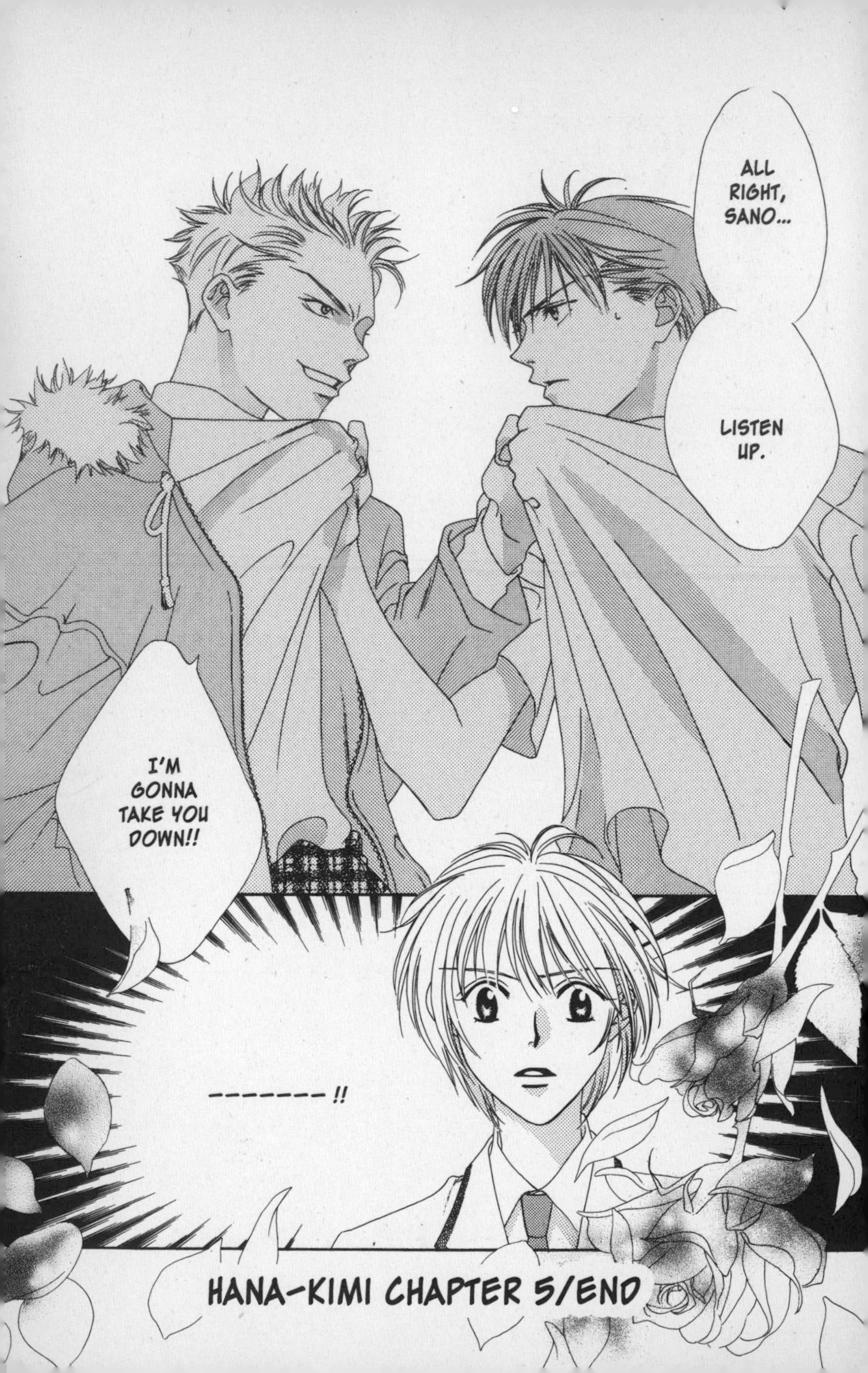
ALL RIGHT, SANO...
LISTEN UP.
I'M GONNA TAKE YOU DOWN!!
--------!!
HANA-KIMI CHAPTER 5/END

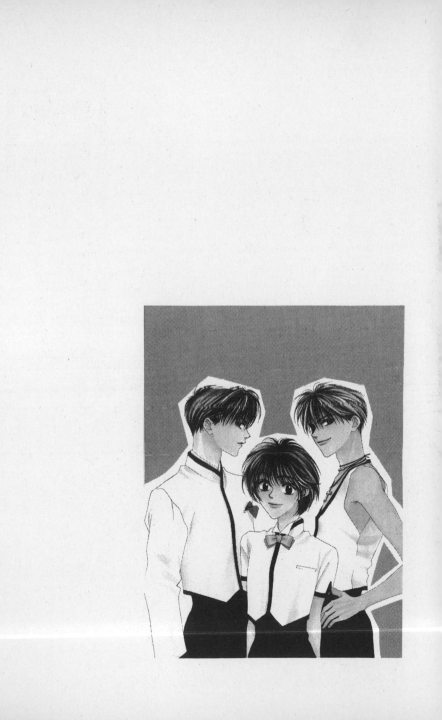

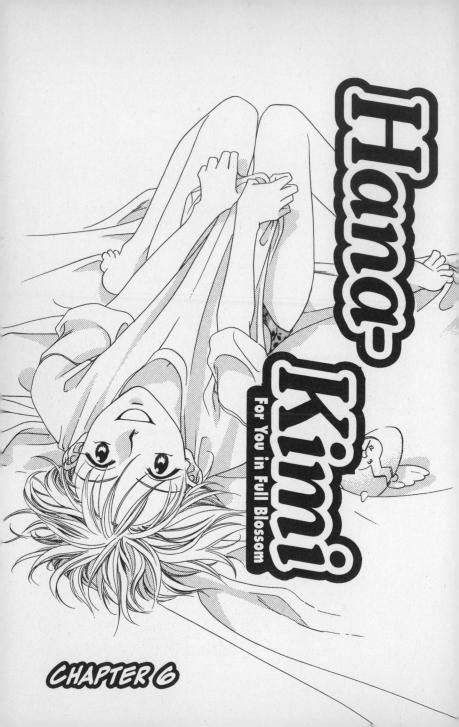

Hana-Kimi
For You in Full Blossom

CHAPTER 6

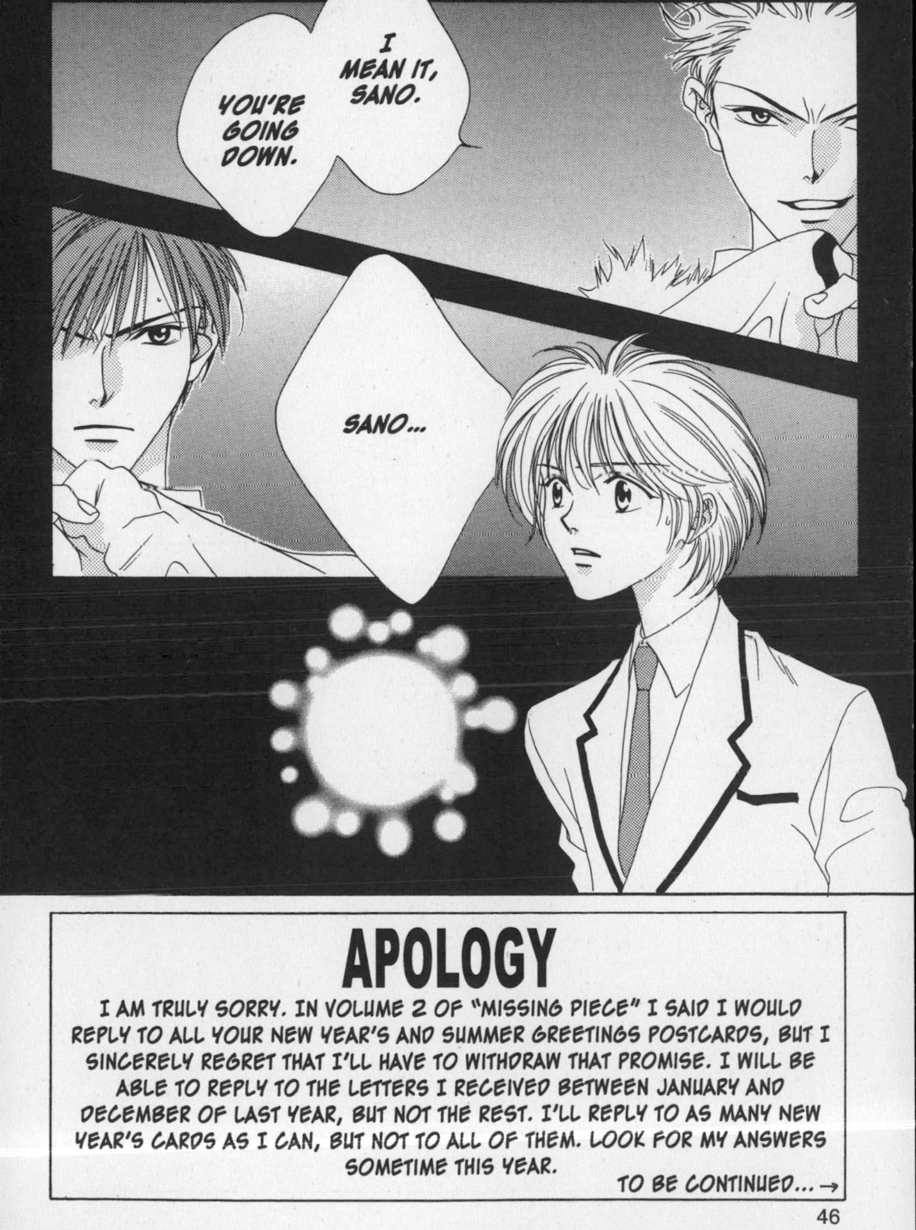
I MEAN IT, SANO.
YOU'RE GOING DOWN.
SANO...

APOLOGY

I AM TRULY SORRY. IN VOLUME 2 OF "MISSING PIECE" I SAID I WOULD REPLY TO ALL YOUR NEW YEAR'S AND SUMMER GREETINGS POSTCARDS, BUT I SINCERELY REGRET THAT I'LL HAVE TO WITHDRAW THAT PROMISE. I WILL BE ABLE TO REPLY TO THE LETTERS I RECEIVED BETWEEN JANUARY AND DECEMBER OF LAST YEAR, BUT NOT THE REST. I'LL REPLY TO AS MANY NEW YEAR'S CARDS AS I CAN, BUT NOT TO ALL OF THEM. LOOK FOR MY ANSWERS SOMETIME THIS YEAR.

TO BE CONTINUED... →

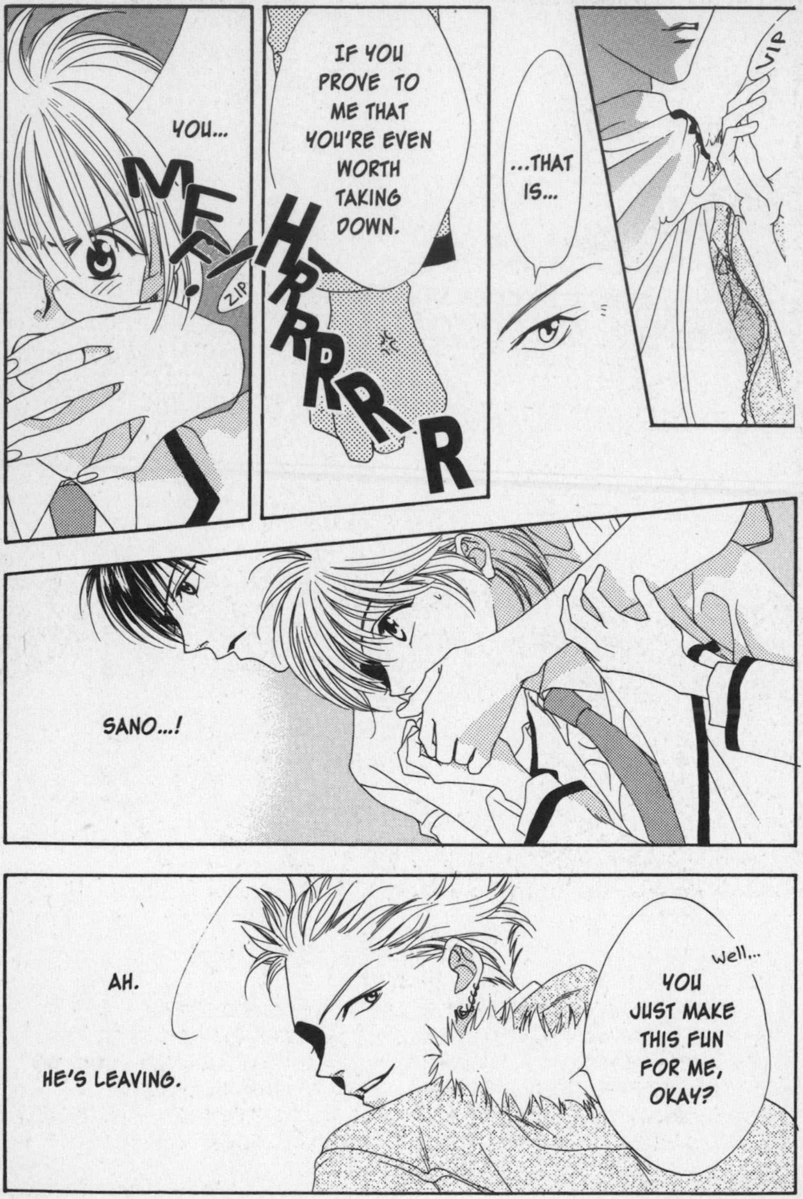
VIP
...THAT IS...
IF YOU PROVE TO ME THAT YOU'RE EVEN WORTH TAKING DOWN.
HRRRRRR
YOU...
MF!
ZIP
SANO...!
Well...
YOU JUST MAKE THIS FUN FOR ME, OKAY?
AH.
HE'S LEAVING.

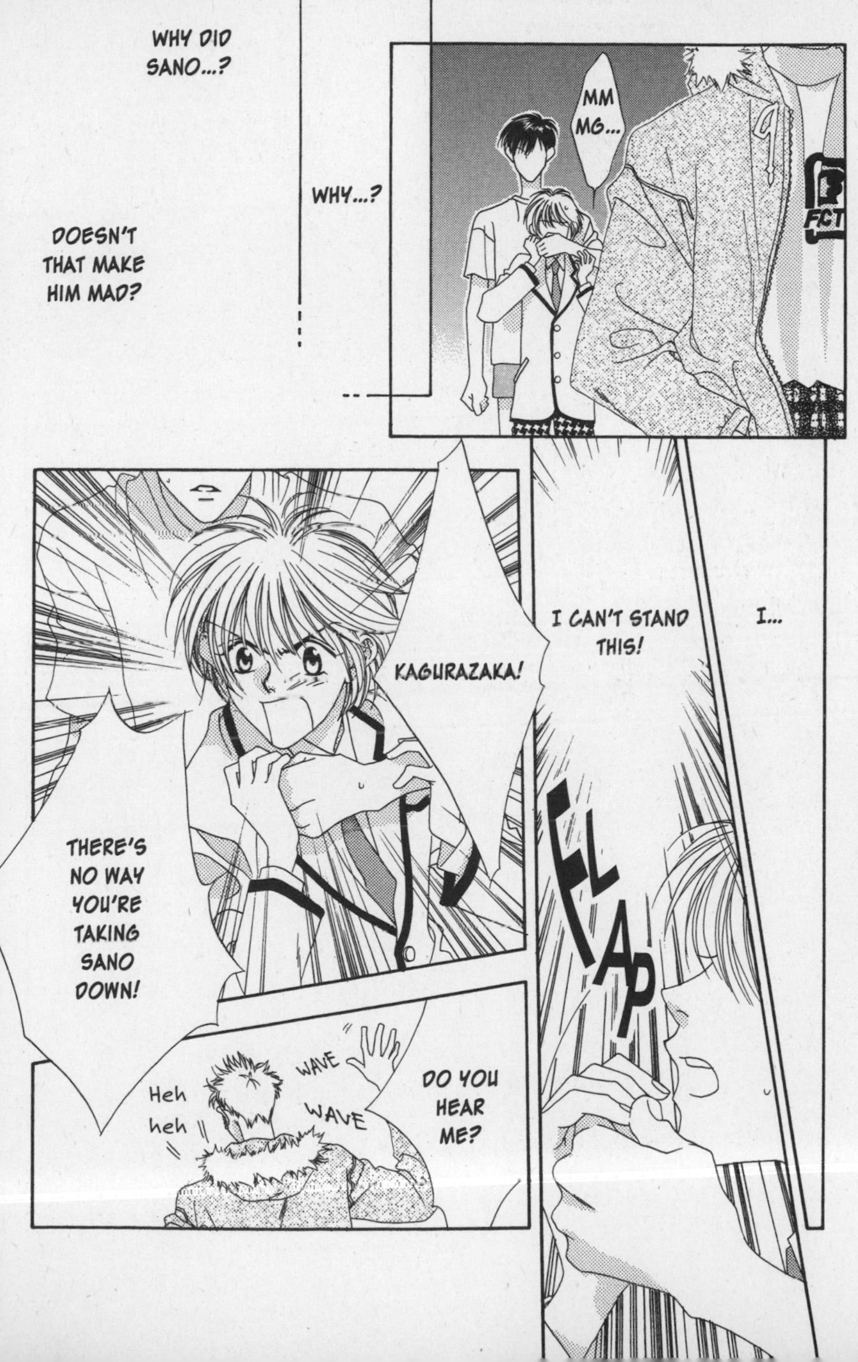
MM MG...
WHY...?
WHY DID SANO...?
DOESN'T THAT MAKE HIM MAD?
I...
I CAN'T STAND THIS!
FLAP
KAGURAZAKA!
THERE'S NO WAY YOU'RE TAKING SANO DOWN!
DO YOU HEAR ME?
WAVE
WAVE
Heh heh

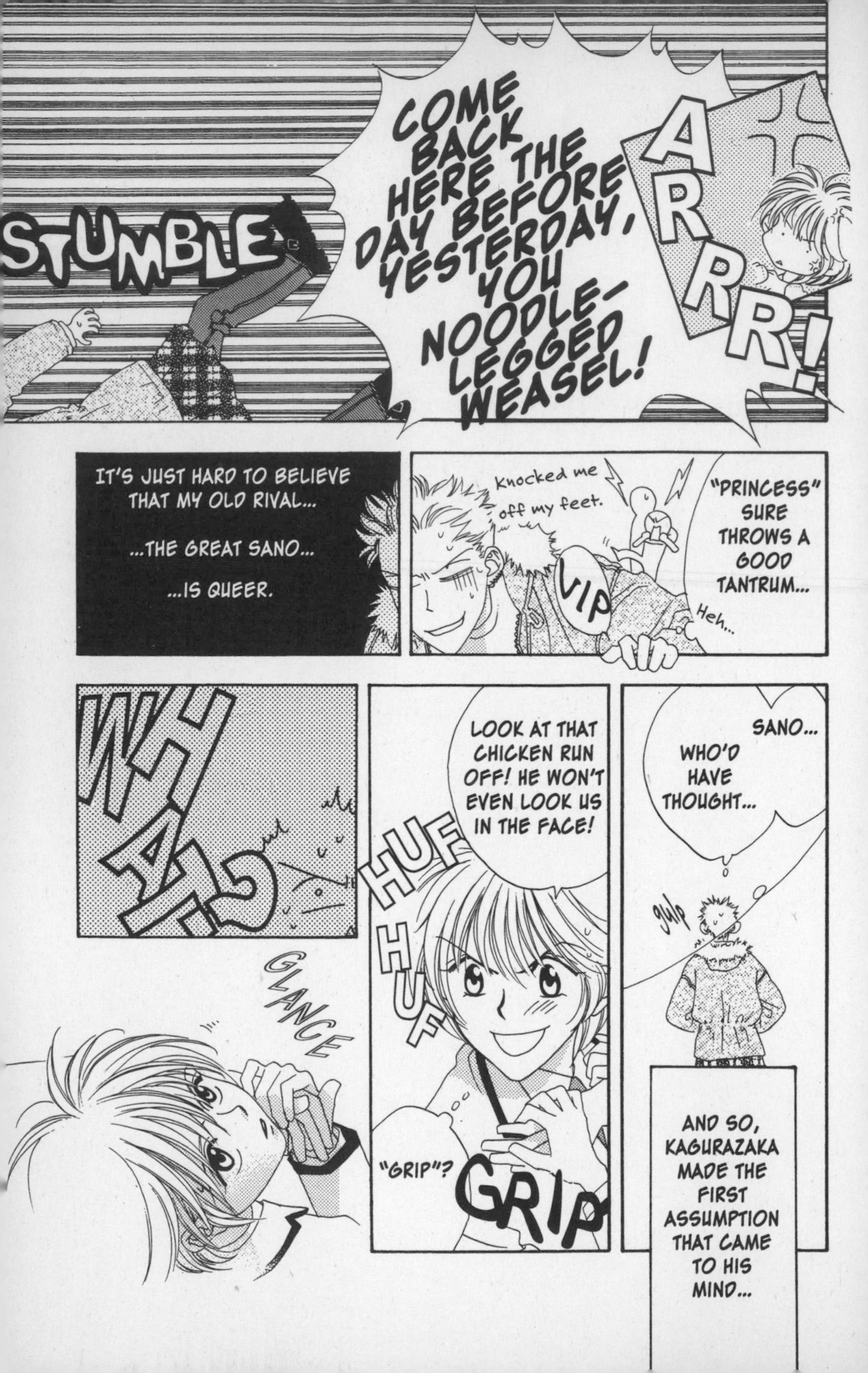
ARRR!
COME BACK HERE THE DAY BEFORE YESTERDAY, YOU NOODLE-LEGGED WEASEL!
STUMBLE
"PRINCESS" SURE THROWS A GOOD TANTRUM...
Knocked me off my feet.
VIP
Heh...
IT'S JUST HARD TO BELIEVE THAT MY OLD RIVAL...
...THE GREAT SANO...
...IS QUEER.
SANO... WHO'D HAVE THOUGHT...
gulp
AND SO, KAGURAZAKA MADE THE FIRST ASSUMPTION THAT CAME TO HIS MIND...
LOOK AT THAT CHICKEN RUN OFF! HE WON'T EVEN LOOK US IN THE FACE!
HUF
HUF
"GRIP"?
GRIP
WHAT?
GLANCE

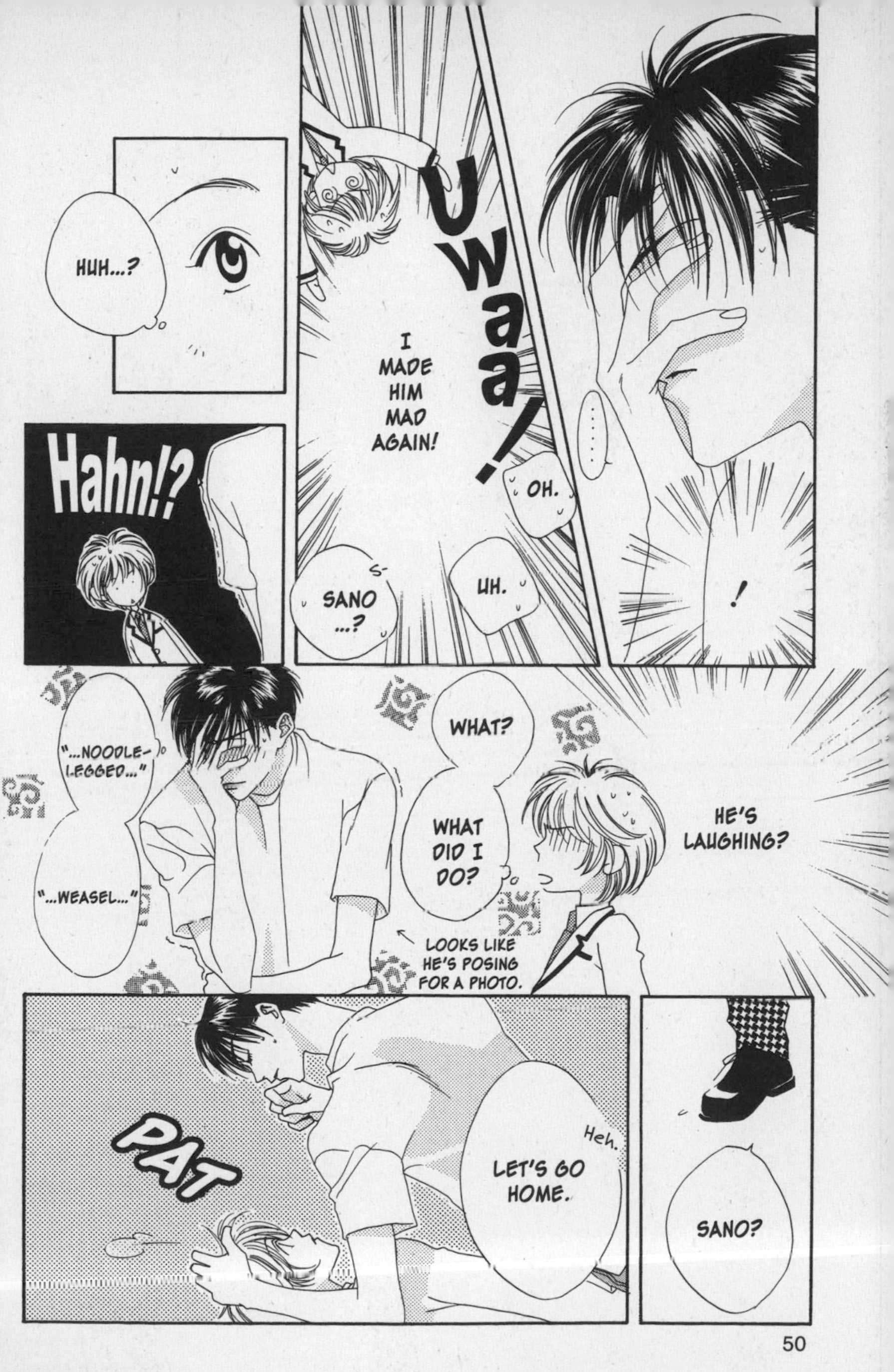
......
!
Uwa!
I MADE HIM MAD AGAIN!
OH.
UH.
S-SANO ...?
HUH...?
Hahn!?
HE'S LAUGHING?
WHAT?
WHAT DID I DO?
LOOKS LIKE HE'S POSING FOR A PHOTO.
"...NOODLE-LEGGED..."
"...WEASEL..."
SANO?
Heh.
LET'S GO HOME.
PAT

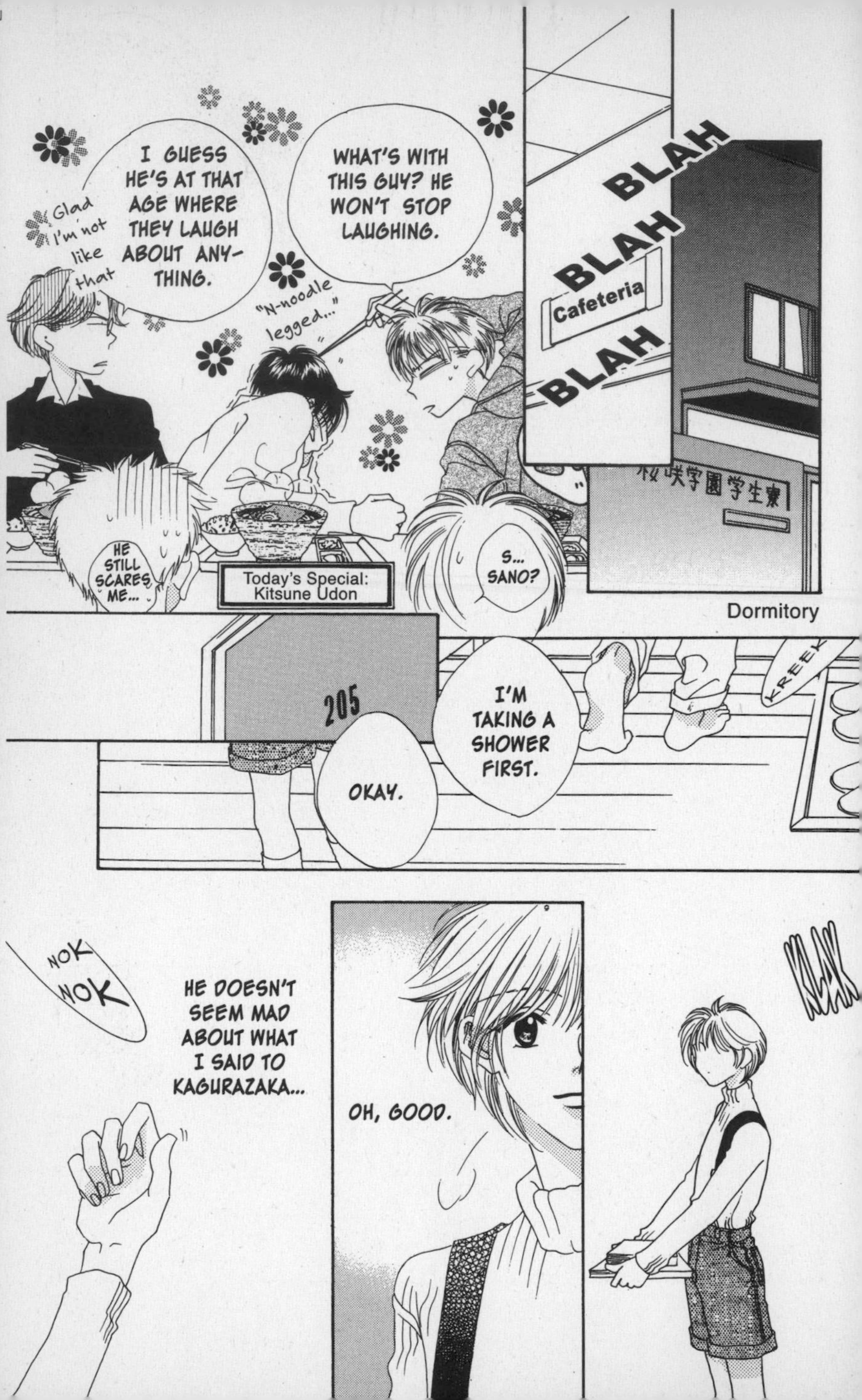
BLAH
BLAH
BLAH
BLAH
Cafeteria
桜咲学園学生寮
Dormitory
WHAT'S WITH THIS GUY? HE WON'T STOP LAUGHING.
I GUESS HE'S AT THAT AGE WHERE THEY LAUGH ABOUT ANYTHING.
Glad I'm not like that
"N-noodle legged..."
S... SANO?
Today's Special: Kitsune Udon
HE STILL SCARES ME...
KREEK
I'M TAKING A SHOWER FIRST.
205
OKAY.
OH, GOOD.
HE DOESN'T SEEM MAD ABOUT WHAT I SAID TO KAGURAZAKA...
NOK NOK

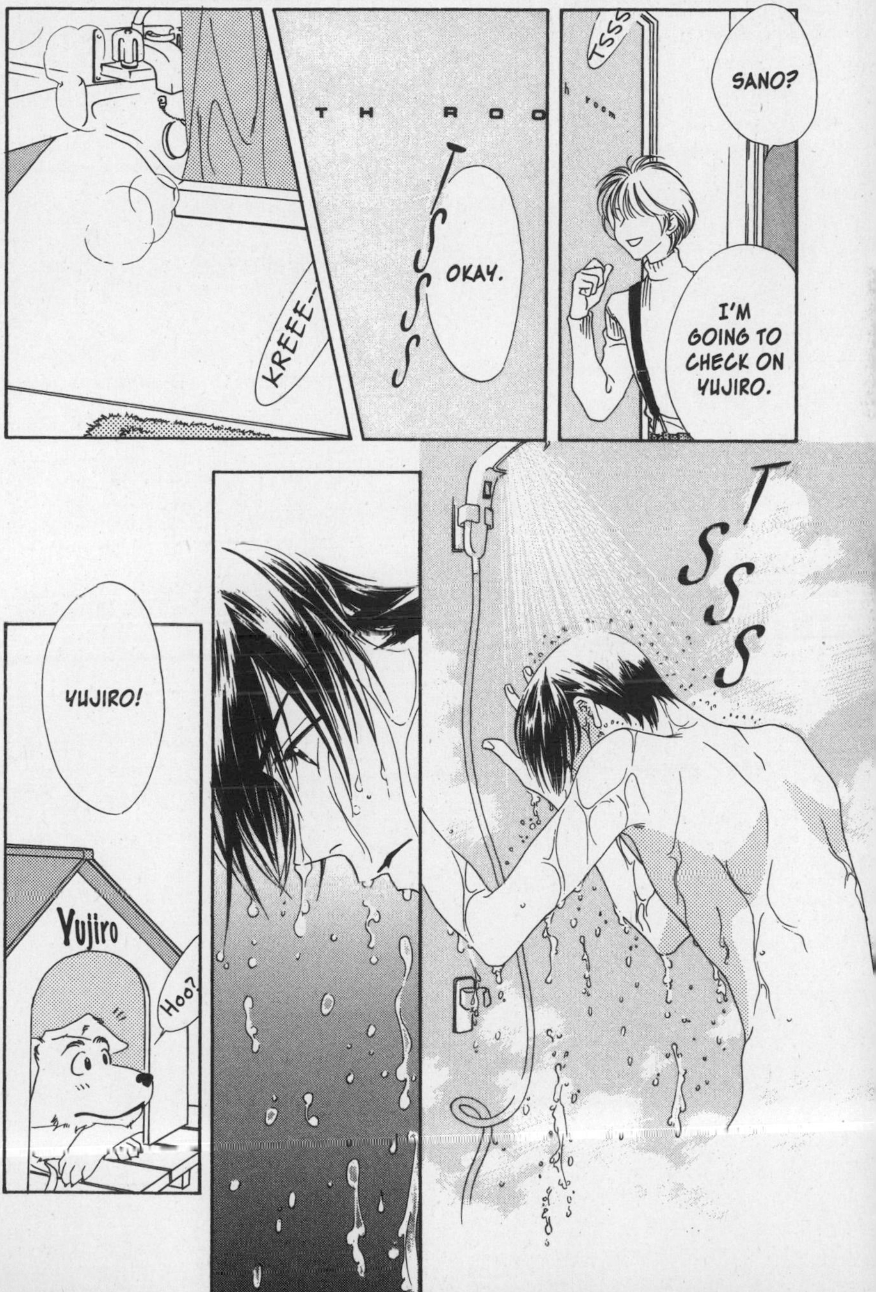

SANO?
TSSS
I'M GOING TO CHECK ON YUJIRO.
OKAY.
TSSSS
KREEEE--
TSSS
YUJIRO!
Yujiro
HOO?

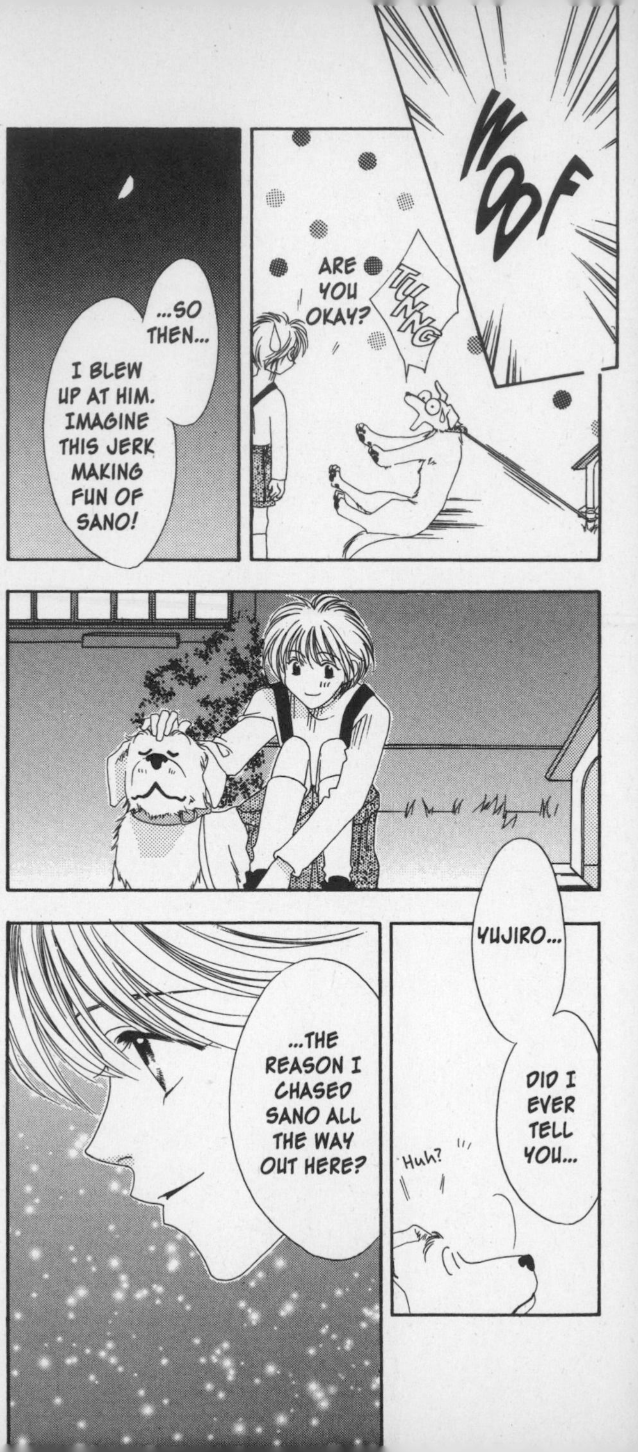
WOOF
TUNNG
ARE YOU OKAY?
...SO THEN...
I BLEW UP AT HIM. IMAGINE THIS JERK MAKING FUN OF SANO!
YUJIRO...
DID I EVER TELL YOU...
Huh?
...THE REASON I CHASED SANO ALL THE WAY OUT HERE?

Whispered Secrets

About Dr. Umeda

AUTHOR'S NOTE: WHAT CAN I SAY ABOUT THIS GUY? (HEH) LIKE NAKATSU, UMEDA IS A CHARACTER I FEEL REALLY COMFORTABLE DRAWING. SO I LIKE HIM A LOT. HE'S VERY POPULAR, TOO. SOME PEOPLE SAY "I'LL FOLLOW HIM FOREVER" WHILE OTHERS SAY "I'D LIKE HIM BETTER IF HE WEREN'T GAY." HE INSPIRES THE MOST INTERESTING RESPONSES. EVEN WHEN I HAD HIM DANCING IN A BIKINI YOU GUYS ALL SAID, "I WAS SHOCKED BUT I THINK IT'S COOL."

DO YOU MEAN IT?

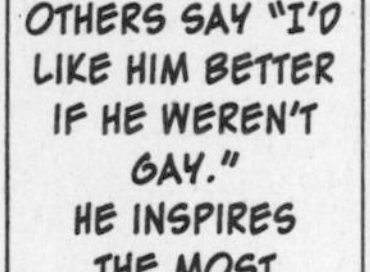
I really like what you're doing with that school doctor.
...
Nanbe Yamada

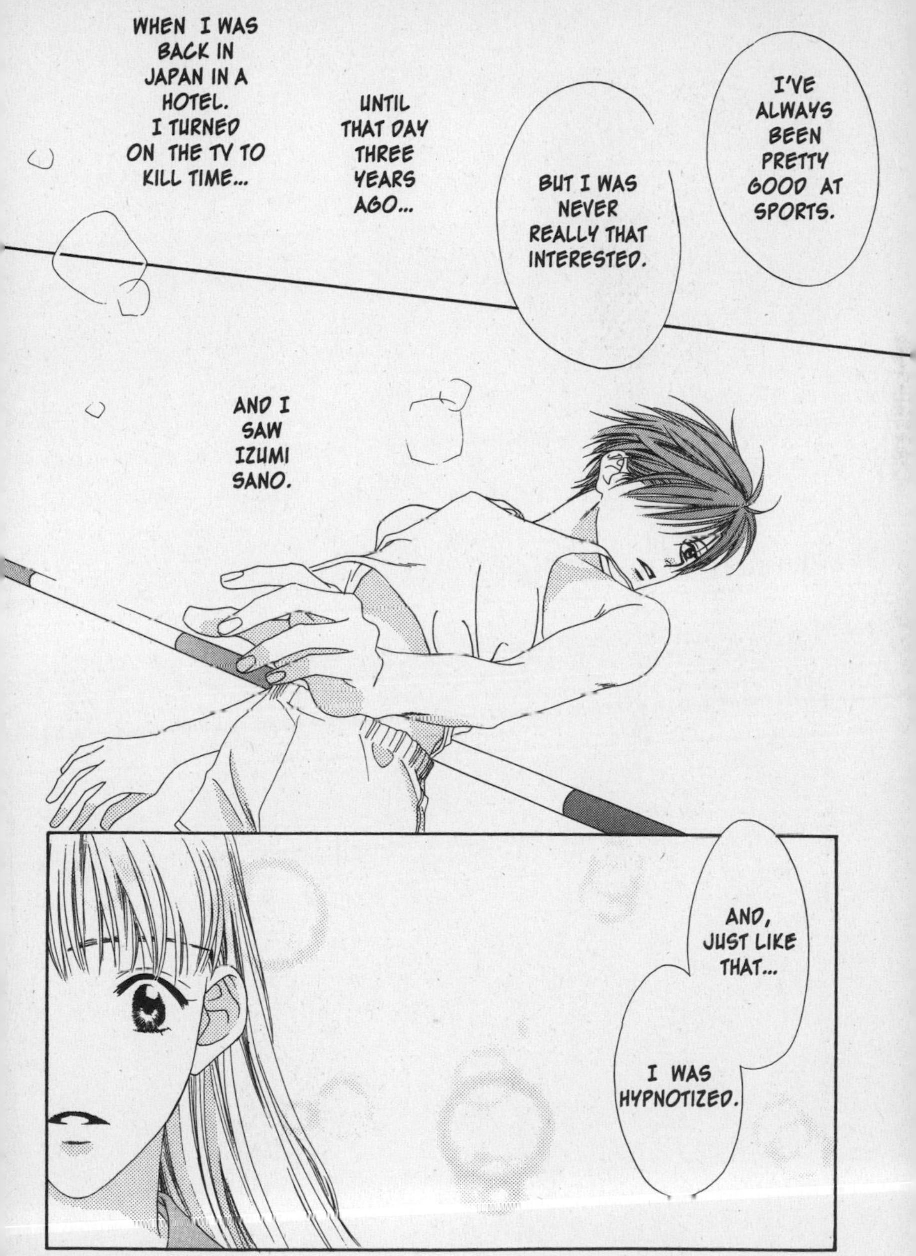
I'VE ALWAYS BEEN PRETTY GOOD AT SPORTS.
BUT I WAS NEVER REALLY THAT INTERESTED.
UNTIL THAT DAY THREE YEARS AGO...
WHEN I WAS BACK IN JAPAN IN A HOTEL. I TURNED ON THE TV TO KILL TIME...
AND I SAW IZUMI SANO.
AND, JUST LIKE THAT...
I WAS HYPNOTIZED.

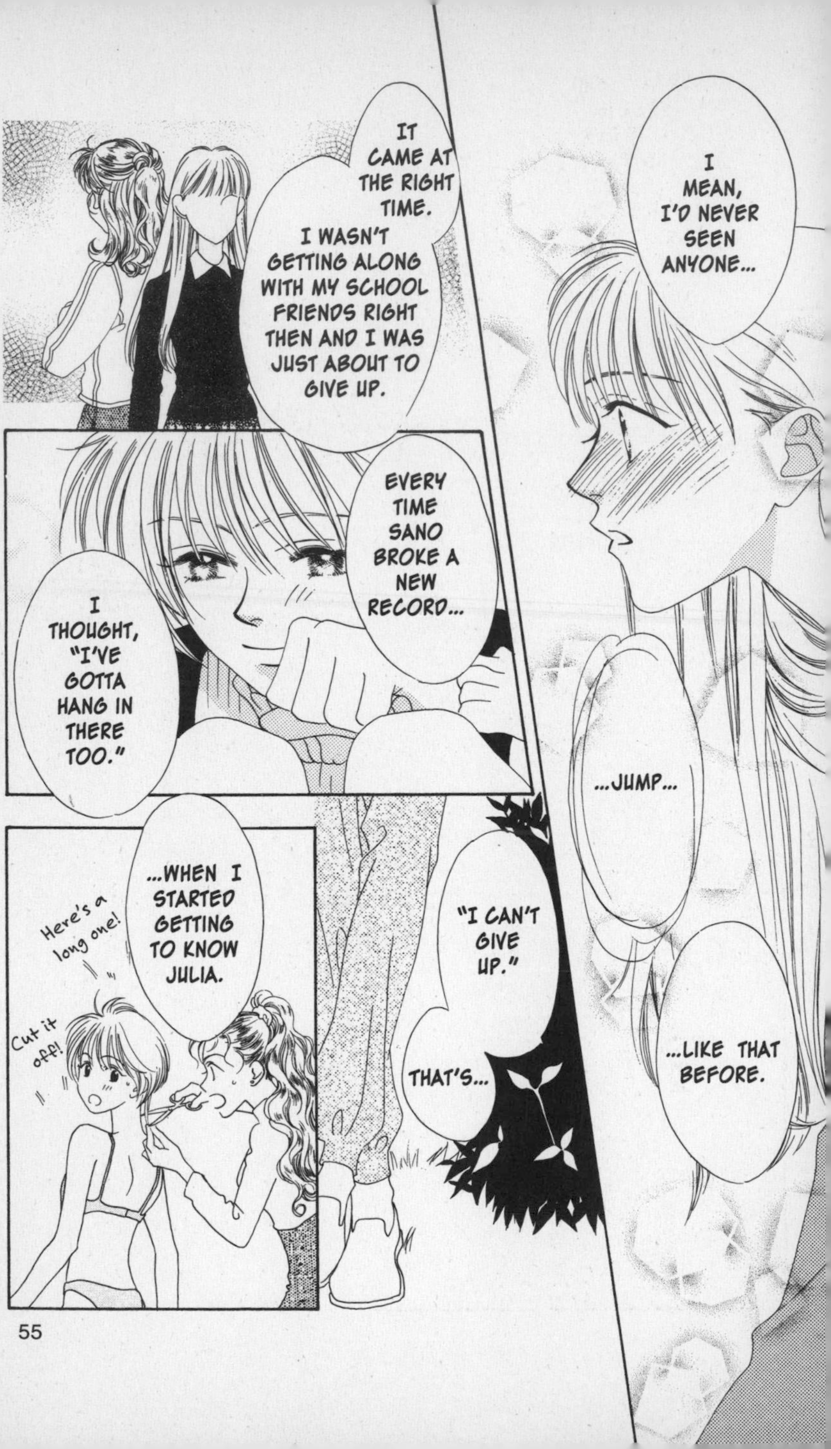
I MEAN, I'D NEVER SEEN ANYONE...
...JUMP...
...LIKE THAT BEFORE.
IT CAME AT THE RIGHT TIME.
I WASN'T GETTING ALONG WITH MY SCHOOL FRIENDS RIGHT THEN AND I WAS JUST ABOUT TO GIVE UP.
EVERY TIME SANO BROKE A NEW RECORD...
I THOUGHT, "I'VE GOTTA HANG IN THERE TOO."
"I CAN'T GIVE UP."
THAT'S...
...WHEN I STARTED GETTING TO KNOW JULIA.
Here's a long one!
Cut it off!

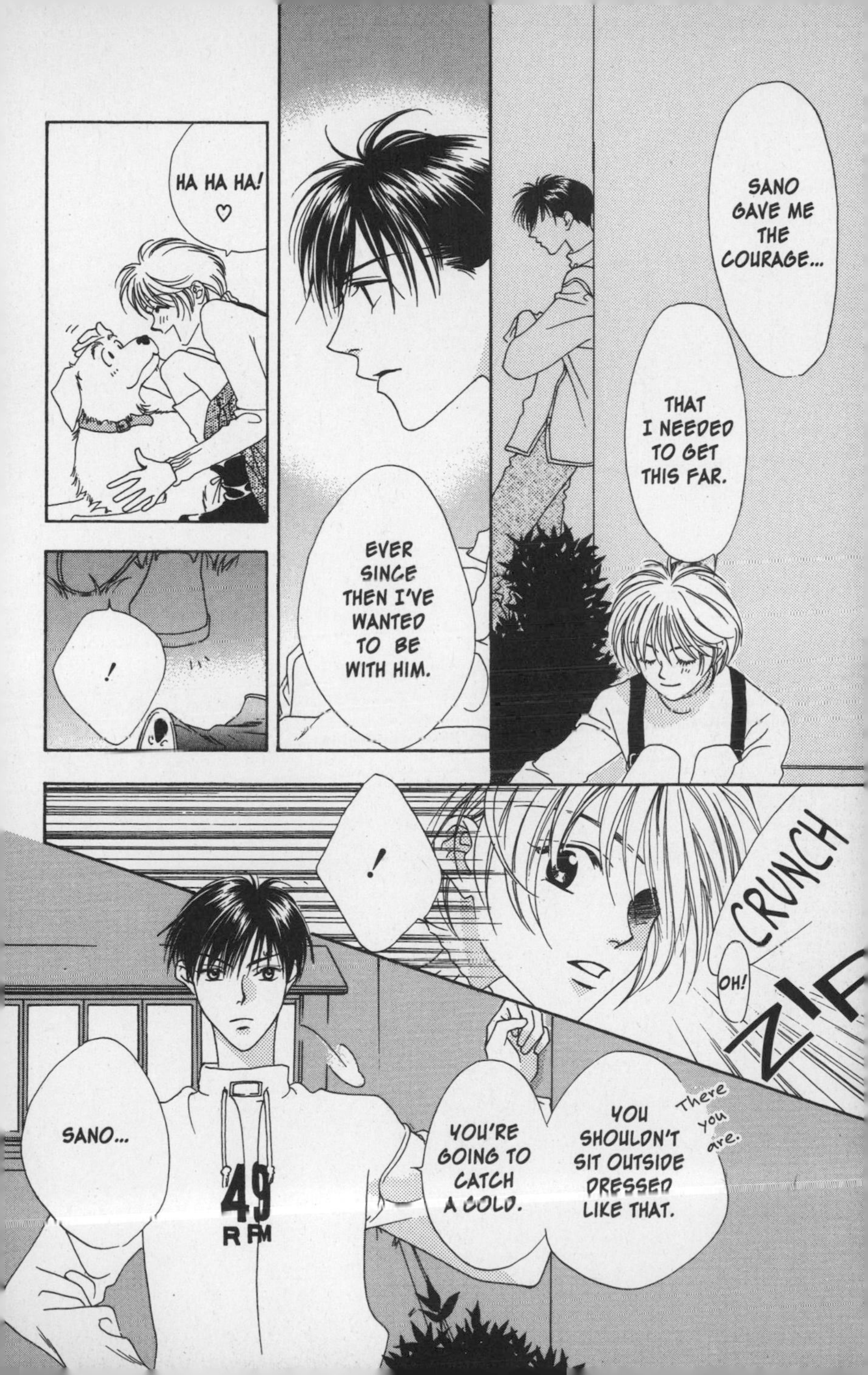
SANO GAVE ME THE COURAGE...
THAT I NEEDED TO GET THIS FAR.
EVER SINCE THEN I'VE WANTED TO BE WITH HIM.
HA HA HA! ♡
!
CRUNCH
OH!
!
There you are.
YOU SHOULDN'T SIT OUTSIDE DRESSED LIKE THAT.
YOU'RE GOING TO CATCH A COLD.
49 R FM
SANO...

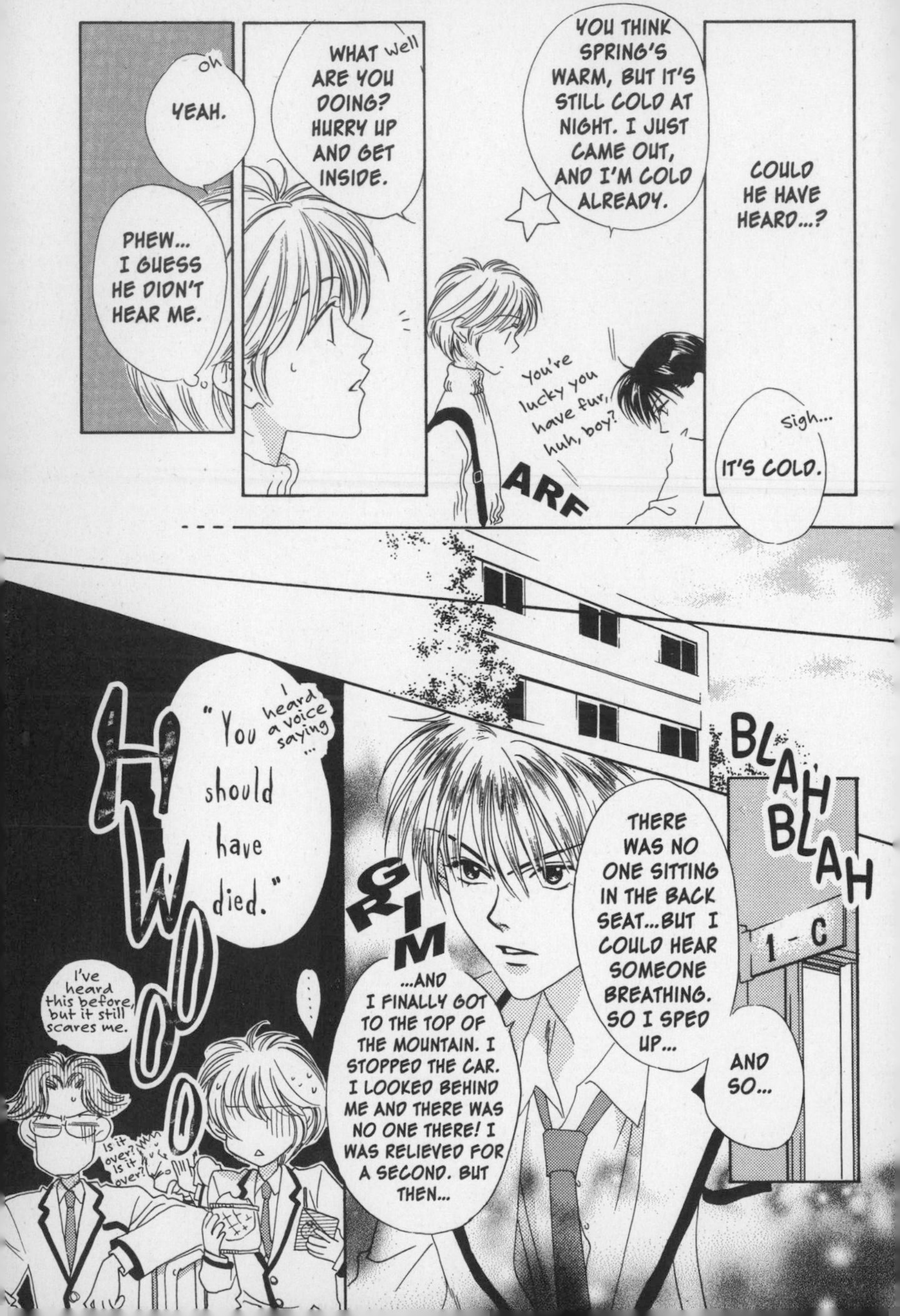
COULD HE HAVE HEARD...?
Sigh...
IT'S COLD.
YOU THINK SPRING'S WARM, BUT IT'S STILL COLD AT NIGHT. I JUST CAME OUT, AND I'M COLD ALREADY.
You're lucky you have fur, huh, boy?
ARF
WHAT well ARE YOU DOING? HURRY UP AND GET INSIDE.
oh YEAH.
PHEW... I GUESS HE DIDN'T HEAR ME.
BLAH BLAH
1-C
THERE WAS NO ONE SITTING IN THE BACK SEAT...BUT I COULD HEAR SOMEONE BREATHING. SO I SPED UP...
AND SO...
GRIM
...AND I FINALLY GOT TO THE TOP OF THE MOUNTAIN. I STOPPED THE CAR. I LOOKED BEHIND ME AND THERE WAS NO ONE THERE! I WAS RELIEVED FOR A SECOND. BUT THEN...
I heard a voice saying...
"You should have died."
HWOOO
...
I've heard this before, but it still scares me.
Is it over? Is it over?

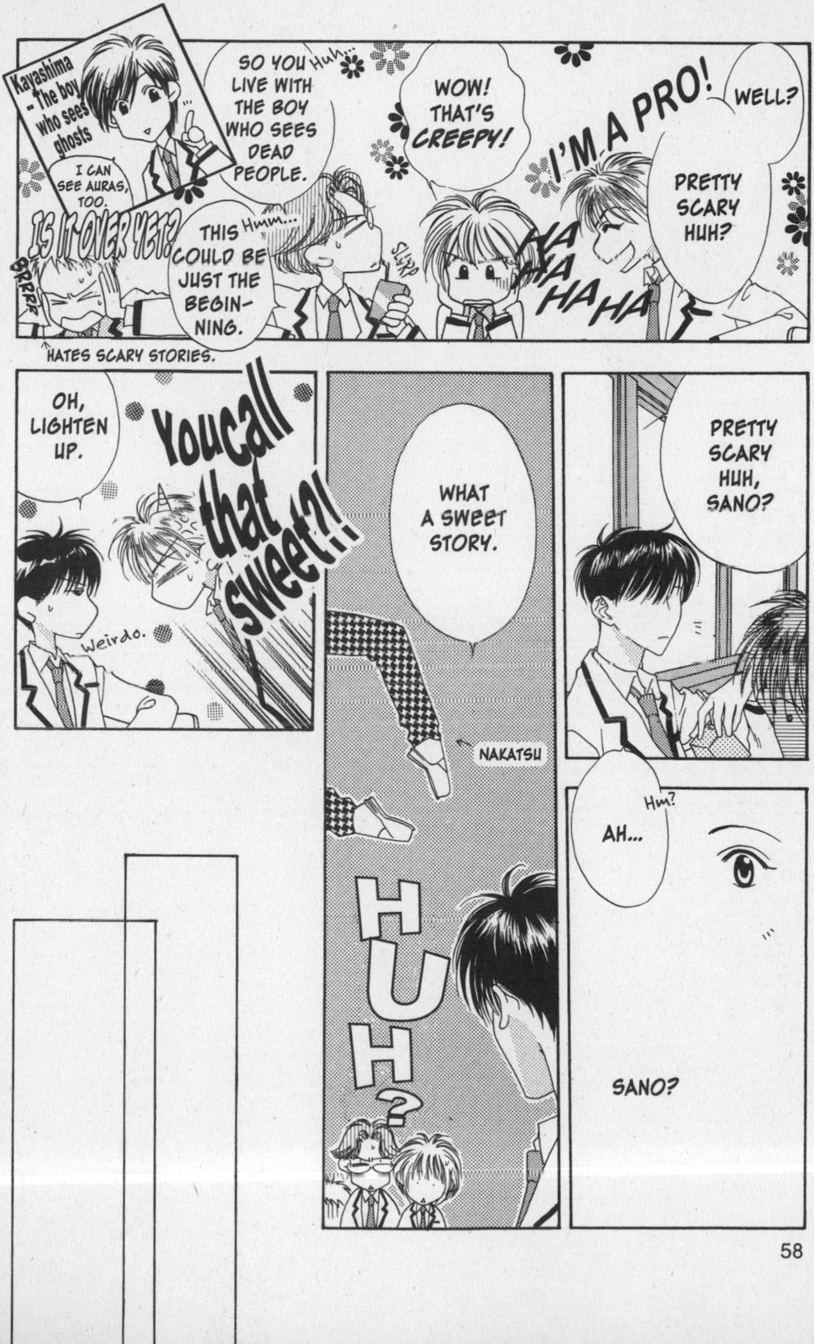
WELL?
PRETTY SCARY HUH?
I'M A PRO!
HA HA HA HA
WOW! THAT'S CREEPY!
SO YOU LIVE WITH THE BOY WHO SEES DEAD PEOPLE.
Huh...
THIS COULD BE JUST THE BEGIN-NING.
Hmm...
SLURP
Kayashima - The boy who sees ghosts
I CAN SEE AURAS, TOO.
IS IT OVER YET?
BRRRR
HATES SCARY STORIES.
PRETTY SCARY HUH, SANO?
AH...
Hm?
SANO?
WHAT A SWEET STORY.
NAKATSU
HUH?
You call that sweet?!
OH, LIGHTEN UP.
Weirdo.

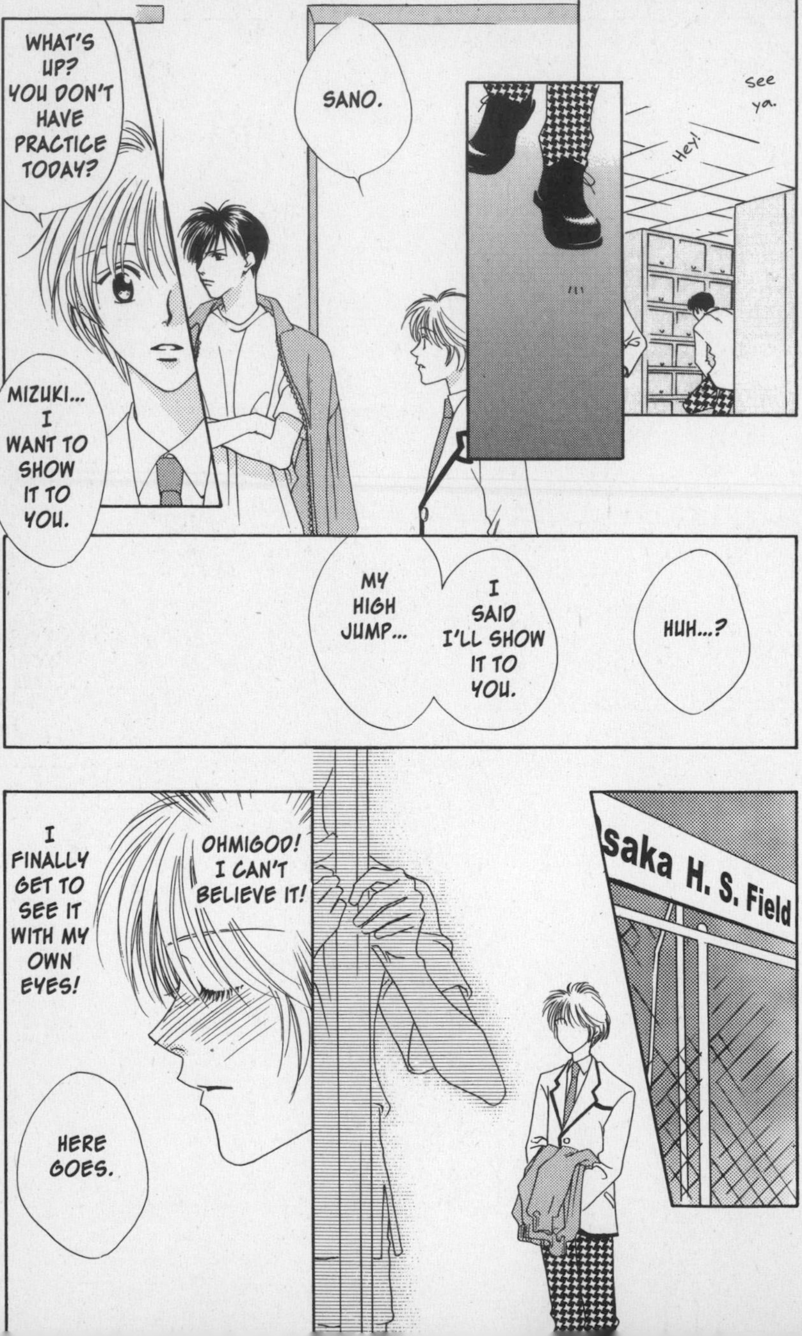
See ya.
Hey!
SANO.
WHAT'S UP? YOU DON'T HAVE PRACTICE TODAY?
MIZUKI... I WANT TO SHOW IT TO YOU.
HUH...?
I SAID I'LL SHOW IT TO YOU.
MY HIGH JUMP...
saka H. S. Field
OHMIGOD! I CAN'T BELIEVE IT!
I FINALLY GET TO SEE IT WITH MY OWN EYES!
HERE GOES.

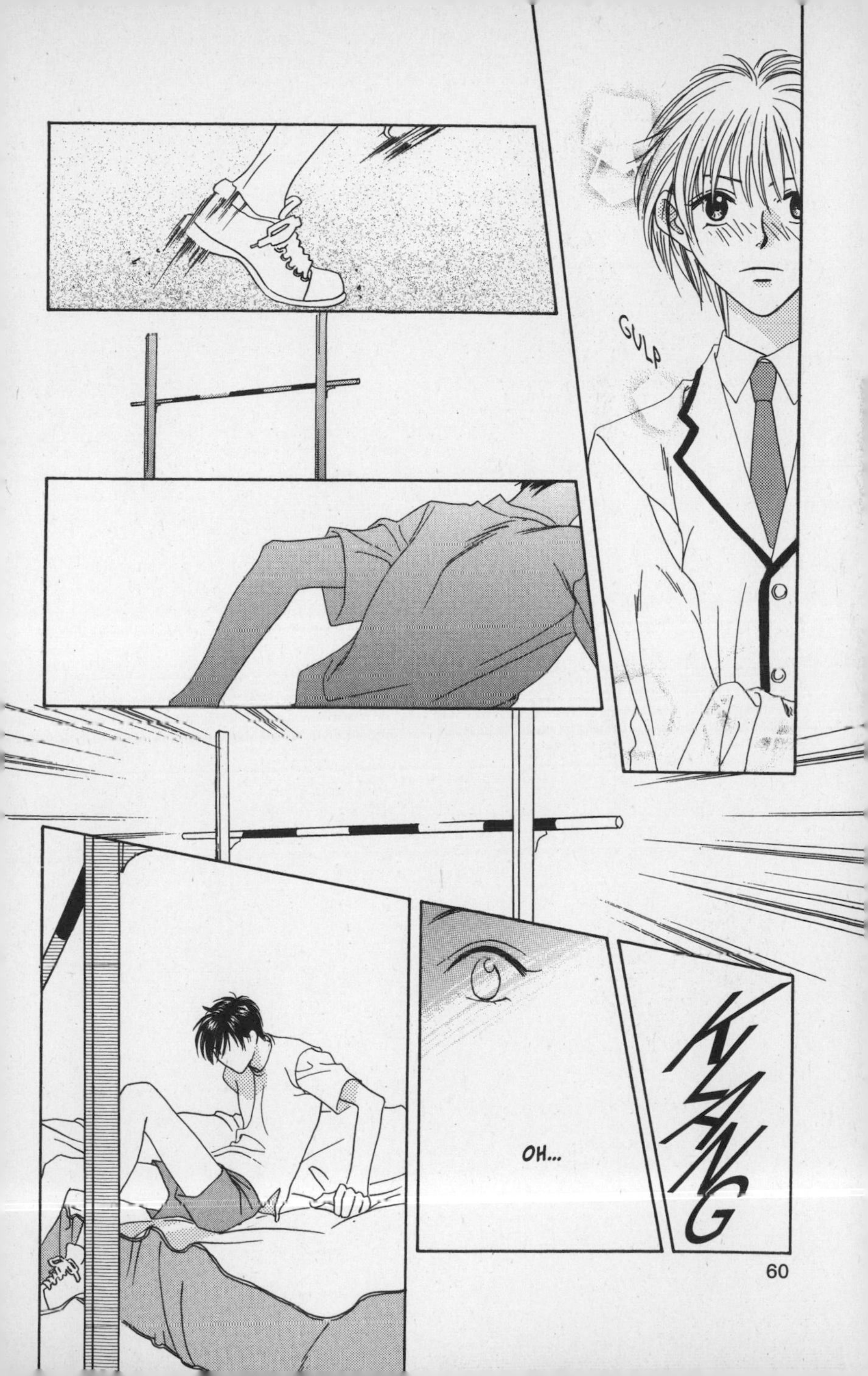
GULP
KLANG
OH...

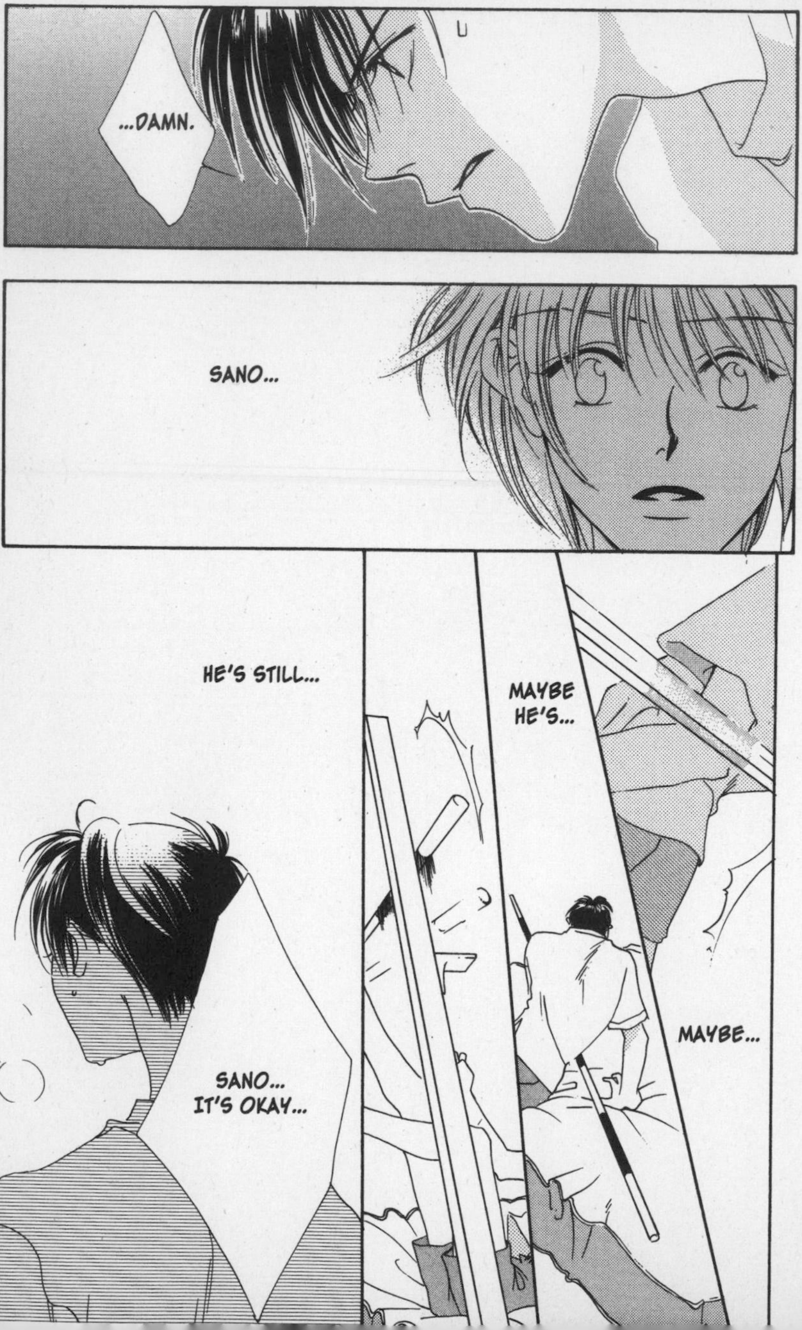
...DAMN.
SANO...
MAYBE...
MAYBE HE'S...
HE'S STILL...
SANO... IT'S OKAY...

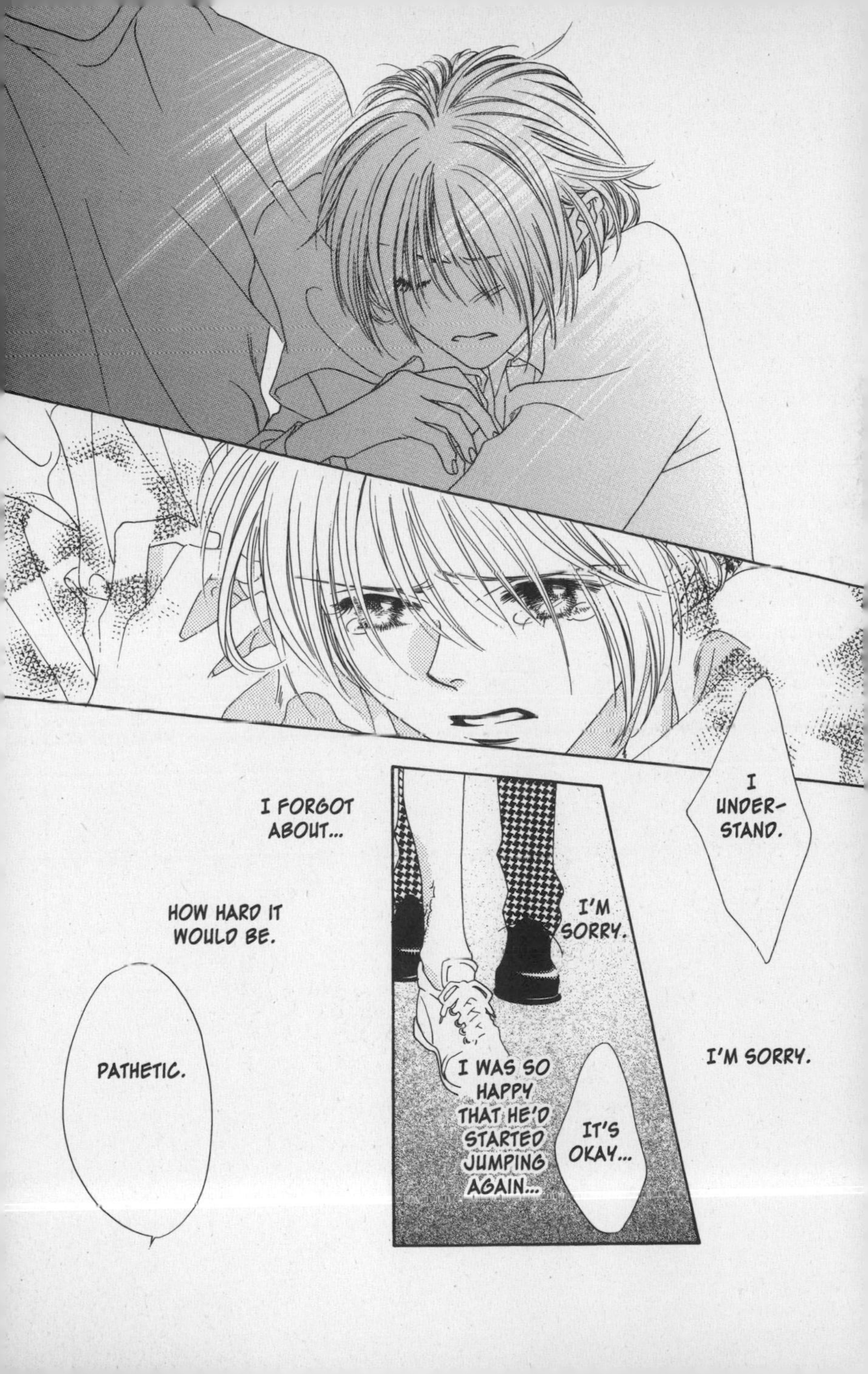
I UNDER-STAND.
I'M SORRY.
I'M SORRY.
IT'S OKAY...
I WAS SO HAPPY THAT HE'D STARTED JUMPING AGAIN...
I FORGOT ABOUT...
HOW HARD IT WOULD BE.
PATHETIC.

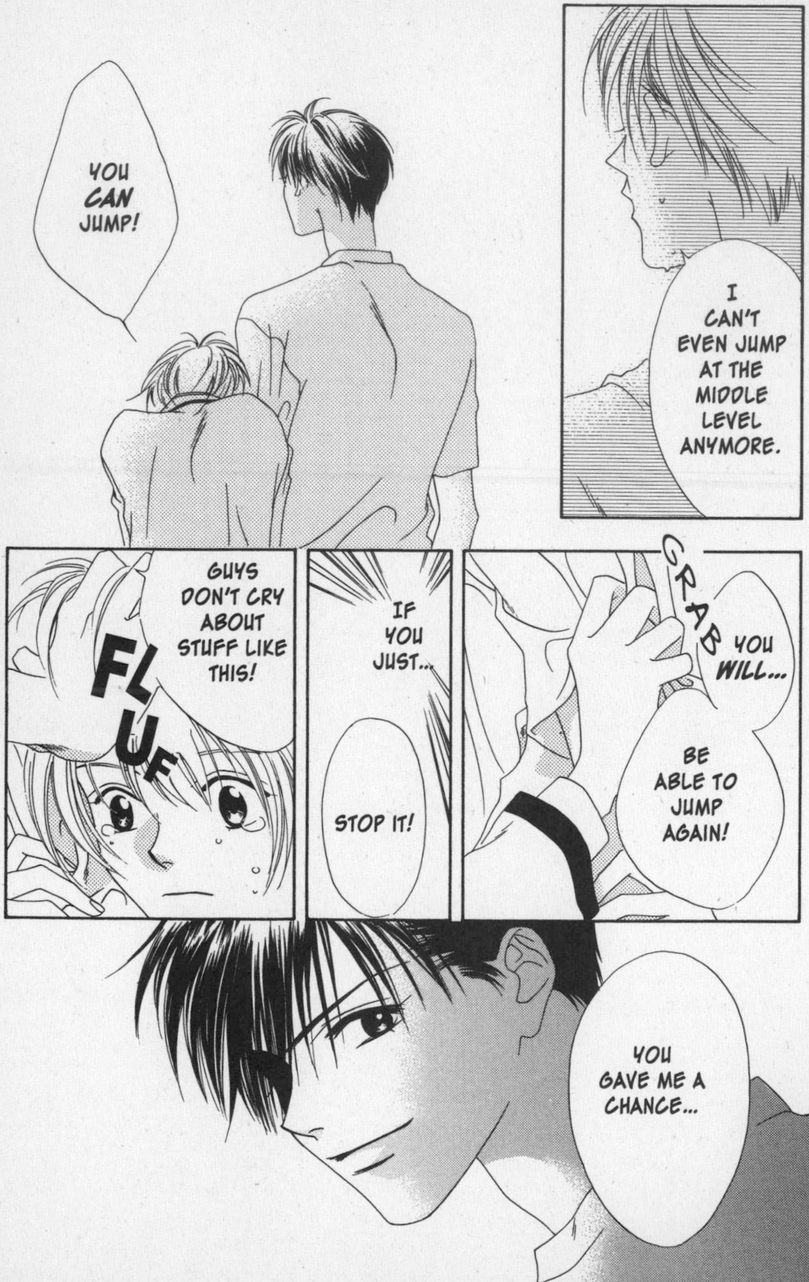
I CAN'T EVEN JUMP AT THE MIDDLE LEVEL ANYMORE.
YOU CAN JUMP!
GRAB
YOU WILL...
BE ABLE TO JUMP AGAIN!
IF YOU JUST...
STOP IT!
GUYS DON'T CRY ABOUT STUFF LIKE THIS!
FLUF
YOU GAVE ME A CHANCE...

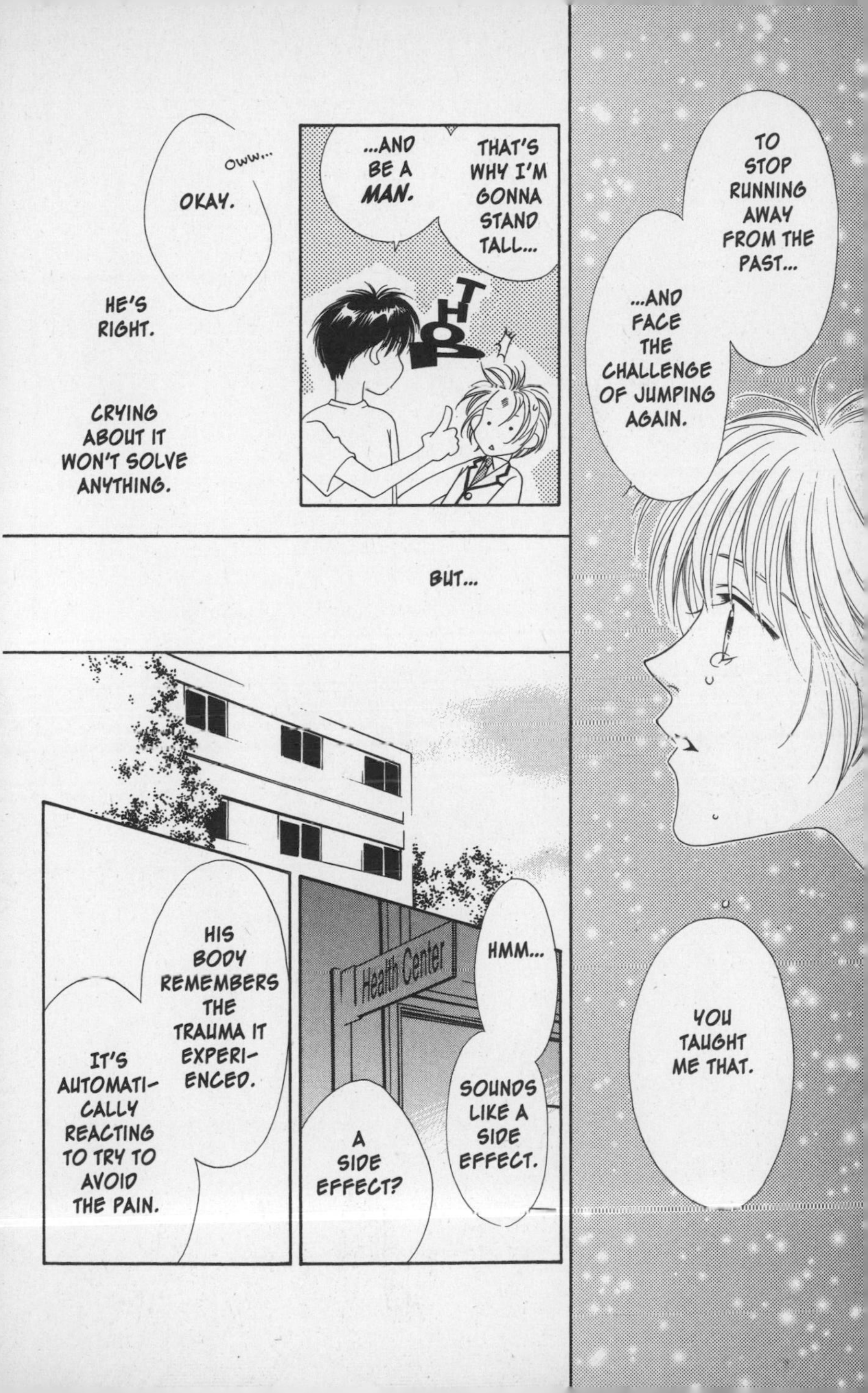
TO STOP RUNNING AWAY FROM THE PAST...
...AND FACE THE CHALLENGE OF JUMPING AGAIN.
YOU TAUGHT ME THAT.
THAT'S WHY I'M GONNA STAND TALL...
...AND BE A MAN.
THOK
OKAY.
OWW...
HE'S RIGHT.
CRYING ABOUT IT WON'T SOLVE ANYTHING.
BUT...
Health Center
HMM...
SOUNDS LIKE A SIDE EFFECT.
A SIDE EFFECT?
HIS BODY REMEMBERS THE TRAUMA IT EXPERI-ENCED.
IT'S AUTOMATI-CALLY REACTING TO TRY TO AVOID THE PAIN.

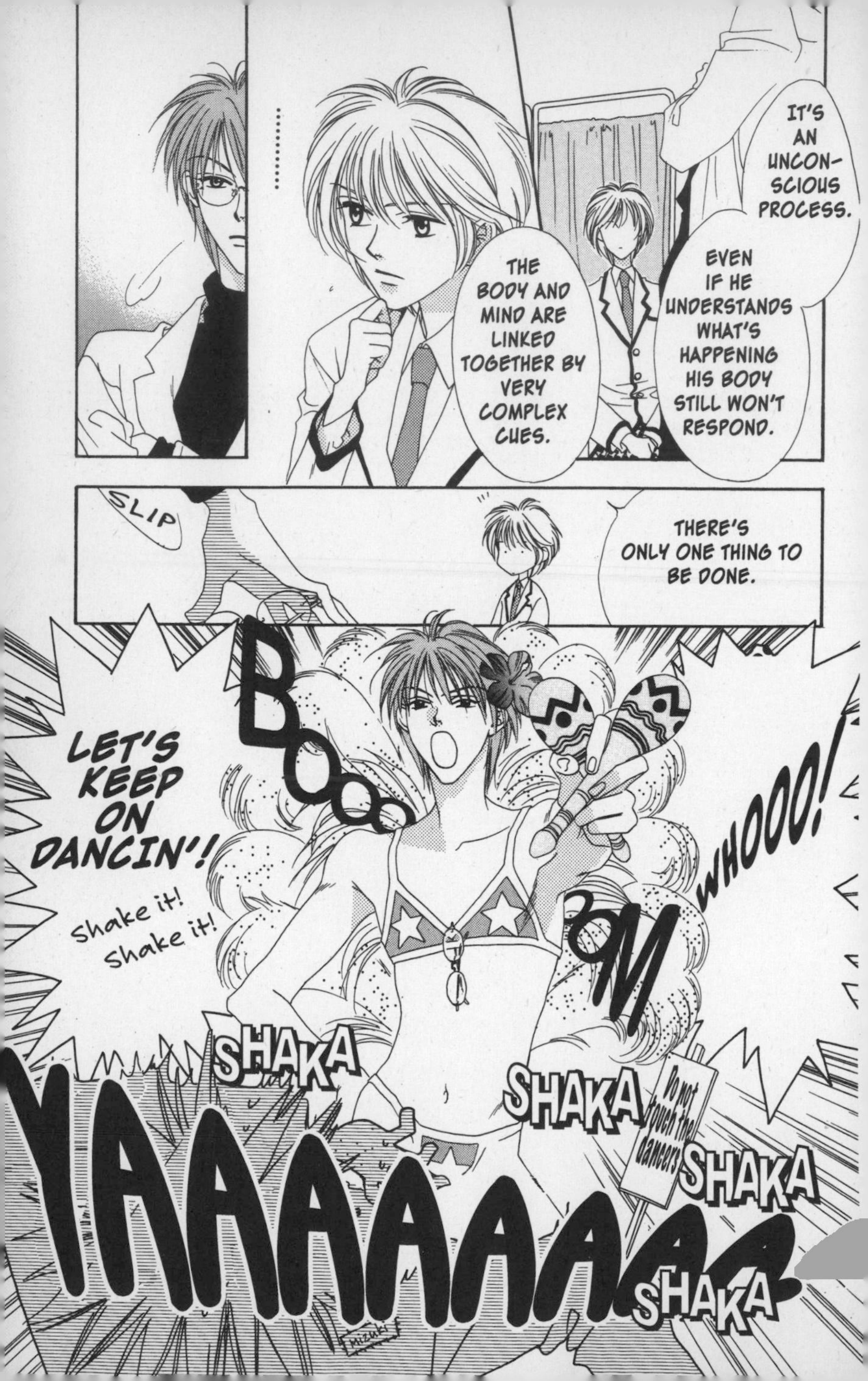
IT'S AN UNCON-SCIOUS PROCESS.
EVEN IF HE UNDERSTANDS WHAT'S HAPPENING HIS BODY STILL WON'T RESPOND.
THE BODY AND MIND ARE LINKED TOGETHER BY VERY COMPLEX CUES.
......
THERE'S ONLY ONE THING TO BE DONE.
SLIP
LET'S KEEP ON DANCIN'!
WHOOO!
BOOOOM
Shake it! Shake it!
SHAKA
SHAKA
Do not touch the dancers
SHAKA
SHAKA
YAAAAAAAA

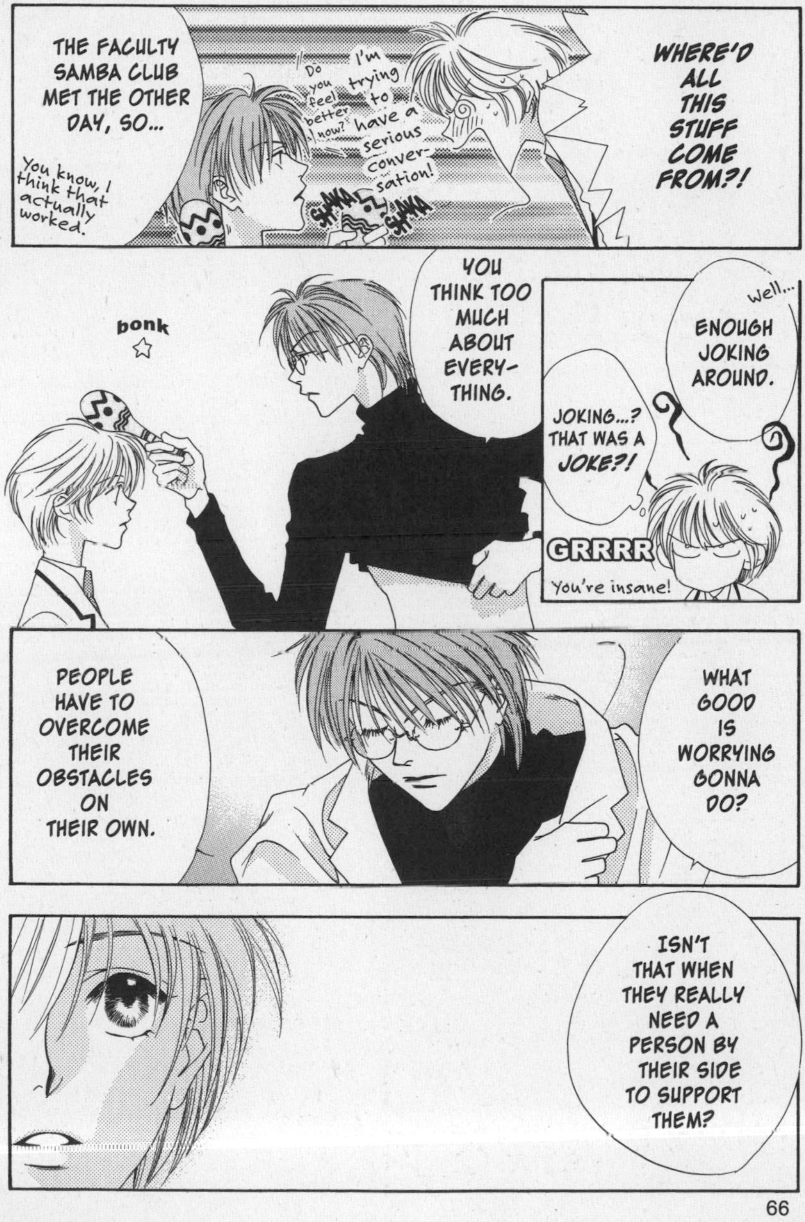
WHERE'D ALL THIS STUFF COME FROM?!
I'm trying to have a serious conver-sation!
Do you feel better now?
SHAKA SHAKA SHAKA
THE FACULTY SAMBA CLUB MET THE OTHER DAY, SO...
You know, I think that actually worked.
Well...
ENOUGH JOKING AROUND.
JOKING...? THAT WAS A JOKE?!
GRRRR
You're insane!
YOU THINK TOO MUCH ABOUT EVERY-THING.
bonk
WHAT GOOD IS WORRYING GONNA DO?
PEOPLE HAVE TO OVERCOME THEIR OBSTACLES ON THEIR OWN.
ISN'T THAT WHEN THEY REALLY NEED A PERSON BY THEIR SIDE TO SUPPORT THEM?

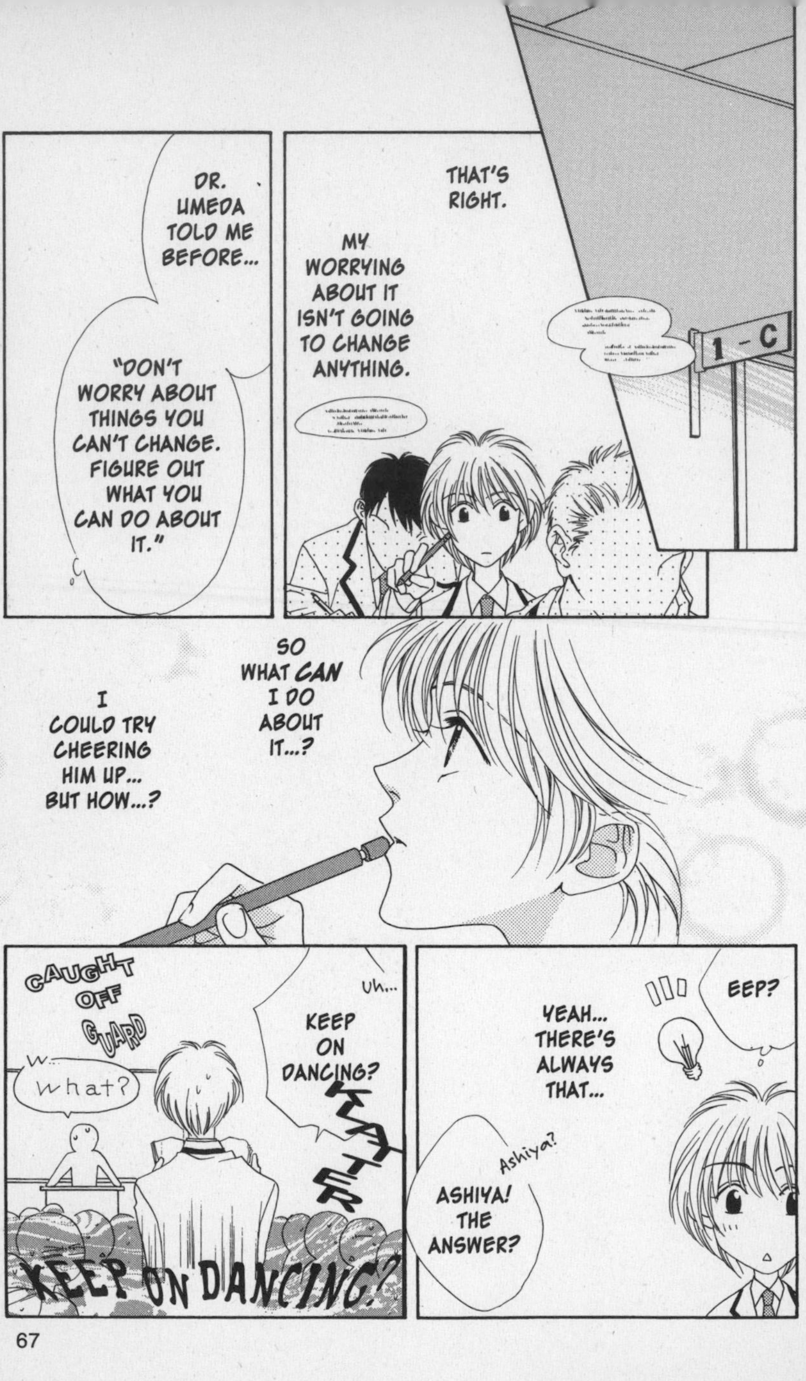
1-C
THAT'S RIGHT.
MY WORRYING ABOUT IT ISN'T GOING TO CHANGE ANYTHING.
DR. UMEDA TOLD ME BEFORE...
"DON'T WORRY ABOUT THINGS YOU CAN'T CHANGE. FIGURE OUT WHAT YOU CAN DO ABOUT IT."
SO WHAT CAN I DO ABOUT IT...?
I COULD TRY CHEERING HIM UP... BUT HOW...?
EEP?
YEAH... THERE'S ALWAYS THAT...
Ashiya?
ASHIYA! THE ANSWER?
Uh...
KEEP ON DANCING?
KLATTER
CAUGHT OFF GUARD
W... what?
KEEP ON DANCING!?

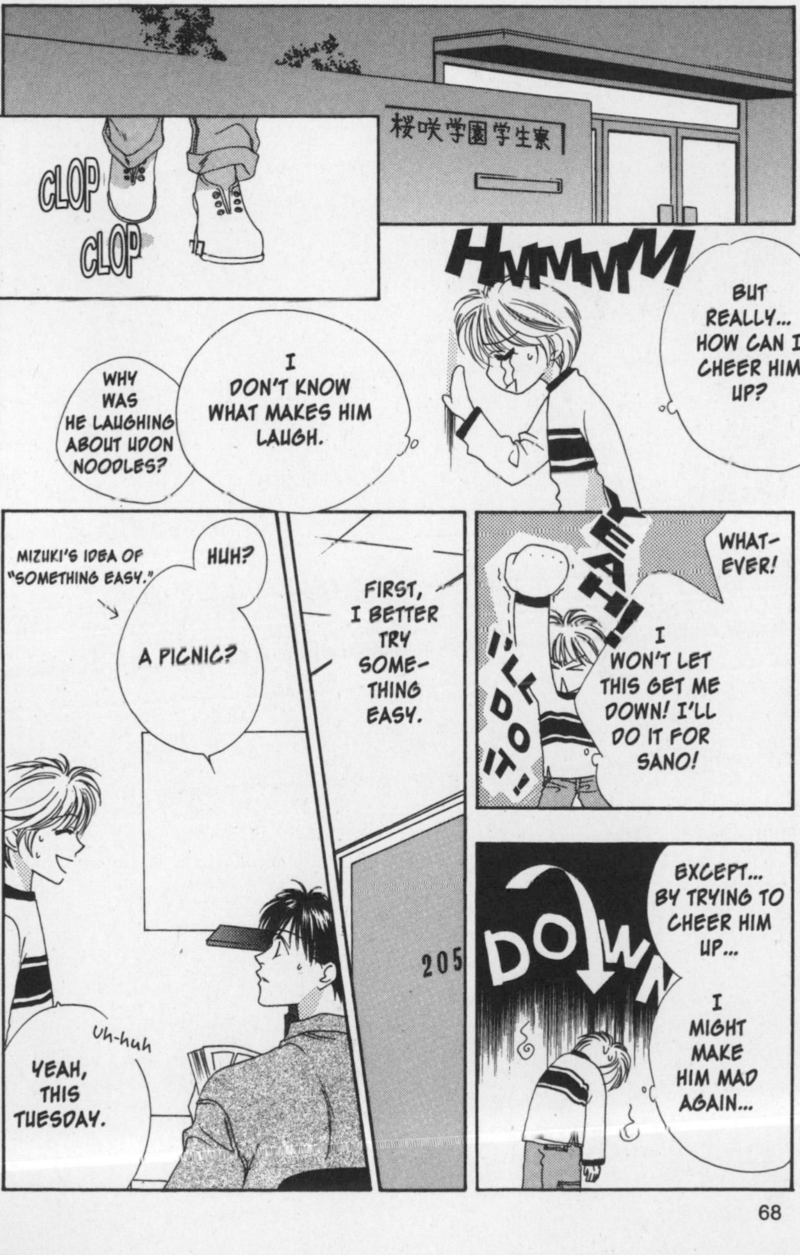

桜咲学園学生寮
CLOP
CLOP
HMMMM
BUT REALLY... HOW CAN I CHEER HIM UP?
I DON'T KNOW WHAT MAKES HIM LAUGH.
WHY WAS HE LAUGHING ABOUT UDON NOODLES?
WHAT-EVER!
YEAH!
I WON'T LET THIS GET ME DOWN! I'LL DO IT FOR SANO!
I'LL DO IT!
EXCEPT... BY TRYING TO CHEER HIM UP...
DOWN
I MIGHT MAKE HIM MAD AGAIN...
FIRST, I BETTER TRY SOME-THING EASY.
HUH?
A PICNIC?
MIZUKI'S IDEA OF "SOMETHING EASY."
205
Uh-huh
YEAH, THIS TUESDAY.

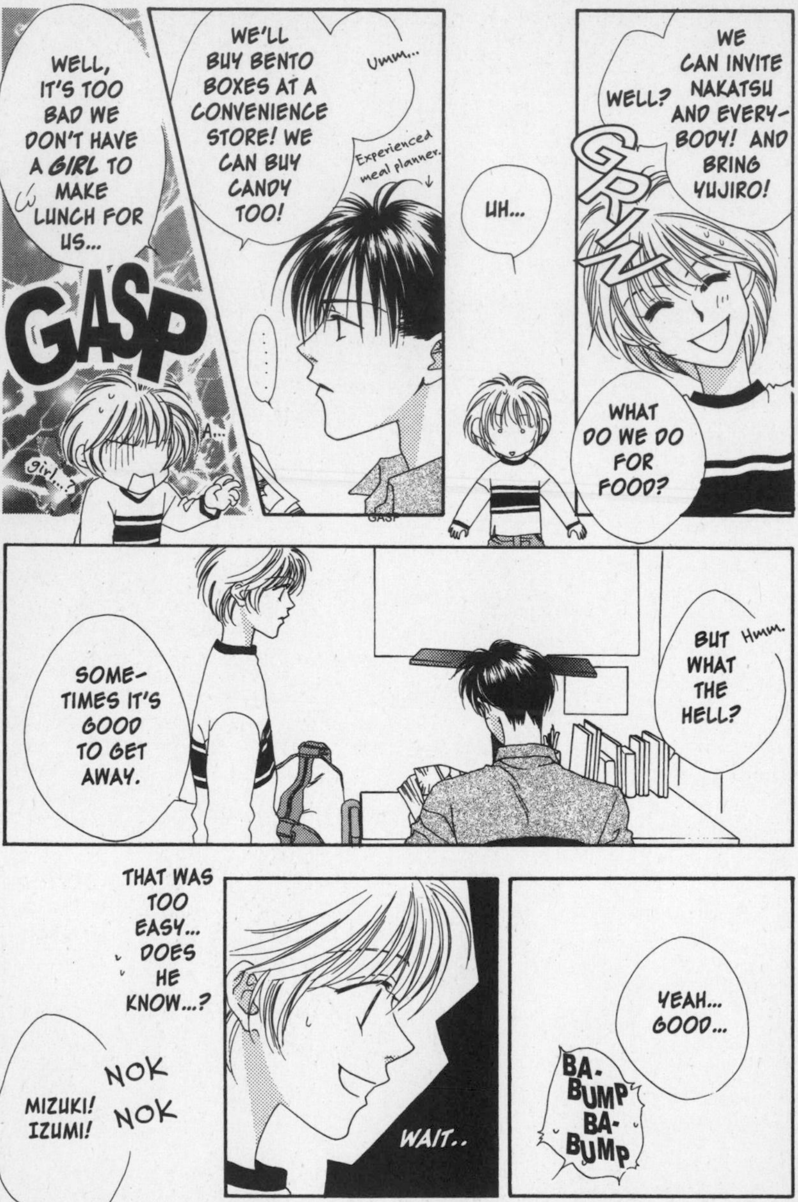
WE CAN INVITE NAKATSU AND EVERY-BODY! AND BRING YUJIRO!
WELL?
GRIN
WHAT DO WE DO FOR FOOD?
UH...
WE'LL BUY BENTO BOXES AT A CONVENIENCE STORE! WE CAN BUY CANDY TOO!
Umm...
Experienced meal planner.
...
GASP
WELL, IT'S TOO BAD WE DON'T HAVE A GIRL TO MAKE LUNCH FOR US...
GASP
A...
girl...?
BUT WHAT THE HELL?
Hmm.
SOME-TIMES IT'S GOOD TO GET AWAY.
YEAH... GOOD...
BA-BUMP BA-BUMP
THAT WAS TOO EASY... DOES HE KNOW...?
WAIT..
NOK NOK
MIZUKI! IZUMI!

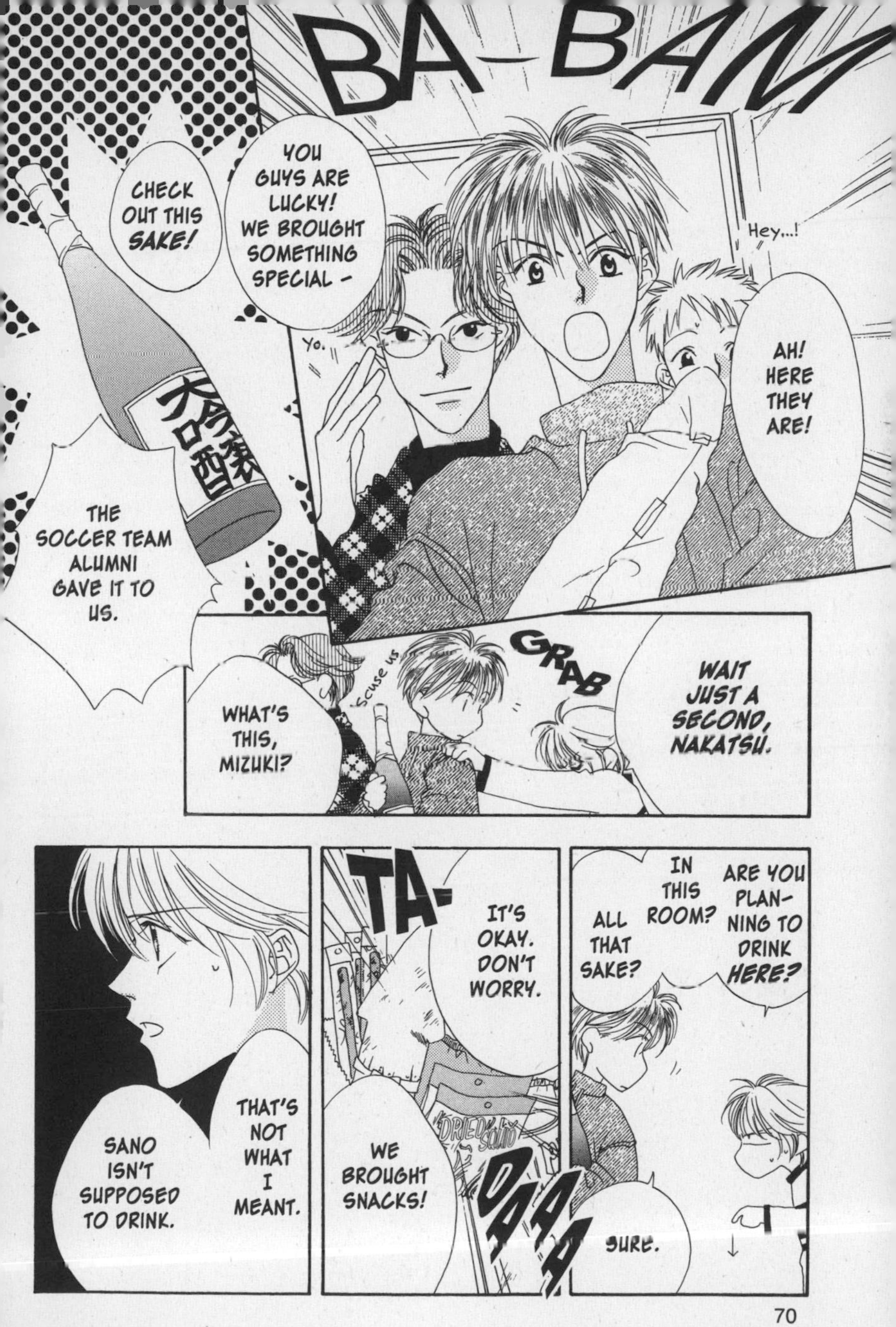
BA-BAM
Hey...!
AH! HERE THEY ARE!
YOU GUYS ARE LUCKY! WE BROUGHT SOMETHING SPECIAL –
Yo.
CHECK OUT THIS SAKE!
大吟醸
THE SOCCER TEAM ALUMNI GAVE IT TO US.
WAIT JUST A SECOND, NAKATSU.
GRAB
Scuse us
WHAT'S THIS, MIZUKI?
ARE YOU PLANNING TO DRINK HERE?
IN THIS ROOM?
ALL THAT SAKE?
SURE.
TA-
IT'S OKAY. DON'T WORRY.
DRIED SQUID
WE BROUGHT SNACKS!
DAAA
THAT'S NOT WHAT I MEANT.
SANO ISN'T SUPPOSED TO DRINK.

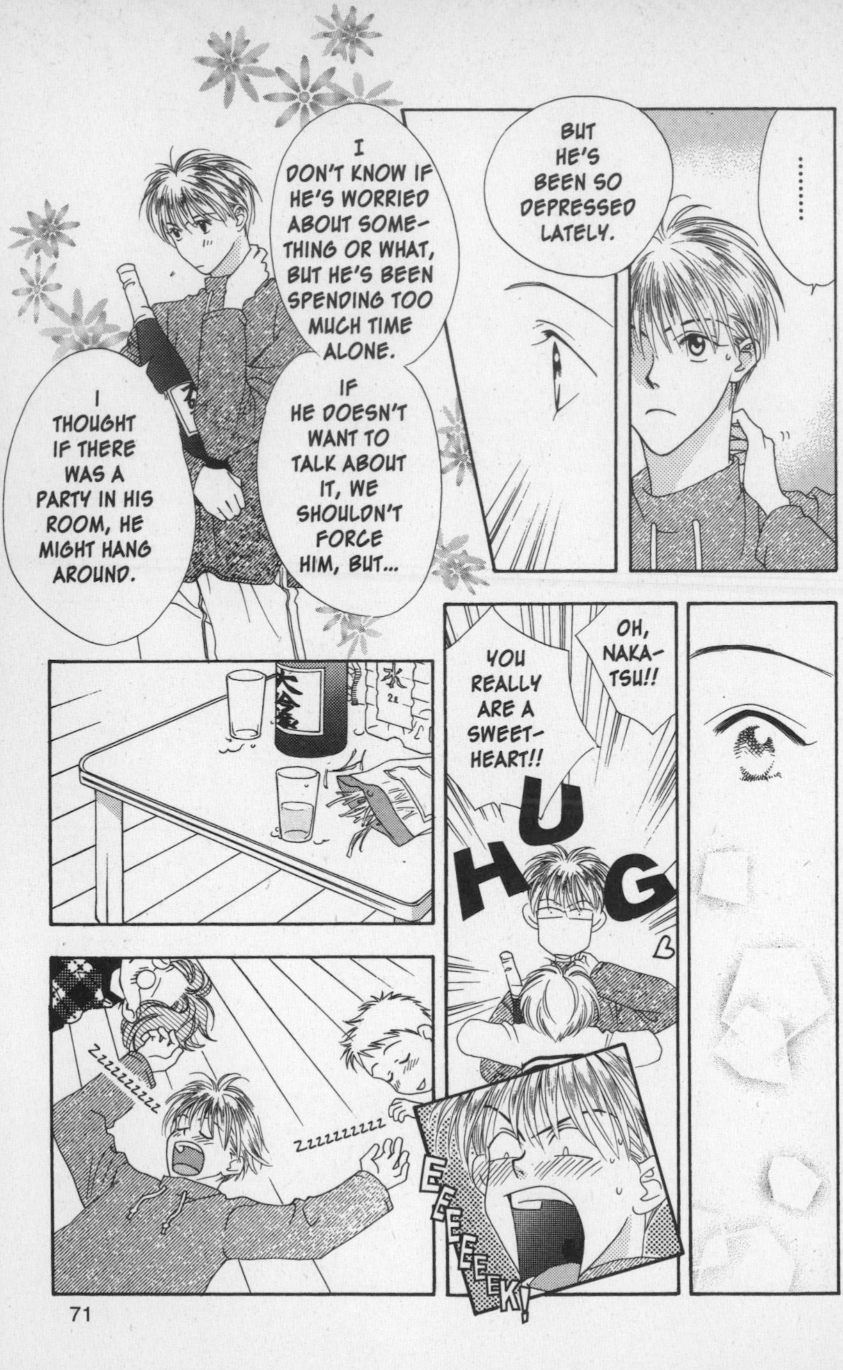
......
BUT HE'S BEEN SO DEPRESSED LATELY.
I DON'T KNOW IF HE'S WORRIED ABOUT SOME-THING OR WHAT, BUT HE'S BEEN SPENDING TOO MUCH TIME ALONE.
IF HE DOESN'T WANT TO TALK ABOUT IT, WE SHOULDN'T FORCE HIM, BUT...
I THOUGHT IF THERE WAS A PARTY IN HIS ROOM, HE MIGHT HANG AROUND.
OH, NAKA-TSU!!
YOU REALLY ARE A SWEET-HEART!!
HUG
EEEEEEK!
ZZZZZZZZZZ
ZZZZZZZZZZ

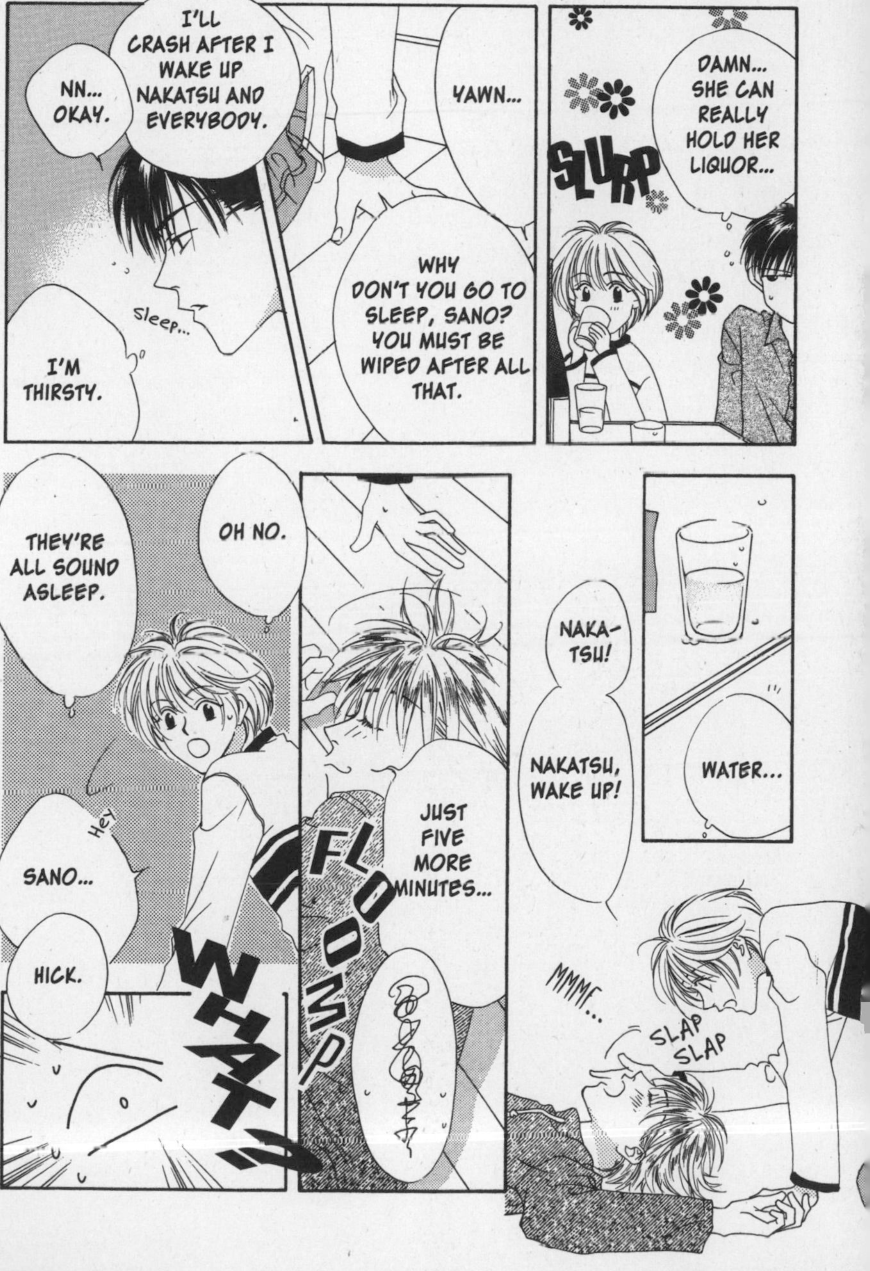
DAMN... SHE CAN REALLY HOLD HER LIQUOR...
SLURP
YAWN...
WHY DON'T YOU GO TO SLEEP, SANO? YOU MUST BE WIPED AFTER ALL THAT.
I'LL CRASH AFTER I WAKE UP NAKATSU AND EVERYBODY.
NN... OKAY.
Sleep...
I'M THIRSTY.
WATER...
NAKA-TSU!
NAKATSU, WAKE UP!
MMMF...
SLAP SLAP
JUST FIVE MORE MINUTES...
FLOOMP
OH NO.
THEY'RE ALL SOUND ASLEEP.
Hey
SANO...
HICK.
WHAT?!

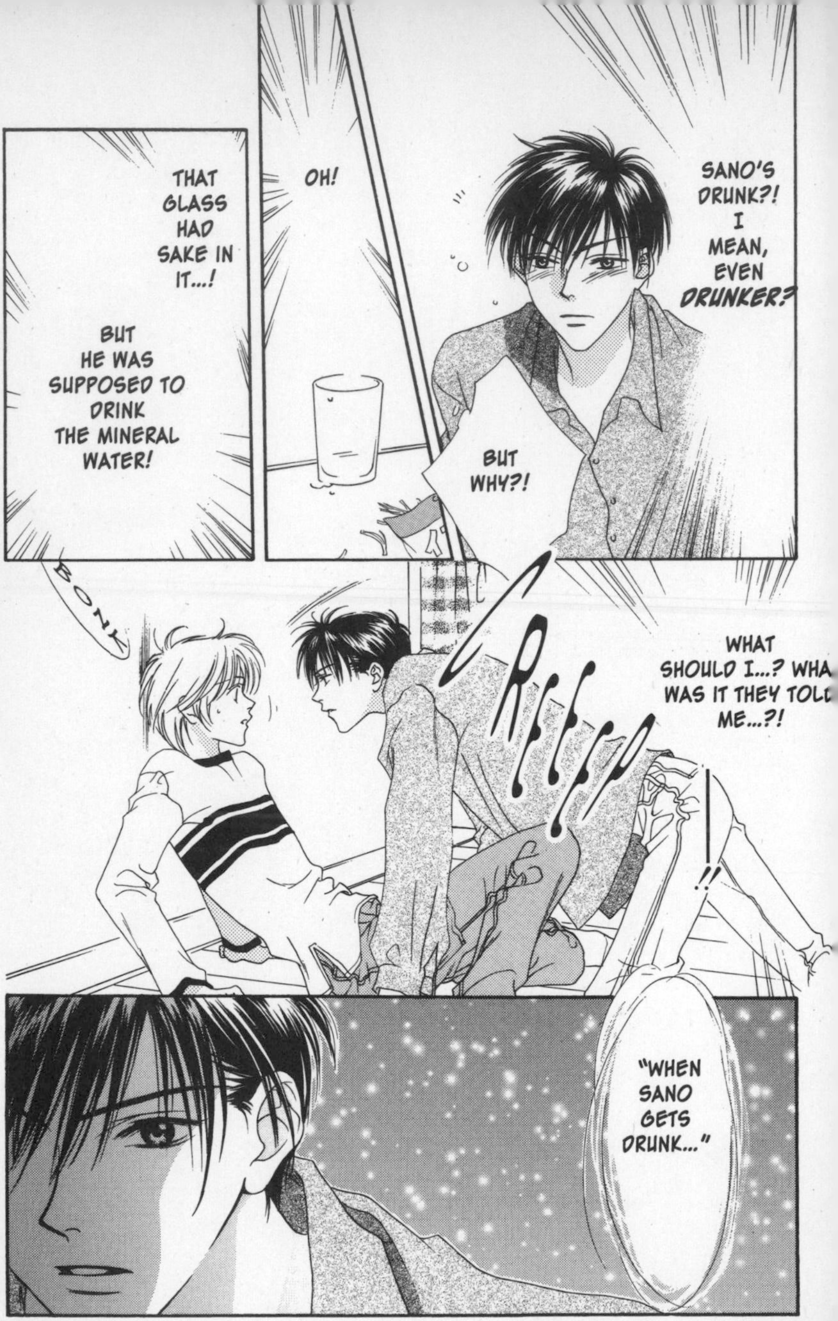
SANO'S DRUNK?! I MEAN, EVEN DRUNKER?
OH!
BUT WHY?!
THAT GLASS HAD SAKE IN IT...!
BUT HE WAS SUPPOSED TO DRINK THE MINERAL WATER!
WHAT SHOULD I...? WHA WAS IT THEY TOLD ME...?!
CREEP
!!
BONK
"WHEN SANO GETS DRUNK..."

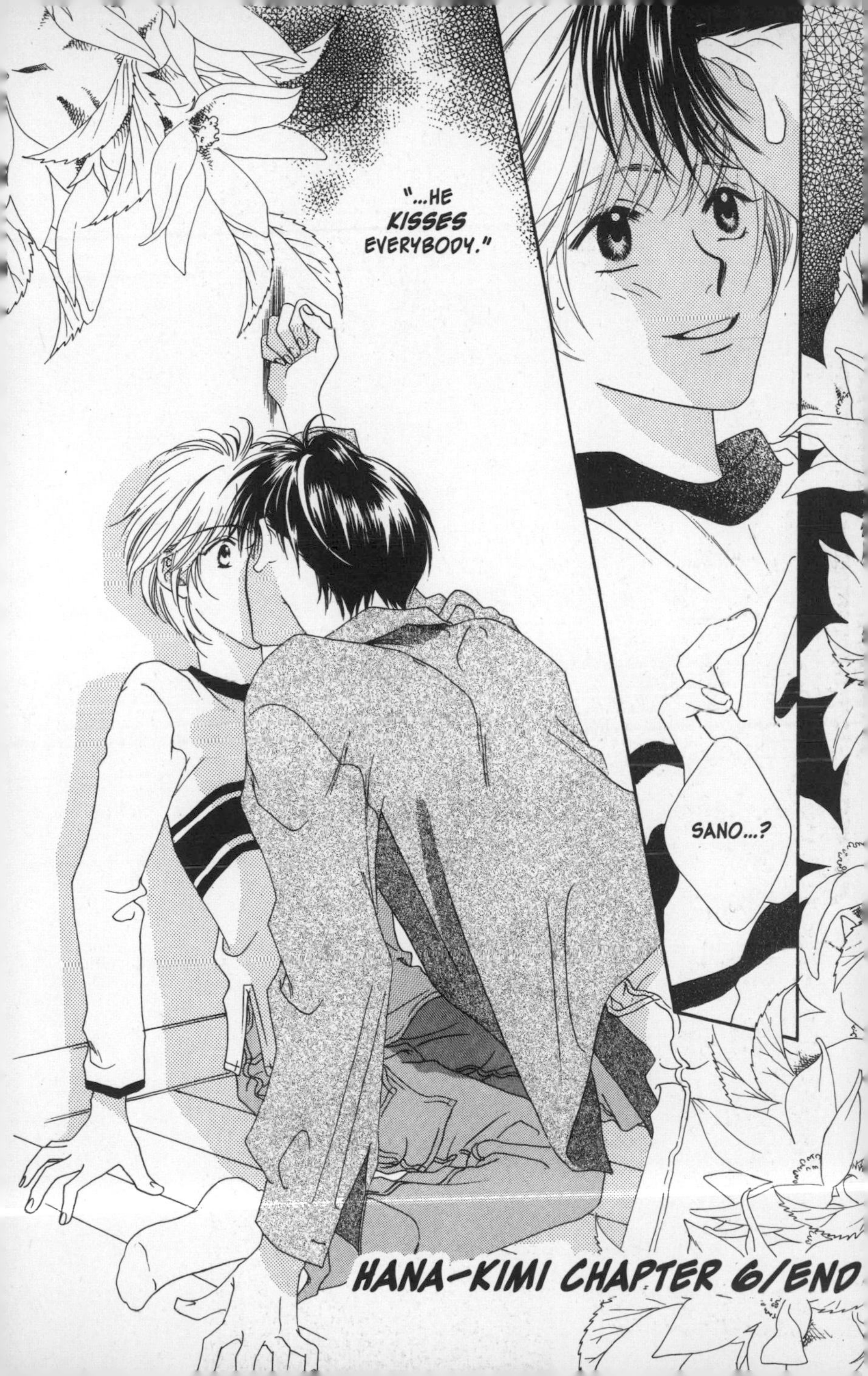
SANO...?
"...HE KISSES EVERYBODY."
HANA-KIMI CHAPTER 6/END

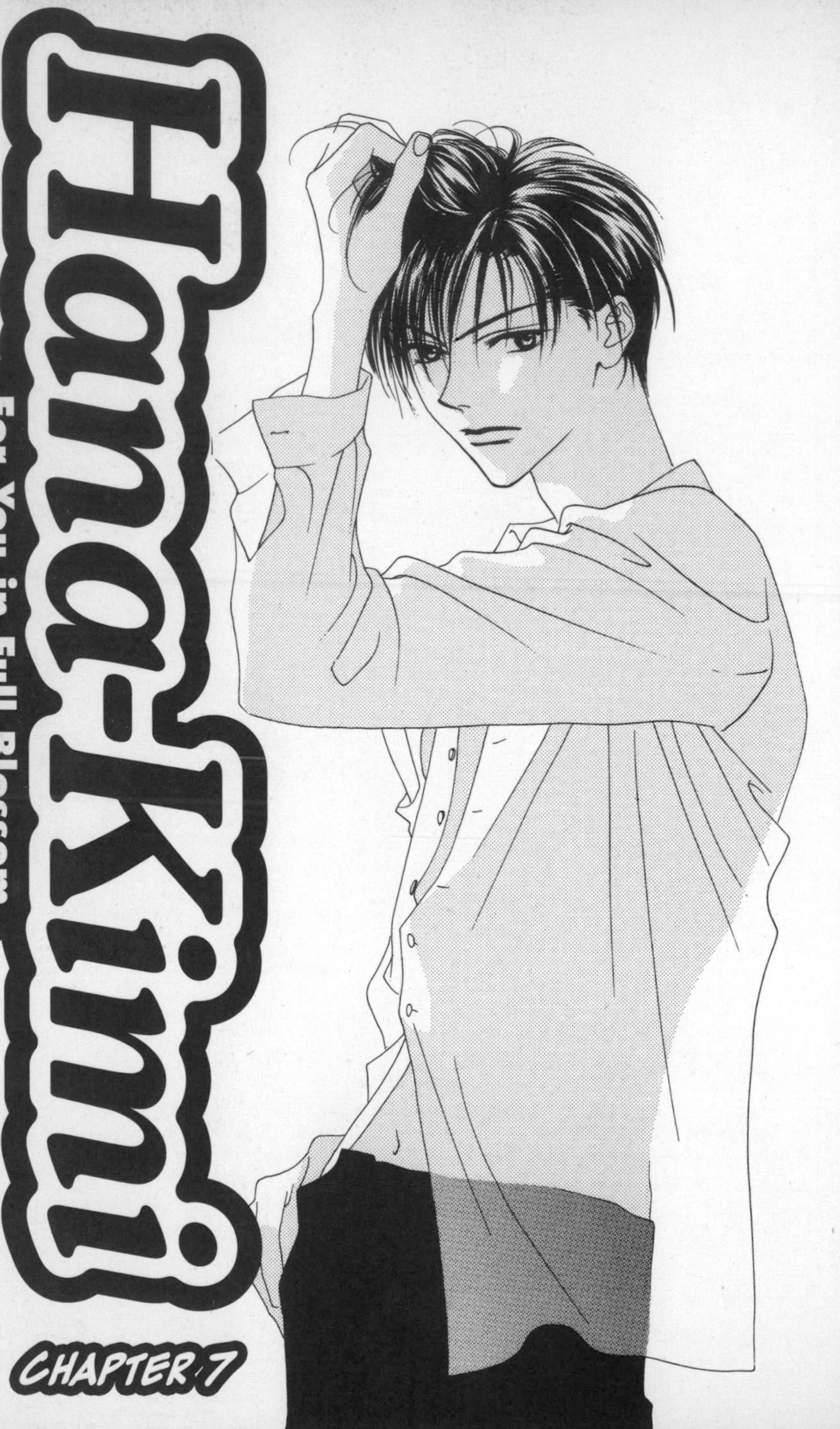
Hana-Kimi
For You in Full Blossom
CHAPTER 7

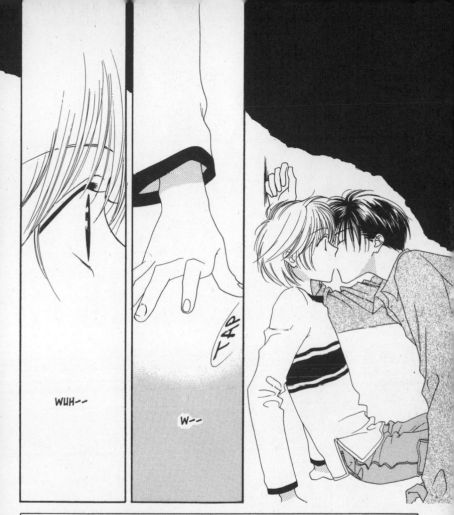

APOLOGY Part 2

AUTHOR'S NOTE:
I JUST DON'T HAVE TIME TO WRITE AND STAMP ALL OF
THE NEW YEAR'S CARDS AND SUMMER GREETINGS CARDS. (ESPECIALLY
THE NEW YEAR'S CARDS!) I'M REALLY SORRY. I KNOW IT'S BAD BUT I'LL
REPLY NEXT YEAR TO THE LETTERS I RECEIVED THIS YEAR. I MADE A
PROMISE I COULDN'T KEEP AND I FEEL REALLY STUPID. I'LL MAKE SURE IT
DOESN'T HAPPEN AGAIN. PLEASE FORGIVE ME! BE PATIENT AND I'LL TRY
TO ANSWER BY NEXT DECEMBER! I'M SO SORRY!

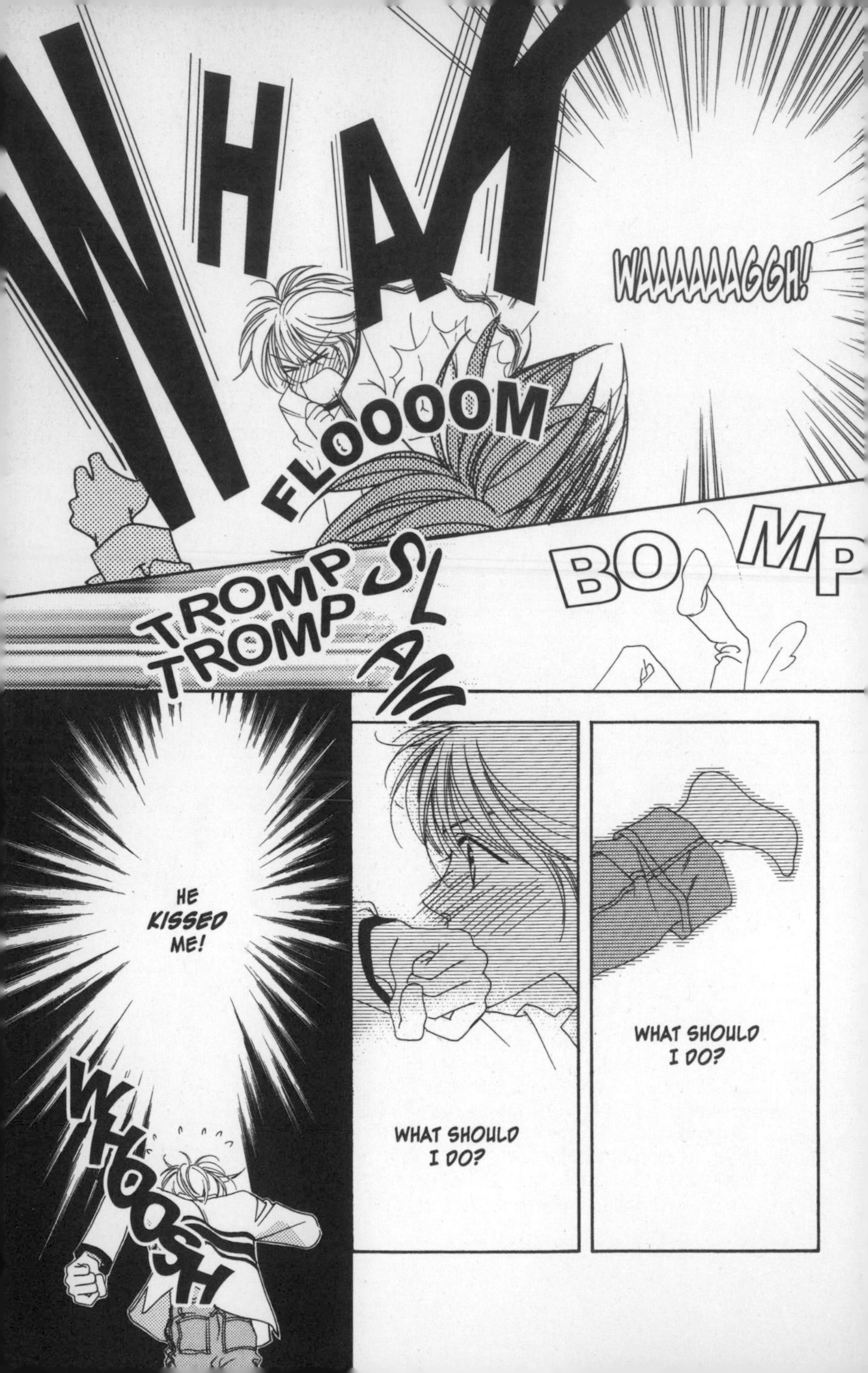
WHAK
WAAAAAAGGH!
FLOOOOM
BOMP
TROMP TROMP
SLAM
WHAT SHOULD I DO?
WHAT SHOULD I DO?
HE KISSED ME!
WHOOSH

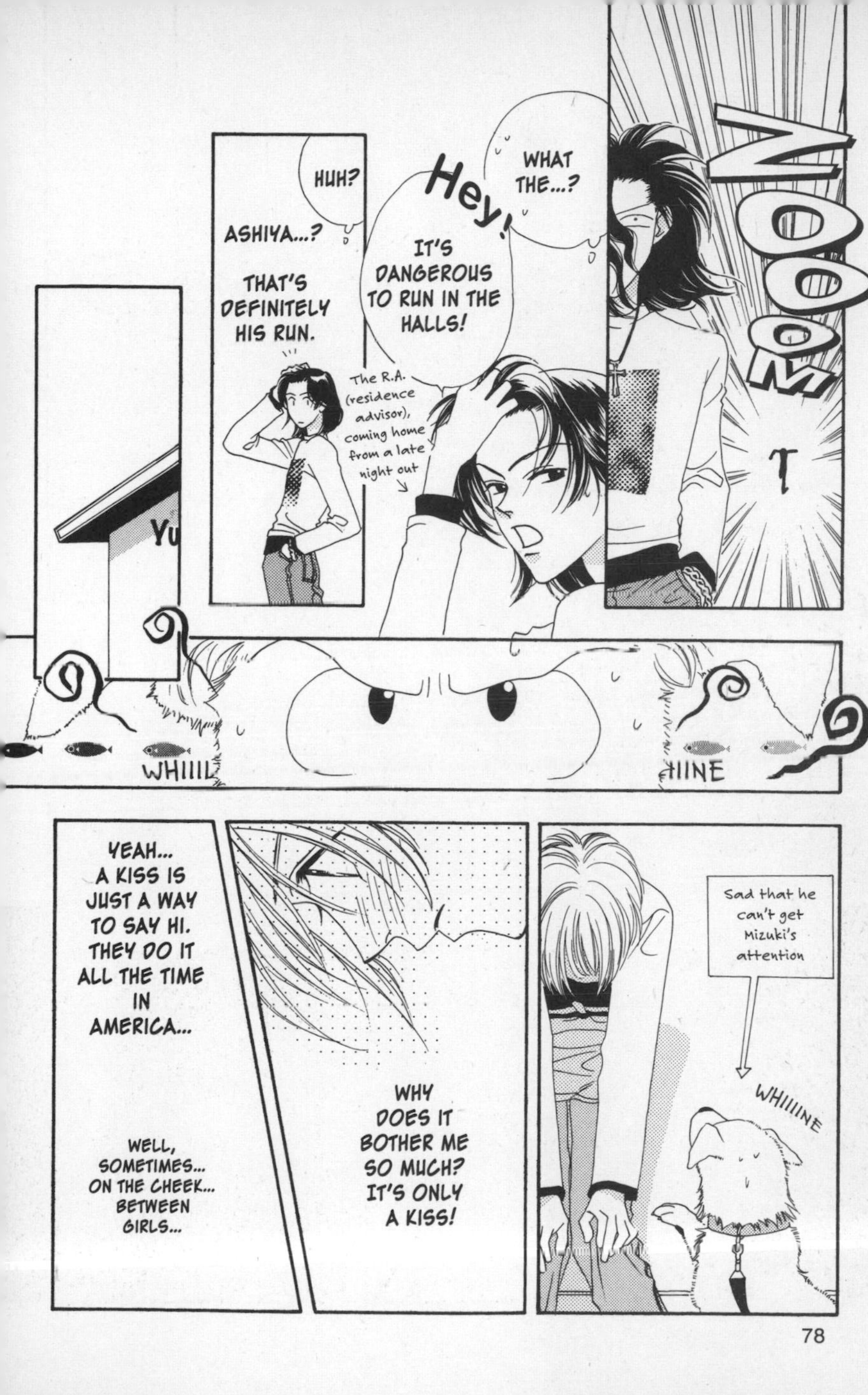
VOOOM
T
WHAT THE...?
Hey!
IT'S DANGEROUS TO RUN IN THE HALLS!
The R.A. (residence advisor), coming home from a late night out
HUH?
ASHIYA...?
THAT'S DEFINITELY HIS RUN.
Yu
WHIIIL
IINE
Sad that he can't get Mizuki's attention
WHIIIINE
WHY DOES IT BOTHER ME SO MUCH? IT'S ONLY A KISS!
YEAH... A KISS IS JUST A WAY TO SAY HI. THEY DO IT ALL THE TIME IN AMERICA...
WELL, SOMETIMES... ON THE CHEEK... BETWEEN GIRLS...

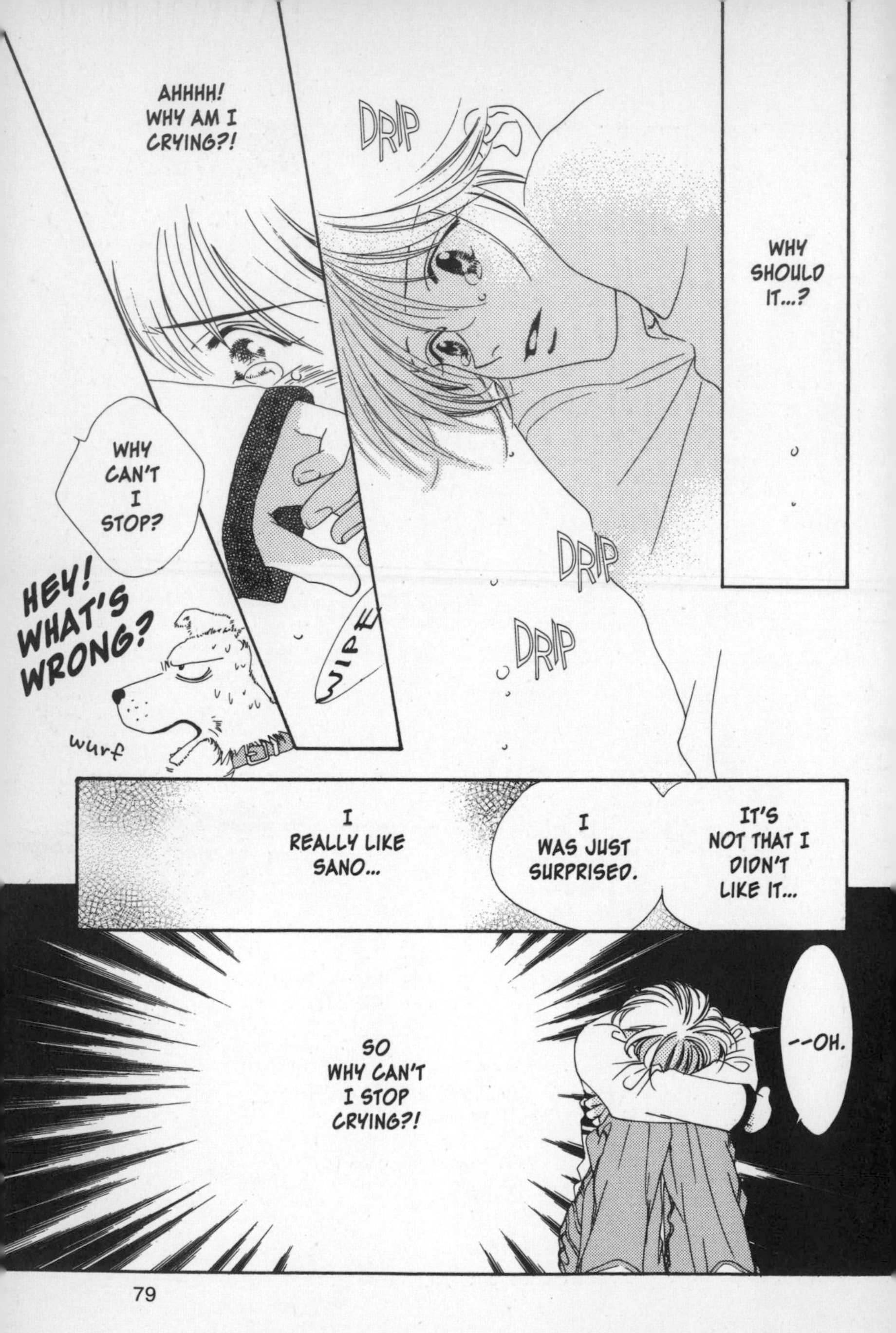
WHY SHOULD IT...?
DRIP
DRIP
DRIP
WIPE
AHHHH! WHY AM I CRYING?!
WHY CAN'T I STOP?
HEY! WHAT'S WRONG?
wurf
IT'S NOT THAT I DIDN'T LIKE IT...
I WAS JUST SURPRISED.
I REALLY LIKE SANO...
--OH.
SO WHY CAN'T I STOP CRYING?!

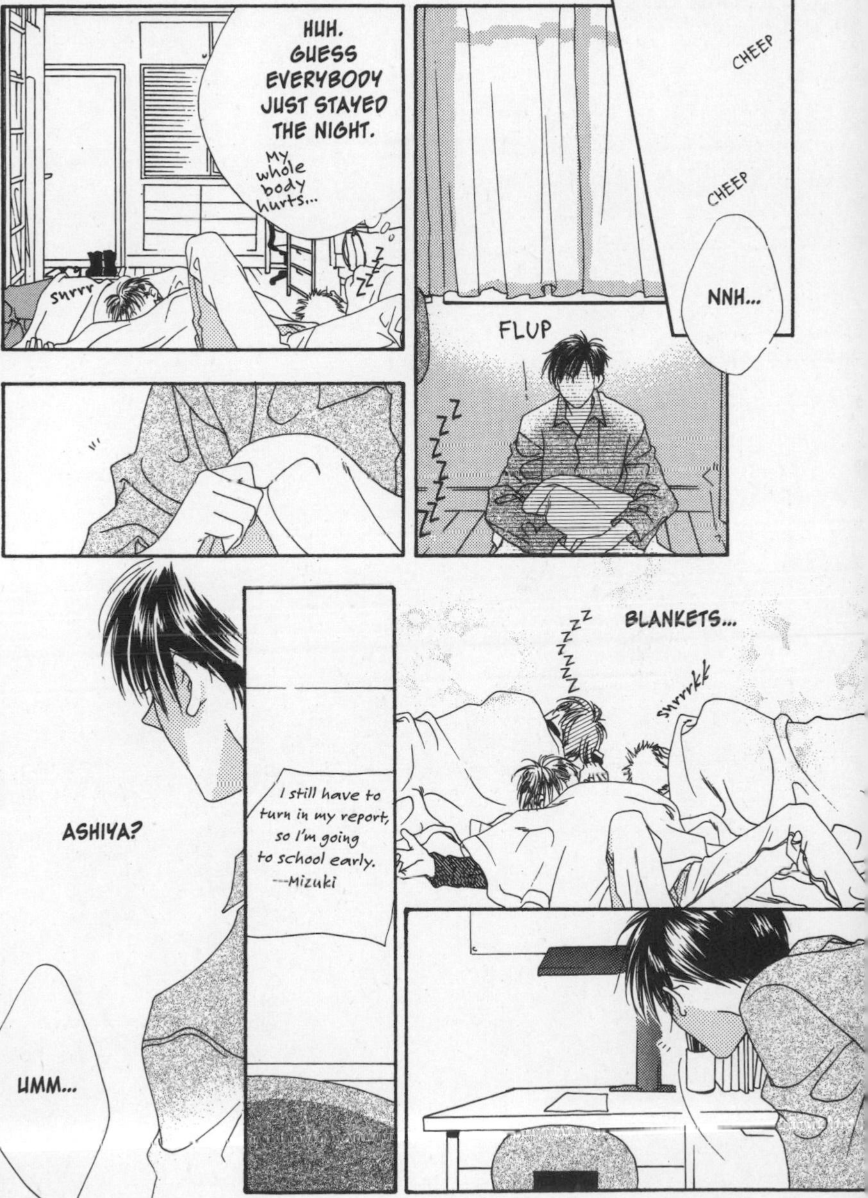
CHEEP
CHEEP
NNH...
FLUP
HUH. GUESS EVERYBODY JUST STAYED THE NIGHT.
My whole body hurts...
Snrrr
BLANKETS...
Snrrrkk
ASHIYA?
I still have to turn in my report, so I'm going to school early. ---Mizuki
UMM...

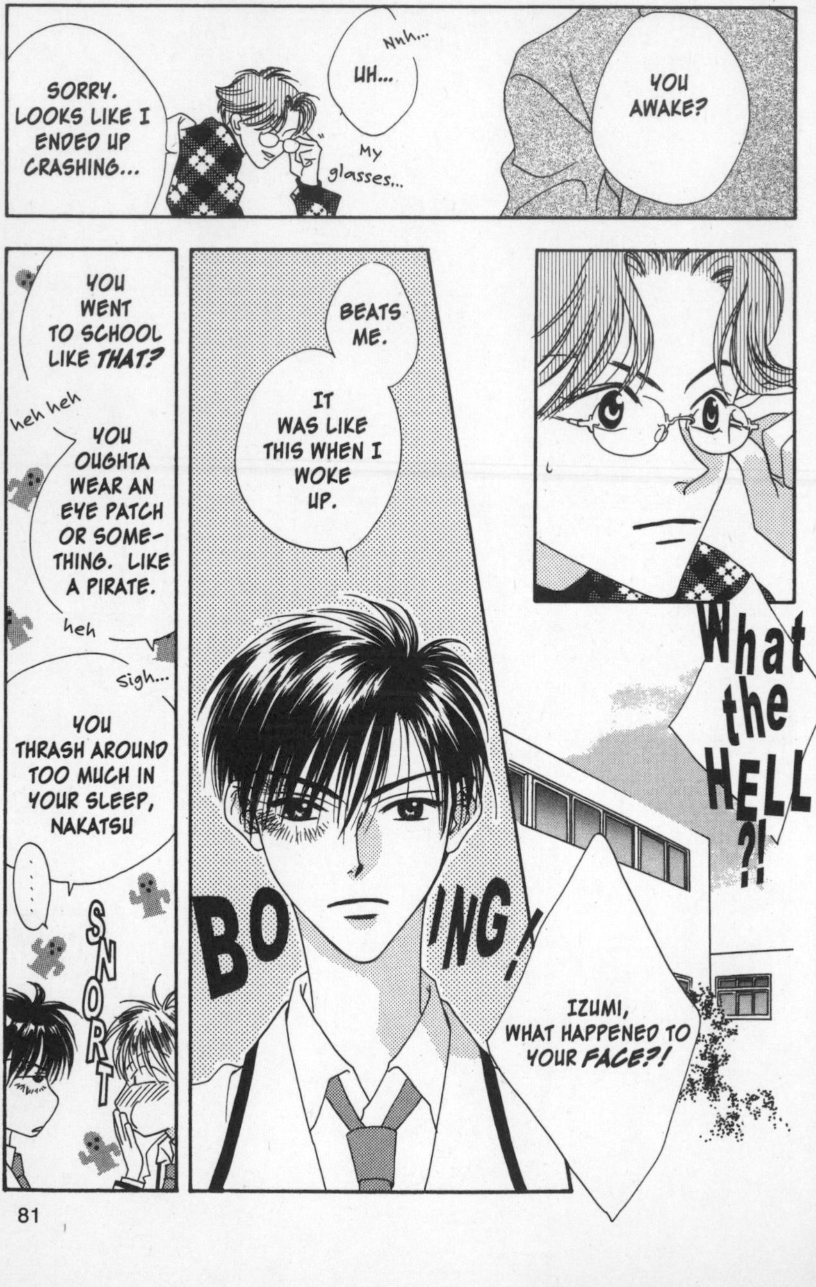
YOU AWAKE?
Nnh...
UH...
My glasses...
SORRY. LOOKS LIKE I ENDED UP CRASHING...
What the HELL?!
IZUMI, WHAT HAPPENED TO YOUR FACE?!
BEATS ME.
IT WAS LIKE THIS WHEN I WOKE UP.
BO
ING!
YOU WENT TO SCHOOL LIKE THAT?
heh heh
YOU OUGHTA WEAR AN EYE PATCH OR SOME-THING. LIKE A PIRATE.
heh
Sigh...
YOU THRASH AROUND TOO MUCH IN YOUR SLEEP, NAKATSU
......
SNORT

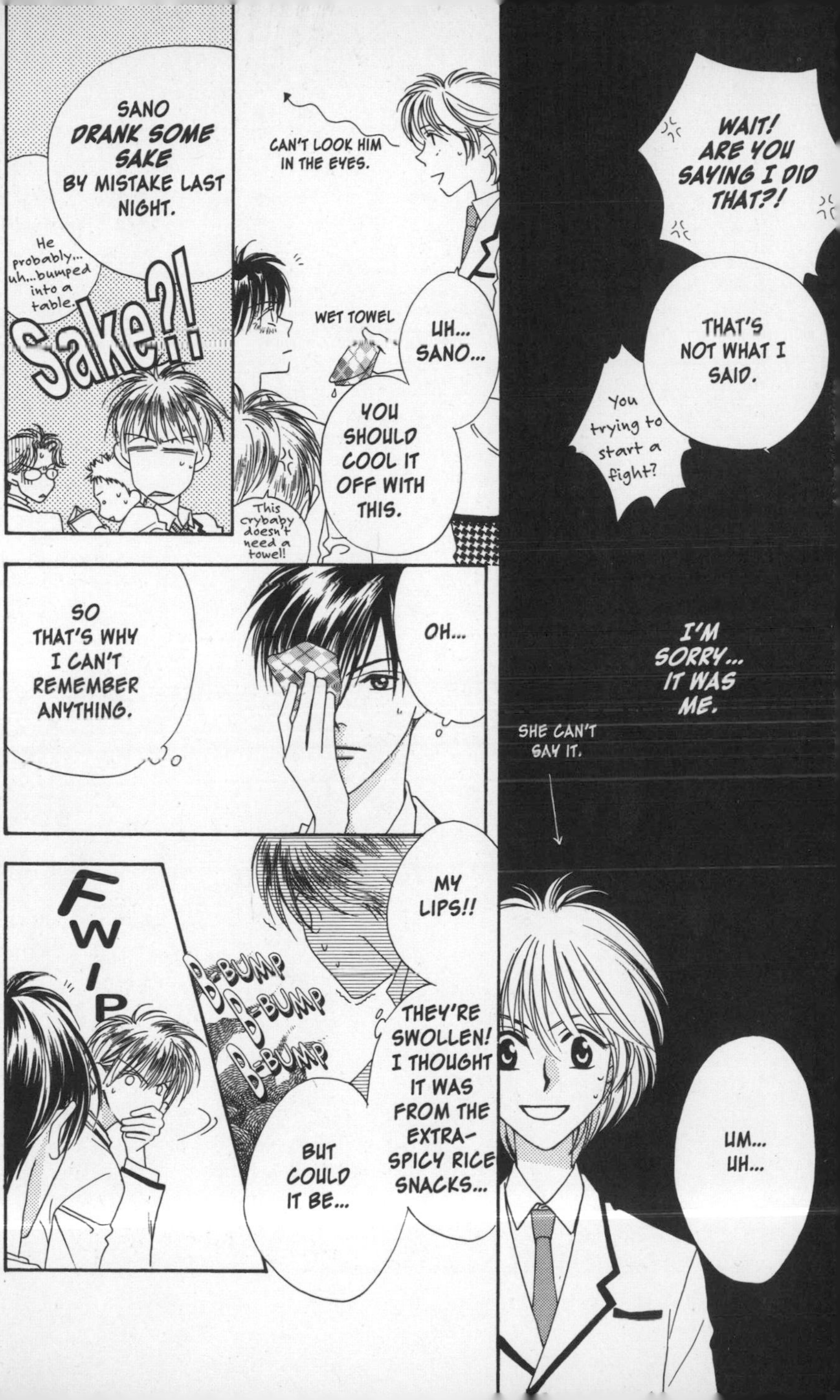
WAIT! ARE YOU SAYING I DID THAT?!
THAT'S NOT WHAT I SAID.
You trying to start a fight?
I'M SORRY... IT WAS ME.
SHE CAN'T SAY IT.
UM... UH...
CAN'T LOOK HIM IN THE EYES.
UH... SANO...
WET TOWEL
YOU SHOULD COOL IT OFF WITH THIS.
This crybaby doesn't need a towel!
SANO DRANK SOME SAKE BY MISTAKE LAST NIGHT.
He probably... uh...bumped into a table.
Sake?!
OH...
SO THAT'S WHY I CAN'T REMEMBER ANYTHING.
MY LIPS!!
THEY'RE SWOLLEN! I THOUGHT IT WAS FROM THE EXTRA-SPICY RICE SNACKS...
B-BUMP
B-BUMP
B-BUMP
BUT COULD IT BE...
FWIP

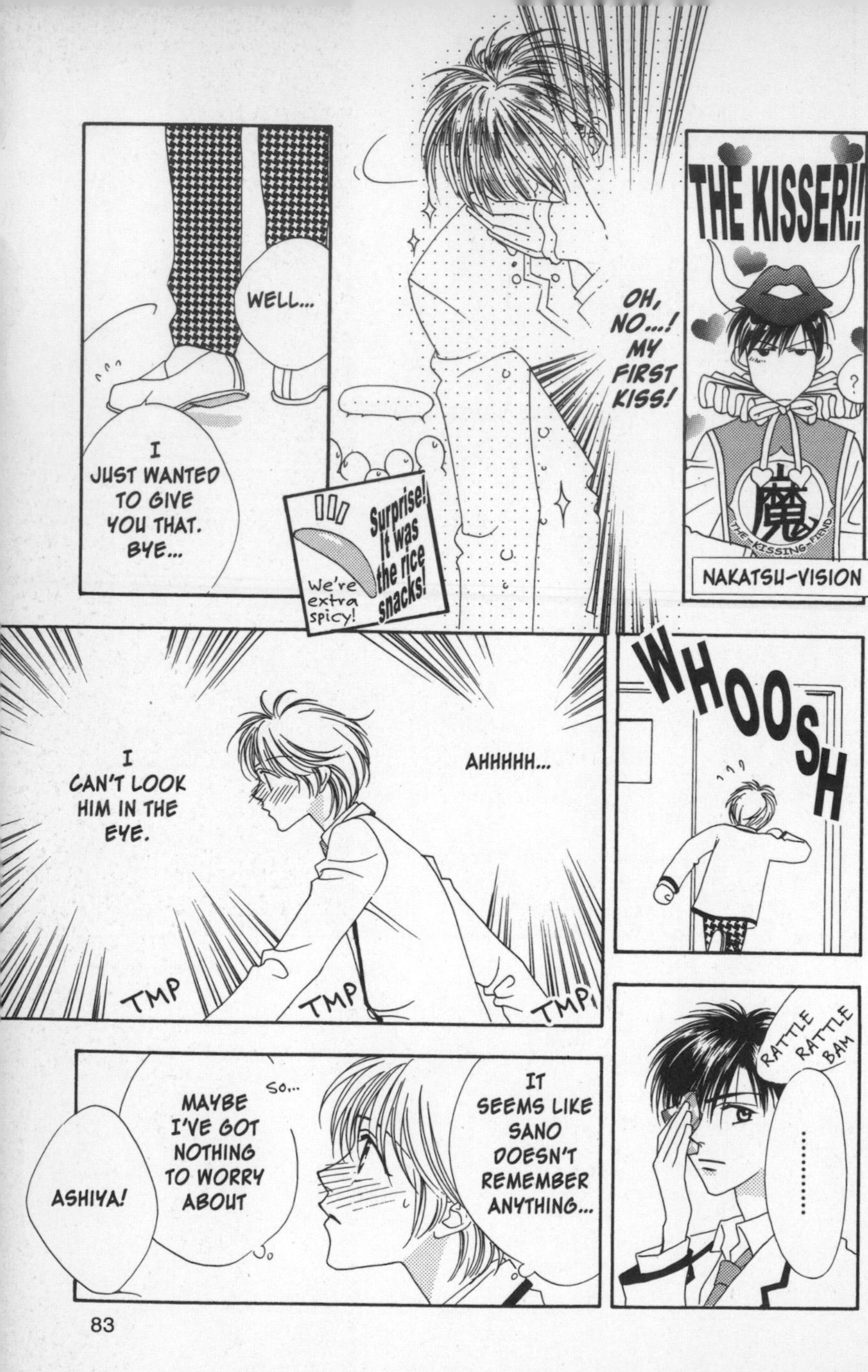
THE KISSER!!
?
魔
THE KISSING FIEND
NAKATSU-VISION
OH, NO...! MY FIRST KISS!
......
Surprise! It was the rice snacks!
We're extra spicy!
WELL...
I JUST WANTED TO GIVE YOU THAT. BYE...
WHOOSH
AHHHHH...
I CAN'T LOOK HIM IN THE EYE.
TMP
TMP
TMP
RATTLE RATTLE BAM
......
IT SEEMS LIKE SANO DOESN'T REMEMBER ANYTHING...
So...
MAYBE I'VE GOT NOTHING TO WORRY ABOUT
ASHIYA!

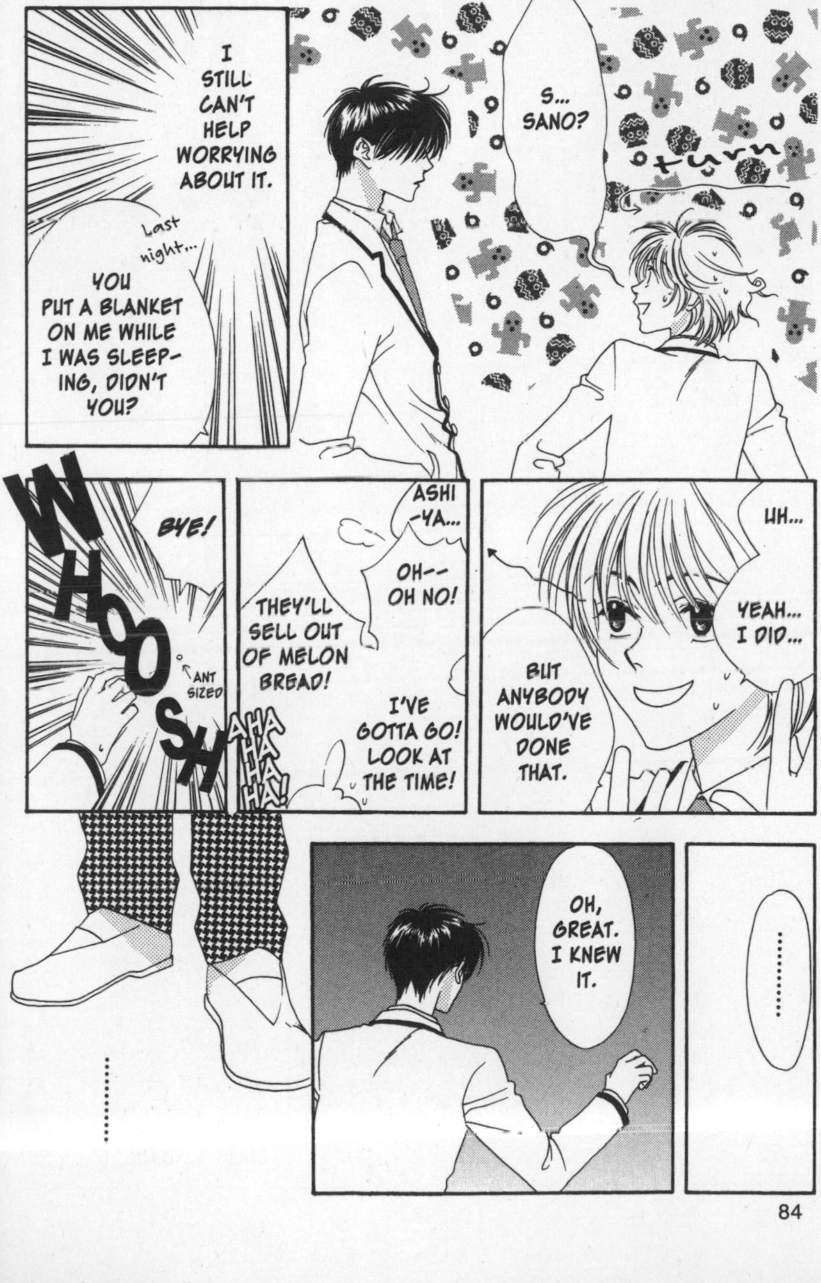
S... SANO?
turn
I STILL CAN'T HELP WORRYING ABOUT IT.
Last night...
YOU PUT A BLANKET ON ME WHILE I WAS SLEEP-ING, DIDN'T YOU?
UH...
YEAH... I DID...
BUT ANYBODY WOULD'VE DONE THAT.
ASHI-YA...
OH-- OH NO!
THEY'LL SELL OUT OF MELON BREAD!
I'VE GOTTA GO! LOOK AT THE TIME!
BYE!
WHOOSH
ANT SIZED
AHAHAHAHA!
....
OH, GREAT. I KNEW IT.
....

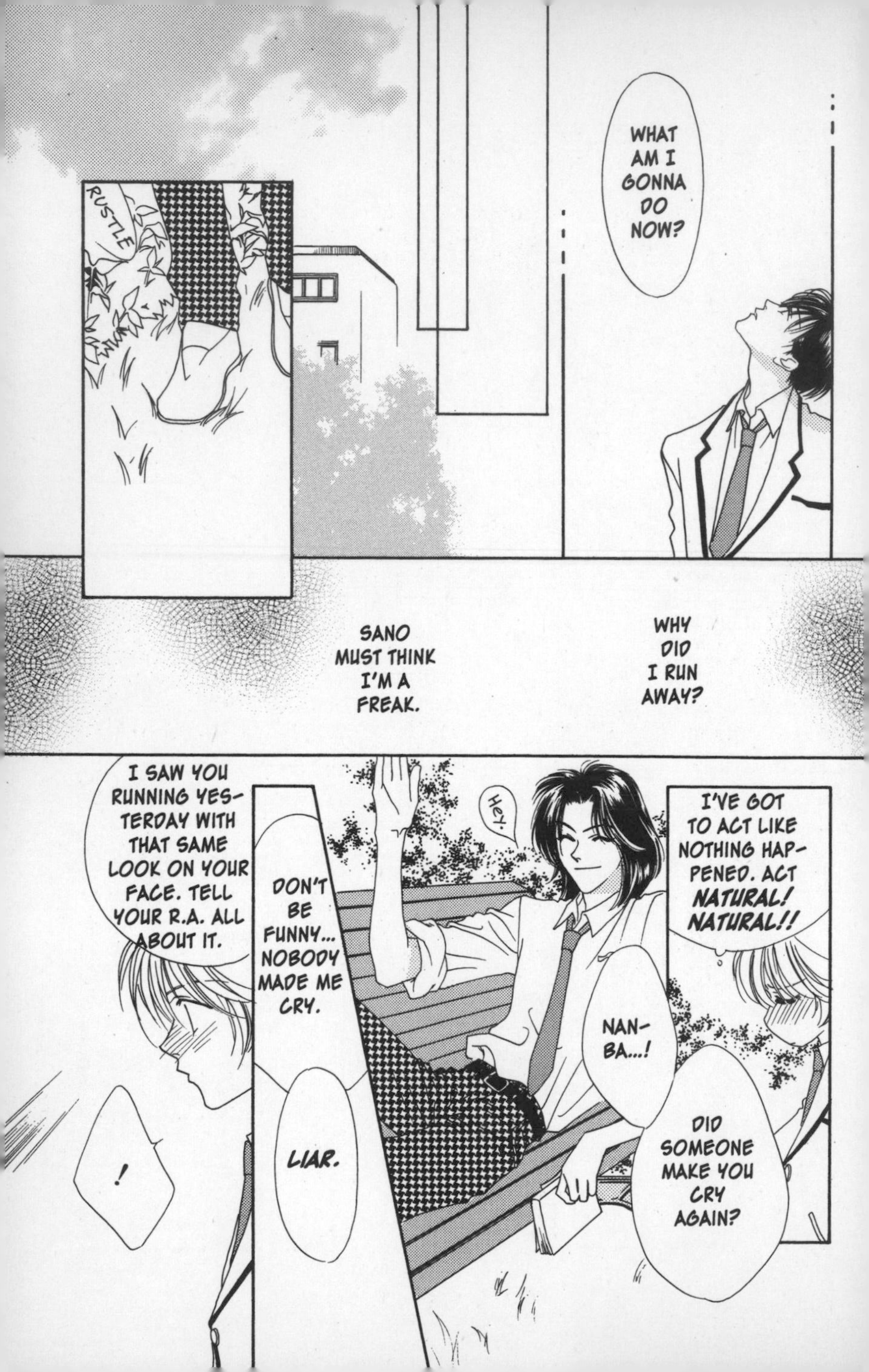
...
WHAT AM I GONNA DO NOW?
...
RUSTLE
WHY DID I RUN AWAY?
SANO MUST THINK I'M A FREAK.
I'VE GOT TO ACT LIKE NOTHING HAPPENED. ACT *NATURAL! NATURAL!!*
Hey.
NAN-BA...!
DID SOMEONE MAKE YOU CRY AGAIN?
DON'T BE FUNNY... NOBODY MADE ME CRY.
LIAR.
I SAW YOU RUNNING YESTERDAY WITH THAT SAME LOOK ON YOUR FACE. TELL YOUR R.A. ALL ABOUT IT.
!

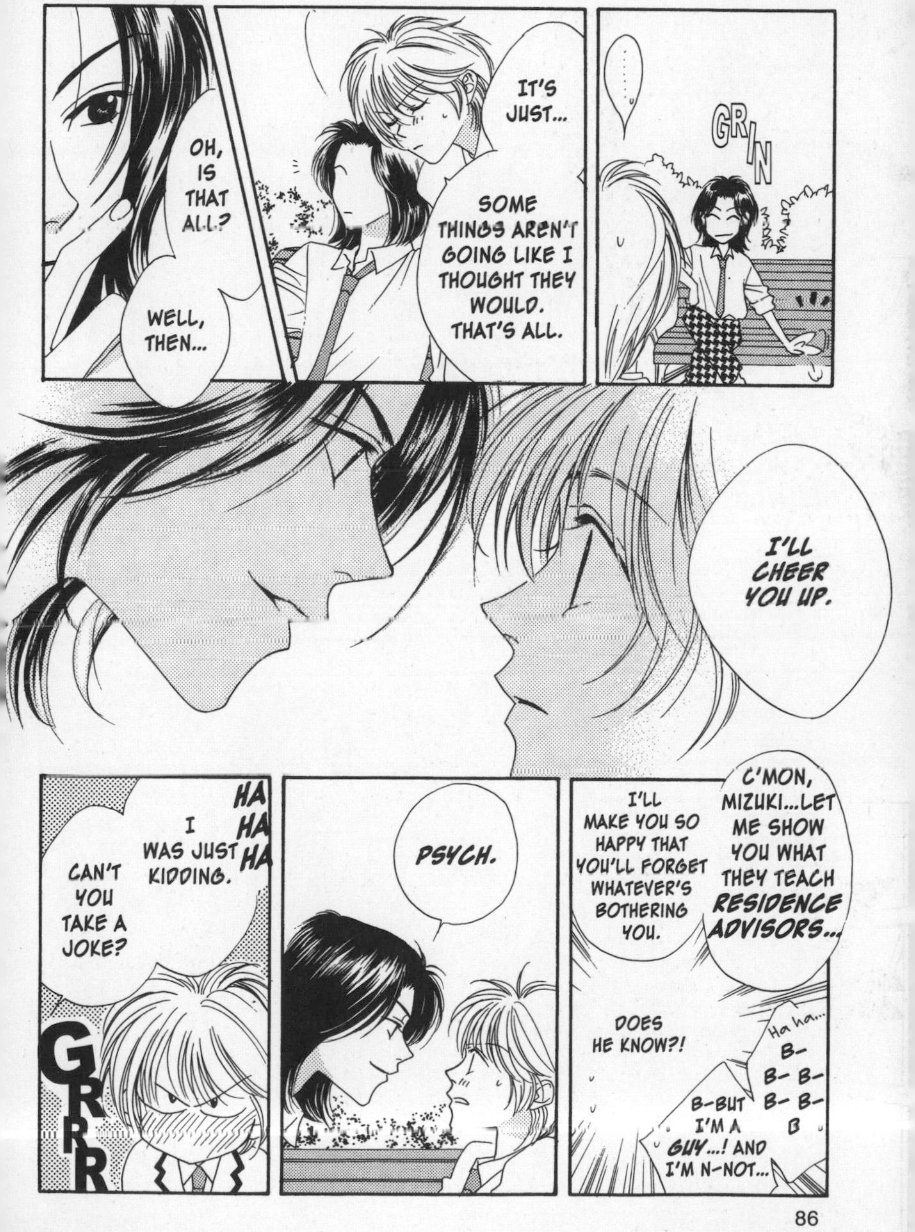
GRIN
IT'S JUST...
SOME THINGS AREN'T GOING LIKE I THOUGHT THEY WOULD. THAT'S ALL.
OH, IS THAT ALL?
WELL, THEN...
I'LL CHEER YOU UP.
C'MON, MIZUKI...LET ME SHOW YOU WHAT THEY TEACH RESIDENCE ADVISORS...
I'LL MAKE YOU SO HAPPY THAT YOU'LL FORGET WHATEVER'S BOTHERING YOU.
DOES HE KNOW?!
Ha ha...
B- B- B- B- B- B
B-BUT I'M A GUY...! AND I'M N-NOT...
PSYCH.
HA HA HA
I WAS JUST KIDDING.
CAN'T YOU TAKE A JOKE?
GRRR

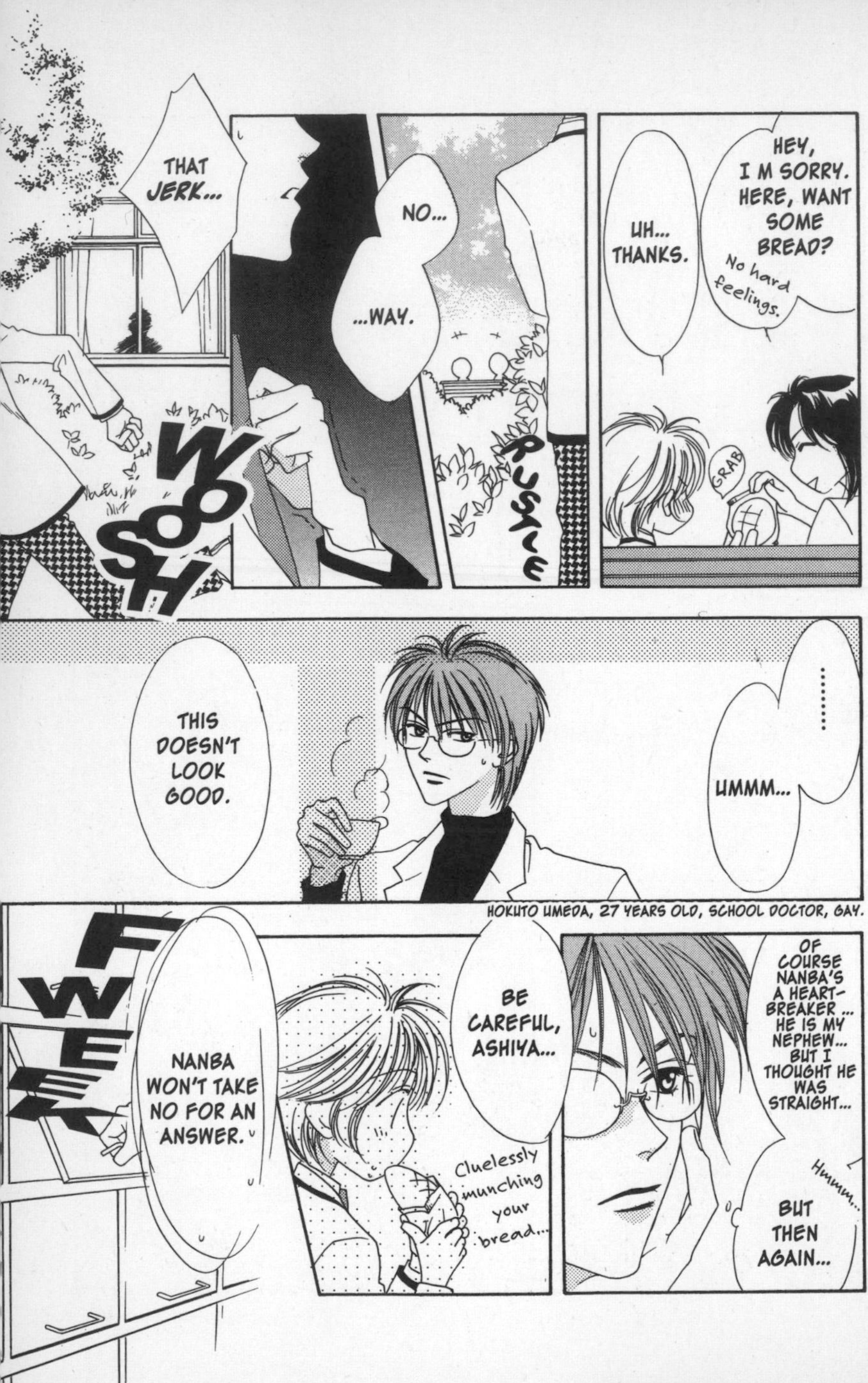
HEY, I M SORRY. HERE, WANT SOME BREAD?
No hard feelings.
GRAB
UH... THANKS.
RUSTLE
NO...
...WAY.
THAT JERK...
WOOSH
......
UMMM...
THIS DOESN'T LOOK GOOD.
HOKUTO UMEDA, 27 YEARS OLD, SCHOOL DOCTOR, GAY.
OF COURSE NANBA'S A HEART-BREAKER ... HE IS MY NEPHEW... BUT I THOUGHT HE WAS STRAIGHT...
Hmmm...
BUT THEN AGAIN...
BE CAREFUL, ASHIYA...
Cluelessly munching your bread...
NANBA WON'T TAKE NO FOR AN ANSWER.
FWEEK

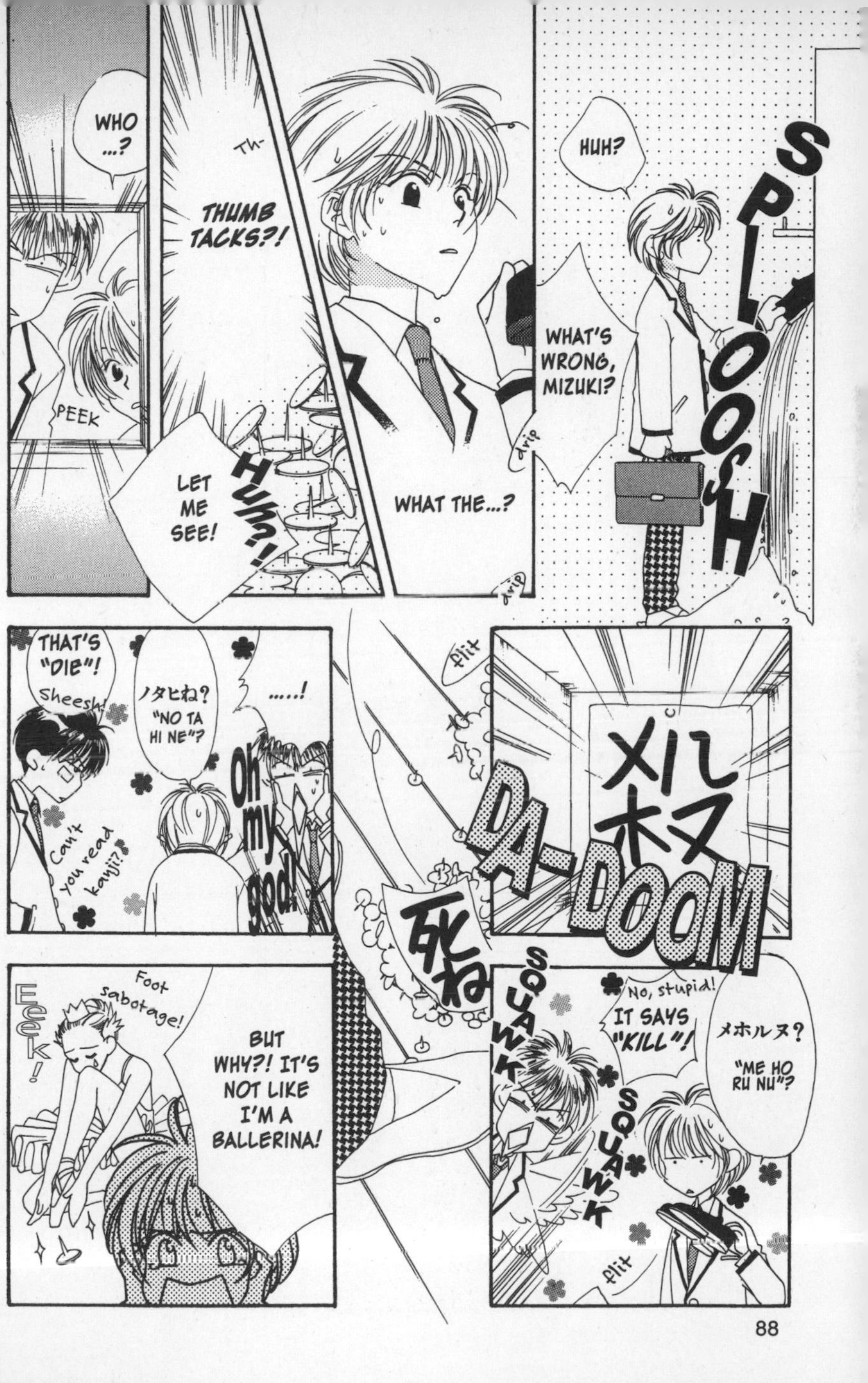
SPLOOSH
HUH?
WHAT'S WRONG, MIZUKI?
drip
drip
Th-
THUMB TACKS?!
WHAT THE...?
WHO ...?
PEEK
LET ME SEE!
HUH?!
DA-DOOM
flit
ノタヒね?
"NO TA HI NE"?
......!
Oh my god!
THAT'S "DIE"!
Sheesh!
Can't you read kanji?
メホルヌ?
"ME HO RU NU"?
No, stupid!
IT SAYS "KILL"!
SQUAWK
SQUAWK
flit
死ね
BUT WHY?! IT'S NOT LIKE I'M A BALLERINA!
Foot sabotage!
Eeek!

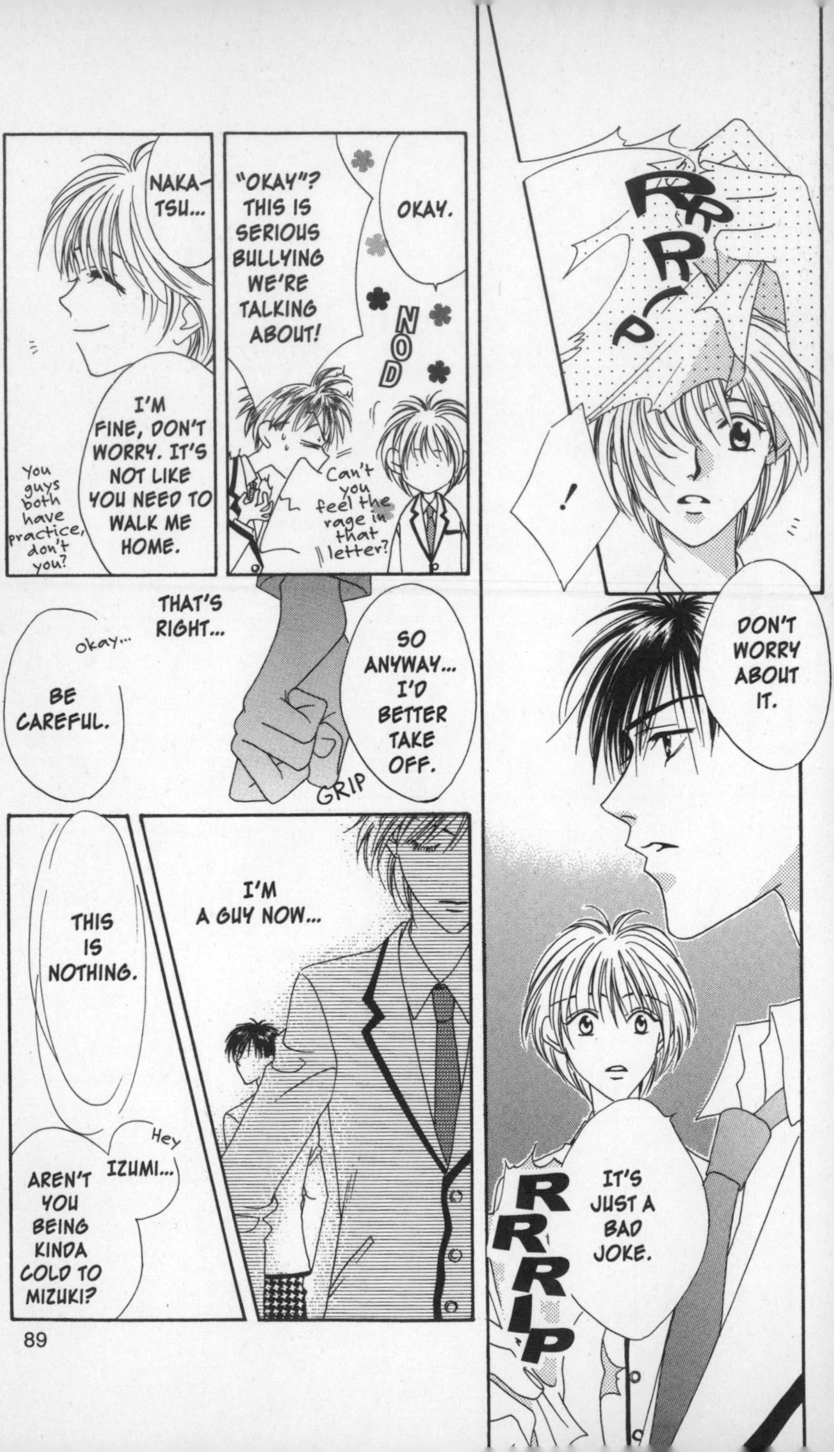
RRRIP
!
DON'T WORRY ABOUT IT.
IT'S JUST A BAD JOKE.
RRRIP
OKAY.
NOD
"OKAY"? THIS IS SERIOUS BULLYING WE'RE TALKING ABOUT!
Can't you feel the rage in that letter?
NAKA-TSU...
I'M FINE, DON'T WORRY. IT'S NOT LIKE YOU NEED TO WALK ME HOME.
You guys both have practice, don't you?
SO ANYWAY... I'D BETTER TAKE OFF.
GRIP
THAT'S RIGHT...
okay...
BE CAREFUL.
I'M A GUY NOW...
THIS IS NOTHING.
Hey
IZUMI...
AREN'T YOU BEING KINDA COLD TO MIZUKI?

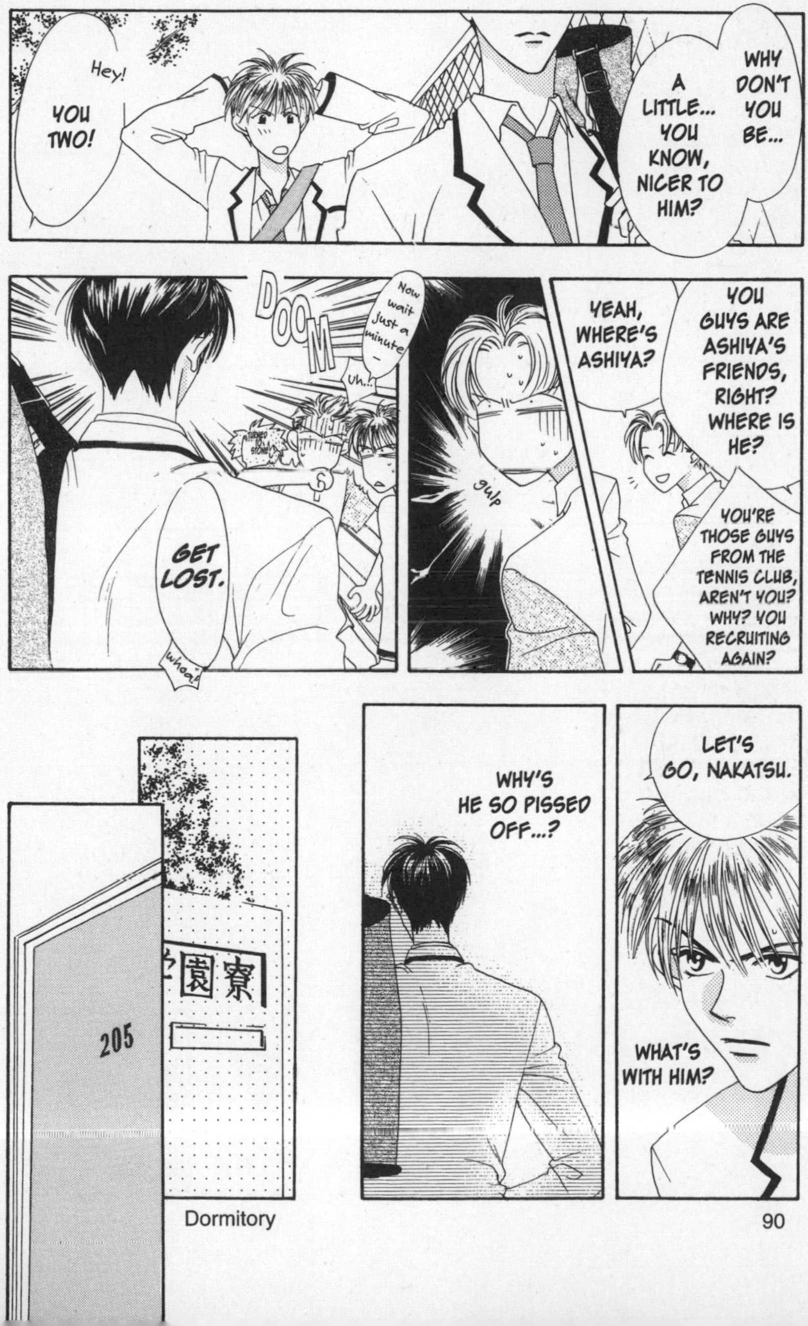
WHY DON'T YOU BE...
A LITTLE... YOU KNOW, NICER TO HIM?
Hey! YOU TWO!
YOU GUYS ARE ASHIYA'S FRIENDS, RIGHT? WHERE IS HE?
YEAH, WHERE'S ASHIYA?
YOU'RE THOSE GUYS FROM THE TENNIS CLUB, AREN'T YOU? WHY? YOU RECRUITING AGAIN?
gulp
DOOM
Now wait just a minute—
uh...
TURNED TO STONE
GET LOST.
whoa!
LET'S GO, NAKATSU.
WHAT'S WITH HIM?
WHY'S HE SO PISSED OFF...?
205

Dormitory

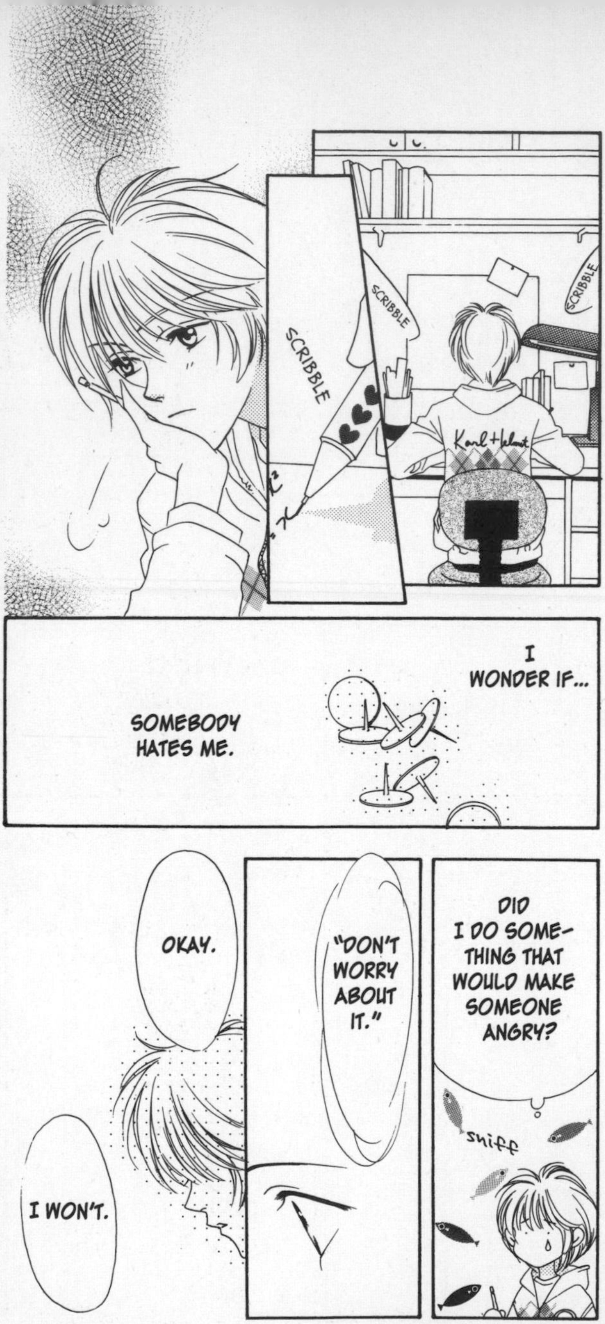
SCRIBBLE
SCRIBBLE
SCRIBBLE
Karl+Helmut
I WONDER IF...
SOMEBODY HATES ME.
DID I DO SOMETHING THAT WOULD MAKE SOMEONE ANGRY?
sniff
"DON'T WORRY ABOUT IT."
OKAY.
I WON'T.

Whispered Secrets

Moving

I FINALLY DID IT! I GOT MY OWN CASTLE!...THAT IS, MY OWN OFFICE. I USED TO WORK FROM HOME, BUT I COULDN'T TAKE THE NOISE FROM MY FAMILY UPSTAIRS. SO I FINALLY MOVED. (BUT WHY DID THE HOUSE SUDDENLY GET QUIET AS SOON AS I MOVED OUT?) MY NEW PLACE IS ONLY A 20 SECOND WALK FROM MY HOUSE, SO IT'S VERY CONVENIENT. IT WAS HARD TO FIND EVERYTHING I NEEDED, BUT IT WAS FUN TO CREATE MY OWN SPACE FROM SCRATCH. (EXCEPT I STILL HAVEN'T UNPACKED!)

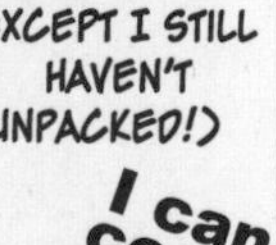
I can cook.
Yeah!

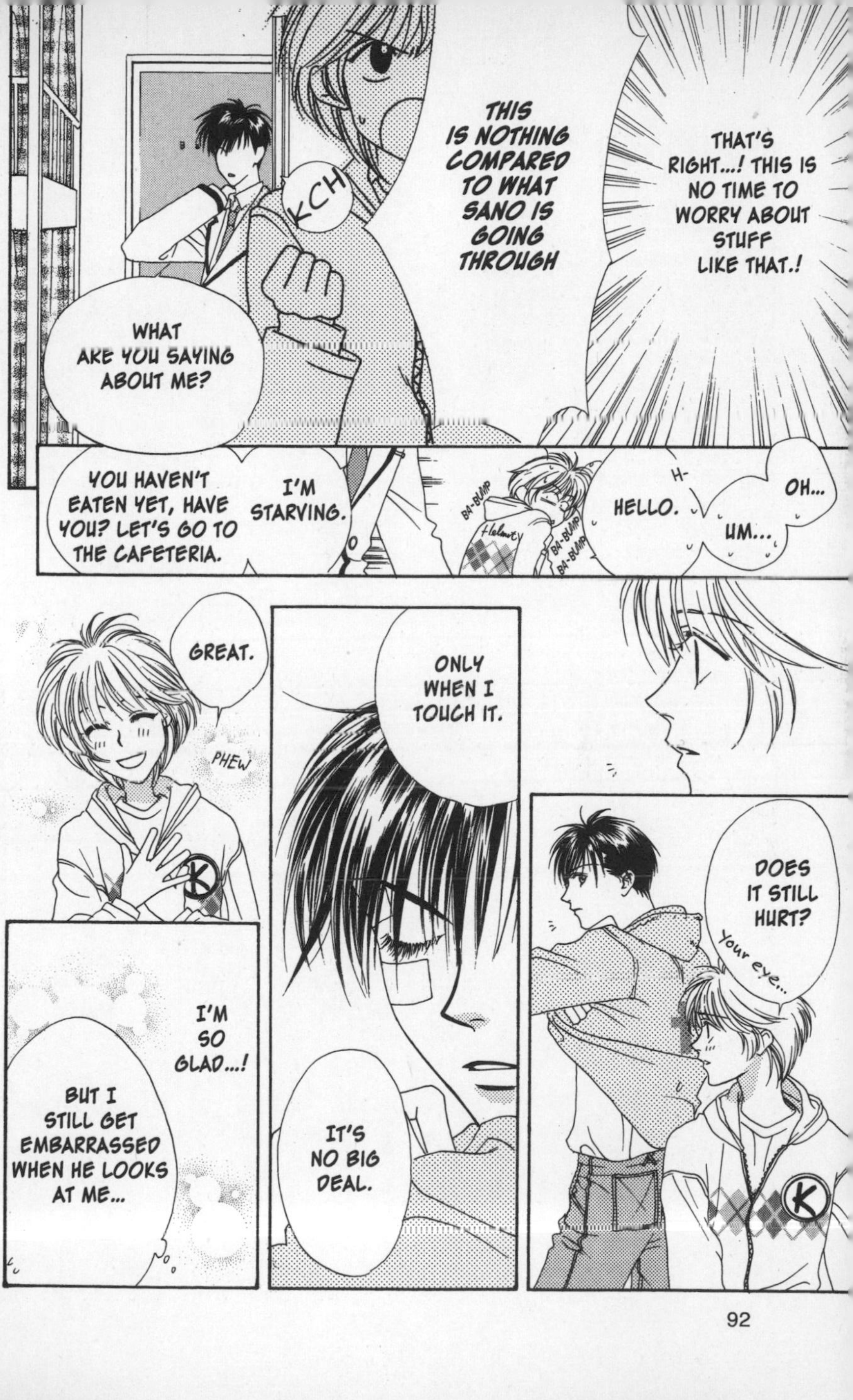
THAT'S RIGHT...! THIS IS NO TIME TO WORRY ABOUT STUFF LIKE THAT.!
THIS IS NOTHING COMPARED TO WHAT SANO IS GOING THROUGH
KCH
WHAT ARE YOU SAYING ABOUT ME?
OH...
UM...
H-
HELLO.
BA-BUMP
BA-BUMP
BA-BUMP
I'M STARVING.
YOU HAVEN'T EATEN YET, HAVE YOU? LET'S GO TO THE CAFETERIA.
DOES IT STILL HURT?
Your eye...
ONLY WHEN I TOUCH IT.
IT'S NO BIG DEAL.
GREAT.
PHEW
I'M SO GLAD...!
BUT I STILL GET EMBARRASSED WHEN HE LOOKS AT ME...

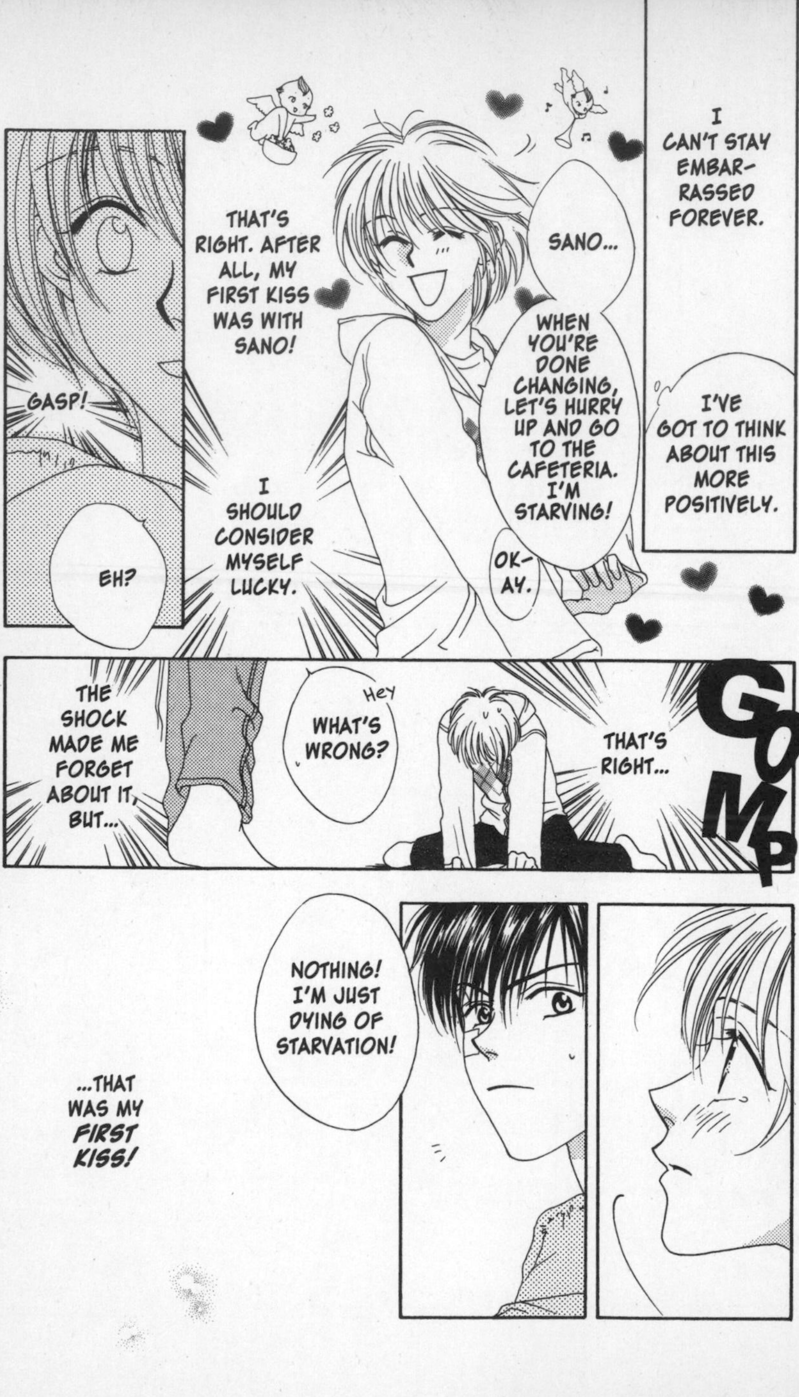
I CAN'T STAY EMBAR-RASSED FOREVER.
I'VE GOT TO THINK ABOUT THIS MORE POSITIVELY.
SANO...
WHEN YOU'RE DONE CHANGING, LET'S HURRY UP AND GO TO THE CAFETERIA. I'M STARVING!
OK-AY.
THAT'S RIGHT. AFTER ALL, MY FIRST KISS WAS WITH SANO!
I SHOULD CONSIDER MYSELF LUCKY.
GASP!
EH?
GOMP
THAT'S RIGHT...
Hey
WHAT'S WRONG?
THE SHOCK MADE ME FORGET ABOUT IT, BUT...
NOTHING! I'M JUST DYING OF STARVATION!
...THAT WAS MY FIRST KISS!

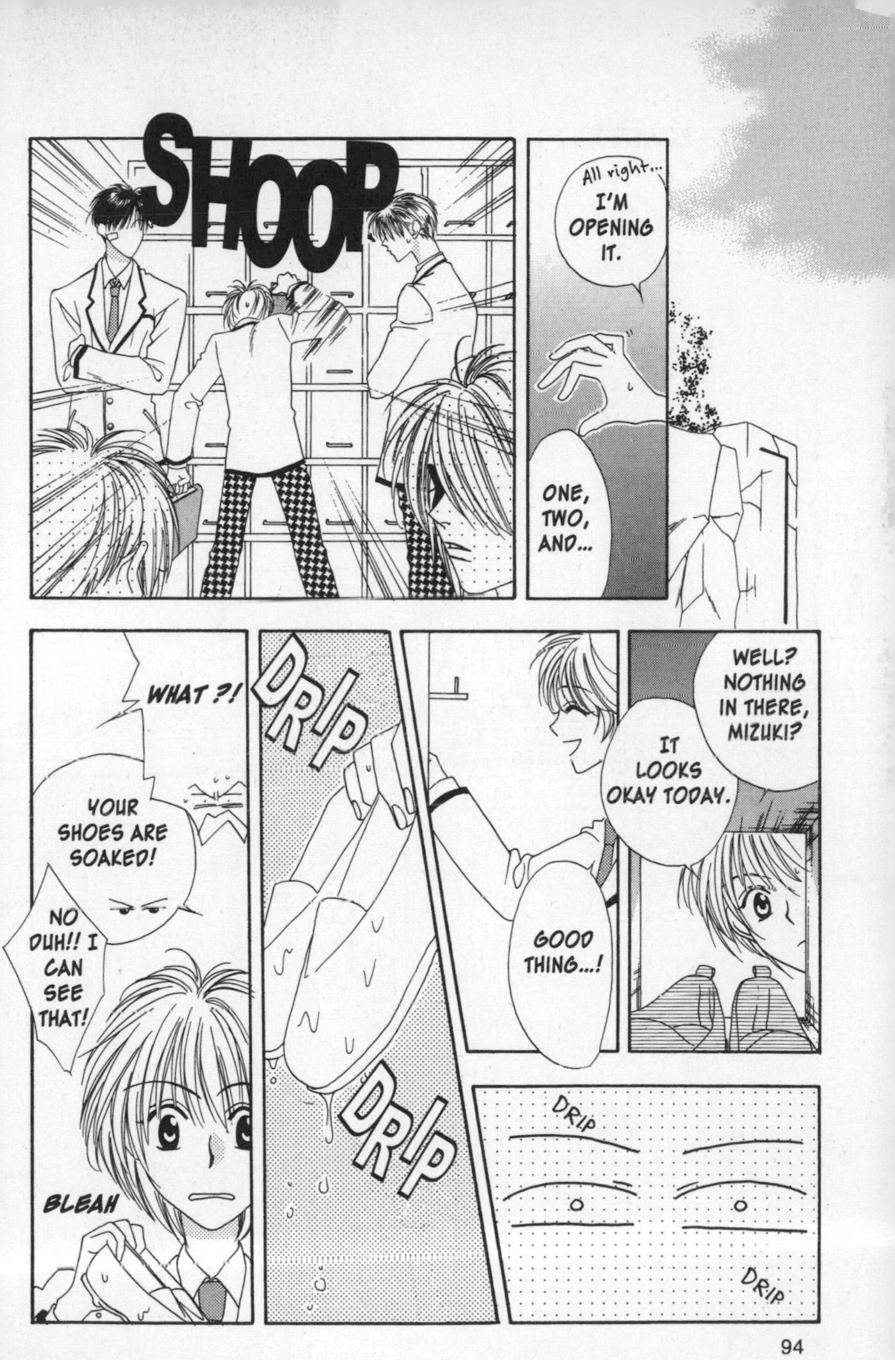
All right...
I'M OPENING IT.
ONE, TWO, AND...
SHOOP
WELL? NOTHING IN THERE, MIZUKI?
IT LOOKS OKAY TODAY.
GOOD THING...!
DRIP
DRIP
DRIP
DRIP
WHAT ?!
YOUR SHOES ARE SOAKED!
NO DUH!! I CAN SEE THAT!
BLEAH

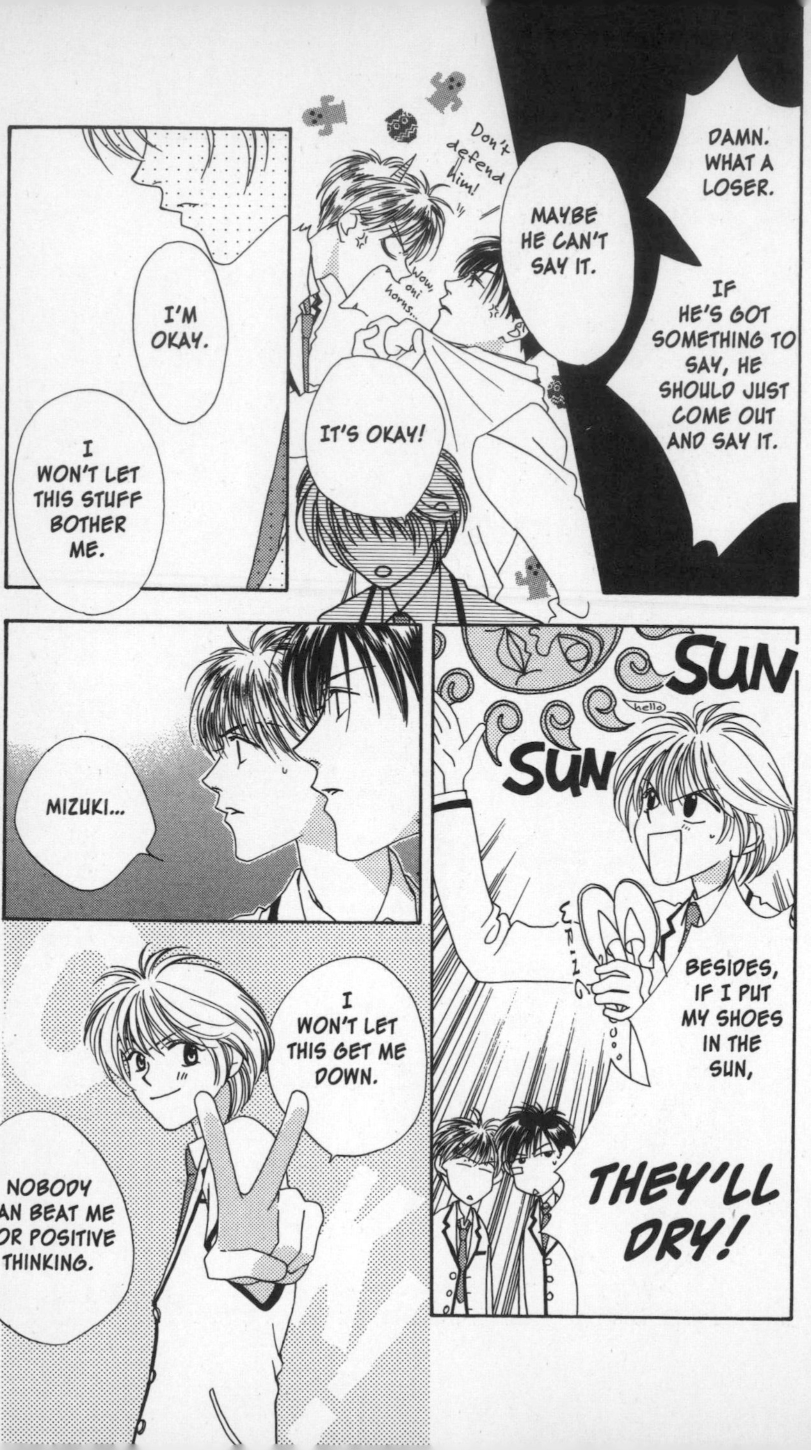
DAMN. WHAT A LOSER.
IF HE'S GOT SOMETHING TO SAY, HE SHOULD JUST COME OUT AND SAY IT.
Don't defend him!
MAYBE HE CAN'T SAY IT.
Wow, oni horns...
IT'S OKAY!
I'M OKAY.
I WON'T LET THIS STUFF BOTHER ME.
SUN
hello
SUN
WRING
BESIDES, IF I PUT MY SHOES IN THE SUN,
THEY'LL DRY!
MIZUKI...
I WON'T LET THIS GET ME DOWN.
NOBODY CAN BEAT ME FOR POSITIVE THINKING.

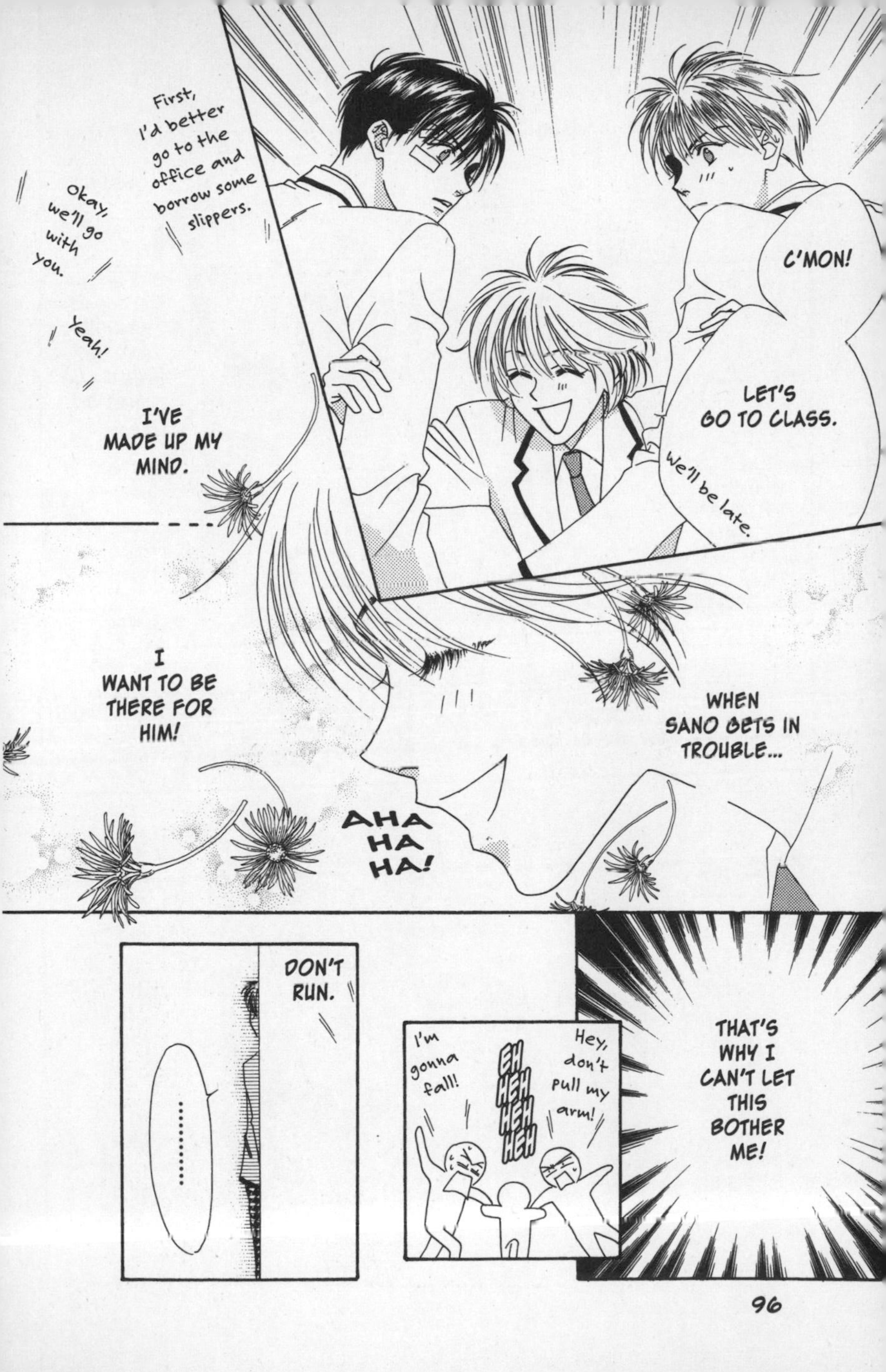
C'MON!
LET'S GO TO CLASS.
We'll be late.
First, I'd better go to the office and borrow some slippers.
Okay, we'll go with you.
Yeah!
I'VE MADE UP MY MIND.
WHEN SANO GETS IN TROUBLE...
I WANT TO BE THERE FOR HIM!
AHA HA HA!
THAT'S WHY I CAN'T LET THIS BOTHER ME!
Hey, don't pull my arm!
EH HEH HEH HEH
I'm gonna fall!
DON'T RUN.
......

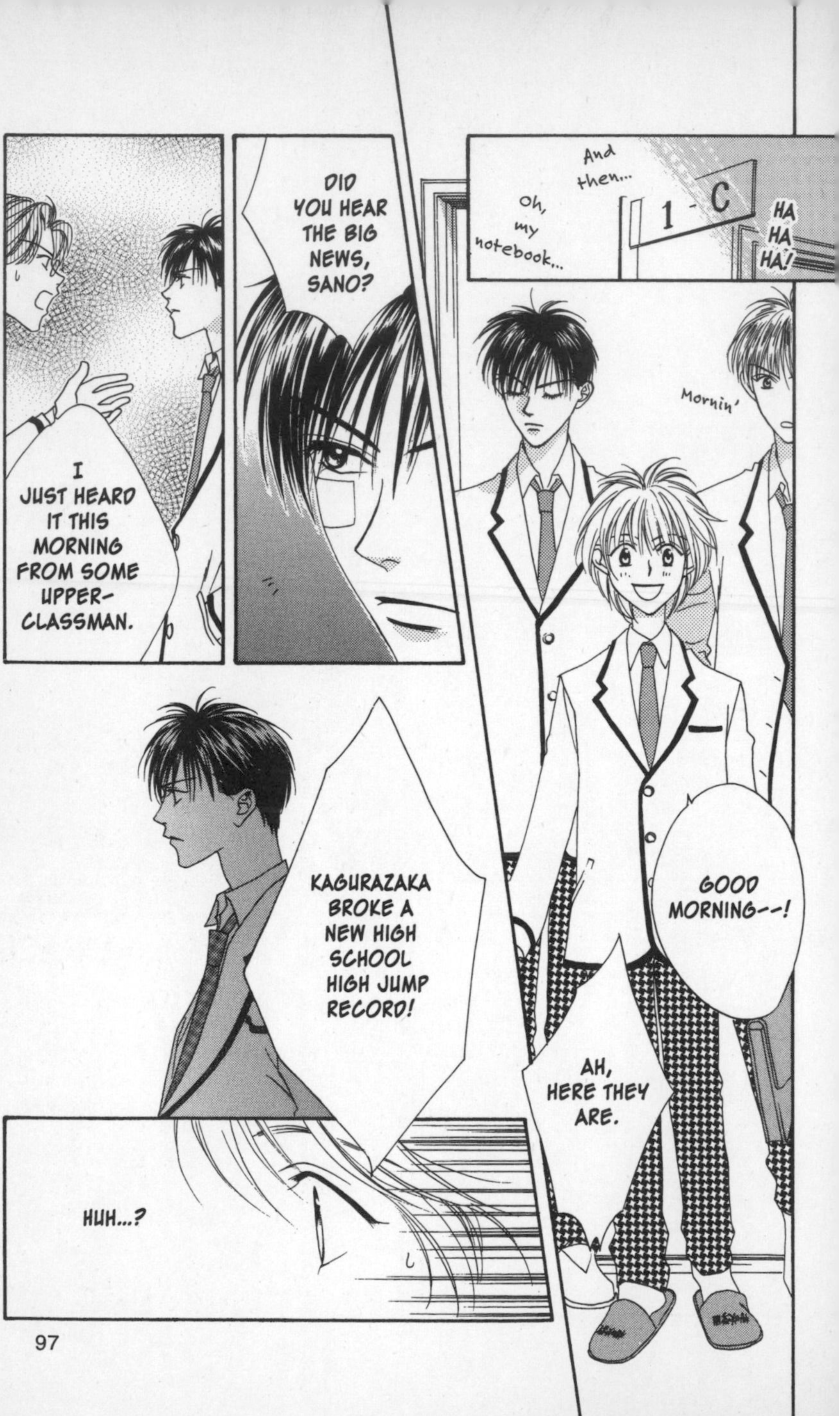
HA HA HA!
And then...
Oh, my notebook...
Mornin'
GOOD MORNING--!
AH, HERE THEY ARE.
DID YOU HEAR THE BIG NEWS, SANO?
I JUST HEARD IT THIS MORNING FROM SOME UPPER-CLASSMAN.
KAGURAZAKA BROKE A NEW HIGH SCHOOL HIGH JUMP RECORD!
HUH...?

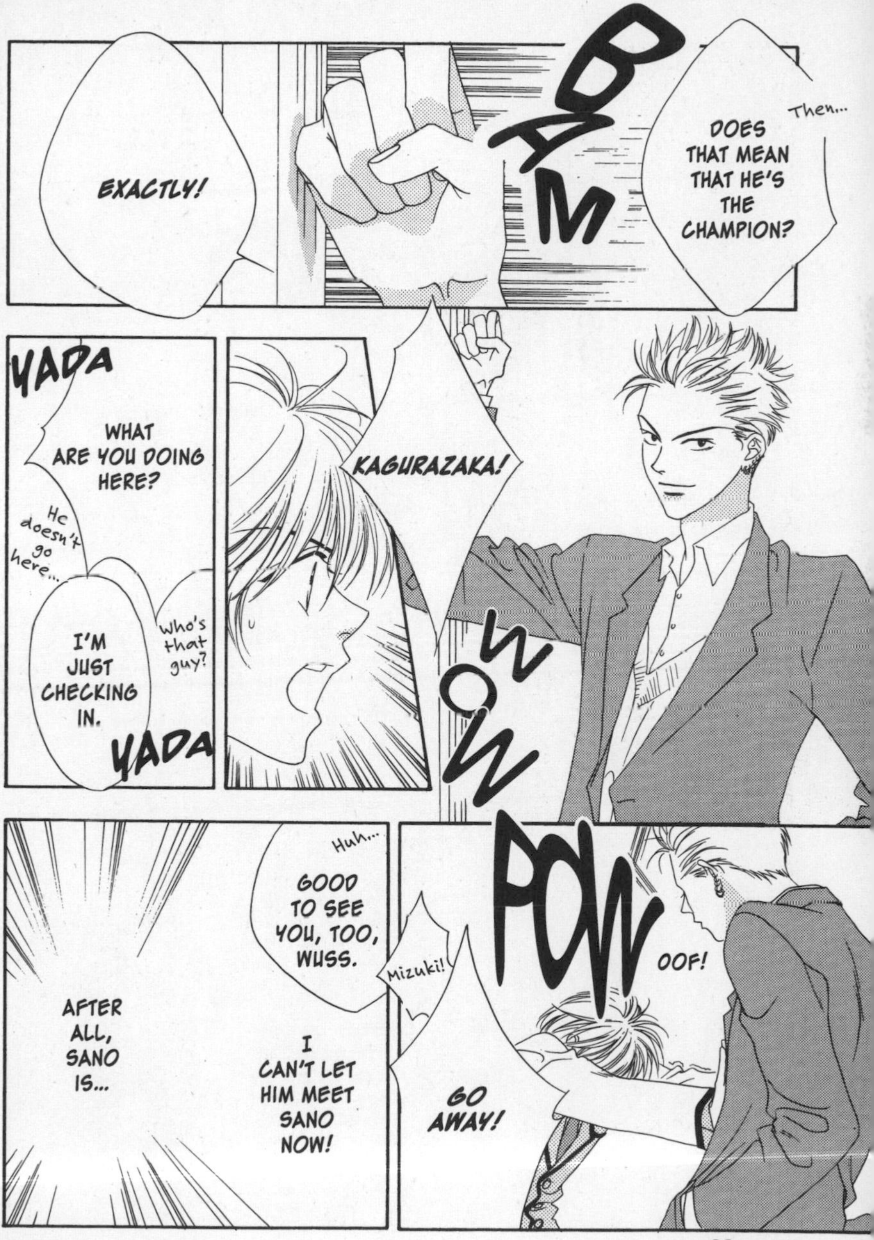
BAM
Then...
DOES THAT MEAN THAT HE'S THE CHAMPION?
EXACTLY!
KAGURAZAKA!
WOW
YADA
WHAT ARE YOU DOING HERE?
He doesn't go here...
Who's that guy?
I'M JUST CHECKING IN.
YADA
POW
OOF!
Mizuki!
GO AWAY!
Huh...
GOOD TO SEE YOU, TOO, WUSS.
I CAN'T LET HIM MEET SANO NOW!
AFTER ALL, SANO IS...

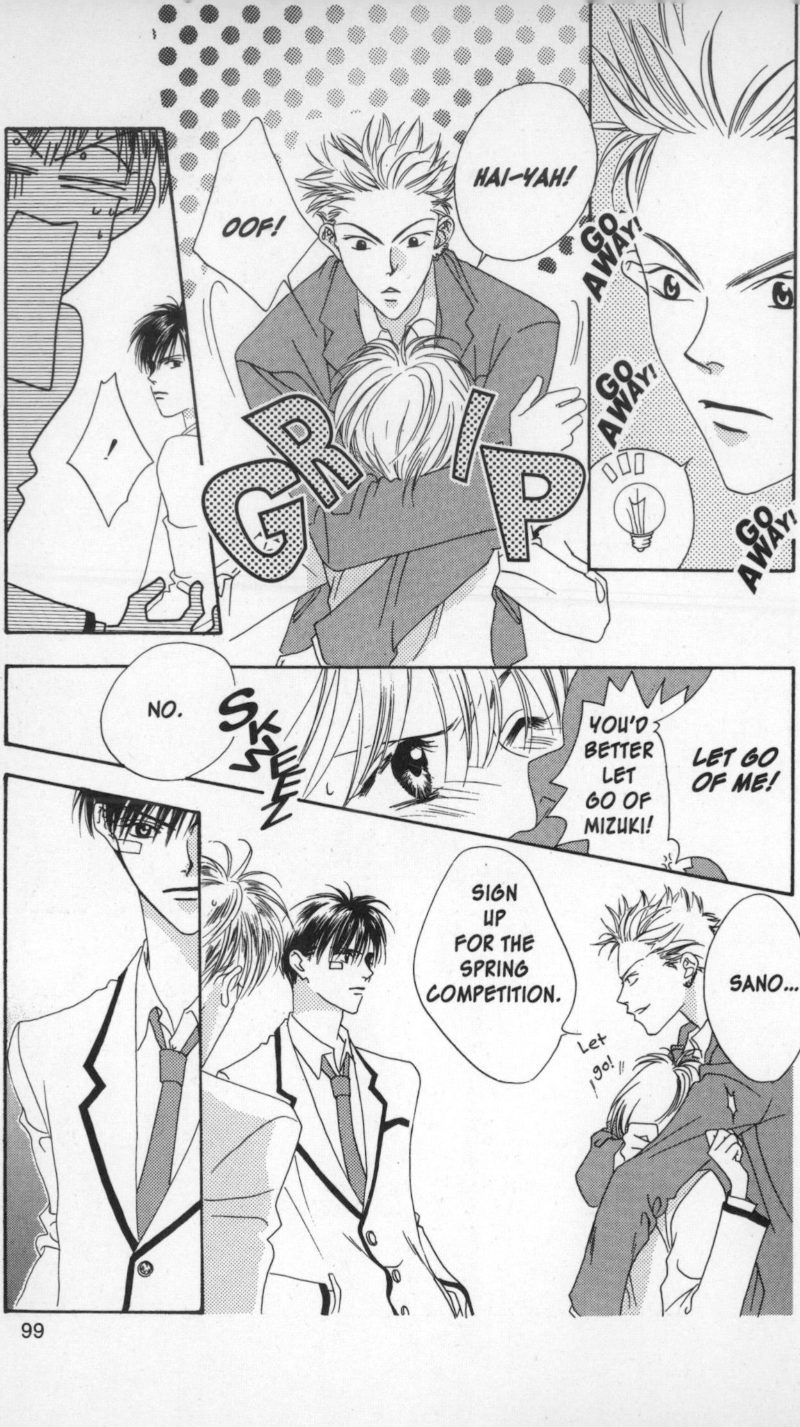
GO AWAY!
GO AWAY!
GO AWAY!
HAI-YAH!
OOF!
GRIP
!
LET GO OF ME!
YOU'D BETTER LET GO OF MIZUKI!
SKWEEZ
NO.
SANO...
Let go!
SIGN UP FOR THE SPRING COMPETITION.

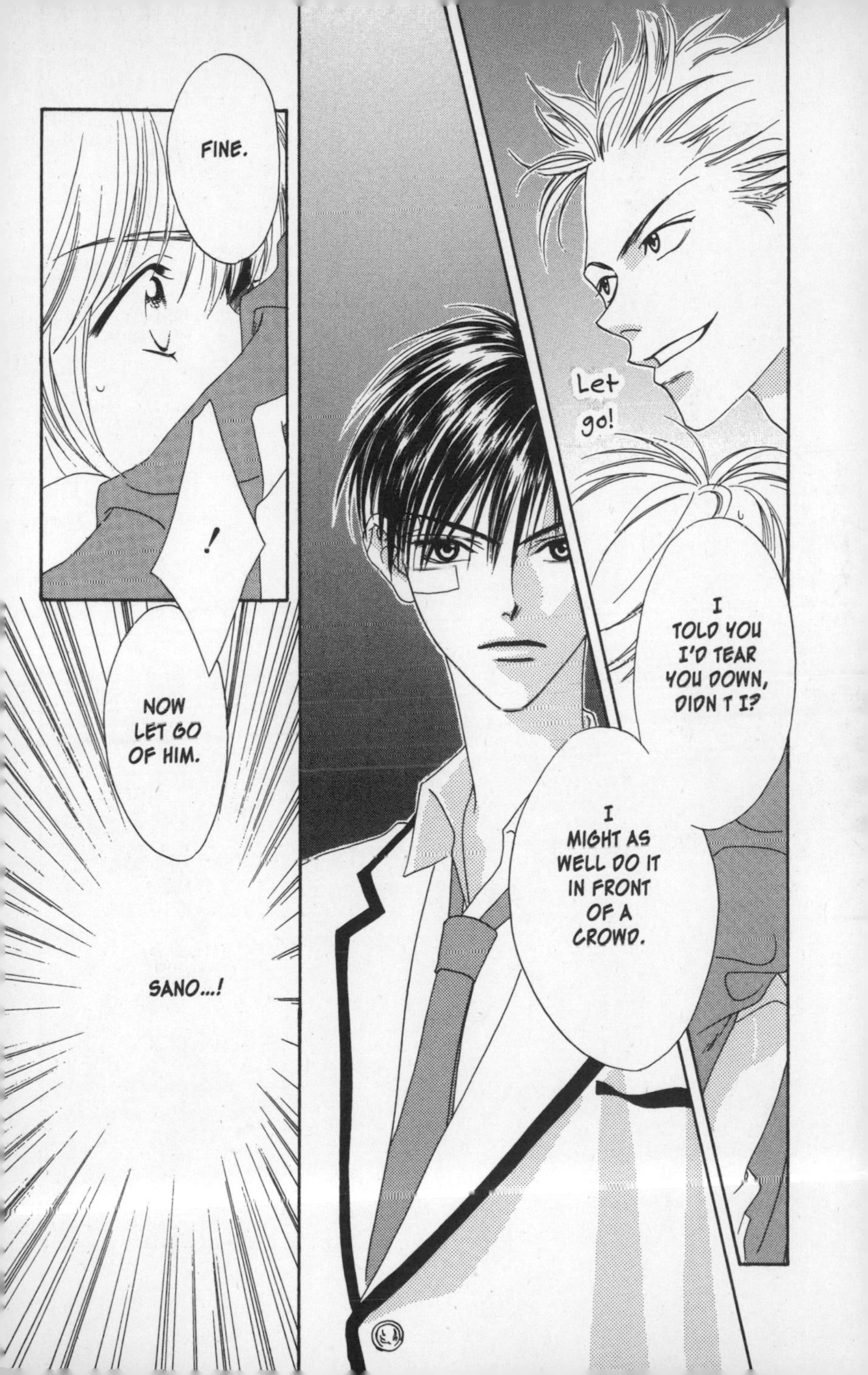
Let go!
I TOLD YOU I'D TEAR YOU DOWN, DIDN T I?
I MIGHT AS WELL DO IT IN FRONT OF A CROWD.
FINE.
!
NOW LET GO OF HIM.
SANO...!

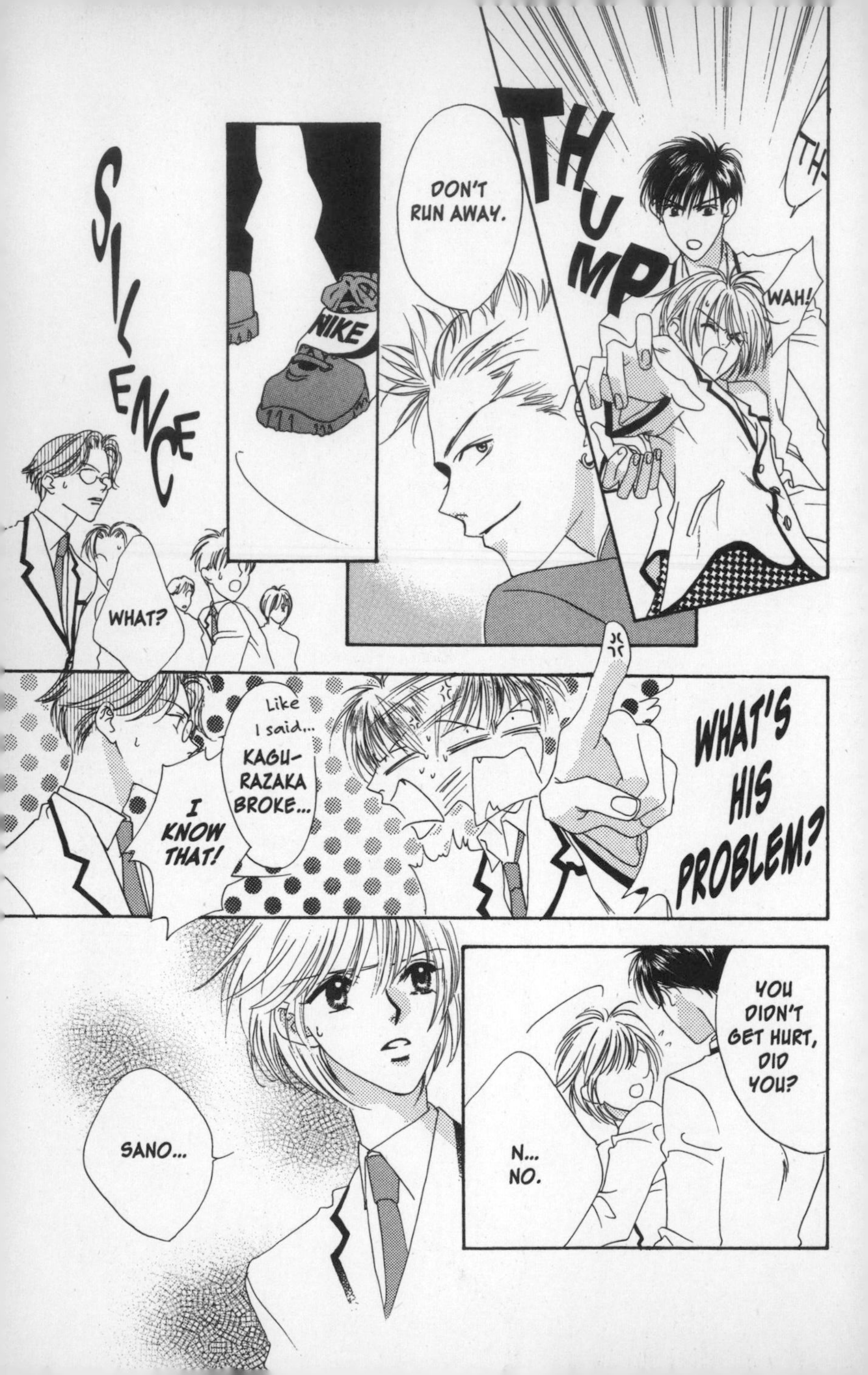
TH-
THUMP
WAH!
DON'T RUN AWAY.
NIKE
SILENCE
WHAT?
WHAT'S HIS PROBLEM?
Like I said... KAGURAZAKA BROKE...
I KNOW THAT!
YOU DIDN'T GET HURT, DID YOU?
N... NO.
SANO...

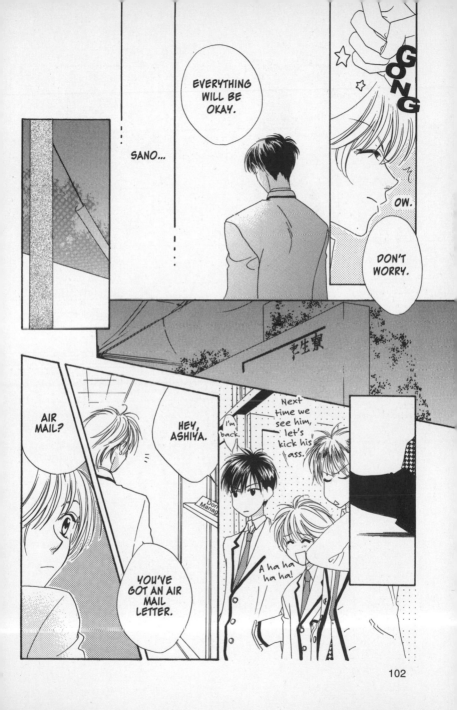

EVERYTHING WILL BE OKAY.

GONG

SANO...

OW.

DON'T WORRY.

AIR MAIL?

HEY, ASHIYA.

I'm back.

Next time we see him, let's kick his ass.

A ha ha ha ha!

YOU'VE GOT AN AIR MAIL LETTER.

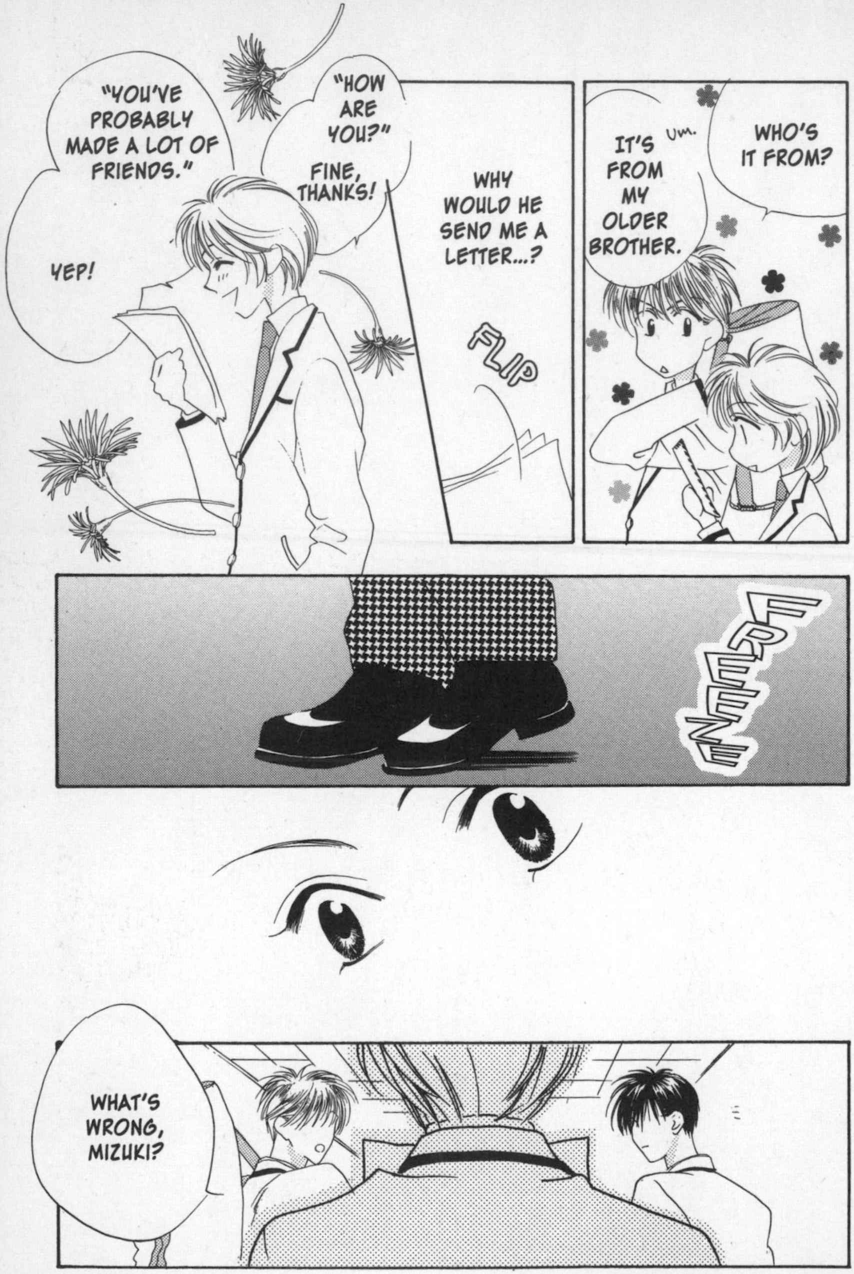
WHO'S IT FROM?
Um.
IT'S FROM MY OLDER BROTHER.
WHY WOULD HE SEND ME A LETTER...?
FLIP
"HOW ARE YOU?"
FINE, THANKS!
"YOU'VE PROBABLY MADE A LOT OF FRIENDS."
YEP!
FREEZE
WHAT'S WRONG, MIZUKI?

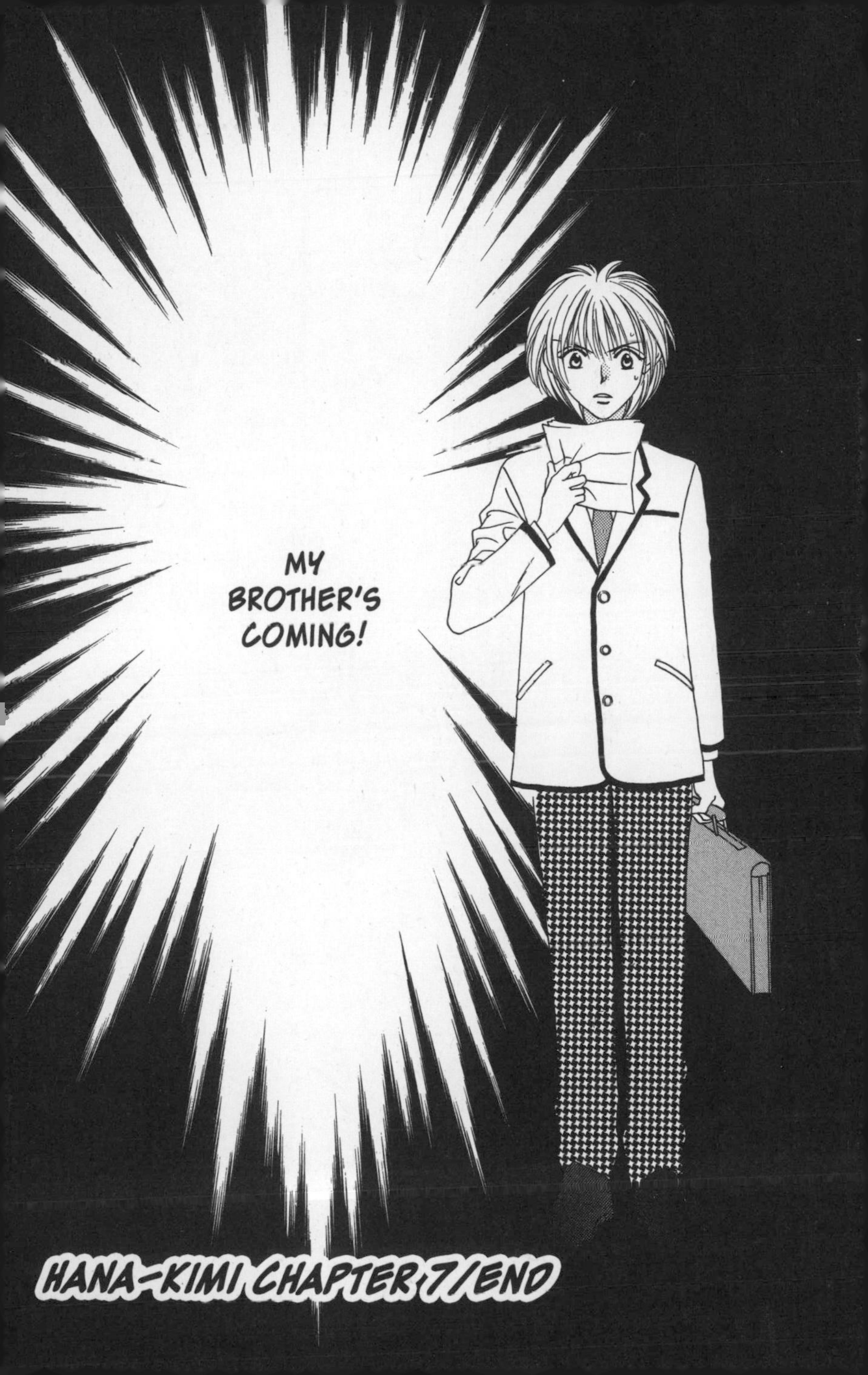
MY BROTHER'S COMING!
HANA-KIMI CHAPTER 7/END

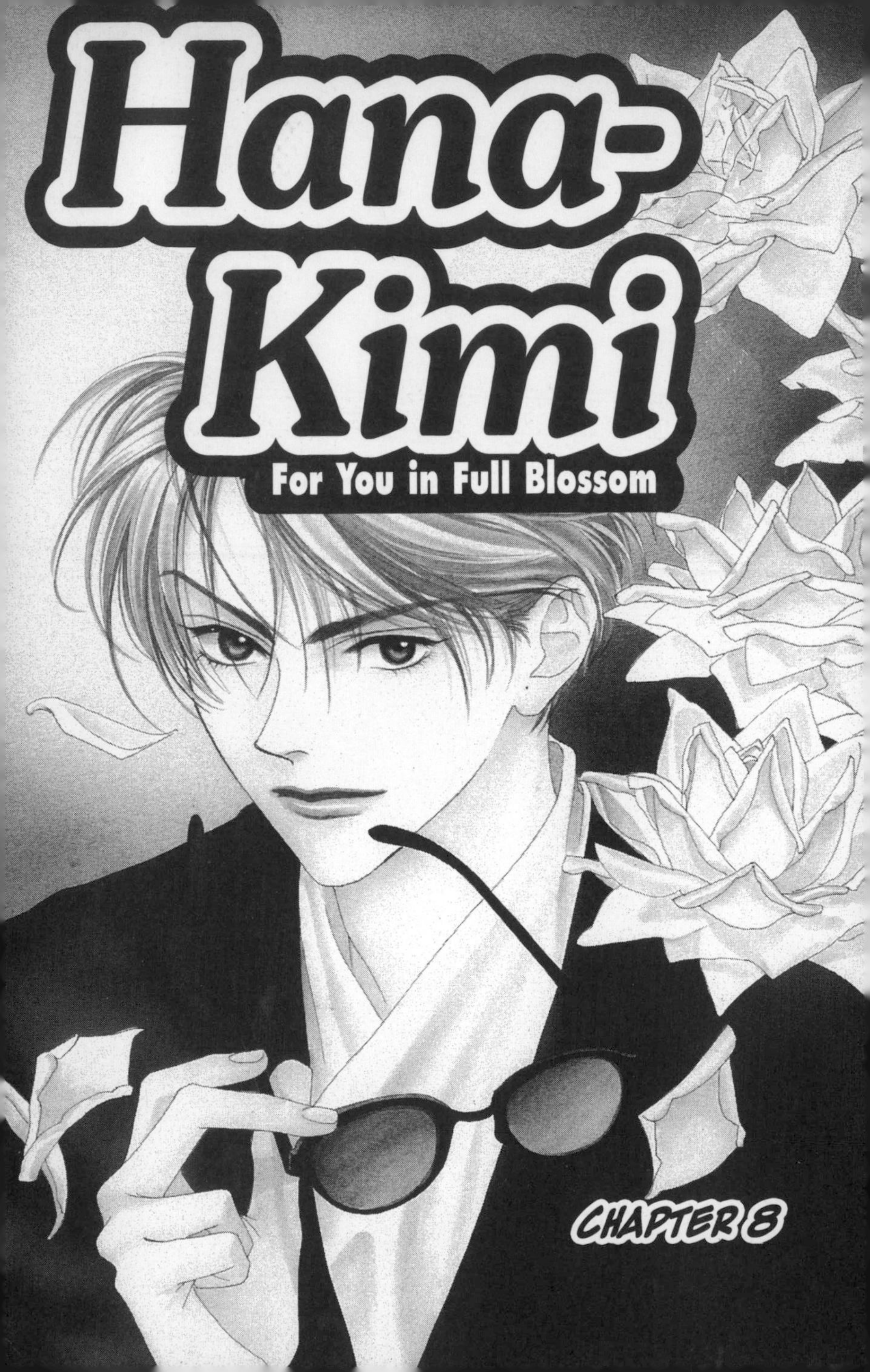
Hana-Kimi
For You in Full Blossom
CHAPTER 8

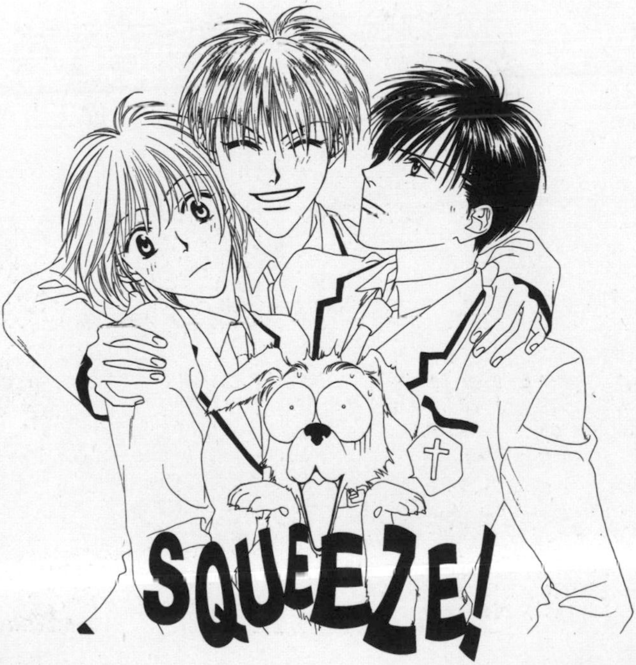
SQUEEZE!

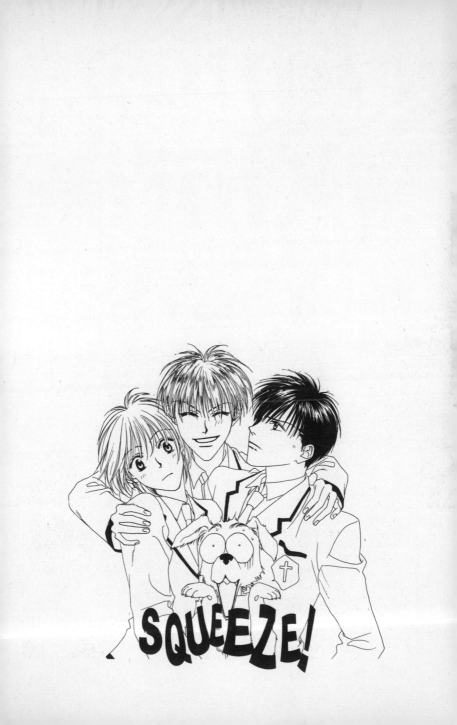

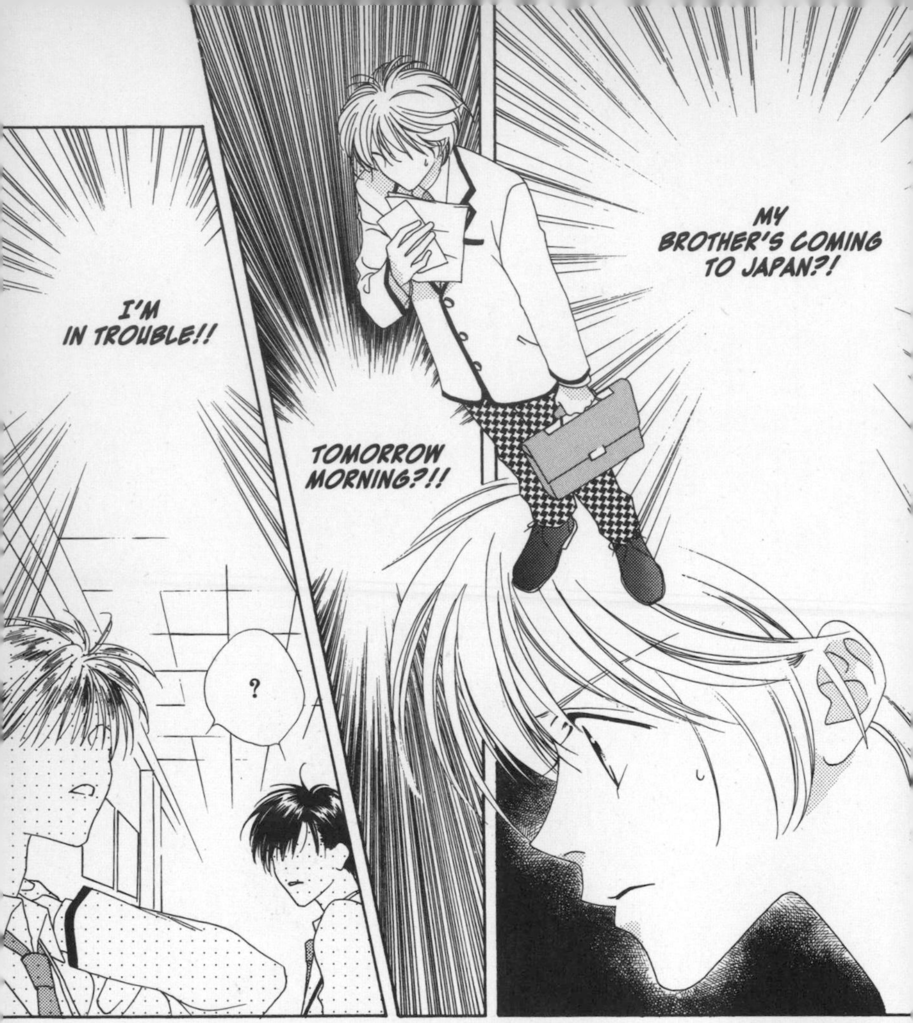
MY BROTHER'S COMING TO JAPAN?!
TOMORROW MORNING?!!
I'M IN TROUBLE!!
?

Confession

...or, my random blabbing...

EVER SINCE DR. UMEDA'S FIRST APPEARANCE, PEOPLE HAVE BEEN WRITING AND ASKING, WHO'S THIS GUY HE LIKES? I ACTUALLY TALKED ABOUT THIS IN THE "HANA TO YUME" (FLOWERS AND DREAMS) QUIZ BOOK...

BUT FOR THOSE OF YOU WHO DIDN'T READ IT, HERE IT IS AGAIN. IT'S ACTUALLY RYOICHI KIJIMA FROM MY FIRST COMIC, "YUMEMIRU HAPPA" (THE DREAMING LEAF)!

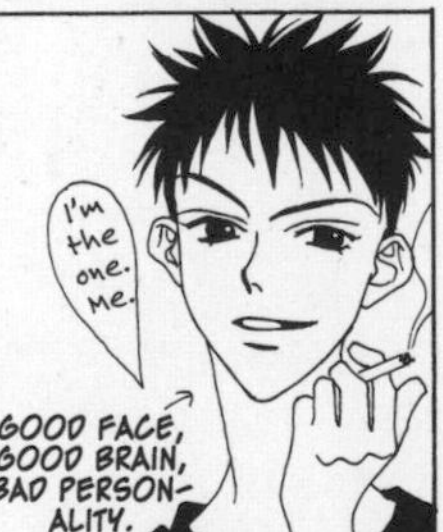
I'm the one. Me.
GOOD FACE, GOOD BRAIN, BAD PERSON-ALITY.

Osaka High School

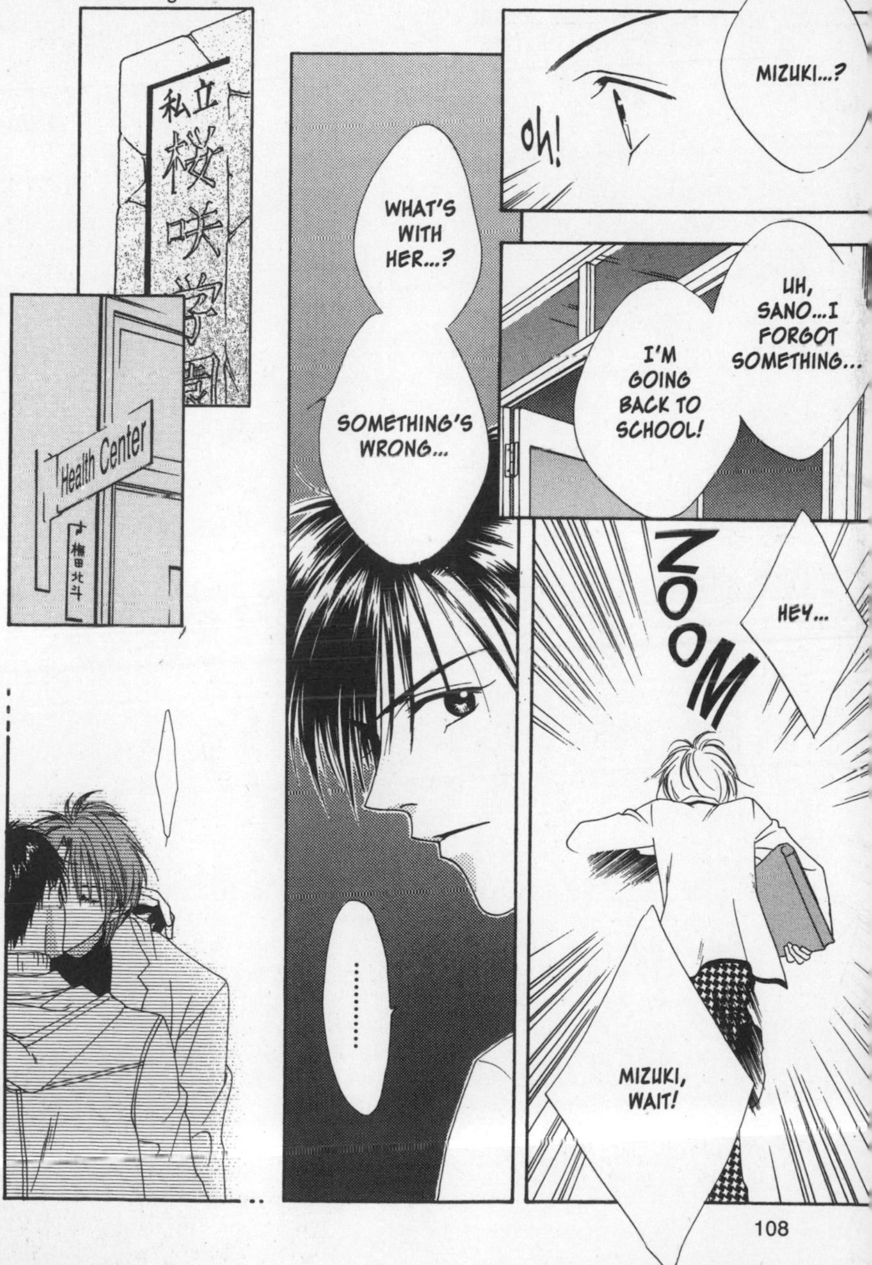
MIZUKI...?
OH!
UH, SANO...I FORGOT SOMETHING...
I'M GOING BACK TO SCHOOL!
HEY...
ZOOM
MIZUKI, WAIT!
WHAT'S WITH HER...?
SOMETHING'S WRONG...
......
私立
桜咲
Health Center
梅田北斗

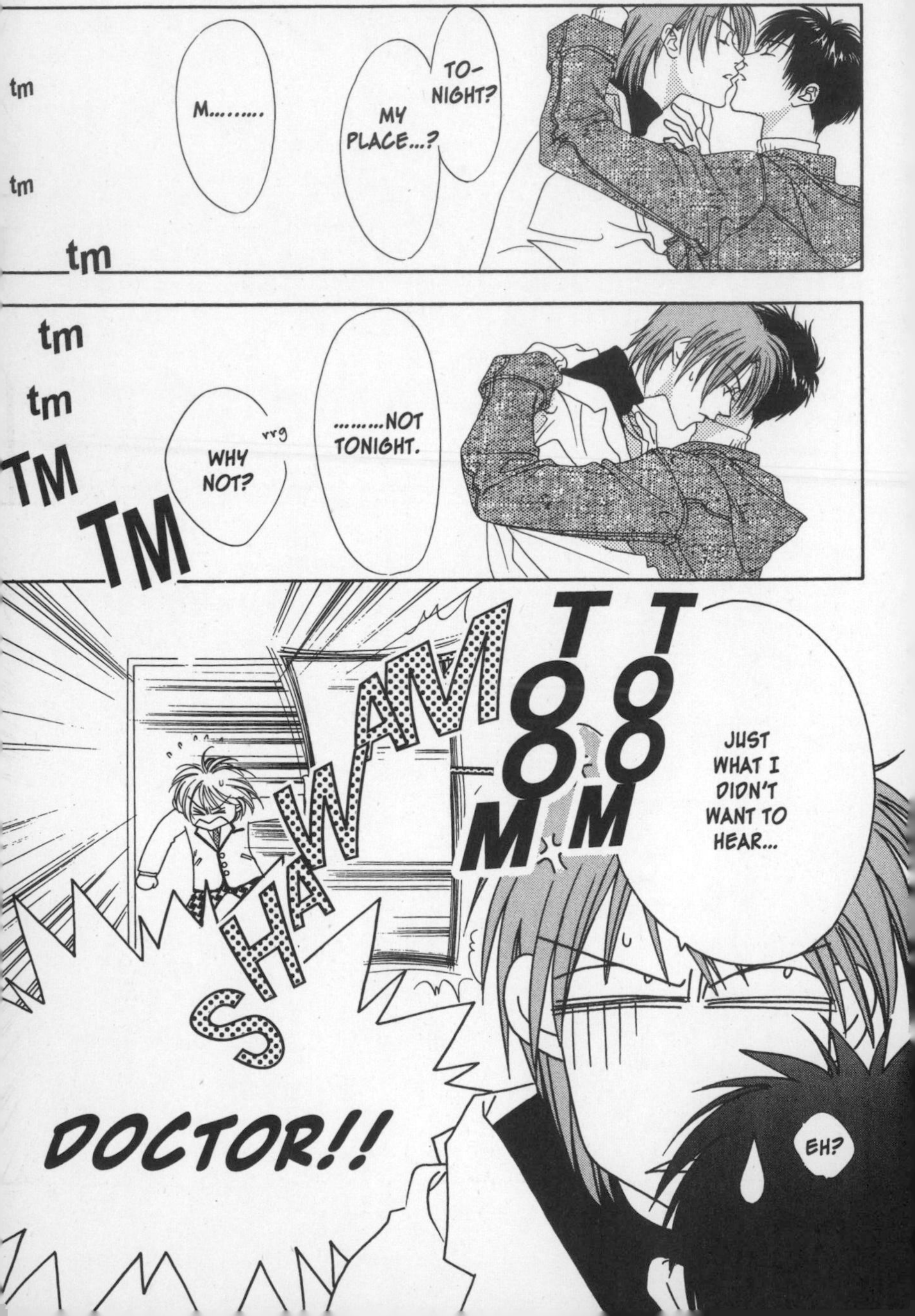
TO-NIGHT?
MY PLACE...?
M.........
tm
tm
tm
.........NOT TONIGHT.
vrg
WHY NOT?
tm
tm
TM
TM
JUST WHAT I DIDN'T WANT TO HEAR...
TOOM
TOOM
SHAWAM
DOCTOR!!
EH?

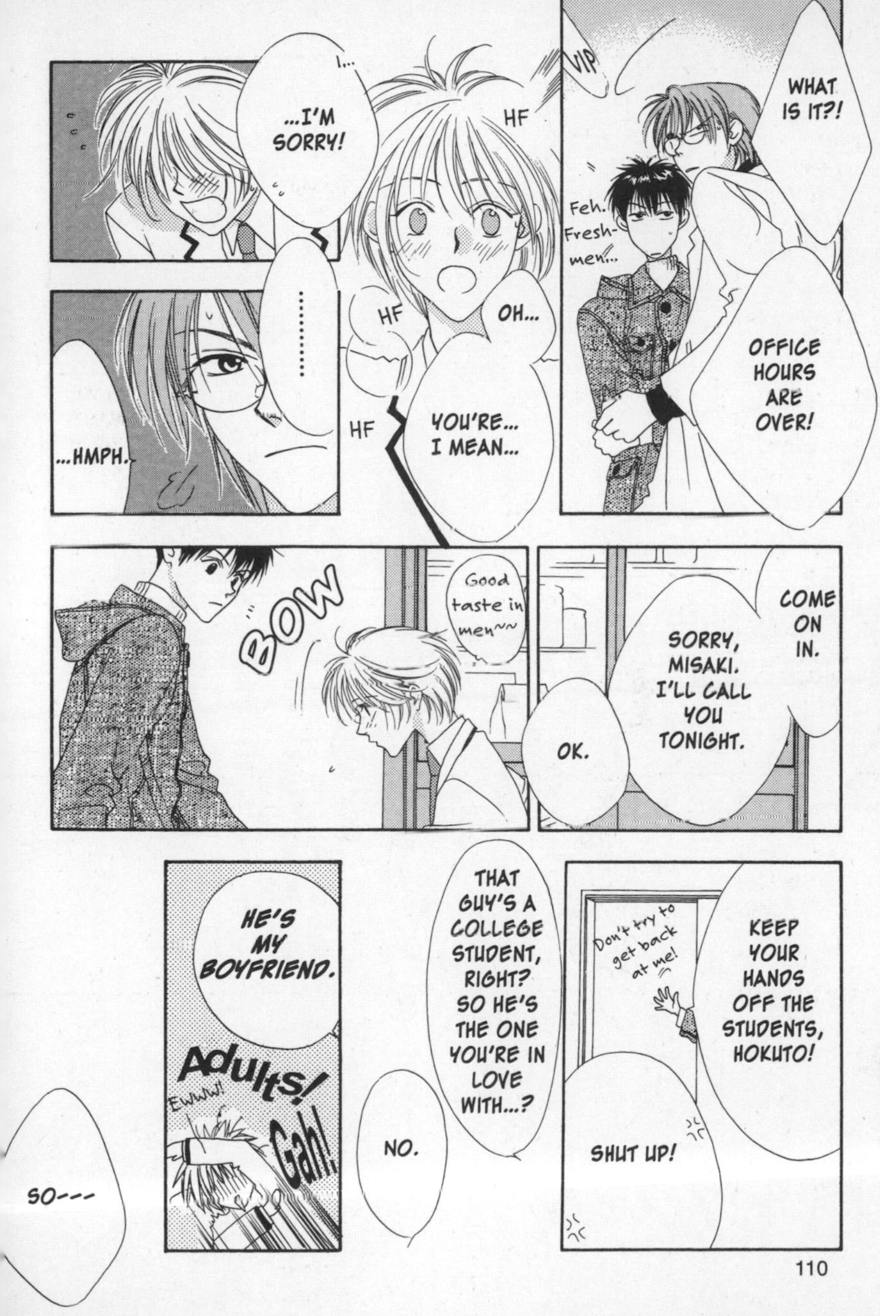
VIP
WHAT IS IT?!
Feh. Freshmen...
OFFICE HOURS ARE OVER!
HF
OH...
HF
HF
YOU'RE... I MEAN...
I...
...I'M SORRY!
......
...HMPH..
COME ON IN.
SORRY, MISAKI. I'LL CALL YOU TONIGHT.
OK.
Good taste in men~~
BOW
KEEP YOUR HANDS OFF THE STUDENTS, HOKUTO!
Don't try to get back at me!
SHUT UP!
THAT GUY'S A COLLEGE STUDENT, RIGHT? SO HE'S THE ONE YOU'RE IN LOVE WITH...?
NO.
HE'S MY BOYFRIEND.
Adults!
Ewww!
Gah!
SO---

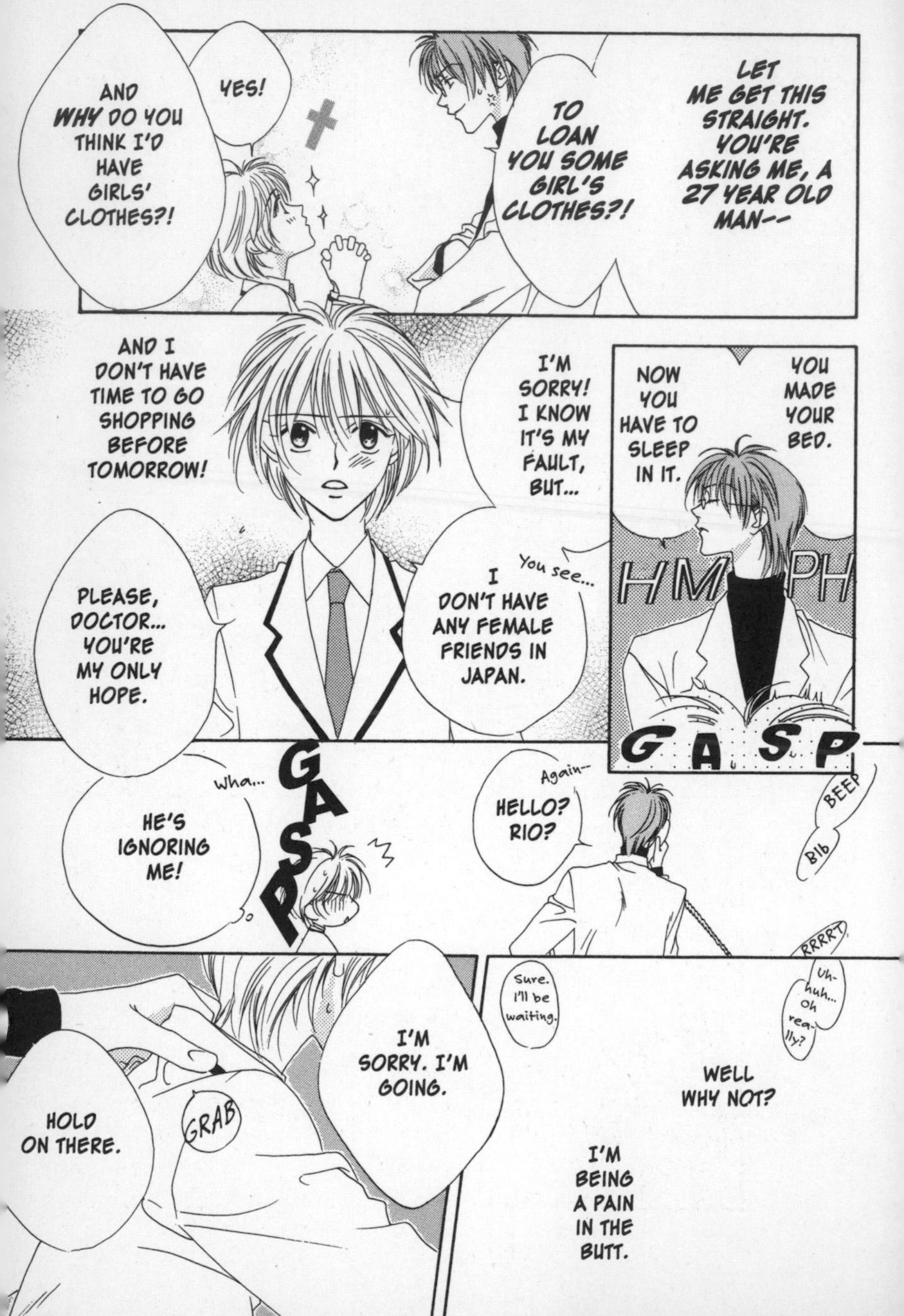
LET ME GET THIS STRAIGHT. YOU'RE ASKING ME, A 27 YEAR OLD MAN--
TO LOAN YOU SOME GIRL'S CLOTHES?!
YES!
AND WHY DO YOU THINK I'D HAVE GIRLS' CLOTHES?!
YOU MADE YOUR BED.
NOW YOU HAVE TO SLEEP IN IT.
HMPH
GASP
I'M SORRY! I KNOW IT'S MY FAULT, BUT...
You see...
I DON'T HAVE ANY FEMALE FRIENDS IN JAPAN.
AND I DON'T HAVE TIME TO GO SHOPPING BEFORE TOMORROW!
PLEASE, DOCTOR... YOU'RE MY ONLY HOPE.
BEEP
Blb
Again--
HELLO? RIO?
GASP
Wha...
HE'S IGNORING ME!
RRRRT
Uh-huh... Oh really?
Sure. I'll be waiting.
WELL WHY NOT?
I'M BEING A PAIN IN THE BUTT.
I'M SORRY. I'M GOING.
GRAB
HOLD ON THERE.

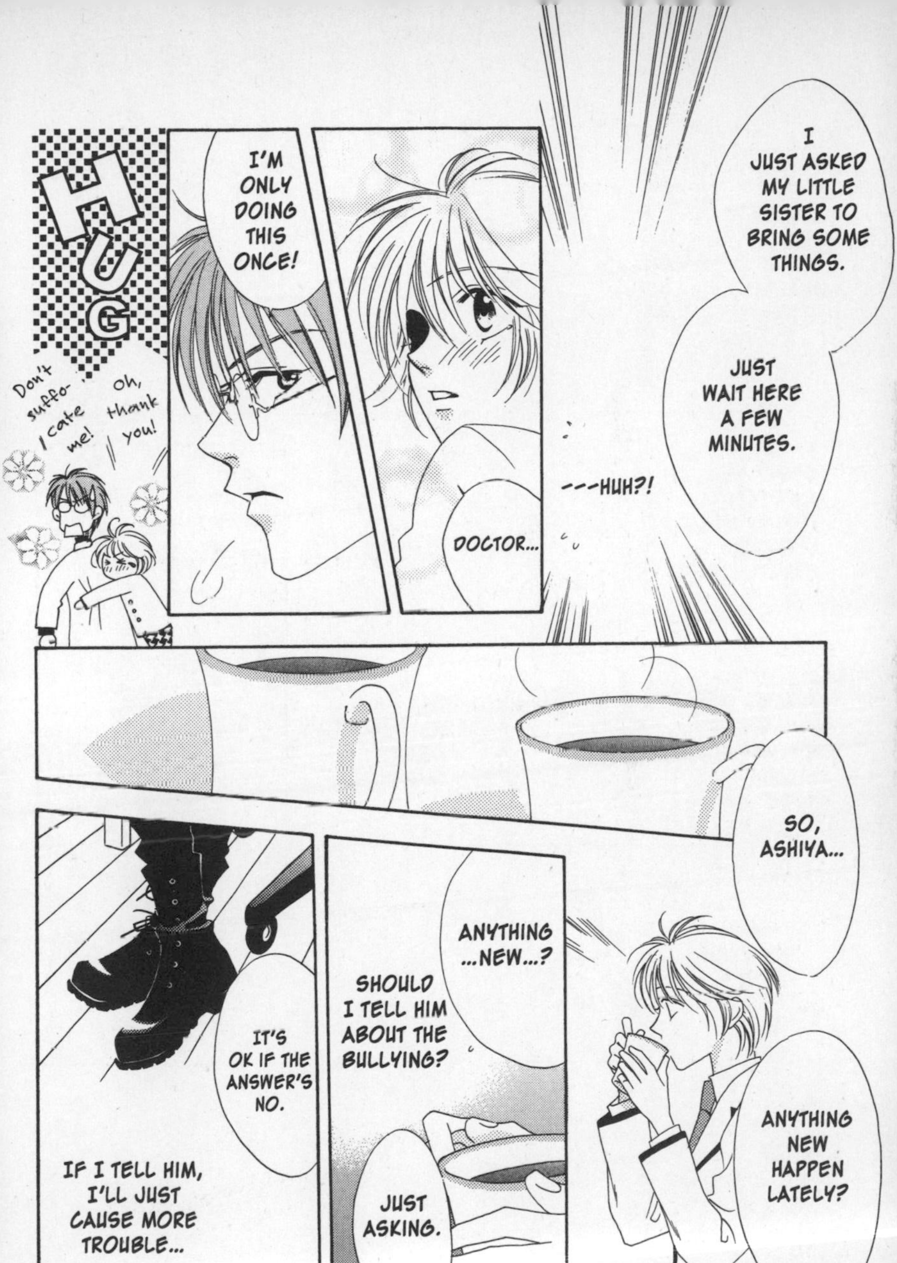
I JUST ASKED MY LITTLE SISTER TO BRING SOME THINGS.
JUST WAIT HERE A FEW MINUTES.
---HUH?!
DOCTOR...
I'M ONLY DOING THIS ONCE!
HUG
Oh, thank you!
Don't suffo- cate me!
SO, ASHIYA...
ANYTHING NEW HAPPEN LATELY?
ANYTHING ...NEW...?
SHOULD I TELL HIM ABOUT THE BULLYING?
IT'S OK IF THE ANSWER'S NO.
JUST ASKING.
IF I TELL HIM, I'LL JUST CAUSE MORE TROUBLE...

WHISPERED SECRETS
Characters

FOR THIS STORY, I DREW EVERYTHING I FELT LIKE DRAWING. MIZUKI DRESSED AS A GIRL, HER FAMILY, UMEDA'S BOYFRIEND, ETC. SO FAR, WE'D ONLY SEEN MIZUKI AS A GIRL AT THE VERY BEGINNING AND IN FLASHBACKS. MY ASSISTANT OGI'S SISTER HELPED ME PICK OUT THE CLOTHES. (THANKS!) MIZUKI'S BROTHER LOVES HER SO MUCH. WHY DOES HE HAVE BLOND HAIR, EVEN THOUGH HE'S HALF JAPANESE? I KNOW HALF JAPANESE/HALF CAUCASIAN PEOPLE USUALLY HAVE MORE ASIAN FEATURES, BUT MY FRIEND WHO WAS HALF GERMAN AND HALF JAPANESE HAD BLONDE HAIR....

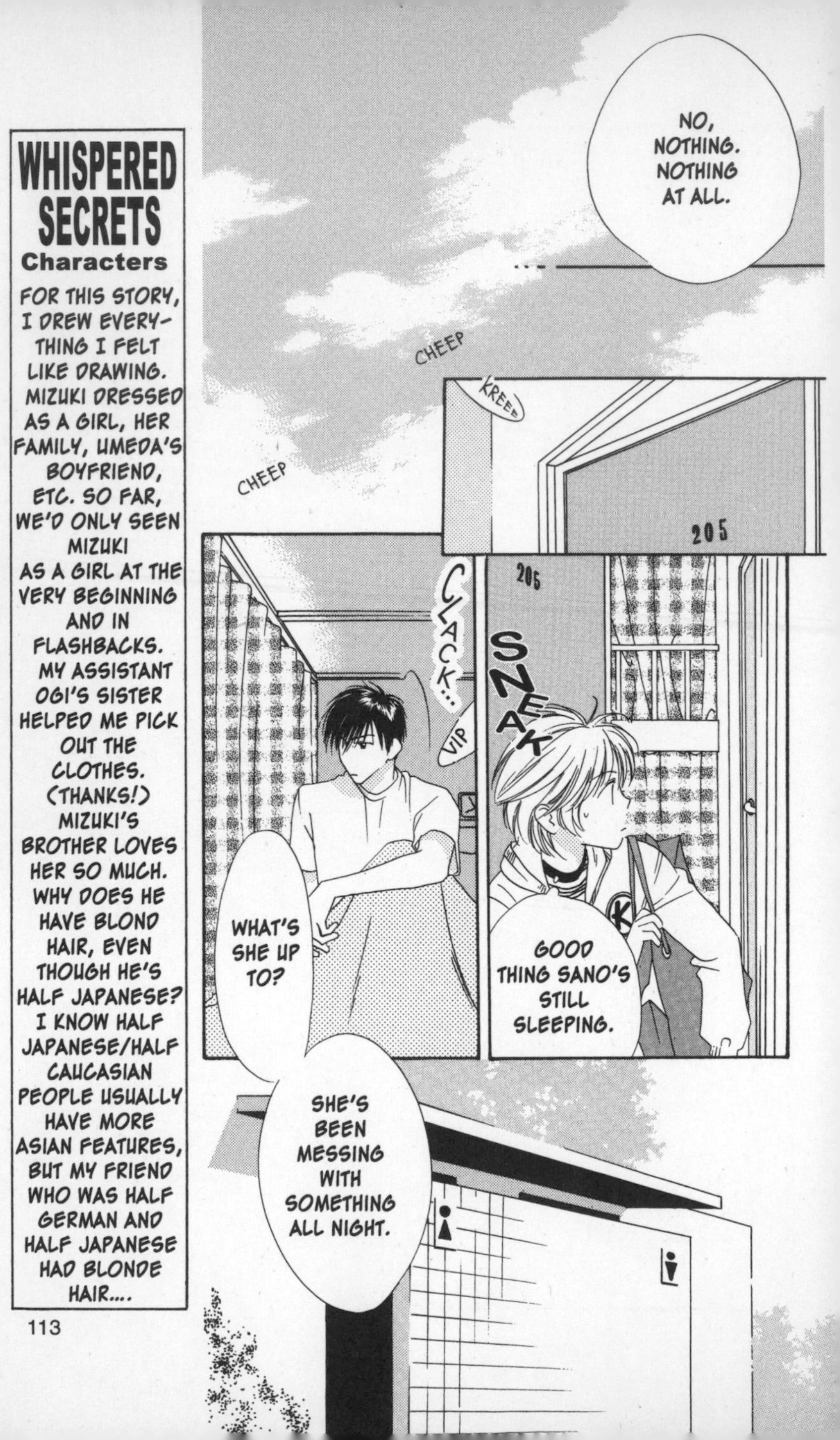
NO, NOTHING. NOTHING AT ALL.
CHEEP
CHEEP
KREEE
205
205
SNEAK
GOOD THING SANO'S STILL SLEEPING.
CLACK...
VIP
WHAT'S SHE UP TO?
SHE'S BEEN MESSING WITH SOMETHING ALL NIGHT.

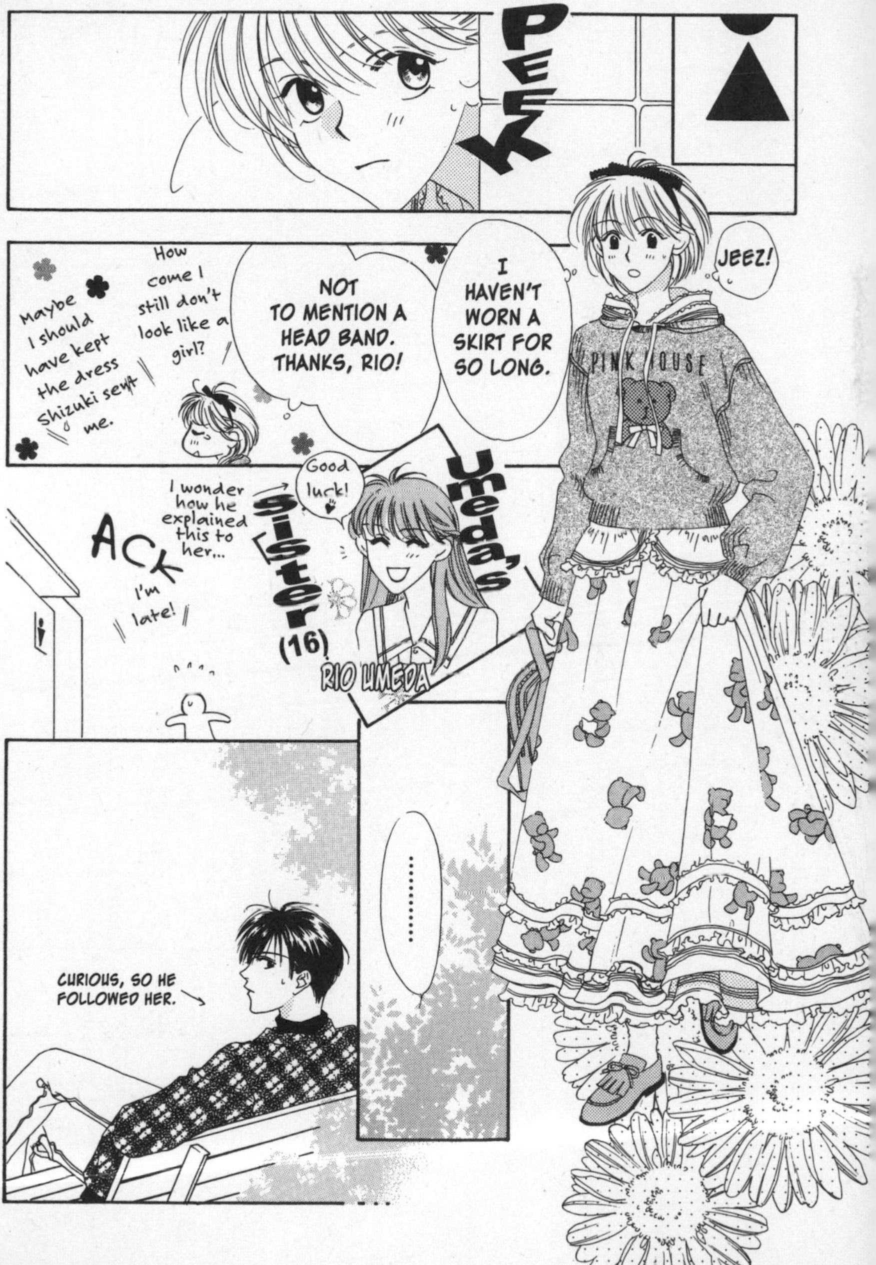
PEEK
JEEZ!
I HAVEN'T WORN A SKIRT FOR SO LONG.
NOT TO MENTION A HEAD BAND. THANKS, RIO!
How come I still don't look like a girl?
Maybe I should have kept the dress Shizuki sent me.
Umeda's Sister (16)
RIO UMEDA
Good luck!
I wonder how he explained this to her...
ACK
I'm late!
......
CURIOUS, SO HE FOLLOWED HER.

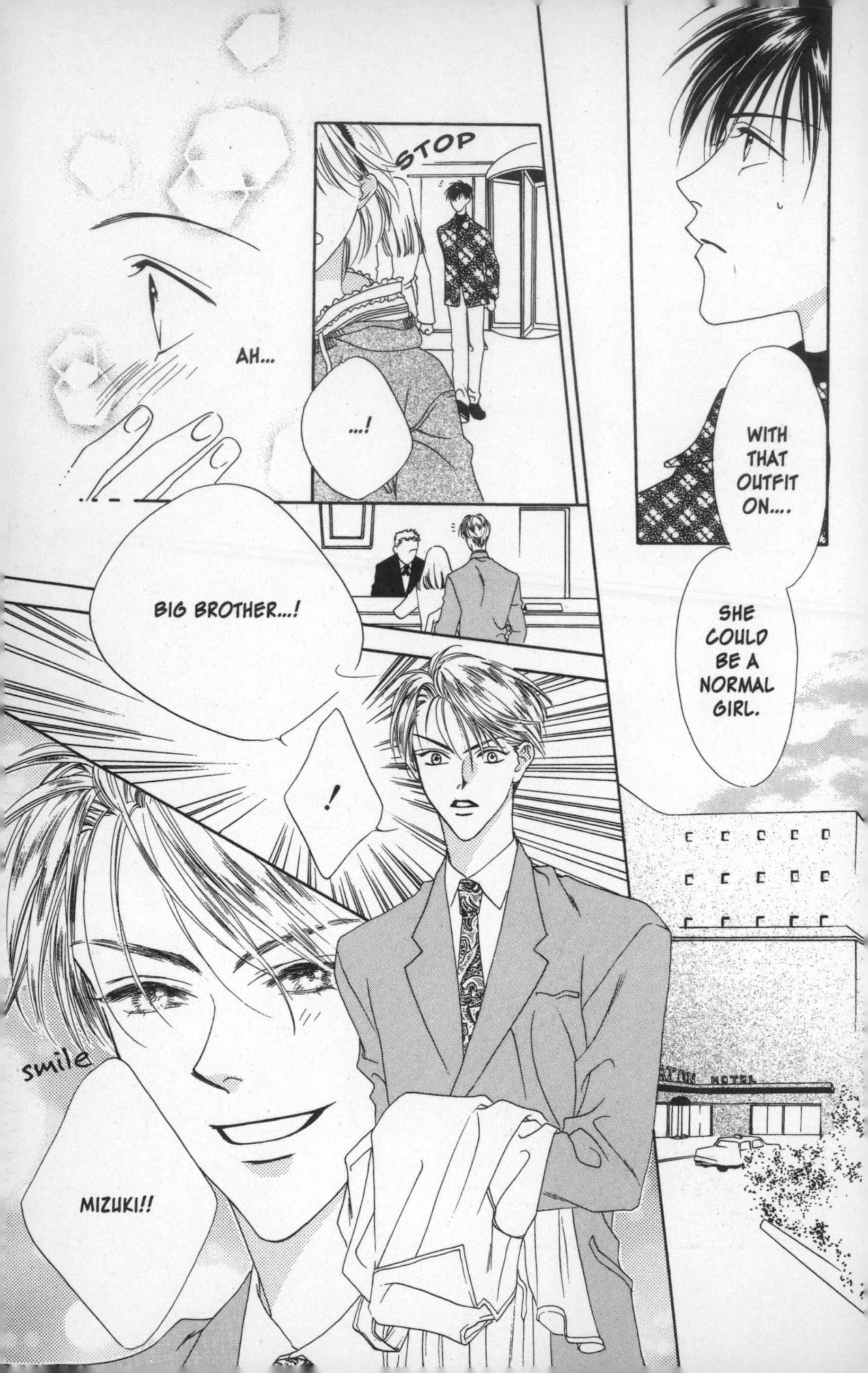
WITH THAT OUTFIT ON....
SHE COULD BE A NORMAL GIRL.
STOP
...!
AH...
BIG BROTHER...!
!
smile
MIZUKI!!

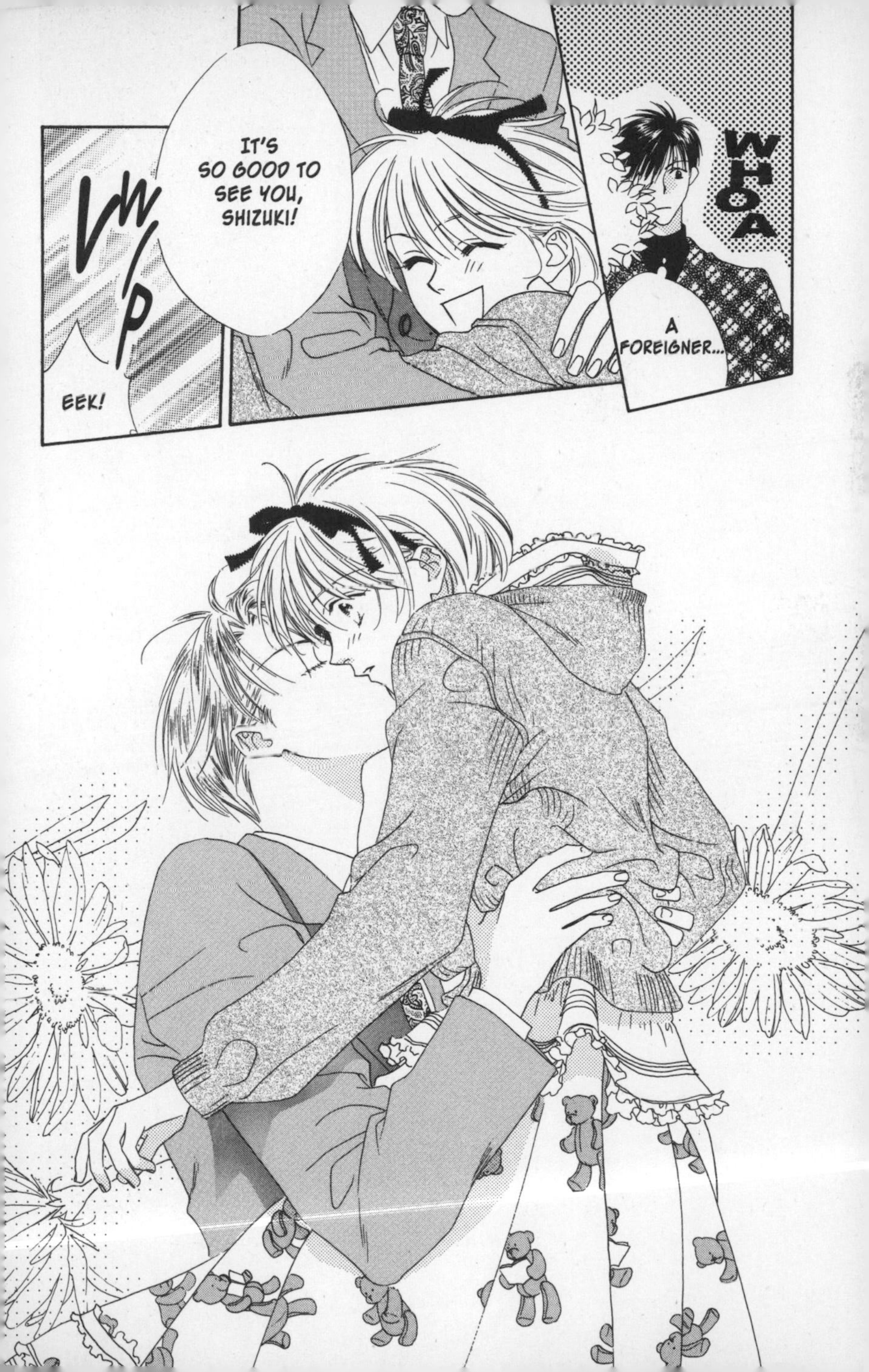
WHOA
A FOREIGNER...
IT'S SO GOOD TO SEE YOU, SHIZUKI!
VWIP
EEK!

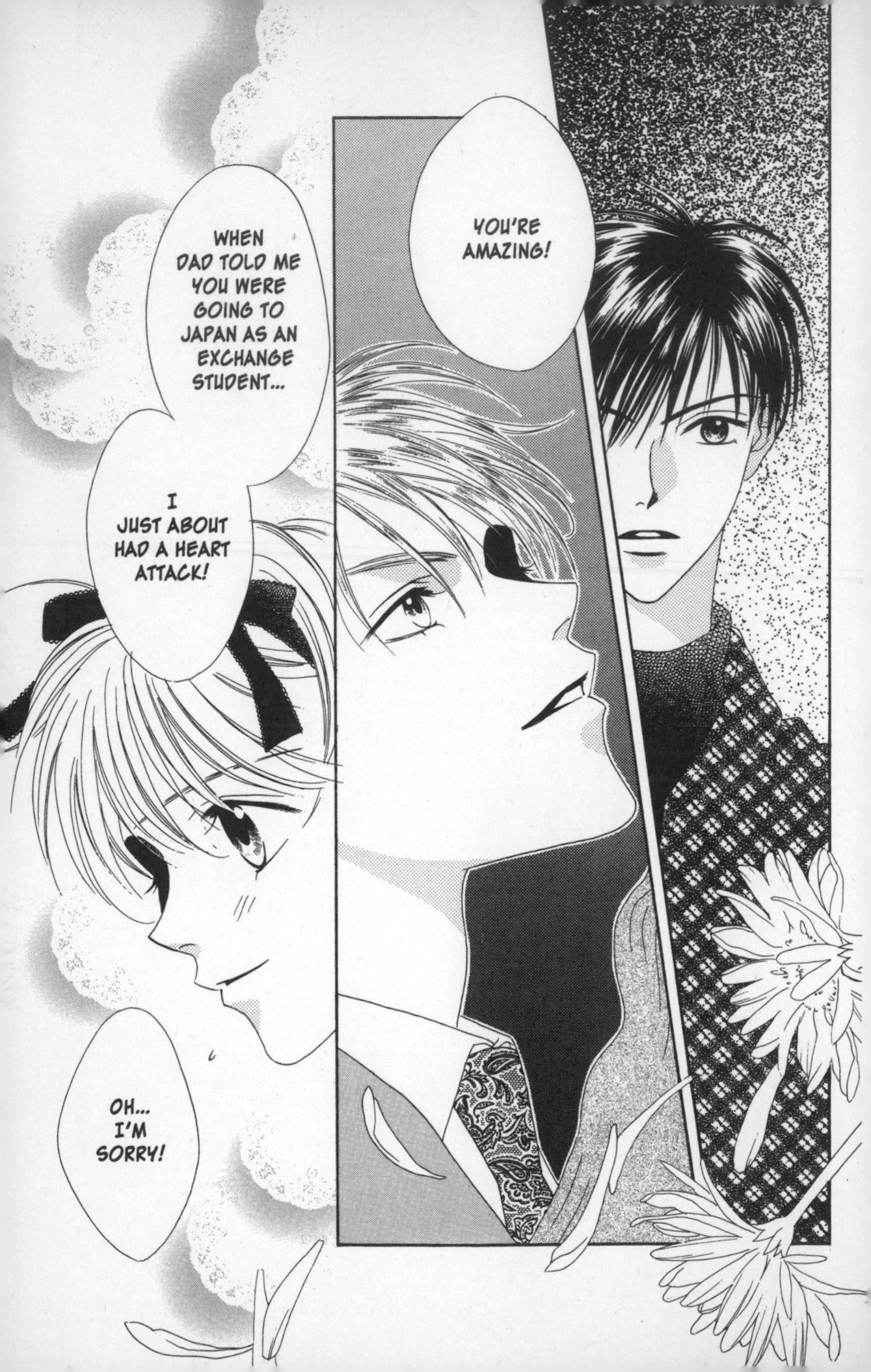
YOU'RE AMAZING!
WHEN DAD TOLD ME YOU WERE GOING TO JAPAN AS AN EXCHANGE STUDENT...
I JUST ABOUT HAD A HEART ATTACK!
OH... I'M SORRY!

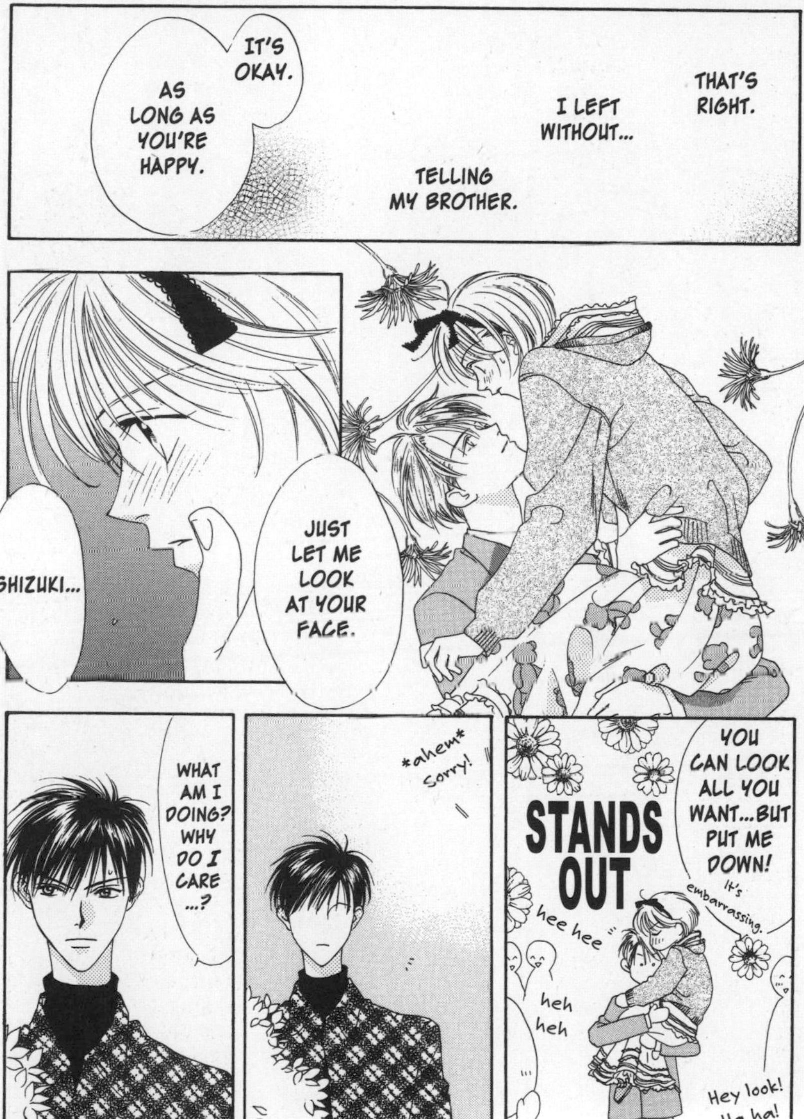
THAT'S RIGHT.
I LEFT WITHOUT...
TELLING MY BROTHER.
IT'S OKAY.
AS LONG AS YOU'RE HAPPY.
JUST LET ME LOOK AT YOUR FACE.
SHIZUKI...
YOU CAN LOOK ALL YOU WANT...BUT PUT ME DOWN!
It's embarrassing.
STANDS OUT
hee hee
heh heh
Hey look! Ha ha!
ahem Sorry!
WHAT AM I DOING? WHY DO I CARE ...?

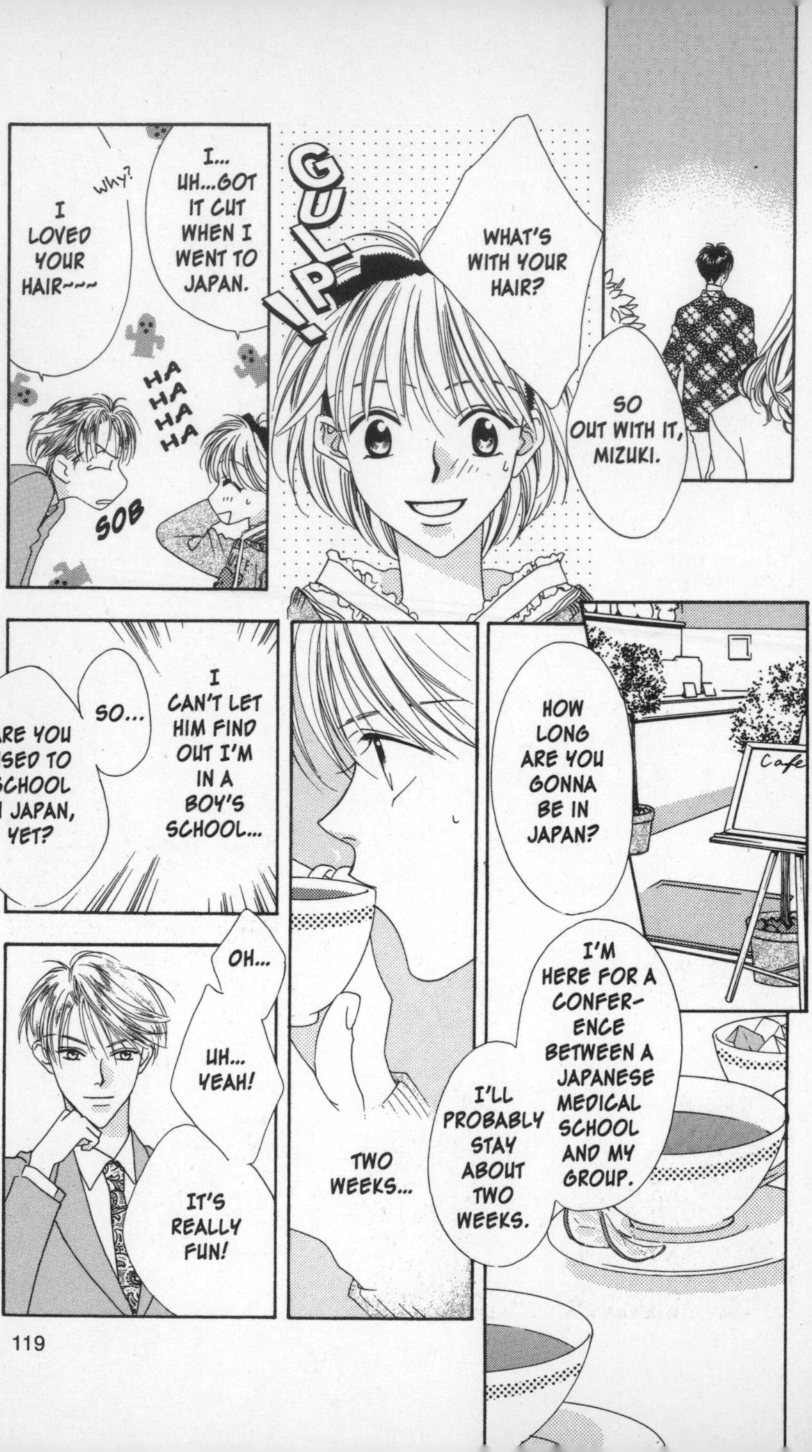
SO OUT WITH IT, MIZUKI.
WHAT'S WITH YOUR HAIR?
GULP!
I... UH...GOT IT CUT WHEN I WENT TO JAPAN.
why?
I LOVED YOUR HAIR~~~
HA HA HA HA
SOB
HOW LONG ARE YOU GONNA BE IN JAPAN?
I'M HERE FOR A CONFER-ENCE BETWEEN A JAPANESE MEDICAL SCHOOL AND MY GROUP.
I'LL PROBABLY STAY ABOUT TWO WEEKS.
Cafe
TWO WEEKS...
I CAN'T LET HIM FIND OUT I'M IN A BOY'S SCHOOL...
SO...
ARE YOU USED TO SCHOOL IN JAPAN, YET?
OH...
UH... YEAH!
IT'S REALLY FUN!

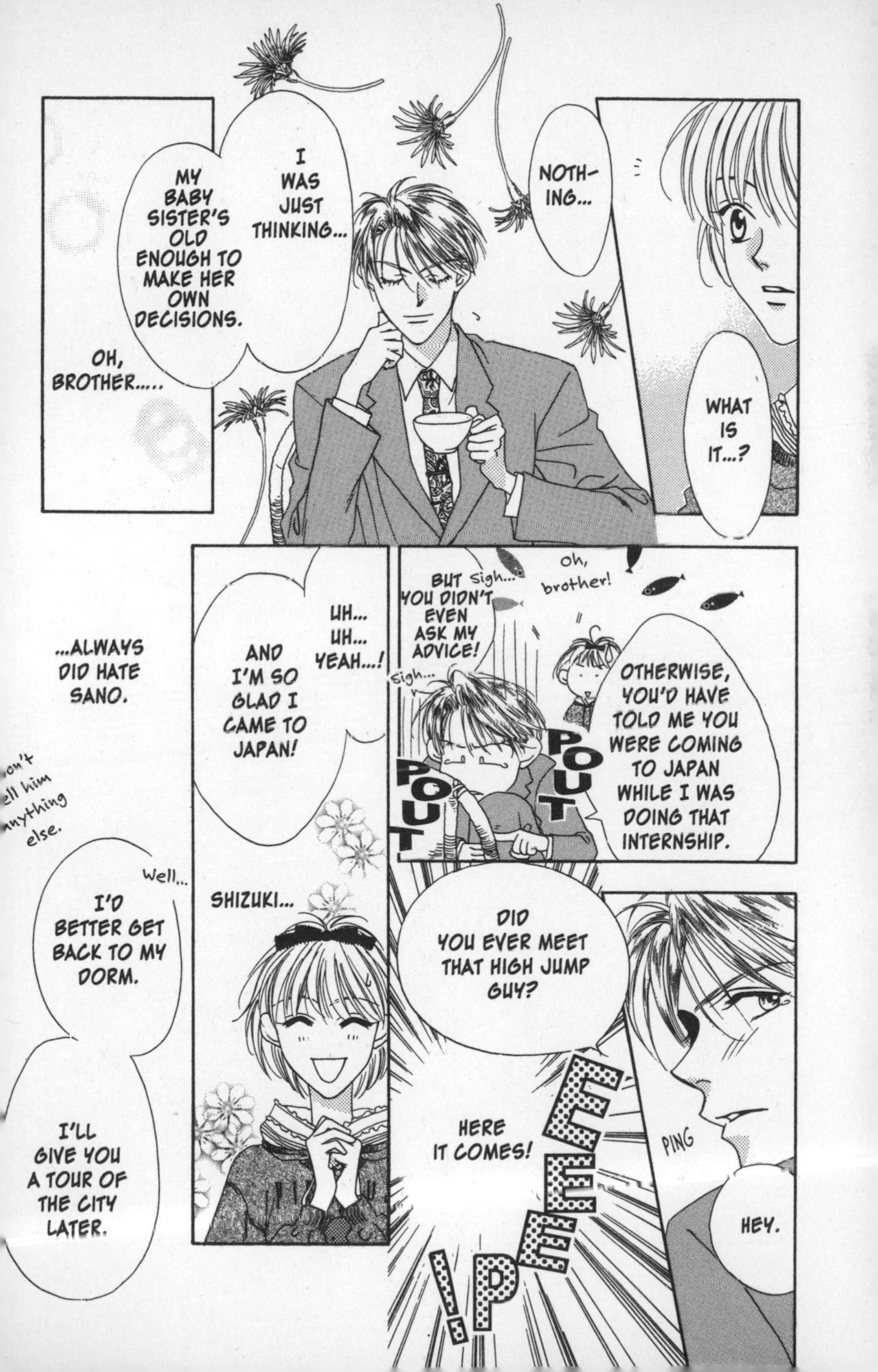
WHAT IS IT...?
NOTH-ING...
I WAS JUST THINKING...
MY BABY SISTER'S OLD ENOUGH TO MAKE HER OWN DECISIONS.
OH, BROTHER.....
Oh, brother!
BUT YOU DIDN'T EVEN ASK MY ADVICE!
Sigh...
Sigh...
OTHERWISE, YOU'D HAVE TOLD ME YOU WERE COMING TO JAPAN WHILE I WAS DOING THAT INTERNSHIP.
POUT
POUT
UH... UH... YEAH...!
AND I'M SO GLAD I CAME TO JAPAN!
SHIZUKI...
DID YOU EVER MEET THAT HIGH JUMP GUY?
PING
HEY.
PEEE!
HERE IT COMES!
...ALWAYS DID HATE SANO.
on't ell him nything else.
Well...
I'D BETTER GET BACK TO MY DORM.
I'LL GIVE YOU A TOUR OF THE CITY LATER.

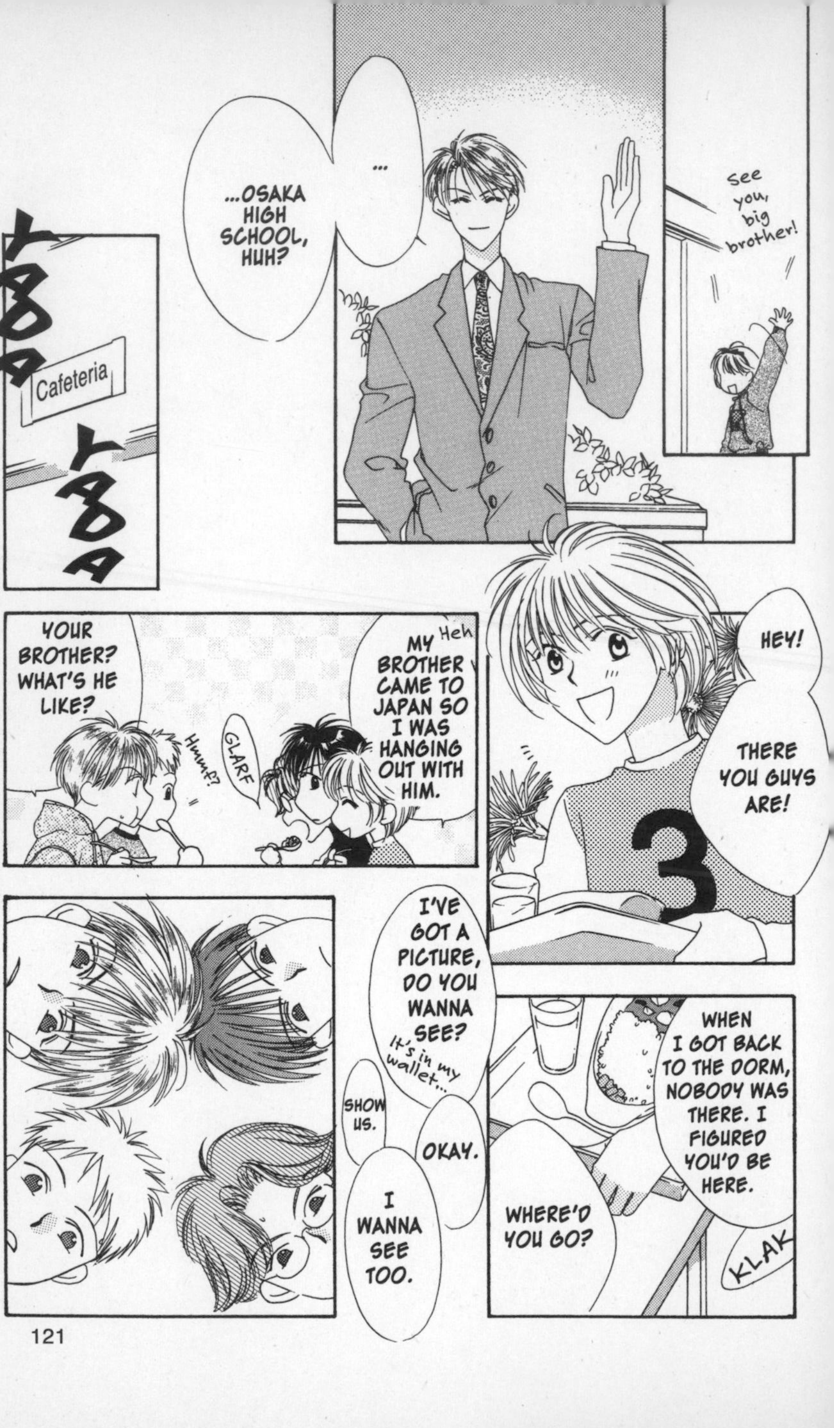

See you, big brother!
...
...OSAKA HIGH SCHOOL, HUH?
Cafeteria
HEY!
THERE YOU GUYS ARE!
WHEN I GOT BACK TO THE DORM, NOBODY WAS THERE. I FIGURED YOU'D BE HERE.
WHERE'D YOU GO?
KLAK
Heh
MY BROTHER CAME TO JAPAN SO I WAS HANGING OUT WITH HIM.
GLARF
Hmmf?
YOUR BROTHER? WHAT'S HE LIKE?
I'VE GOT A PICTURE, DO YOU WANNA SEE?
It's in my wallet...
SHOW US.
OKAY.
I WANNA SEE TOO.

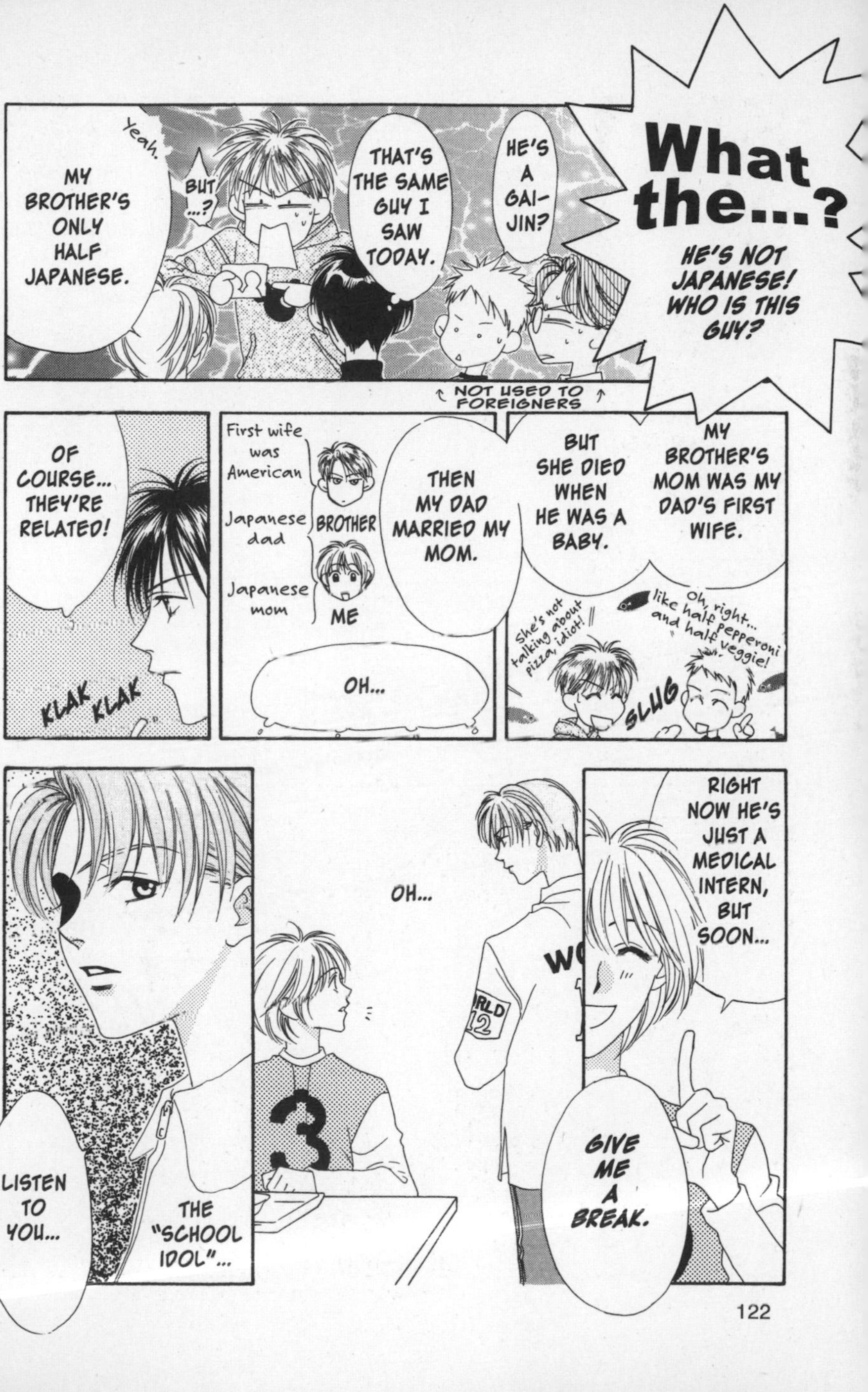
What the...?
HE'S NOT JAPANESE! WHO IS THIS GUY?
HE'S A GAI-JIN?
THAT'S THE SAME GUY I SAW TODAY.
BUT ...?
Yeah.
MY BROTHER'S ONLY HALF JAPANESE.
NOT USED TO FOREIGNERS
MY BROTHER'S MOM WAS MY DAD'S FIRST WIFE.
BUT SHE DIED WHEN HE WAS A BABY.
Oh, right... like half pepperoni and half veggie!
She's not talking about pizza, idiot!
SLUG
THEN MY DAD MARRIED MY MOM.
First wife was American
BROTHER
Japanese dad
Japanese mom
ME
OH...
OF COURSE... THEY'RE RELATED!
KLAK KLAK
RIGHT NOW HE'S JUST A MEDICAL INTERN, BUT SOON...
GIVE ME A BREAK.
OH...
THE "SCHOOL IDOL"...
LISTEN TO YOU...

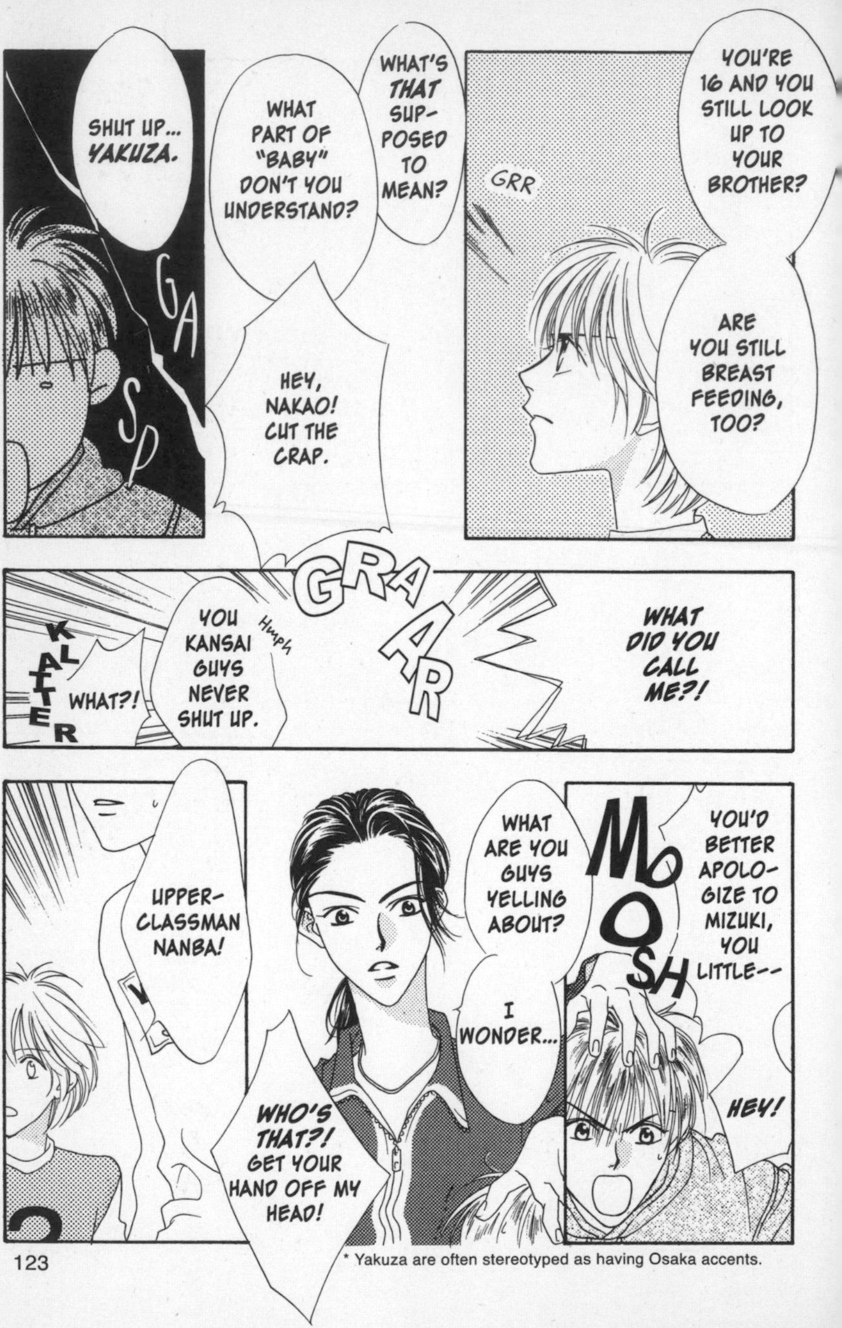
YOU'RE 16 AND YOU STILL LOOK UP TO YOUR BROTHER?
ARE YOU STILL BREAST FEEDING, TOO?
GRR
WHAT'S *THAT* SUPPOSED TO MEAN?
WHAT PART OF "BABY" DON'T YOU UNDERSTAND?
HEY, NAKAO! CUT THE CRAP.
SHUT UP... *YAKUZA.*
GASP
WHAT DID YOU CALL ME?!
GRAAR
Humph
YOU KANSAI GUYS NEVER SHUT UP.
WHAT?!
KLATTER
YOU'D BETTER APOLOGIZE TO MIZUKI, YOU LITTLE--
MOSH
HEY!
WHAT ARE YOU GUYS YELLING ABOUT?
I WONDER...
WHO'S THAT?! GET YOUR HAND OFF MY HEAD!
UPPERCLASSMAN NANBA!

* Yakuza are often stereotyped as having Osaka accents.

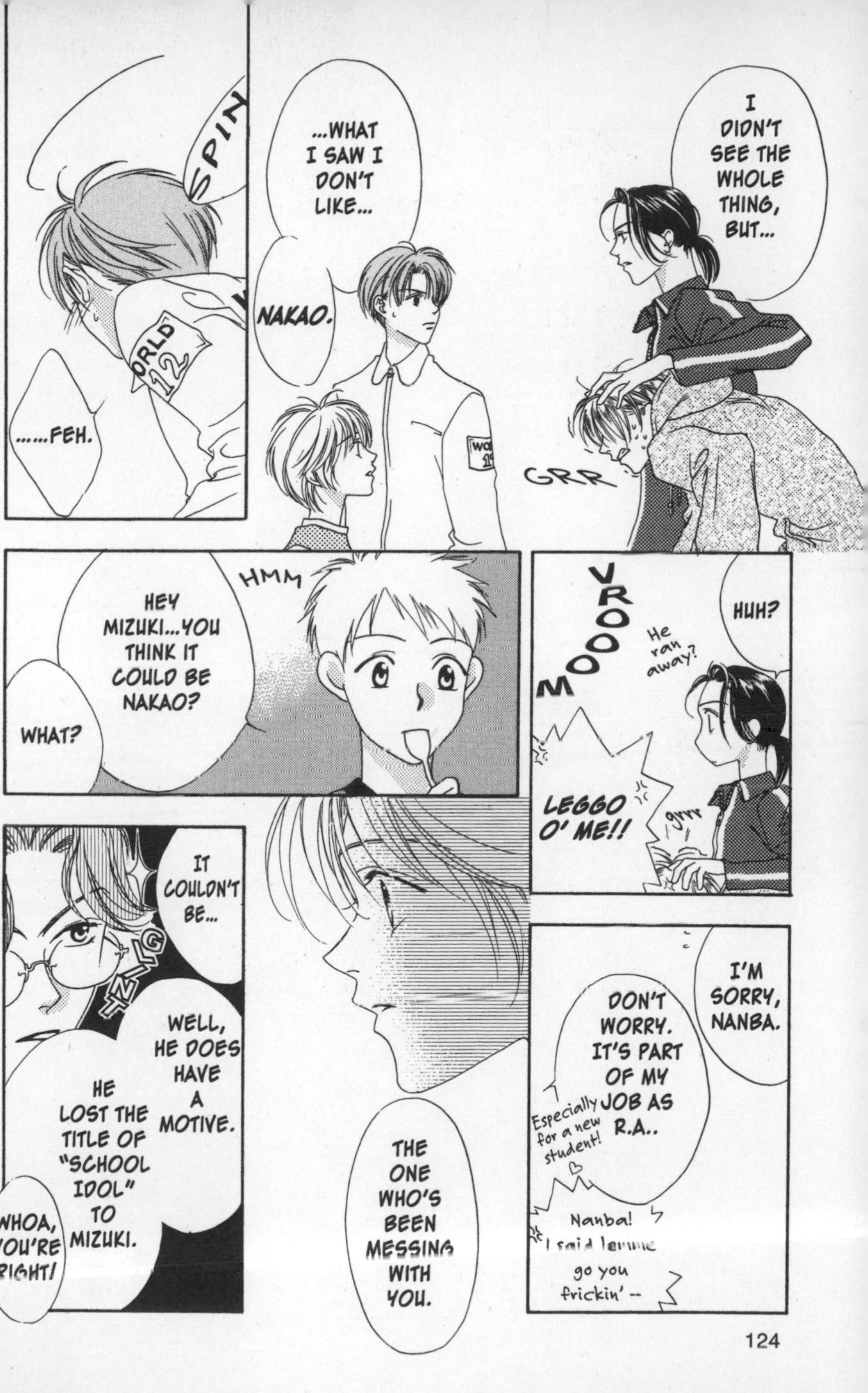
I DIDN'T SEE THE WHOLE THING, BUT...
GRR
...WHAT I SAW I DON'T LIKE...
NAKAO.
SPIN
......FEH.
HUH?
VROOOM
He ran away?
LEGGO O' ME!!
grrr
HMM
HEY MIZUKI...YOU THINK IT COULD BE NAKAO?
WHAT?
I'M SORRY, NANBA.
DON'T WORRY. IT'S PART OF MY JOB AS R.A..
Especially for a new student!
Nanba! I said lemme go you frickin' --
THE ONE WHO'S BEEN MESSING WITH YOU.
IT COULDN'T BE...
WELL, HE DOES HAVE A MOTIVE.
HE LOST THE TITLE OF "SCHOOL IDOL" TO MIZUKI.
WHOA, YOU'RE RIGHT!

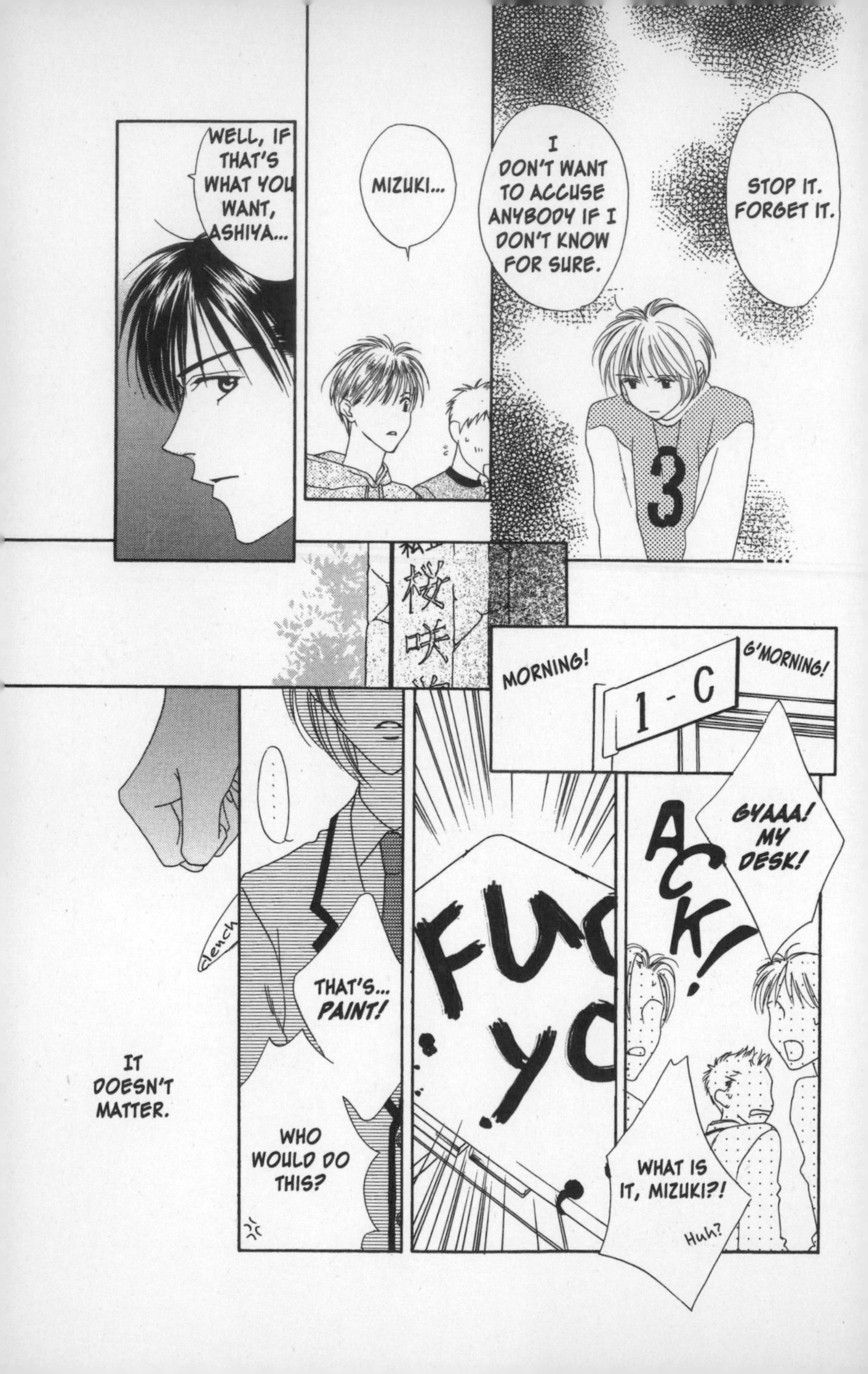
STOP IT. FORGET IT.
I DON'T WANT TO ACCUSE ANYBODY IF I DON'T KNOW FOR SURE.
3
MIZUKI...
WELL, IF THAT'S WHAT YOU WANT, ASHIYA...
G'MORNING!
1 - C
MORNING!
桜咲
GYAAA! MY DESK!
ACK!
WHAT IS IT, MIZUKI?!
Huh?
FUC
YO
......
THAT'S... PAINT!
WHO WOULD DO THIS?
clench
IT DOESN'T MATTER.

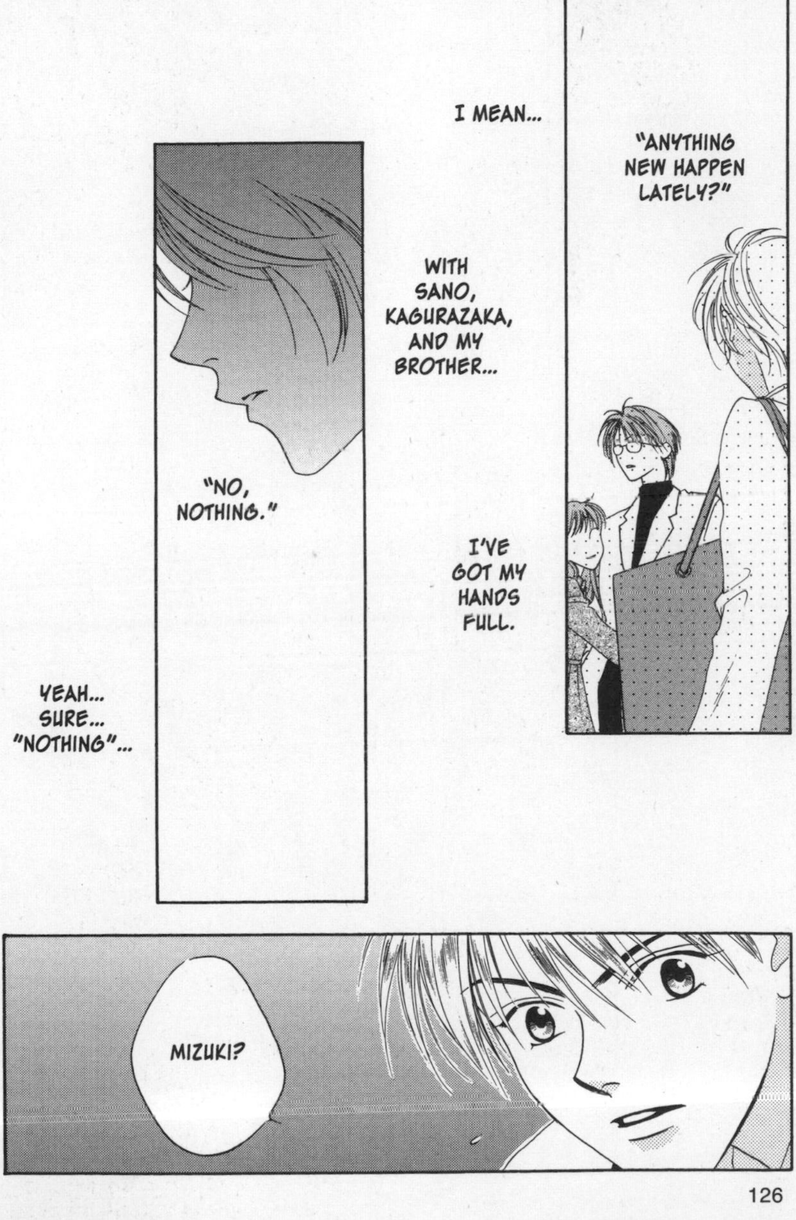
"ANYTHING NEW HAPPEN LATELY?"
I MEAN...
WITH SANO, KAGURAZAKA, AND MY BROTHER...
I'VE GOT MY HANDS FULL.
"NO, NOTHING."
YEAH... SURE... "NOTHING"...
MIZUKI?

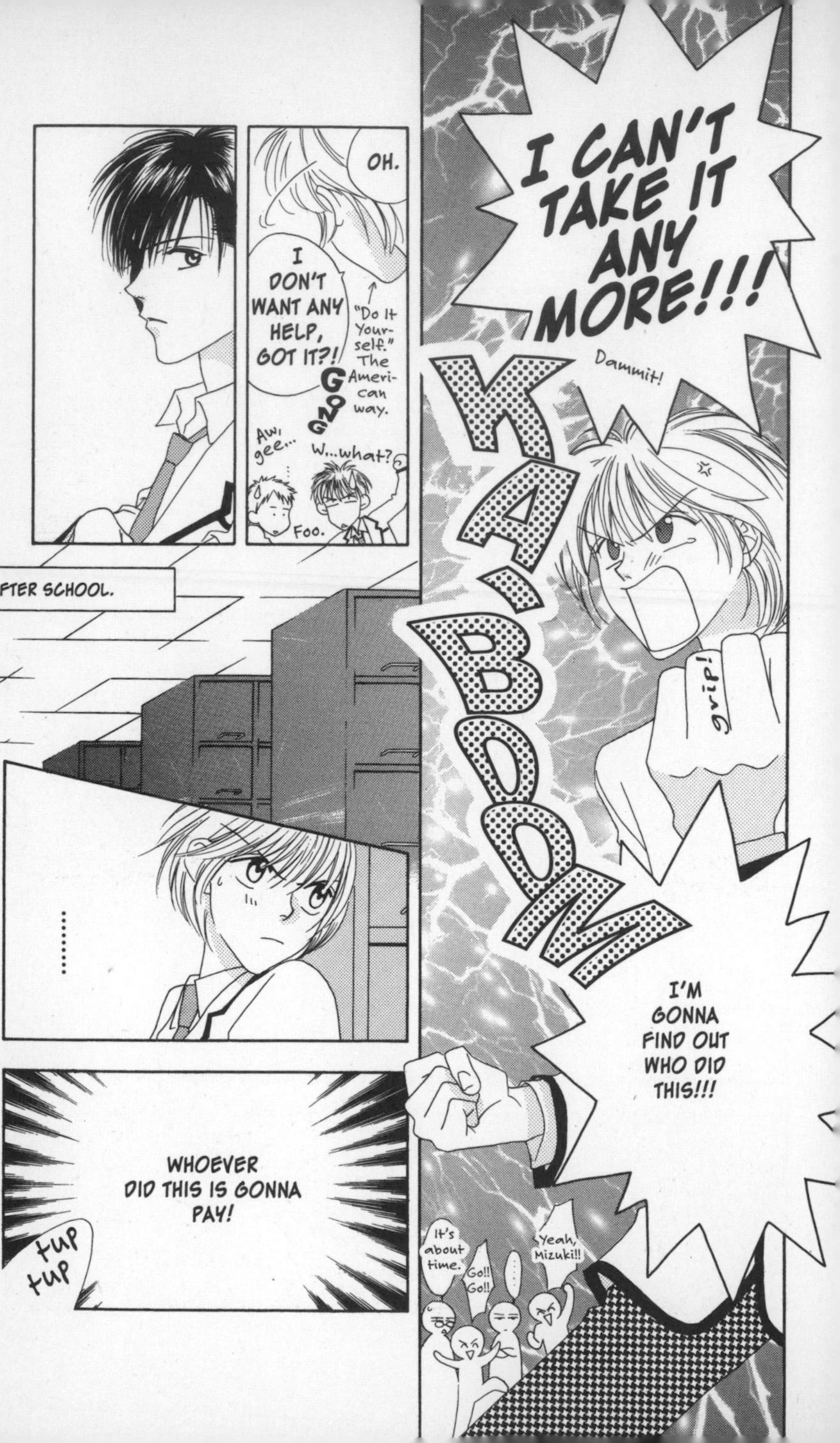
I CAN'T TAKE IT ANY MORE!!!
Dammit!
KA-BOOM
grip!
I'M GONNA FIND OUT WHO DID THIS!!!
It's about time.
Go!! Go!!
...
Yeah, Mizuki!!
OH.
I DON'T WANT ANY HELP, GOT IT?!
"Do It Yourself." The American way.
GONG
W...what?
Aw, gee...
...
Foo.
AFTER SCHOOL.
....
WHOEVER DID THIS IS GONNA PAY!
tup tup

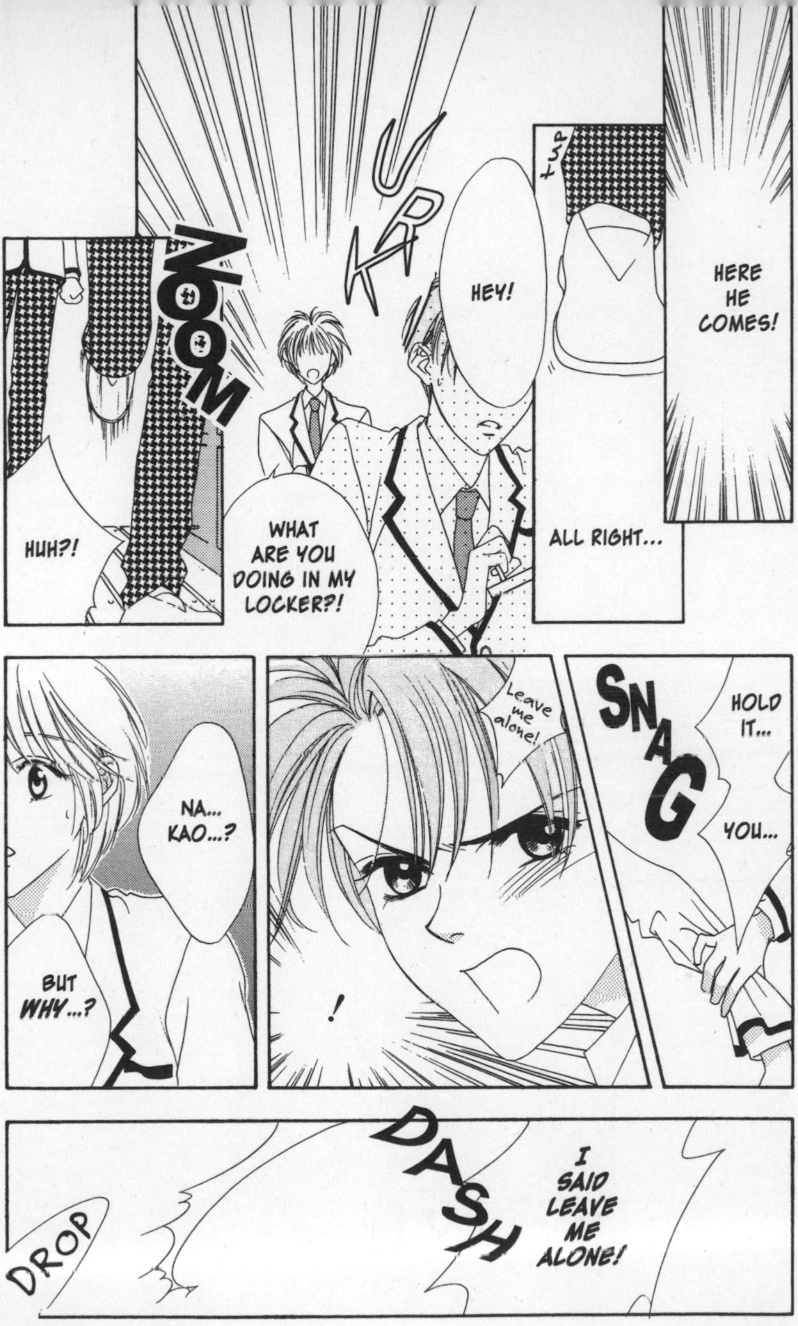
HERE HE COMES!
tup
ALL RIGHT...
URK
HEY!
WHAT ARE YOU DOING IN MY LOCKER?!
NOOM
HUH?!
SNAG
HOLD IT...
YOU...
Leave me alone!
!
NA... KAO...?
BUT WHY...?
I SAID LEAVE ME ALONE!
DASH
DROP

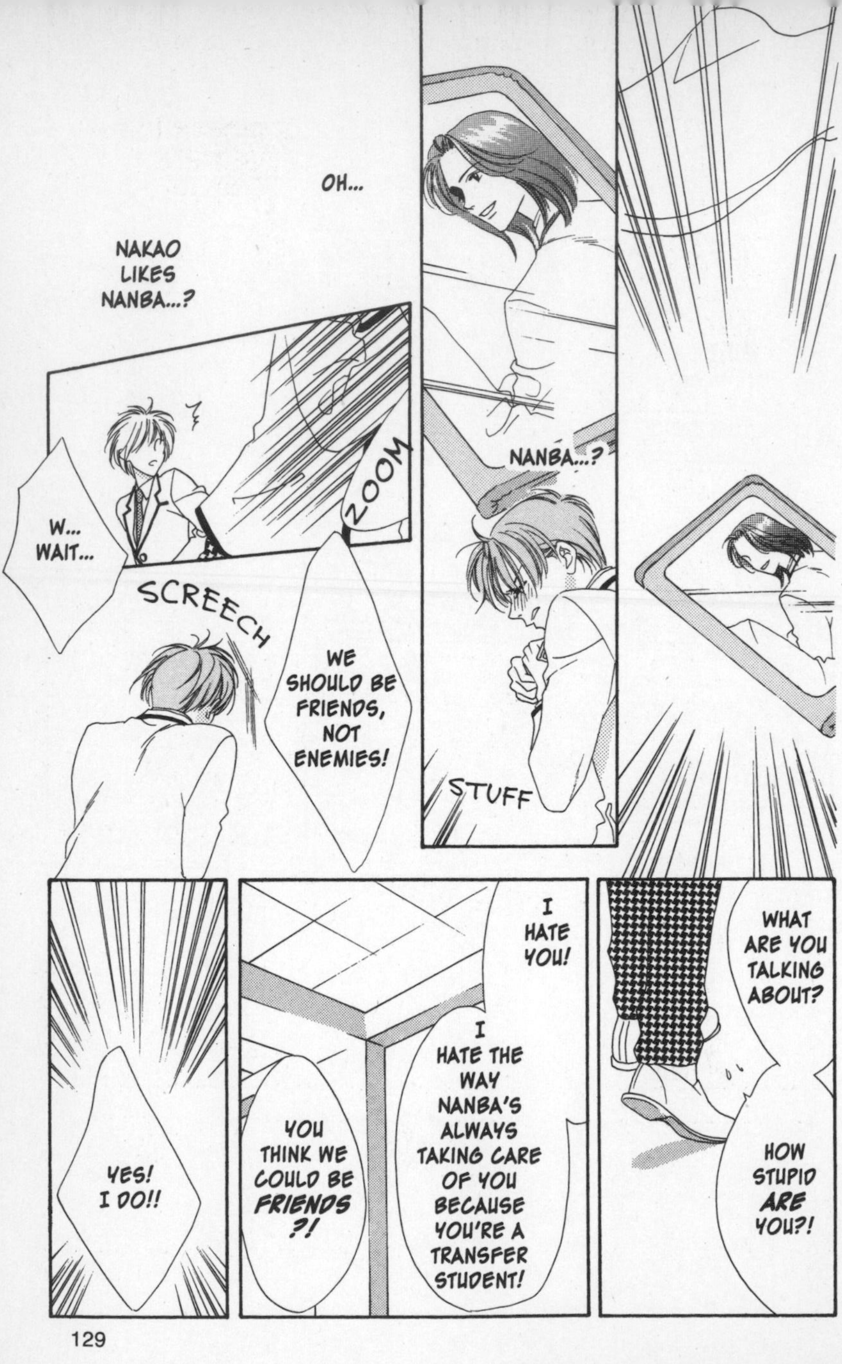
NANBA...?
STUFF
OH...
NAKAO LIKES NANBA...?
ZOOM
W... WAIT...
SCREECH
WE SHOULD BE FRIENDS, NOT ENEMIES!
WHAT ARE YOU TALKING ABOUT?
HOW STUPID ARE YOU?!
I HATE YOU!
I HATE THE WAY NANBA'S ALWAYS TAKING CARE OF YOU BECAUSE YOU'RE A TRANSFER STUDENT!
YOU THINK WE COULD BE FRIENDS?!
YES! I DO!!

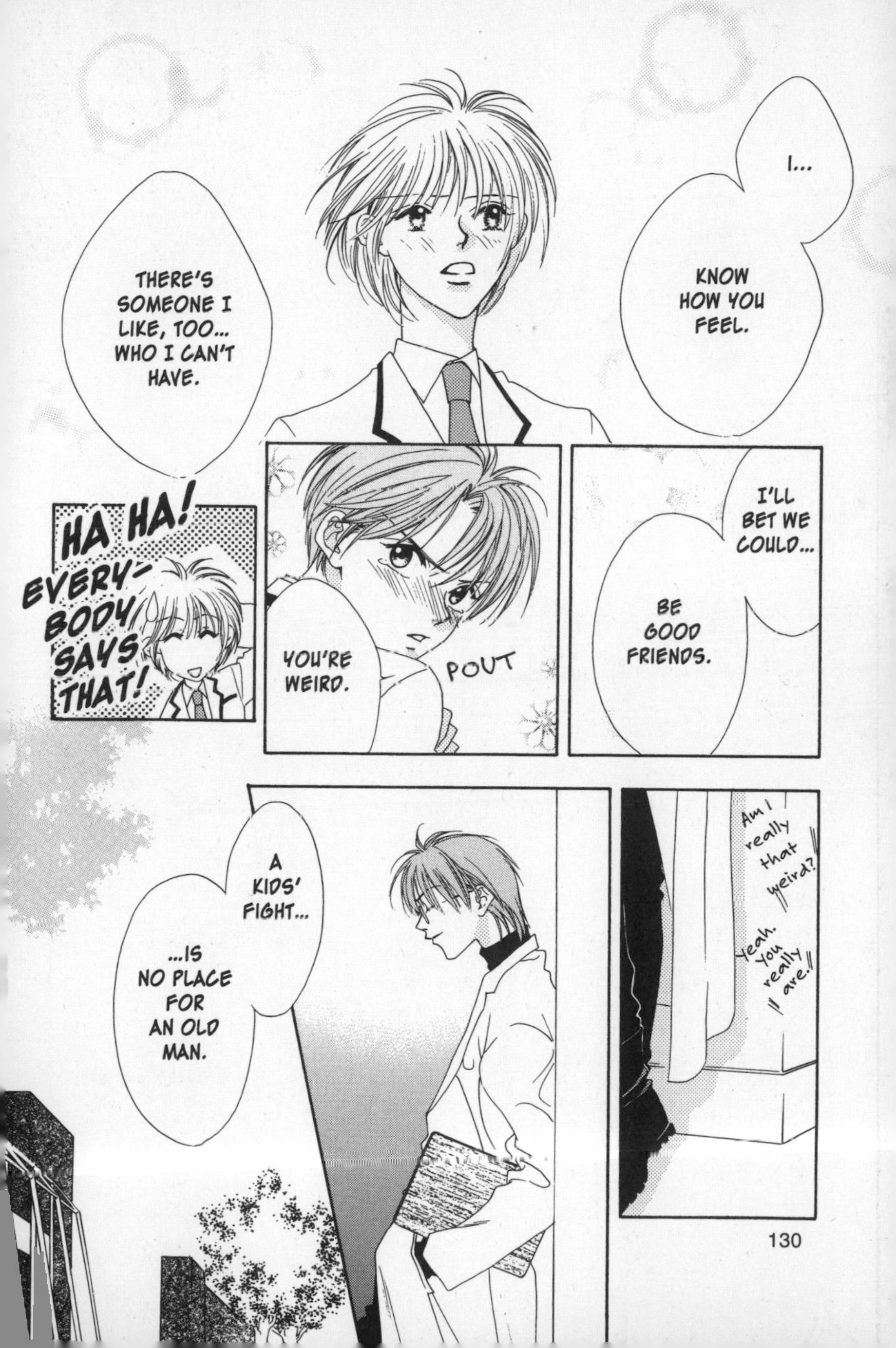
I...
KNOW HOW YOU FEEL.
THERE'S SOMEONE I LIKE, TOO... WHO I CAN'T HAVE.
I'LL BET WE COULD...
BE GOOD FRIENDS.
YOU'RE WEIRD.
POUT
HA HA! EVERY-BODY SAYS THAT!
Am I really that weird?
Yeah. You really are.
A KIDS' FIGHT...
...IS NO PLACE FOR AN OLD MAN.

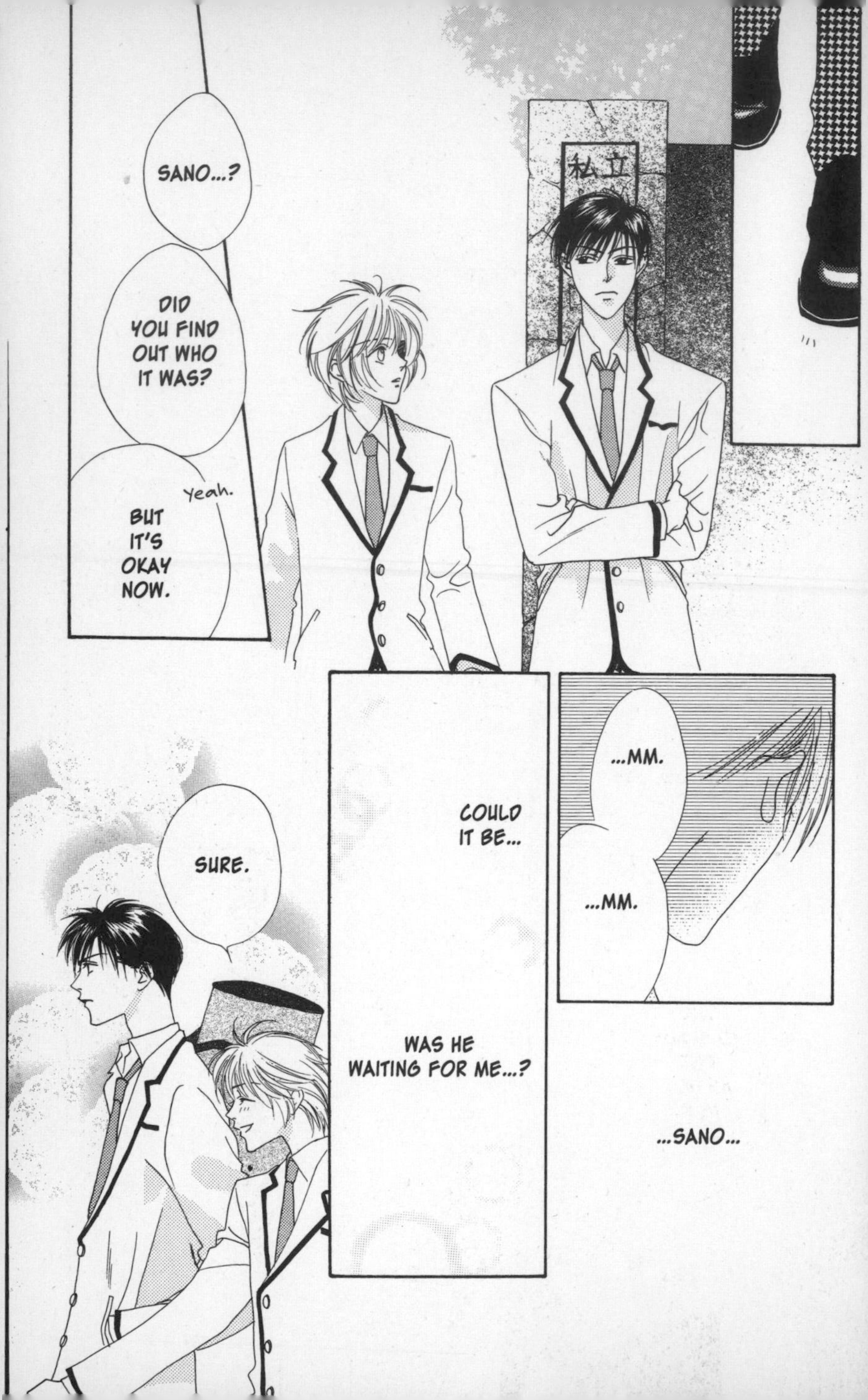
SANO...?
DID YOU FIND OUT WHO IT WAS?
Yeah.
BUT IT'S OKAY NOW.
...MM.
...MM.
...SANO...
COULD IT BE...
WAS HE WAITING FOR ME...?
SURE.

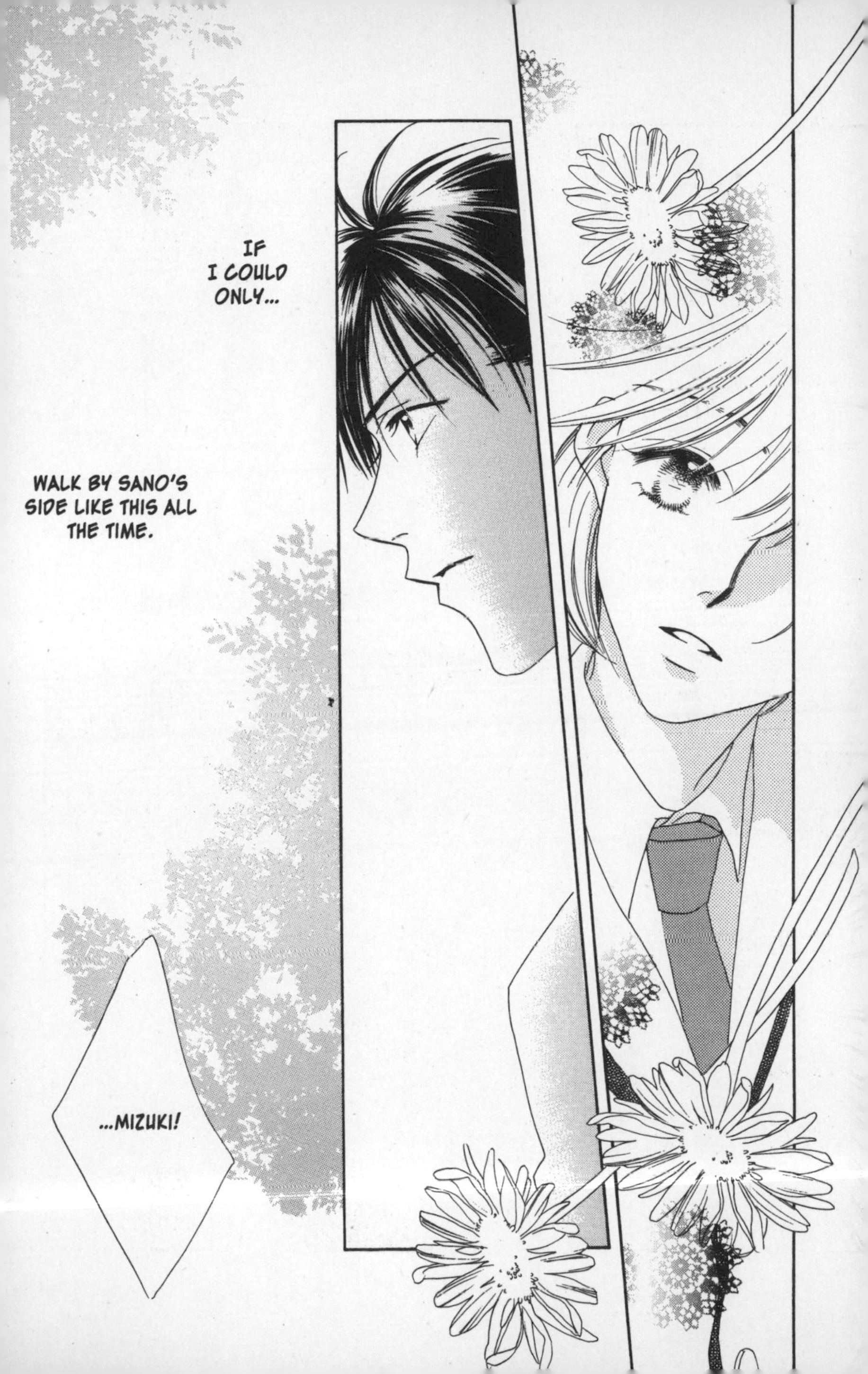
IF I COULD ONLY...
WALK BY SANO'S SIDE LIKE THIS ALL THE TIME.
...MIZUKI!

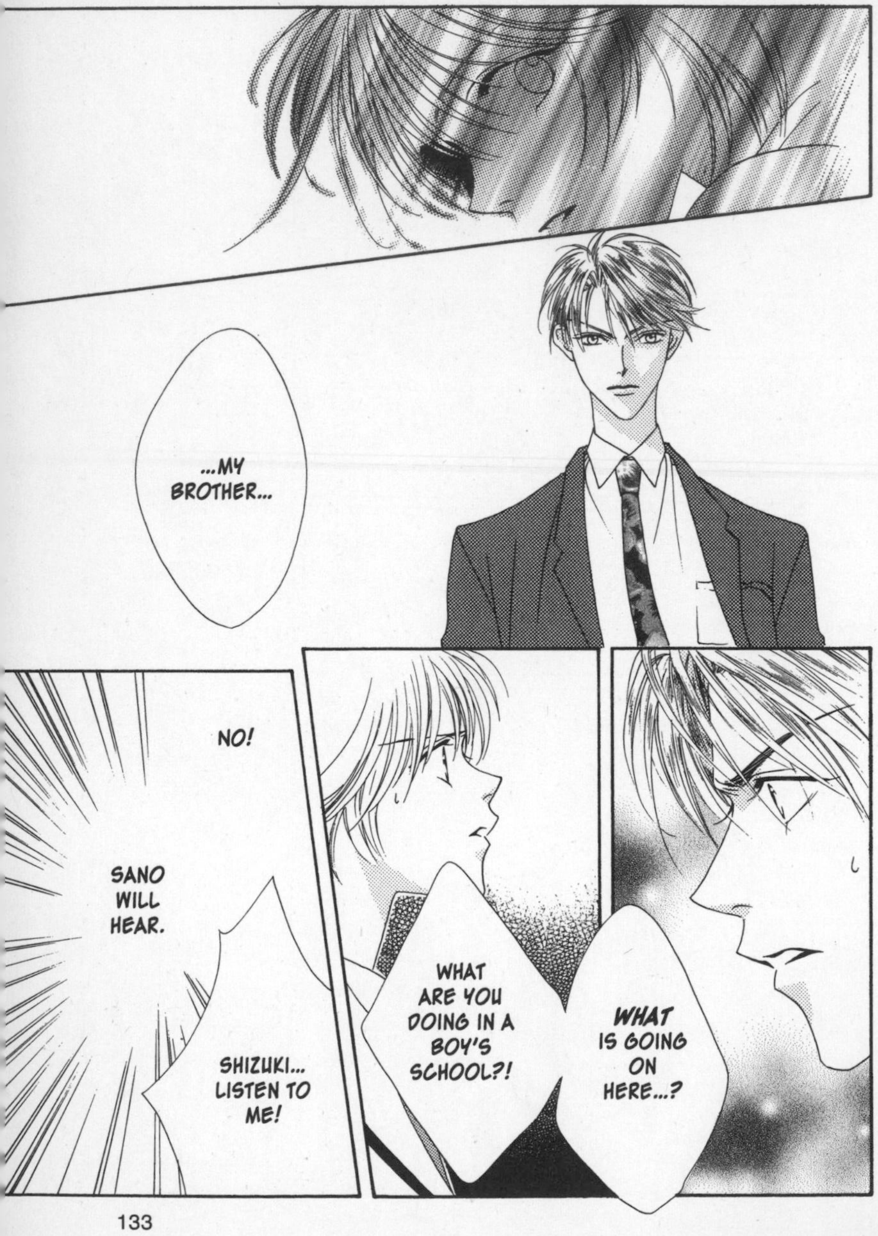
...MY BROTHER...
WHAT IS GOING ON HERE...?
WHAT ARE YOU DOING IN A BOY'S SCHOOL?!
NO!
SANO WILL HEAR.
SHIZUKI... LISTEN TO ME!

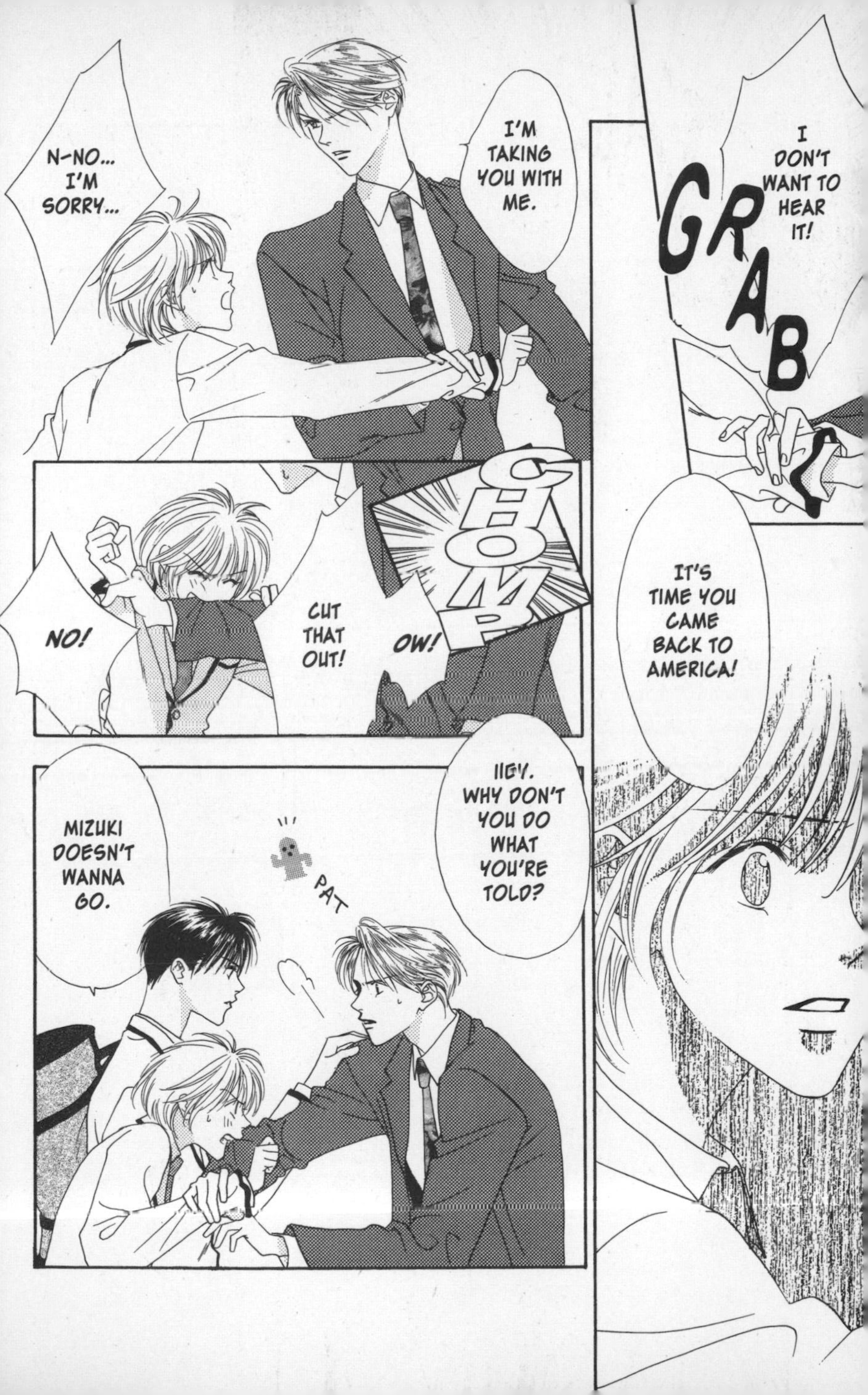
I DON'T WANT TO HEAR IT!
GRAB
IT'S TIME YOU CAME BACK TO AMERICA!
I'M TAKING YOU WITH ME.
N-NO... I'M SORRY...
CHOMP
OW!
CUT THAT OUT!
NO!
WHY DON'T YOU DO WHAT YOU'RE TOLD?
PAT
MIZUKI DOESN'T WANNA GO.

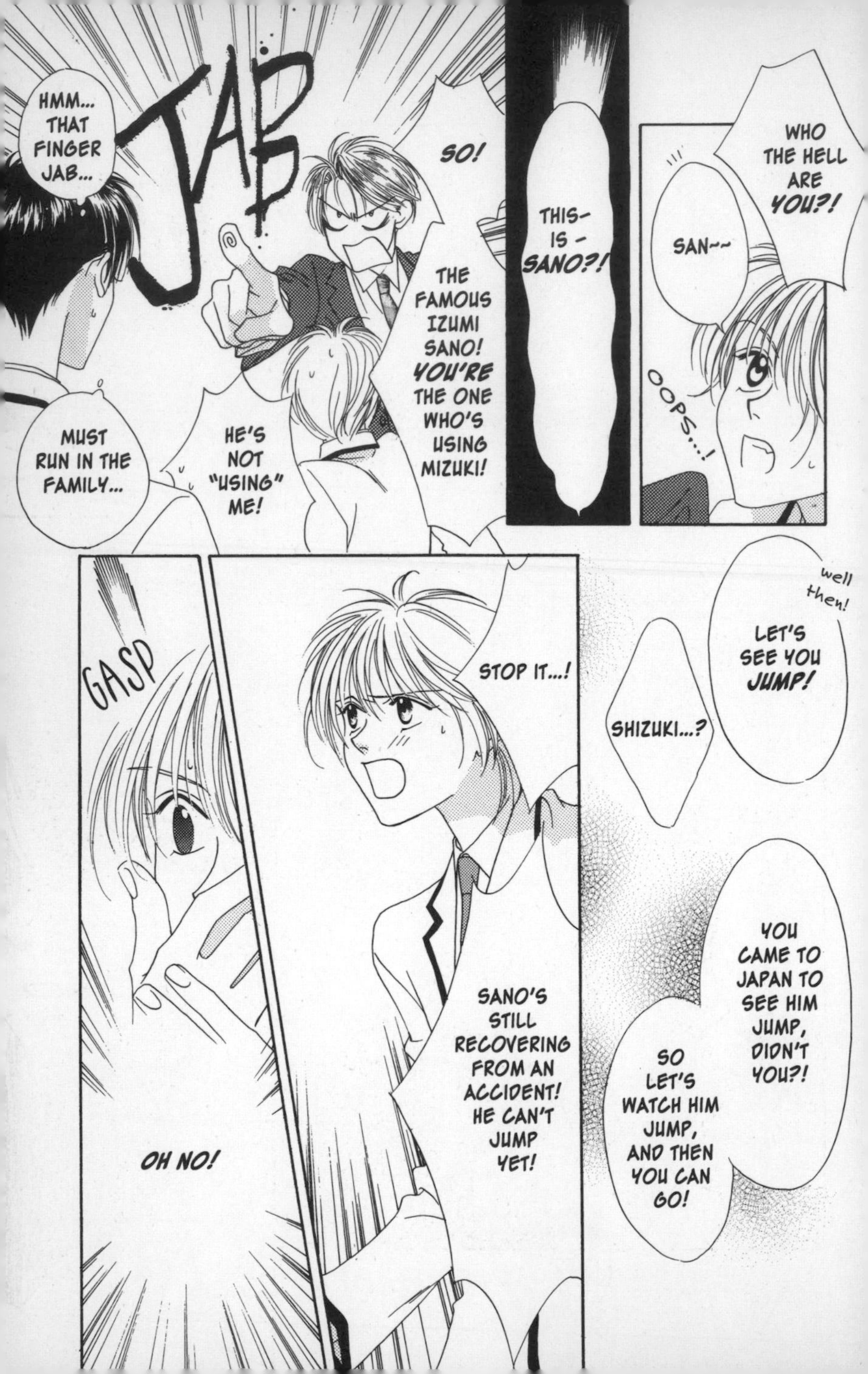
WHO THE HELL ARE YOU?!
SAN--
OOPS...!
THIS- IS - SANO?!
SO!
THE FAMOUS IZUMI SANO! YOU'RE THE ONE WHO'S USING MIZUKI!
JAB
HMM... THAT FINGER JAB...
HE'S NOT "USING" ME!
MUST RUN IN THE FAMILY...
well then!
LET'S SEE YOU JUMP!
SHIZUKI...?
YOU CAME TO JAPAN TO SEE HIM JUMP, DIDN'T YOU?!
SO LET'S WATCH HIM JUMP, AND THEN YOU CAN GO!
STOP IT...!
SANO'S STILL RECOVERING FROM AN ACCIDENT! HE CAN'T JUMP YET!
GASP
OH NO!

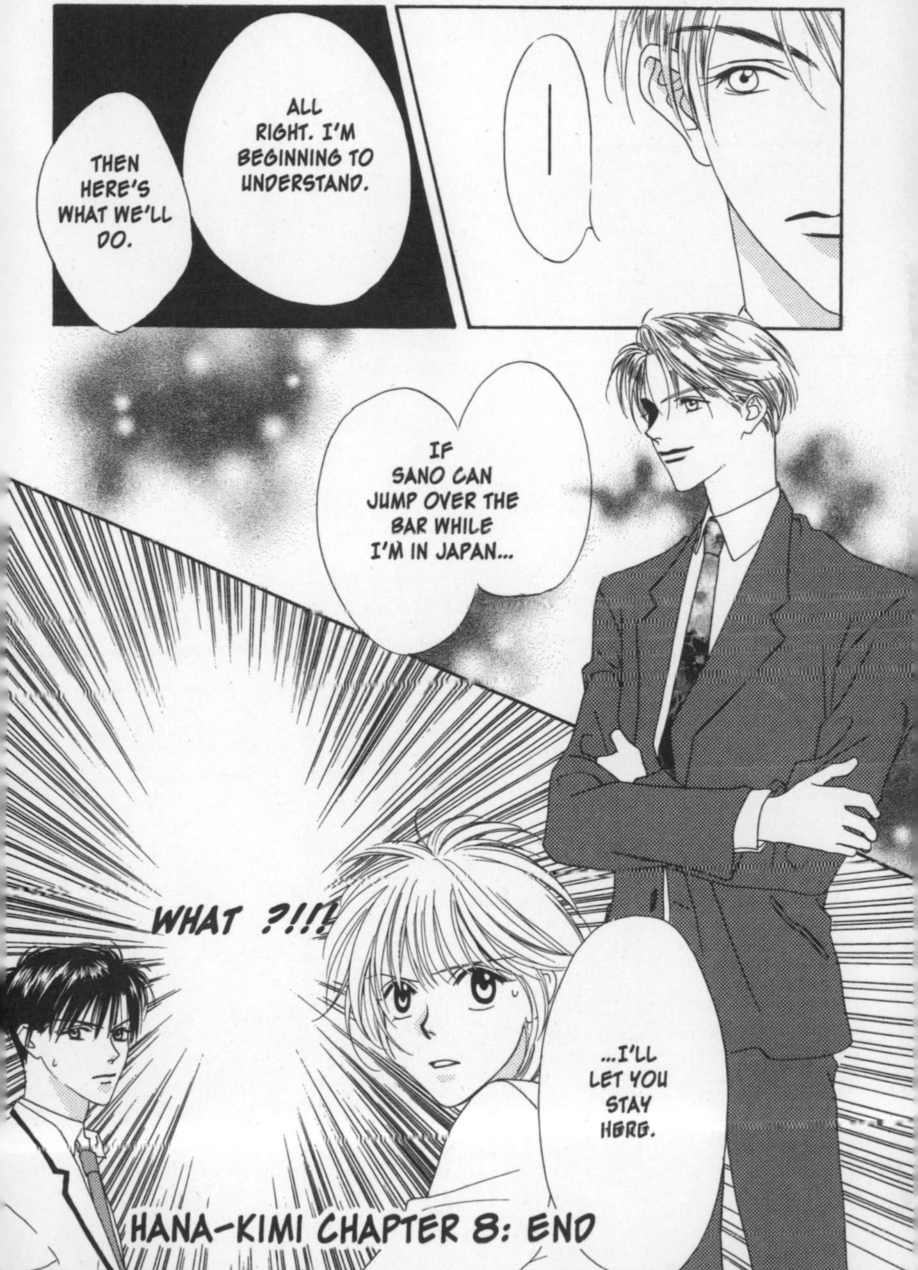
—
ALL RIGHT. I'M BEGINNING TO UNDERSTAND.
THEN HERE'S WHAT WE'LL DO.
IF SANO CAN JUMP OVER THE BAR WHILE I'M IN JAPAN...
...I'LL LET YOU STAY HERE.
WHAT ?!!!
HANA-KIMI CHAPTER 8: END

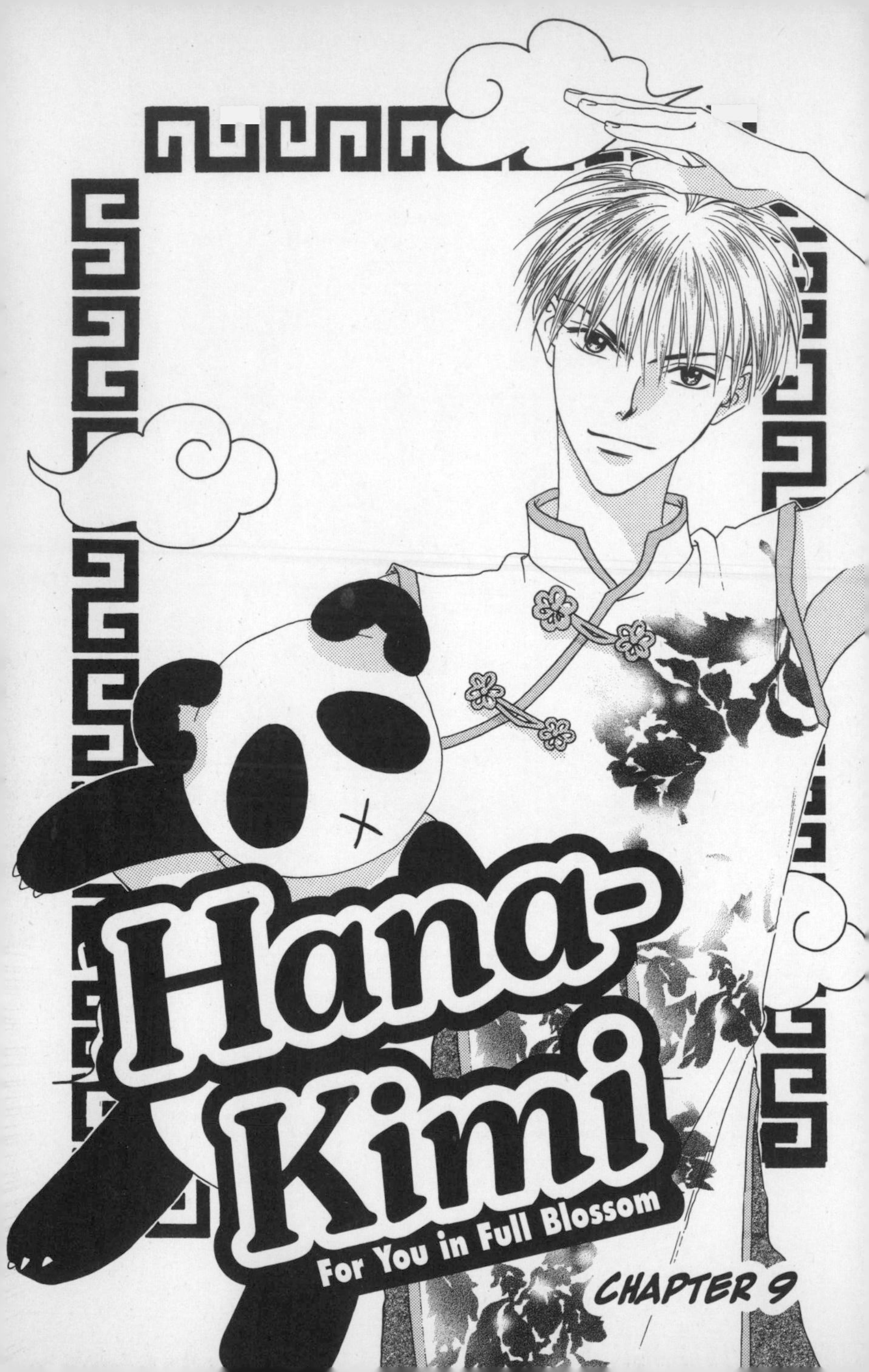
Hana-Kimi
For You in Full Blossom
CHAPTER 9

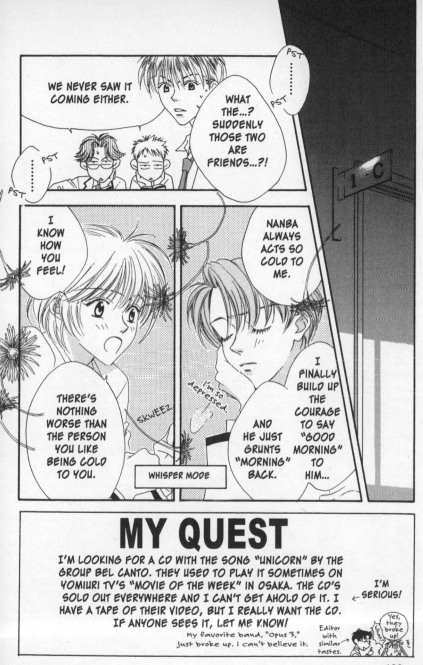

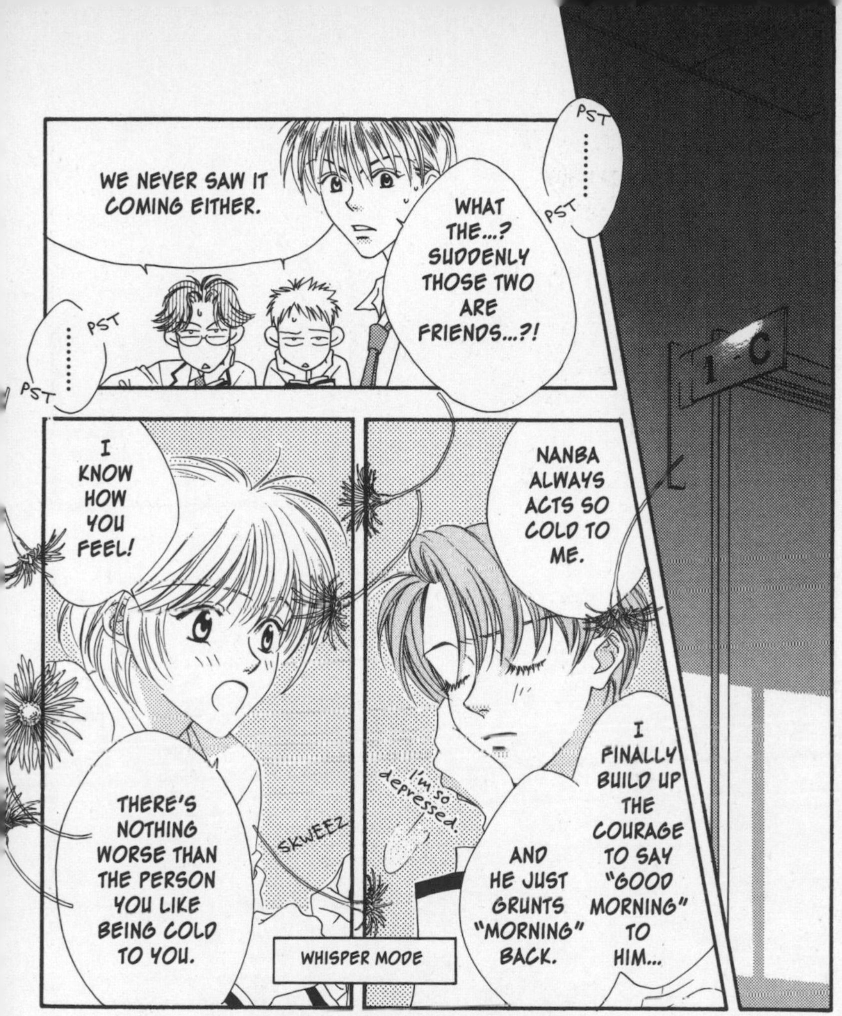
PST ...... PST
WHAT THE...? SUDDENLY THOSE TWO ARE FRIENDS...?!
WE NEVER SAW IT COMING EITHER.
...... PST PST
NANBA ALWAYS ACTS SO COLD TO ME.
I FINALLY BUILD UP THE COURAGE TO SAY "GOOD MORNING" TO HIM...
AND HE JUST GRUNTS "MORNING" BACK.
I'm so depressed.
I KNOW HOW YOU FEEL!
THERE'S NOTHING WORSE THAN THE PERSON YOU LIKE BEING COLD TO YOU.
SKWEEZ
WHISPER MODE

MY QUEST

I'M LOOKING FOR A CD WITH THE SONG "UNICORN" BY THE GROUP BEL CANTO. THEY USED TO PLAY IT SOMETIMES ON YOMIURI TV'S "MOVIE OF THE WEEK" IN OSAKA. THE CD'S SOLD OUT EVERYWHERE AND I CAN'T GET AHOLD OF IT. I HAVE A TAPE OF THEIR VIDEO, BUT I REALLY WANT THE CD. IF ANYONE SEES IT, LET ME KNOW!

← I'M SERIOUS!

My favorite band, "Opus 3," just broke up. I can't believe it.

Editor with similar tastes. →

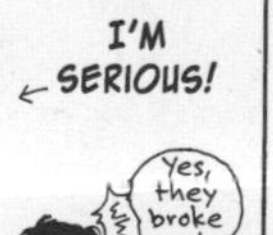
What?
Yes, they broke up!

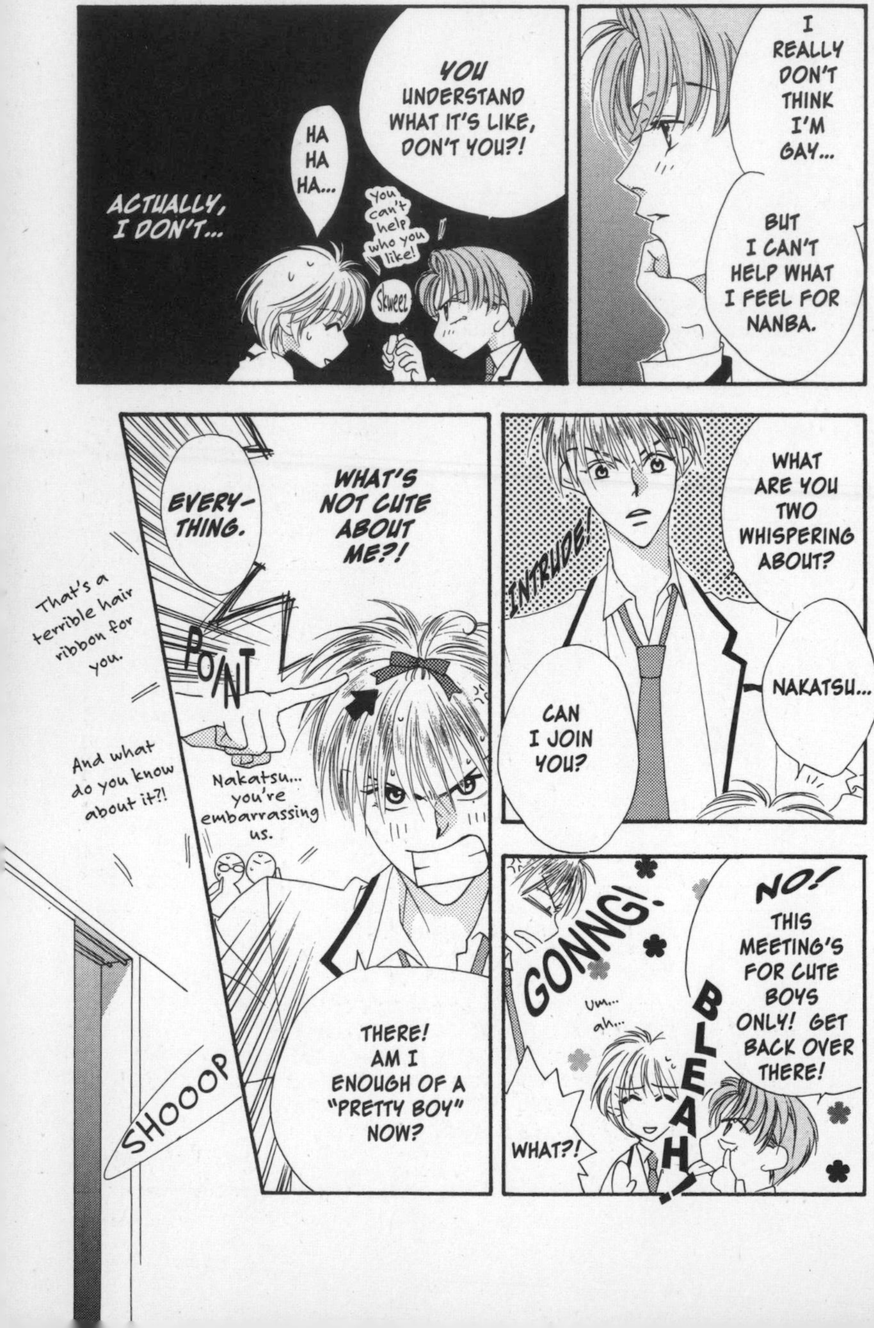
I REALLY DON'T THINK I'M GAY...
BUT I CAN'T HELP WHAT I FEEL FOR NANBA.
YOU UNDERSTAND WHAT IT'S LIKE, DON'T YOU?!
You can't help who you like!
Skweez
HA HA HA...
ACTUALLY, I DON'T...
WHAT ARE YOU TWO WHISPERING ABOUT?
INTRUDE!
NAKATSU...
CAN I JOIN YOU?
NO! THIS MEETING'S FOR CUTE BOYS ONLY! GET BACK OVER THERE!
GONNG!
Um... ah...
BLEAH!
WHAT?!
WHAT'S NOT CUTE ABOUT ME?!
EVERYTHING.
POINT
That's a terrible hair ribbon for you.
And what do you know about it?!
Nakatsu... you're embarrassing us.
THERE! AM I ENOUGH OF A "PRETTY BOY" NOW?
SHOOOP

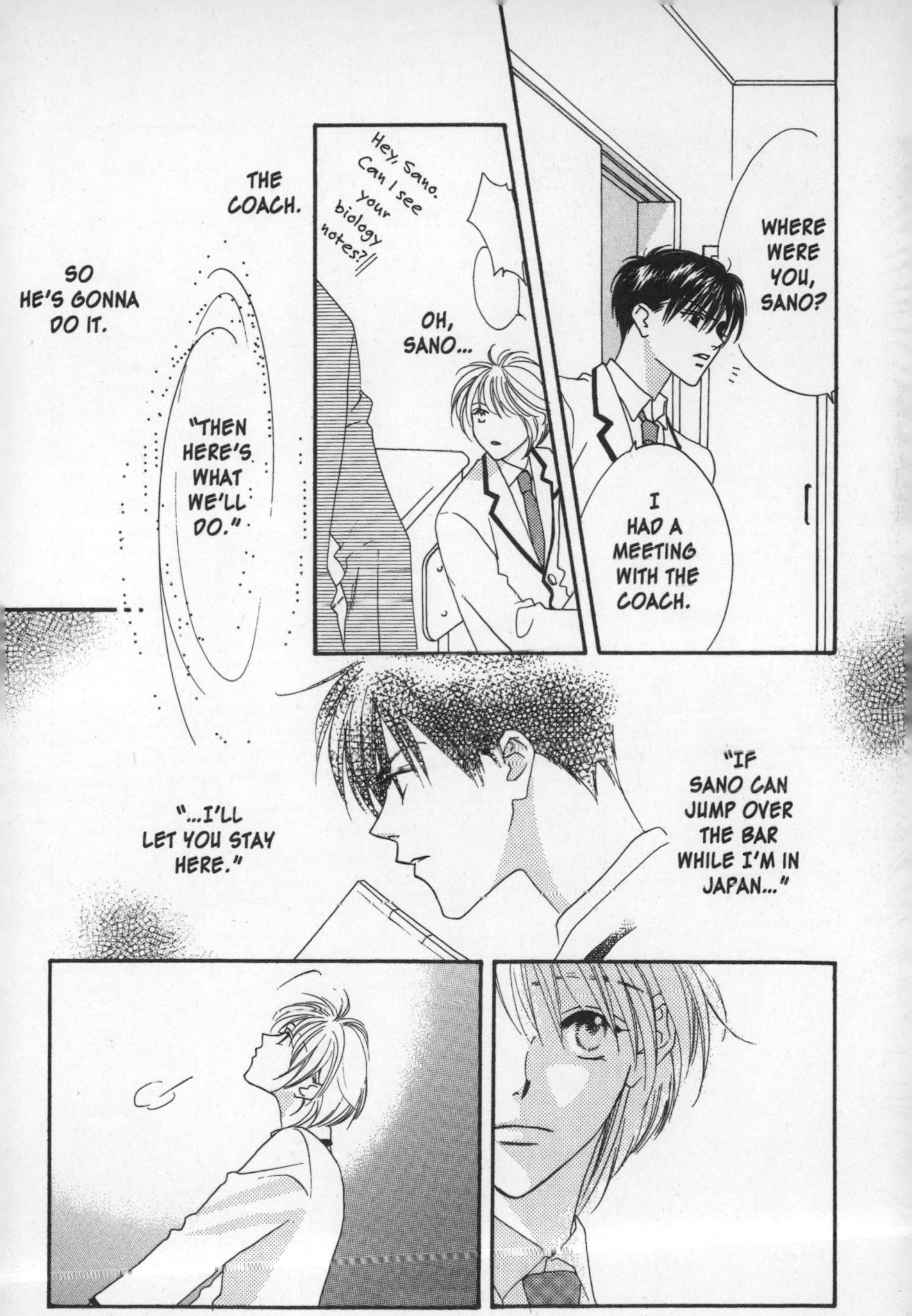
WHERE WERE YOU, SANO?
I HAD A MEETING WITH THE COACH.
Hey, Sano. Can I see your biology notes?!
OH, SANO...
THE COACH.
SO HE'S GONNA DO IT.
"THEN HERE'S WHAT WE'LL DO."
"IF SANO CAN JUMP OVER THE BAR WHILE I'M IN JAPAN..."
"...I'LL LET YOU STAY HERE."

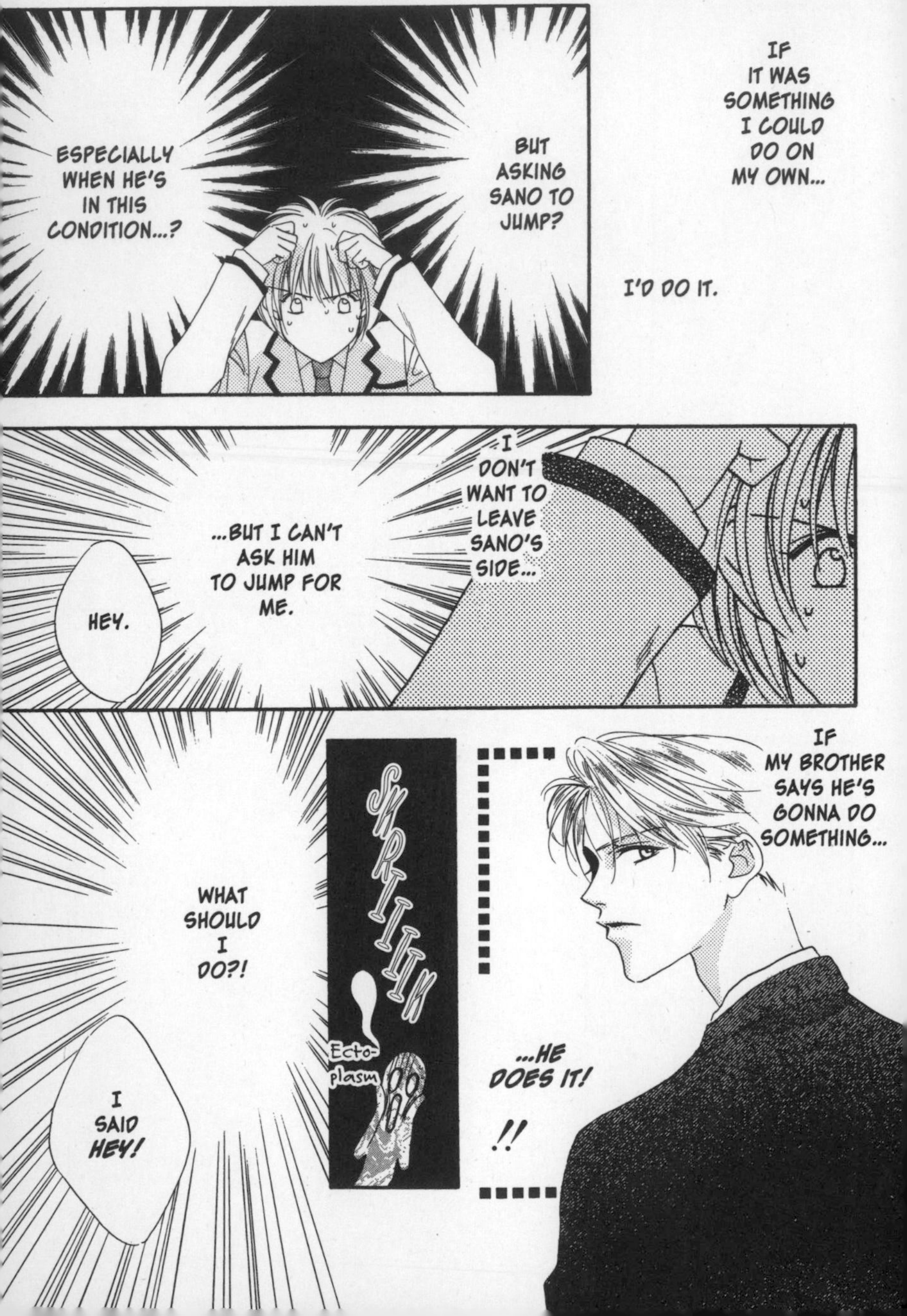
IF IT WAS SOMETHING I COULD DO ON MY OWN...
I'D DO IT.
BUT ASKING SANO TO JUMP?
ESPECIALLY WHEN HE'S IN THIS CONDITION...?
I DON'T WANT TO LEAVE SANO'S SIDE...
...BUT I CAN'T ASK HIM TO JUMP FOR ME.
HEY.
IF MY BROTHER SAYS HE'S GONNA DO SOMETHING...
...HE DOES IT!
!!
SHRIIIIN
Ecto-plasm
WHAT SHOULD I DO?!
I SAID HEY!

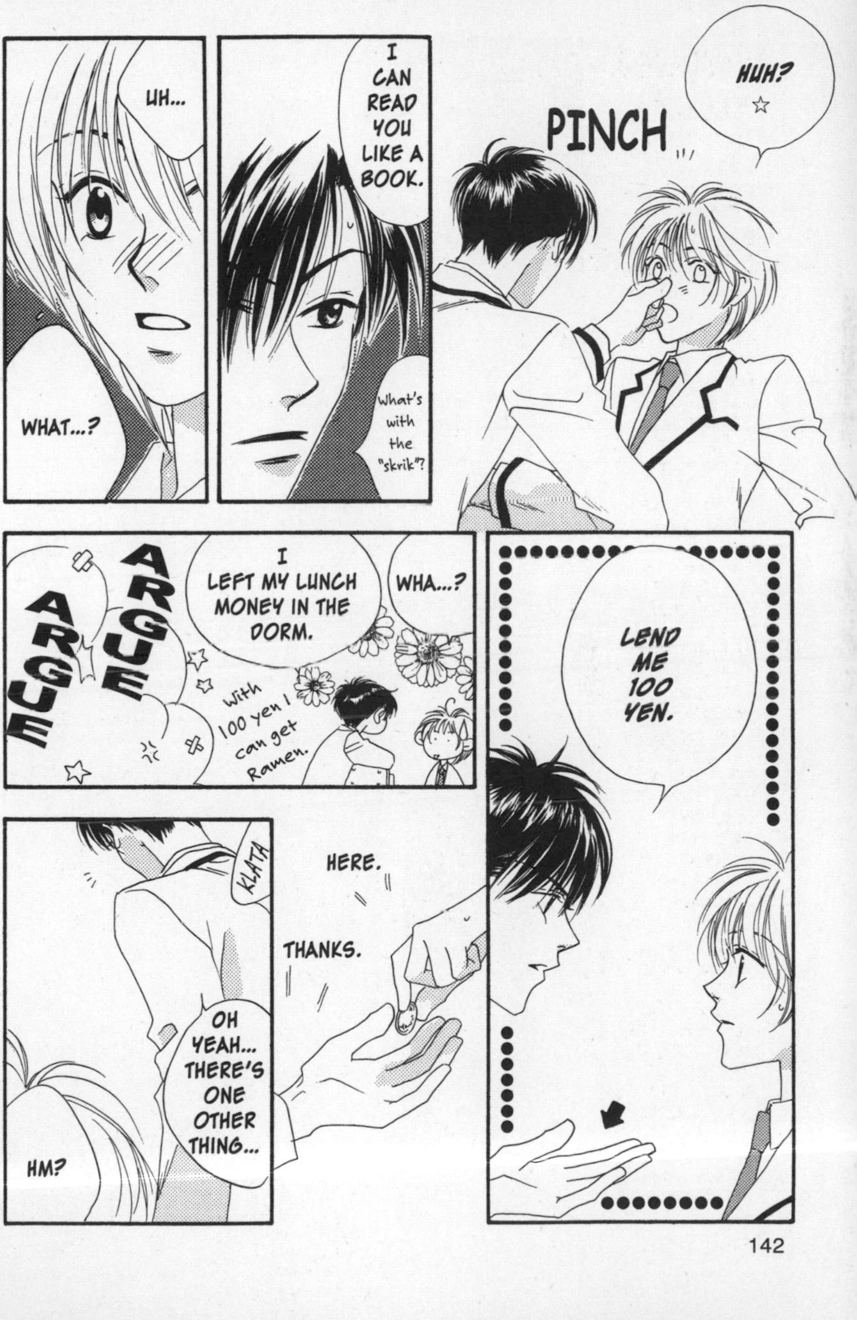
PINCH
HUH? ☆
I CAN READ YOU LIKE A BOOK.
What's with the "skrik"?
UH...
WHAT...?
LEND ME 100 YEN.
WHA...?
I LEFT MY LUNCH MONEY IN THE DORM.
ARGUE ARGUE
With 100 yen I can get Ramen.
KLATA
HERE.
THANKS.
OH YEAH... THERE'S ONE OTHER THING...
HM?

Whispered Secrets

My Favorite Movies

I'VE BECOME A REAL MOVIE GEEK. THERE ARE SO MANY MOVIES I LIKE I CAN'T BEGIN TO NAME THEM. ONE OF MY FAVORITES IS "INDEPENDENCE DAY". IT REMINDS ME OF THE OLD AMERICAN TV SERIES "V". I SAW IT THREE TIMES! HA! (I LOVE JEFF GOLDBLUM.) I ALSO LIKED "THE PROFESSIONAL," "HELLRAISER," "JOHNNY MNEMONIC," "TERMINATOR 2," "SPEED," "TORCH SONG TRILOGY," "ALIEN," "THE HIDDEN," "YOKAI HUNTER HIRUKO," "YANEURA NO HANATACHI," "BARA NO NAMAE," "CAT PEOPLE," "STAND BY ME," "SISTER ACT," "BLACK RAIN," "JURASSIC PARK..." THE LIST GOES ON AND ON. I'M SO EASY. I EVEN LIKED "DUNE," EVEN THOUGH IT GOT SUCH BAD REVIEWS. IT WAS COOL.

THE COMPUTER GRAPHICS WERE COOL. AND SO WAS KEANU!

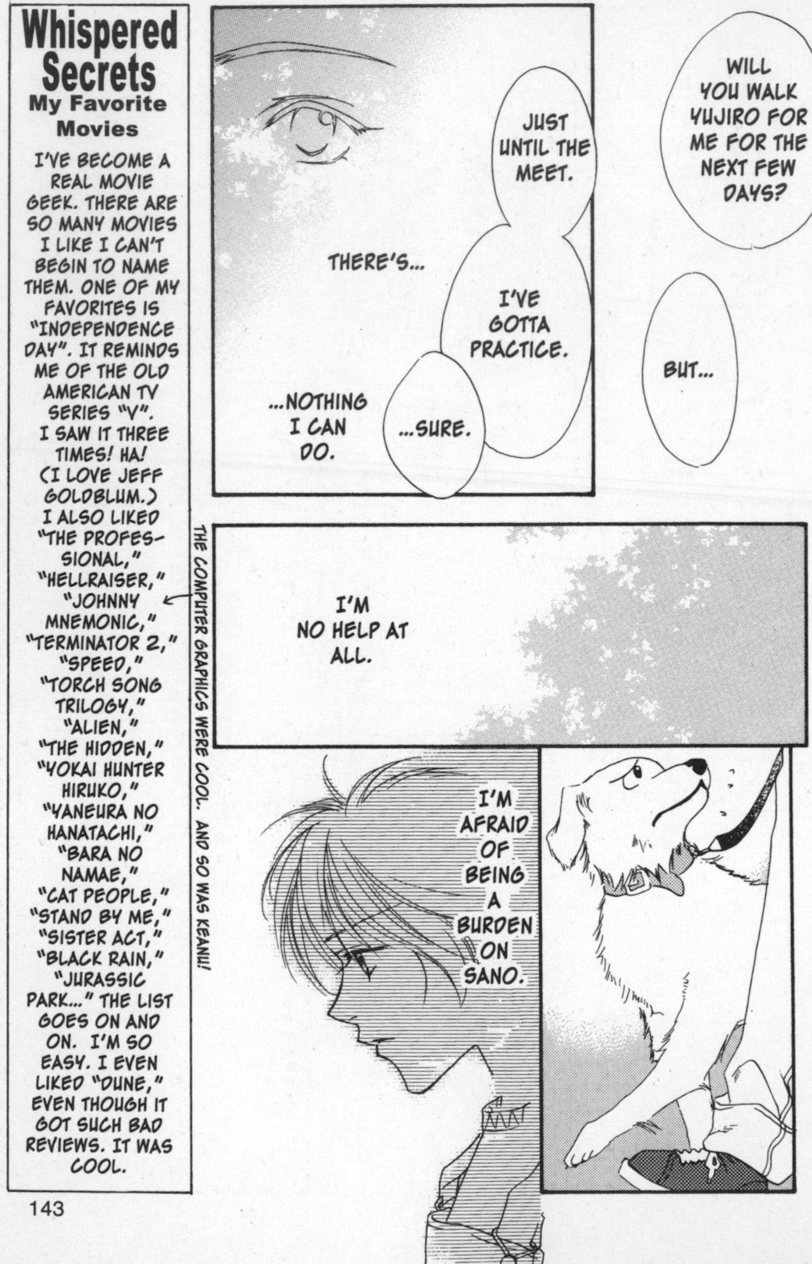
WILL YOU WALK YUJIRO FOR ME FOR THE NEXT FEW DAYS?
BUT...
JUST UNTIL THE MEET.
I'VE GOTTA PRACTICE.
...SURE.
THERE'S...
...NOTHING I CAN DO.
I'M NO HELP AT ALL.
I'M AFRAID OF BEING A BURDEN ON SANO.

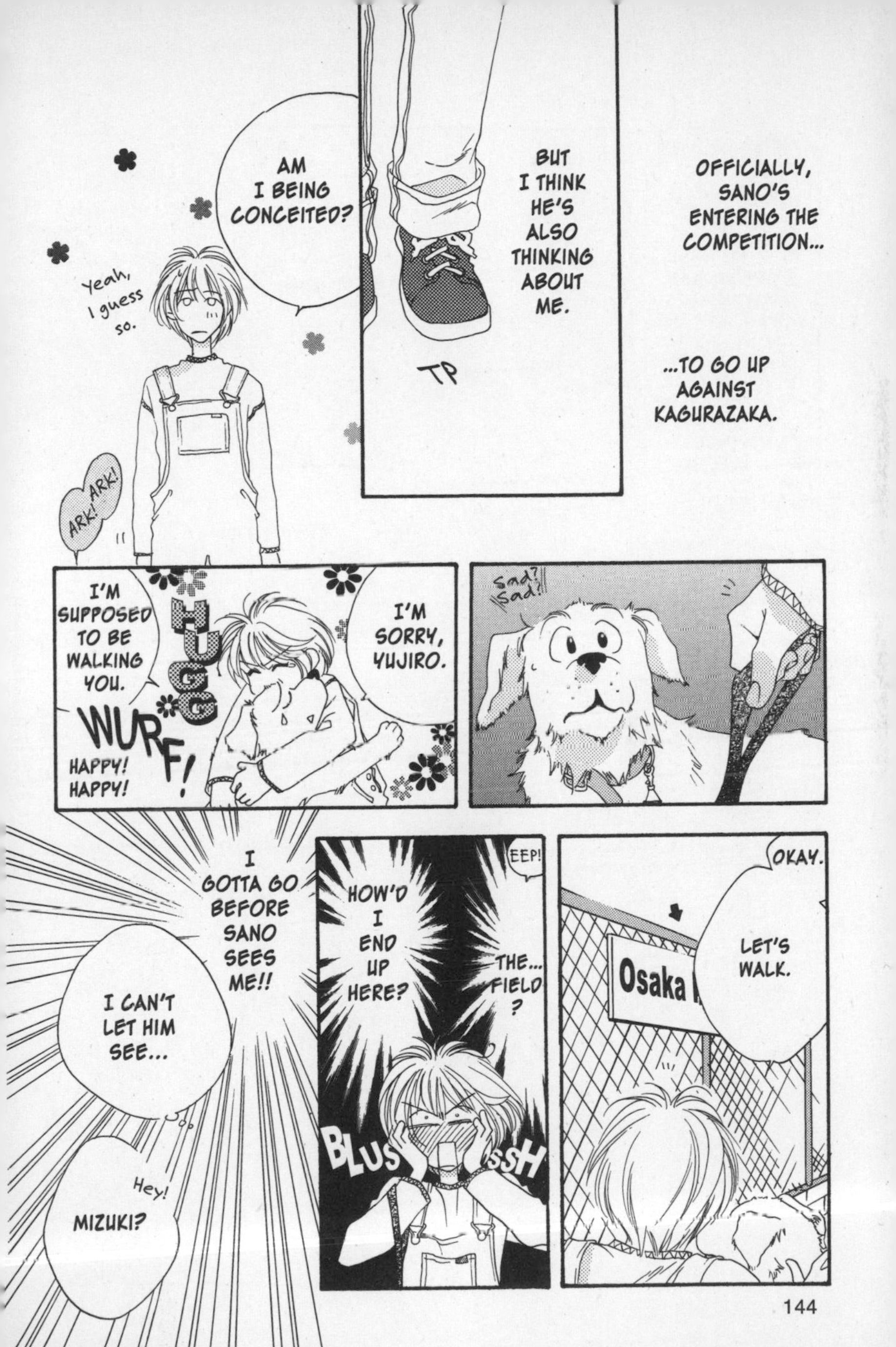
OFFICIALLY, SANO'S ENTERING THE COMPETITION...
...TO GO UP AGAINST KAGURAZAKA.
BUT I THINK HE'S ALSO THINKING ABOUT ME.
TP
AM I BEING CONCEITED?
Yeah, I guess so.
ARK! ARK!
Sad? Sad?
I'M SORRY, YUJIRO.
HUGG
I'M SUPPOSED TO BE WALKING YOU.
WURF!
HAPPY! HAPPY!
OKAY.
LET'S WALK.
Osaka
EEP!
THE... FIELD?
HOW'D I END UP HERE?
BLUSSSH
I GOTTA GO BEFORE SANO SEES ME!!
I CAN'T LET HIM SEE...
Hey!
MIZUKI?

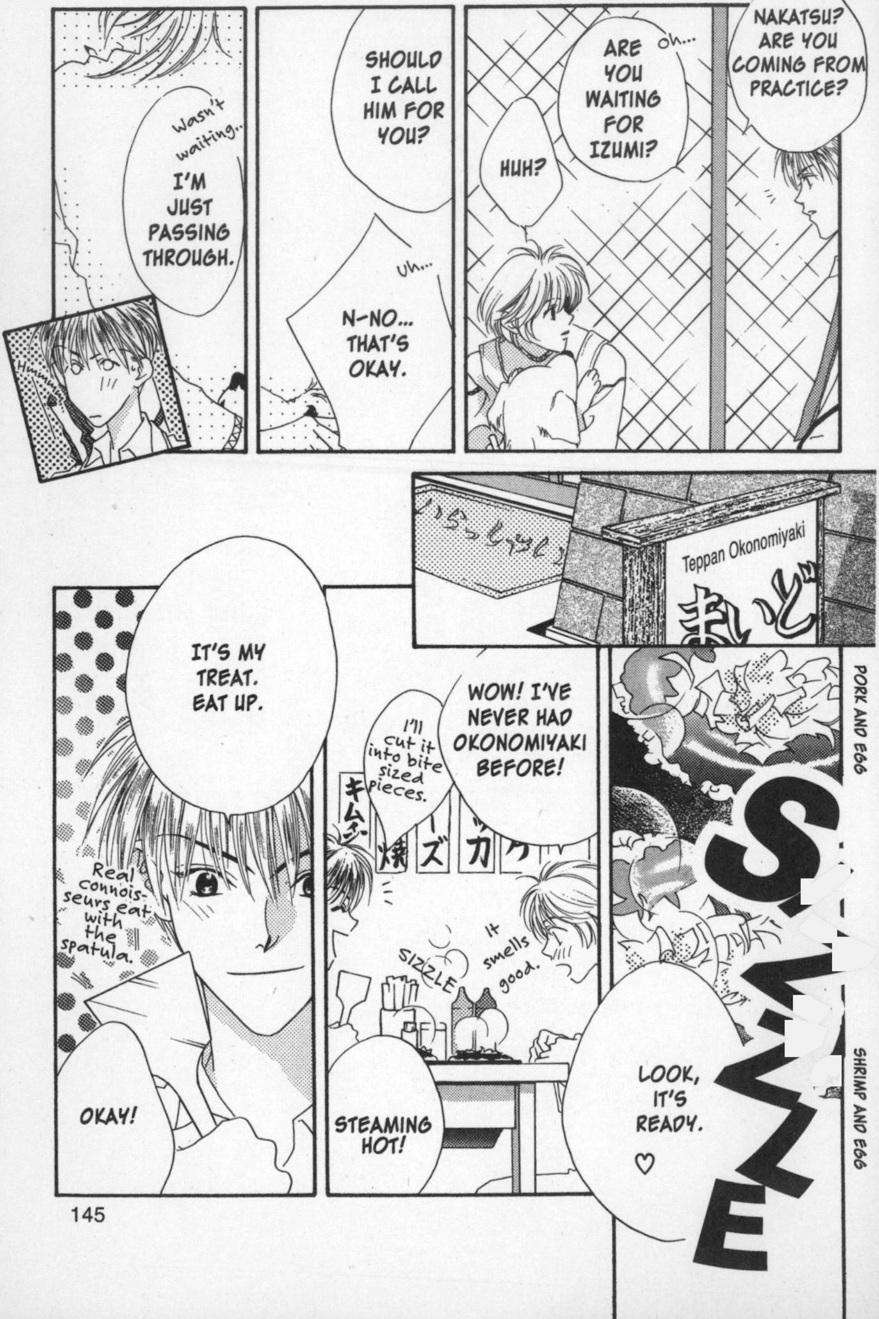
NAKATSU? ARE YOU COMING FROM PRACTICE?
ARE YOU WAITING FOR IZUMI?
Oh...
HUH?
SHOULD I CALL HIM FOR YOU?
Uh...
N-NO... THAT'S OKAY.
Wasn't waiting...
I'M JUST PASSING THROUGH.
いらっしゃい
Teppan Okonomiyaki
まいど
PORK AND EGG
SIZZLE
SHRIMP AND EGG
LOOK, IT'S READY. ♡
WOW! I'VE NEVER HAD OKONOMIYAKI BEFORE!
I'll cut it into bite sized pieces.
キムチ
焼
ズ
カ
It smells good.
SIZZLE
STEAMING HOT!
IT'S MY TREAT. EAT UP.
Real connoisseurs eat with the spatula.
OKAY!

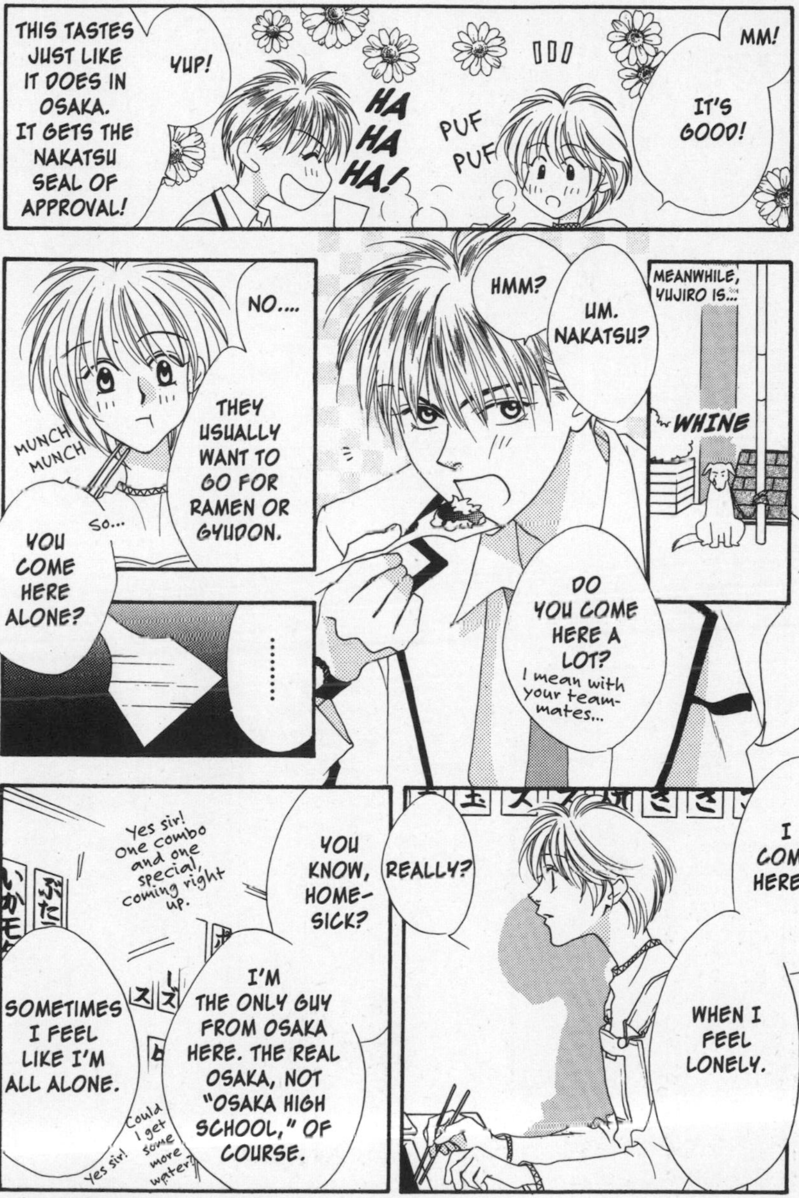
MM!
IT'S GOOD!
!!!
PUF PUF
HA HA HA!
YUP!
THIS TASTES JUST LIKE IT DOES IN OSAKA. IT GETS THE NAKATSU SEAL OF APPROVAL!
MEANWHILE, YUJIRO IS...
WHINE
UM. NAKATSU?
HMM?
DO YOU COME HERE A LOT?
I mean with your team-mates...
NO....
THEY USUALLY WANT TO GO FOR RAMEN OR GYUDON.
MUNCH MUNCH
SO...
YOU COME HERE ALONE?
......
I COME HERE...
WHEN I FEEL LONELY.
REALLY?
YOU KNOW, HOME-SICK?
Yes sir! One combo and one special, coming right up.
I'M THE ONLY GUY FROM OSAKA HERE. THE REAL OSAKA, NOT "OSAKA HIGH SCHOOL," OF COURSE.
SOMETIMES I FEEL LIKE I'M ALL ALONE.
Could I get some more water?
Yes sir!

*OSAKA (AS IN THE CITY) AND OSAKA (AS IN MIZUKI'S SCHOOL) ARE WRITTEN WITH DIFFERENT JAPANESE CHARACTERS

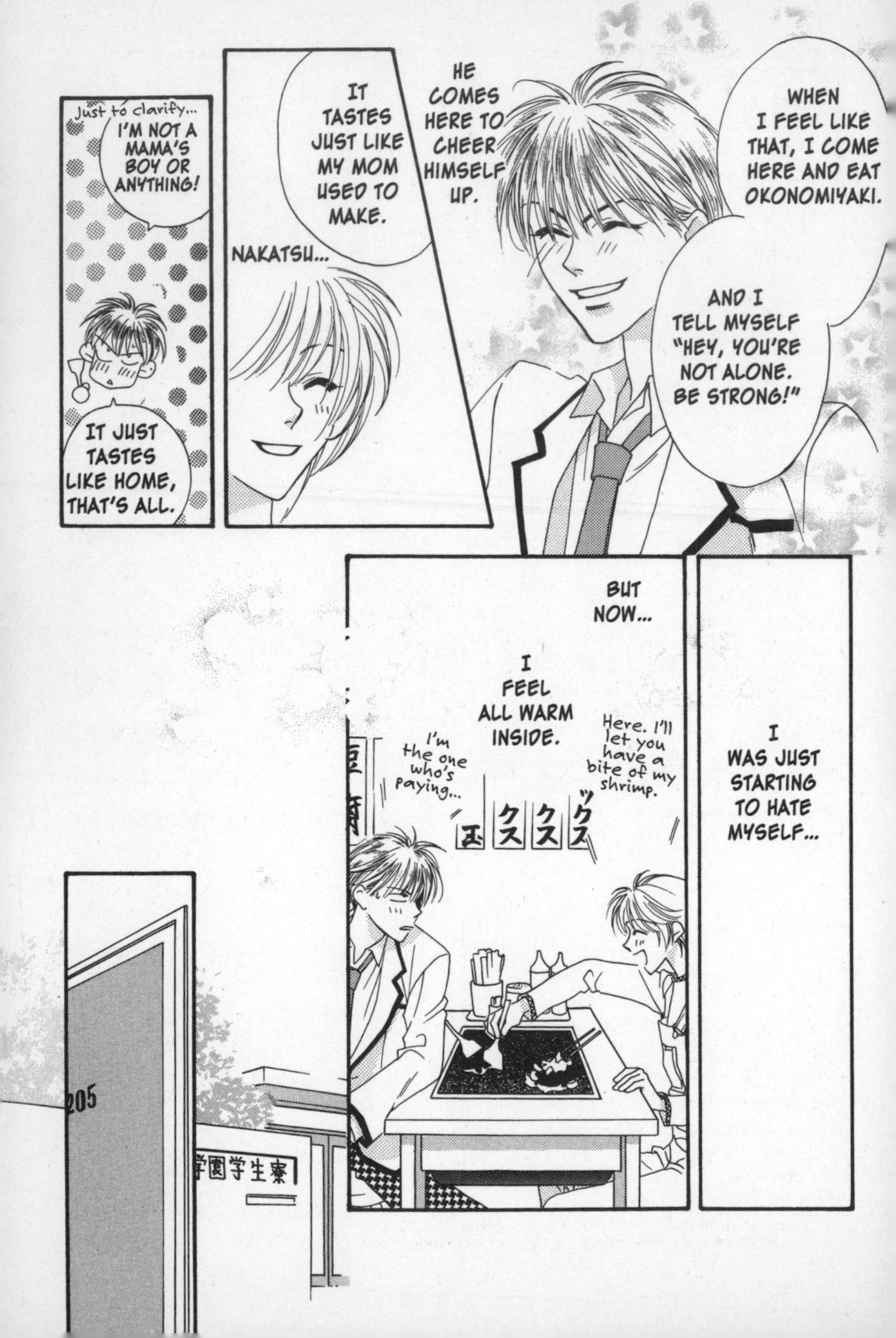
WHEN I FEEL LIKE THAT, I COME HERE AND EAT OKONOMIYAKI.
AND I TELL MYSELF "HEY, YOU'RE NOT ALONE. BE STRONG!"
HE COMES HERE TO CHEER HIMSELF UP.
IT TASTES JUST LIKE MY MOM USED TO MAKE.
NAKATSU...
Just to clarify...
I'M NOT A MAMA'S BOY OR ANYTHING!
IT JUST TASTES LIKE HOME, THAT'S ALL.
I WAS JUST STARTING TO HATE MYSELF...
BUT NOW...
I FEEL ALL WARM INSIDE.
Here. I'll let you have a bite of my shrimp.
I'm the one who's paying...
205
学園学生寮

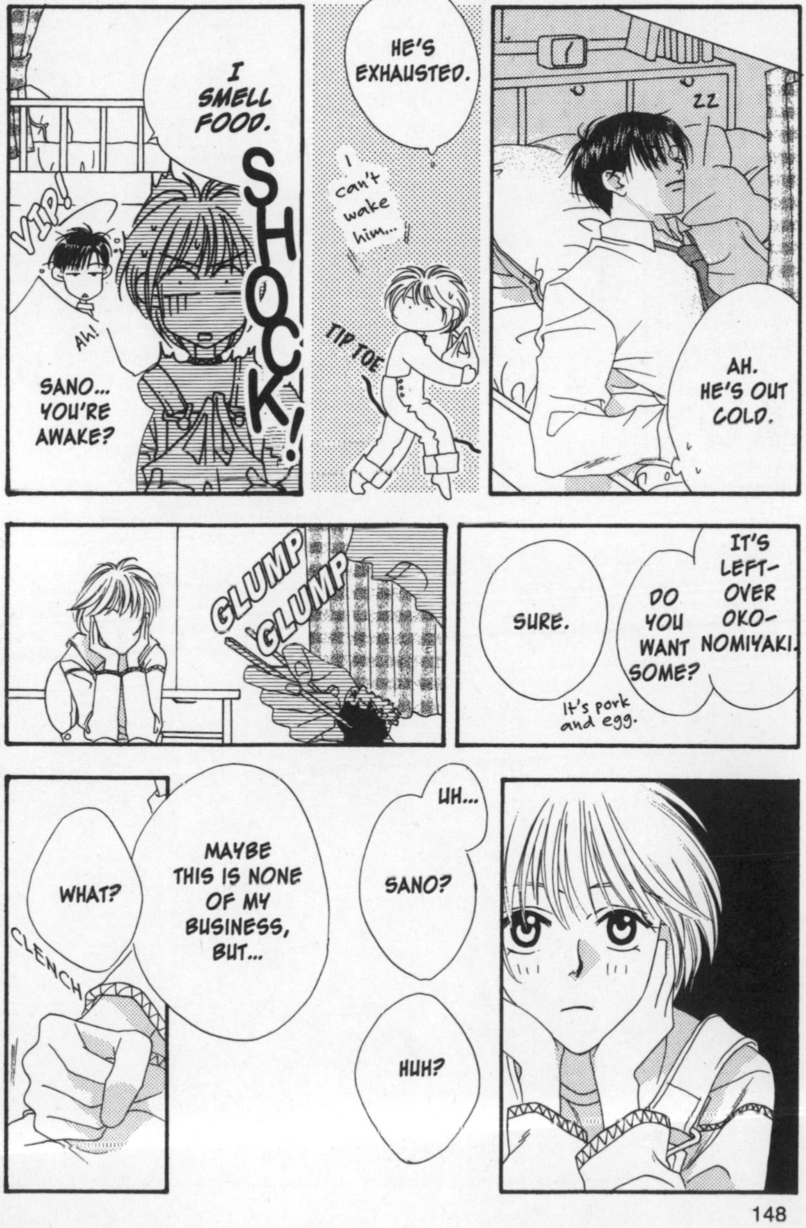
ZZ
AH. HE'S OUT COLD.
HE'S EXHAUSTED.
I can't wake him...
TIP TOE
I SMELL FOOD.
SHOCK!
VIP!
AH!
SANO... YOU'RE AWAKE?
IT'S LEFT-OVER OKO-NOMIYAKI.
DO YOU WANT SOME?
SURE.
It's pork and egg.
GLUMP GLUMP
UH...
SANO?
HUH?
MAYBE THIS IS NONE OF MY BUSINESS, BUT...
WHAT?
CLENCH

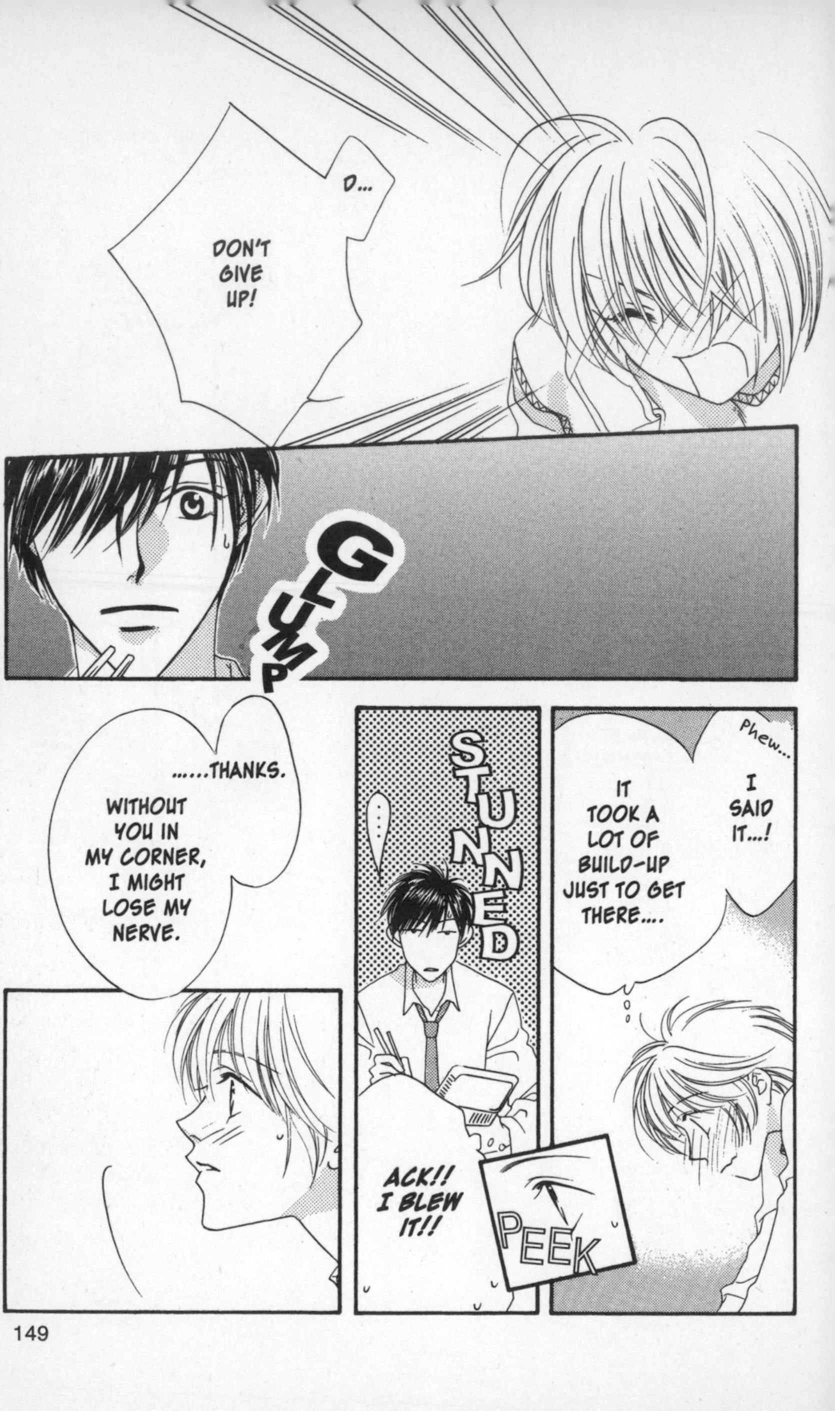
D...
DON'T GIVE UP!
GLUMP
Phew...
I SAID IT...!
IT TOOK A LOT OF BUILD-UP JUST TO GET THERE....
PEEK
STUNNED
...
ACK!! I BLEW IT!!
......THANKS.
WITHOUT YOU IN MY CORNER, I MIGHT LOSE MY NERVE.

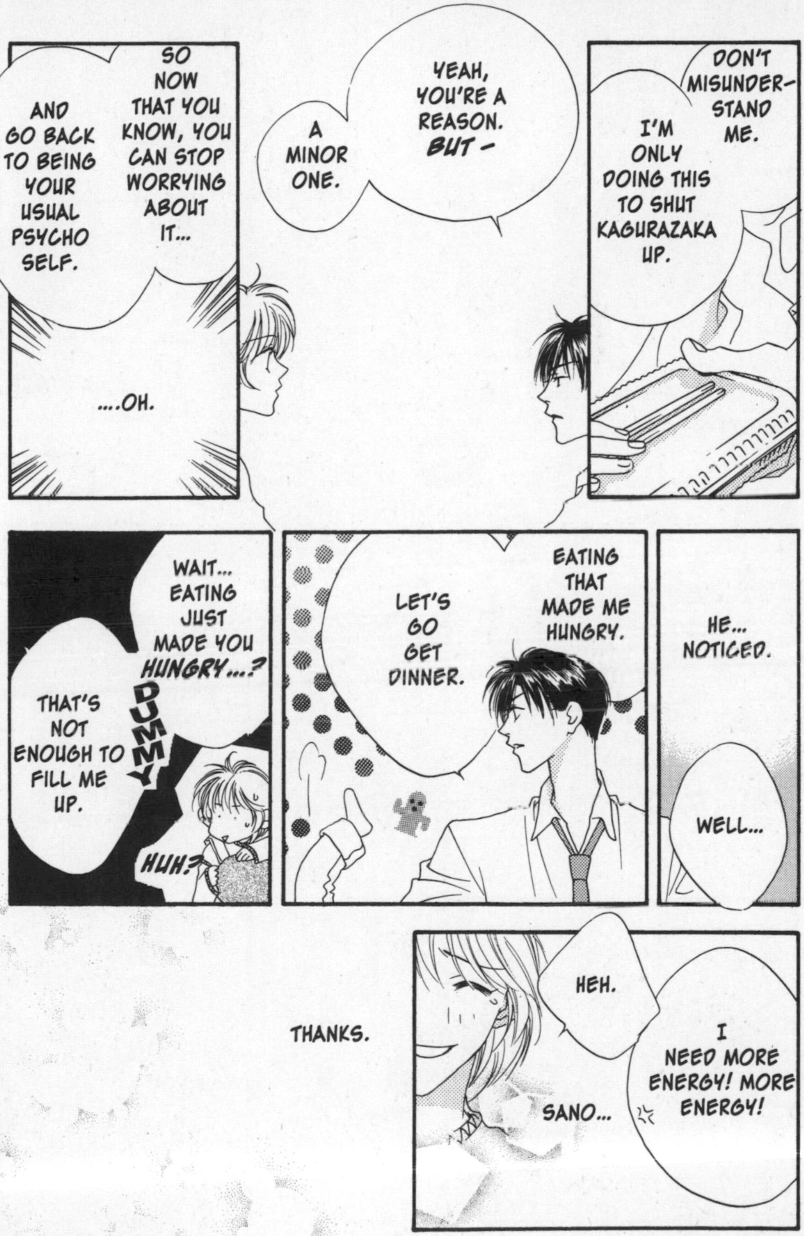
DON'T MISUNDERSTAND ME.
I'M ONLY DOING THIS TO SHUT KAGURAZAKA UP.
YEAH, YOU'RE A REASON. BUT -
A MINOR ONE.
SO NOW THAT YOU KNOW, YOU CAN STOP WORRYING ABOUT IT...
AND GO BACK TO BEING YOUR USUAL PSYCHO SELF.
....OH.
HE... NOTICED.
WELL...
EATING THAT MADE ME HUNGRY.
LET'S GO GET DINNER.
WAIT... EATING JUST MADE YOU HUNGRY...?
DUMMY
THAT'S NOT ENOUGH TO FILL ME UP.
HUH?
I NEED MORE ENERGY! MORE ENERGY!
HEH.
SANO...
THANKS.

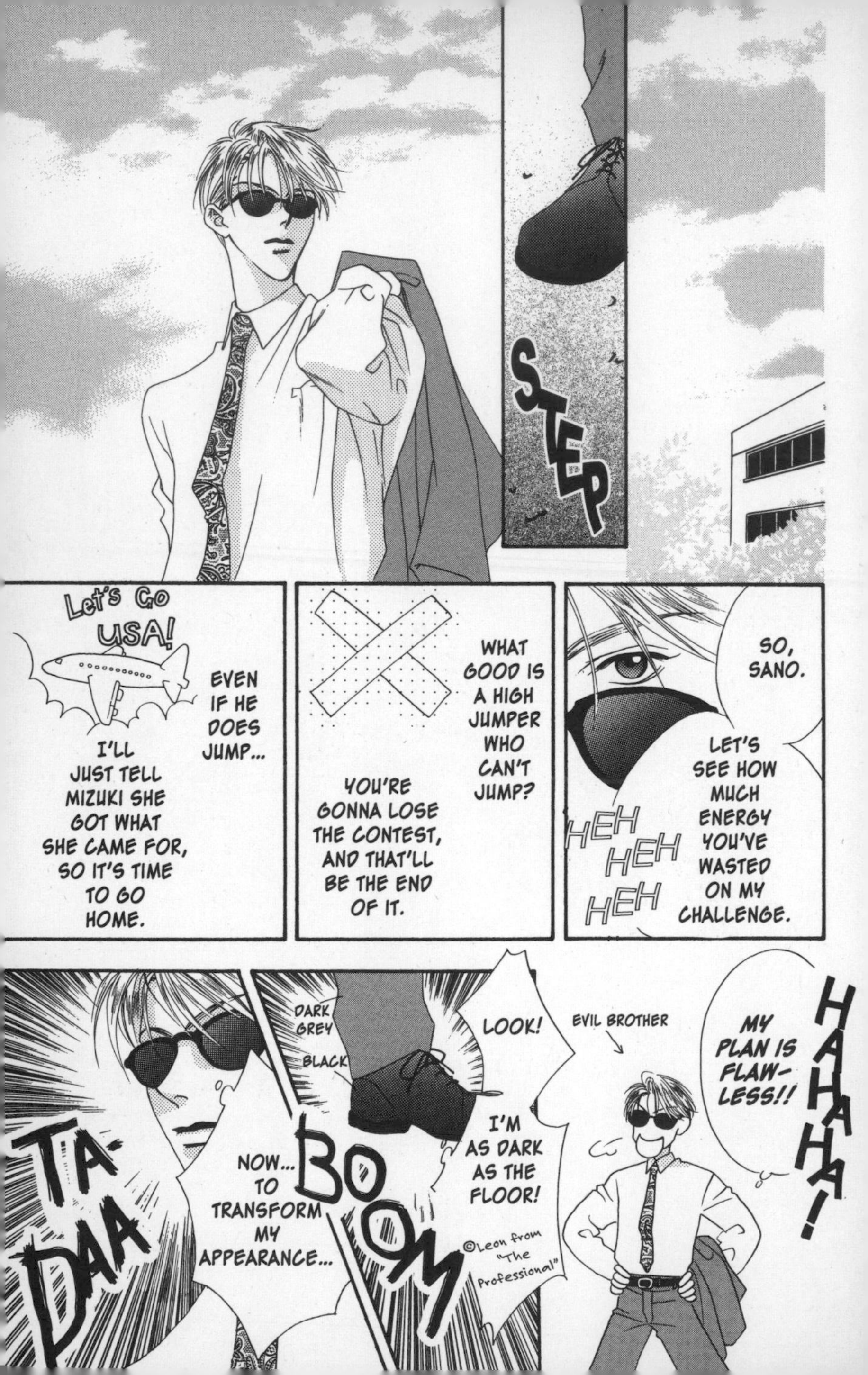
STEP
SO, SANO.
LET'S SEE HOW MUCH ENERGY YOU'VE WASTED ON MY CHALLENGE.
HEH HEH HEH
WHAT GOOD IS A HIGH JUMPER WHO CAN'T JUMP?
YOU'RE GONNA LOSE THE CONTEST, AND THAT'LL BE THE END OF IT.
EVEN IF HE DOES JUMP...
I'LL JUST TELL MIZUKI SHE GOT WHAT SHE CAME FOR, SO IT'S TIME TO GO HOME.
Let's Go USA!
HAHAHA!
MY PLAN IS FLAW-LESS!!
EVIL BROTHER
©Leon from "The Professional"
LOOK!
I'M AS DARK AS THE FLOOR!
DARK GREY
BLACK
BOOM
NOW... TO TRANSFORM MY APPEARANCE...
TA DAA

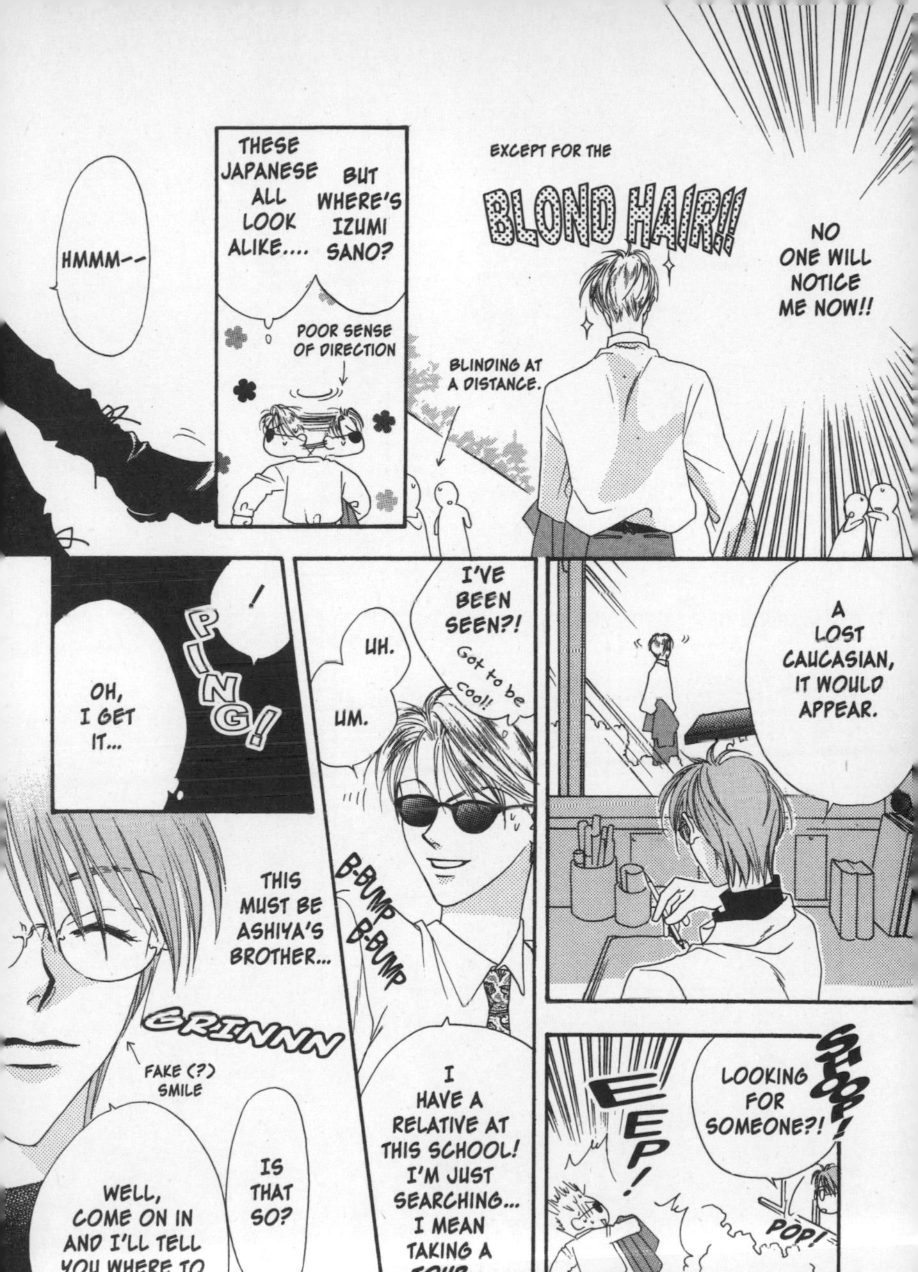
NO ONE WILL NOTICE ME NOW!!
EXCEPT FOR THE
BLOND HAIR!!
BLINDING AT A DISTANCE.
THESE JAPANESE ALL LOOK ALIKE....
BUT WHERE'S IZUMI SANO?
POOR SENSE OF DIRECTION
HMMM--
A LOST CAUCASIAN, IT WOULD APPEAR.
LOOKING FOR SOMEONE?!
SHOOP!
EEP!
POP!
I'VE BEEN SEEN?!
Got to be cool!!
UH.
UM.
B-BUMP B-BUMP
I HAVE A RELATIVE AT THIS SCHOOL! I'M JUST SEARCHING... I MEAN TAKING A TOUR...
!
PING!
OH, I GET IT...
THIS MUST BE ASHIYA'S BROTHER...
GRINNNN
FAKE (?) SMILE
IS THAT SO?
WELL, COME ON IN AND I'LL TELL YOU WHERE TO GO!

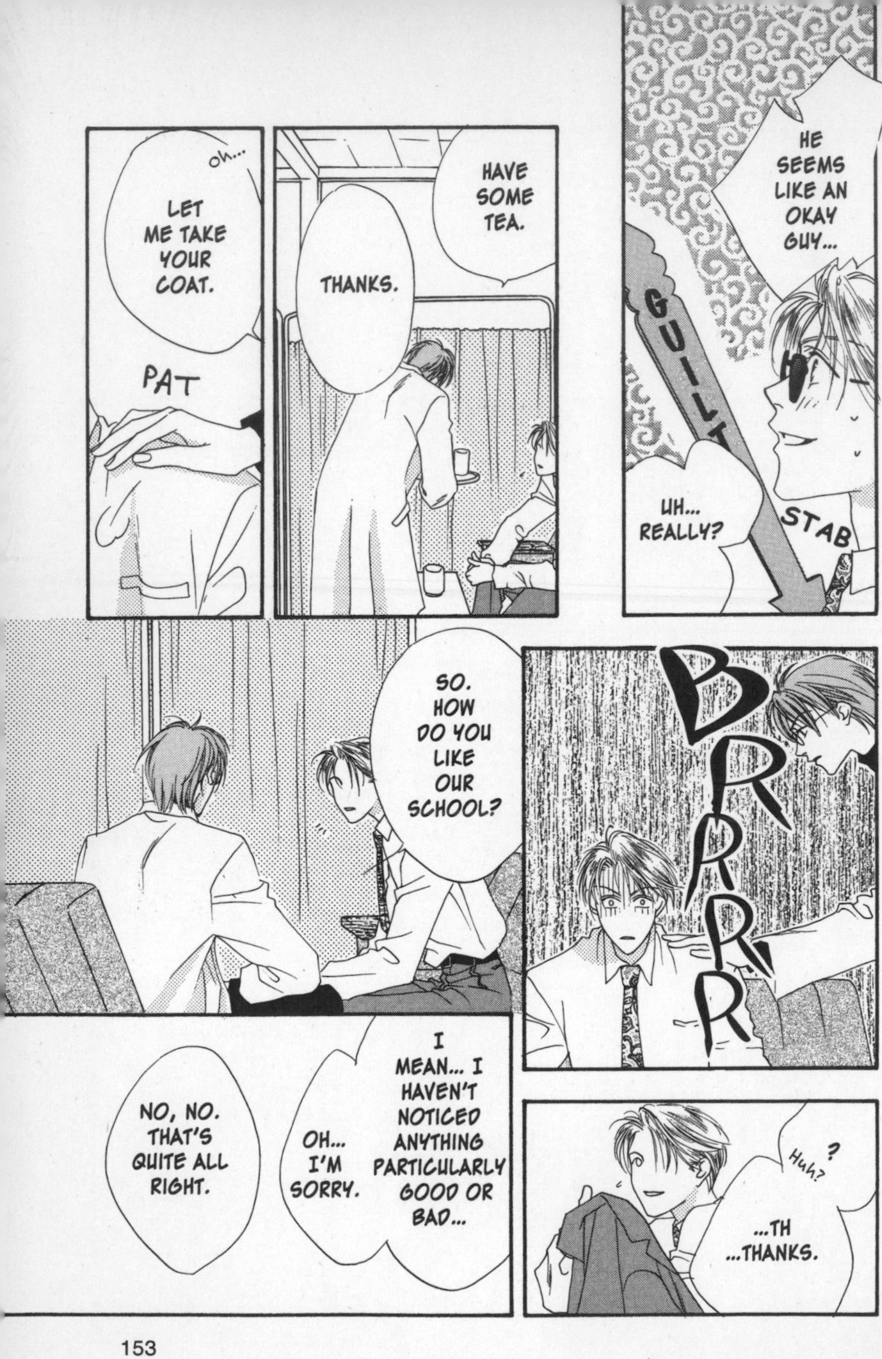
HE SEEMS LIKE AN OKAY GUY...
GUILT
UH... REALLY?
STAB
HAVE SOME TEA.
THANKS.
oh...
LET ME TAKE YOUR COAT.
PAT
BRRRRR
SO. HOW DO YOU LIKE OUR SCHOOL?
Huh? ?
...TH ...THANKS.
I MEAN... I HAVEN'T NOTICED ANYTHING PARTICULARLY GOOD OR BAD...
OH... I'M SORRY.
NO, NO. THAT'S QUITE ALL RIGHT.

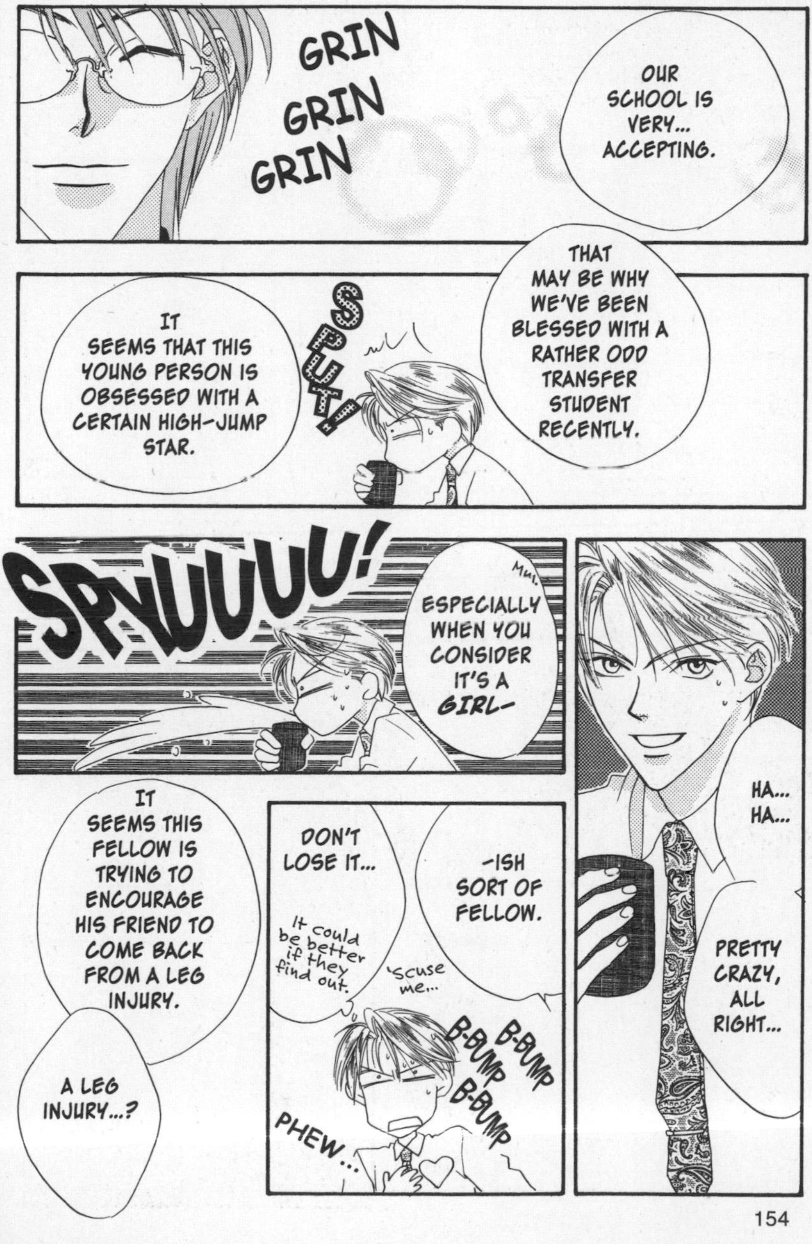
OUR SCHOOL IS VERY... ACCEPTING.
GRIN GRIN GRIN
THAT MAY BE WHY WE'VE BEEN BLESSED WITH A RATHER ODD TRANSFER STUDENT RECENTLY.
SPUT!
IT SEEMS THAT THIS YOUNG PERSON IS OBSESSED WITH A CERTAIN HIGH-JUMP STAR.
HA... HA...
PRETTY CRAZY, ALL RIGHT...
Mu.
ESPECIALLY WHEN YOU CONSIDER IT'S A GIRL-
SPWUUUU!
-ISH SORT OF FELLOW.
DON'T LOSE IT...
'Scuse me...
It could be better if they find out.
B-BUMP B-BUMP B-BUMP
PHEW...
IT SEEMS THIS FELLOW IS TRYING TO ENCOURAGE HIS FRIEND TO COME BACK FROM A LEG INJURY.
A LEG INJURY...?

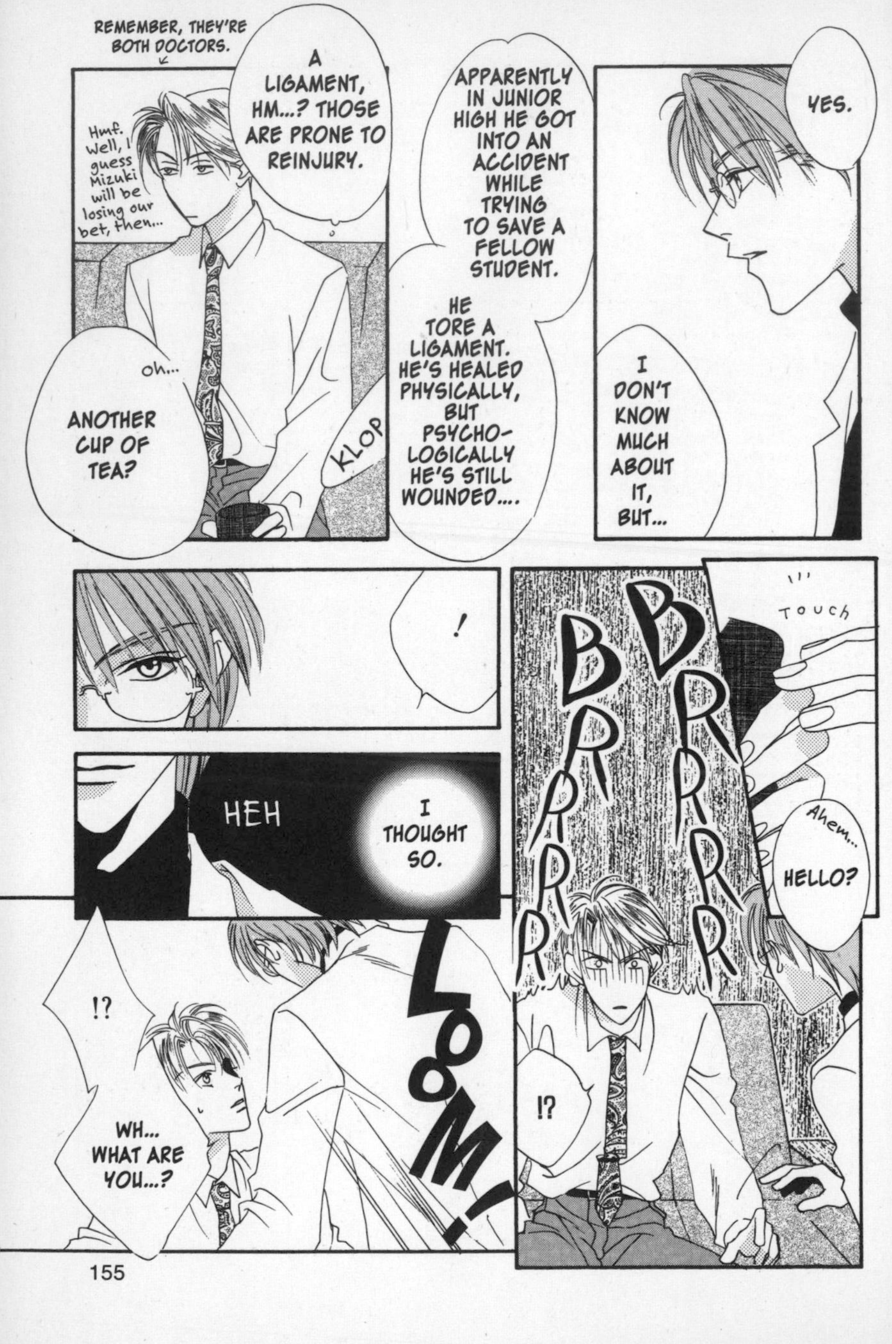
YES.
I DON'T KNOW MUCH ABOUT IT, BUT...
APPARENTLY IN JUNIOR HIGH HE GOT INTO AN ACCIDENT WHILE TRYING TO SAVE A FELLOW STUDENT.
HE TORE A LIGAMENT. HE'S HEALED PHYSICALLY, BUT PSYCHO-LOGICALLY HE'S STILL WOUNDED....
REMEMBER, THEY'RE BOTH DOCTORS.
A LIGAMENT, HM...? THOSE ARE PRONE TO REINJURY.
Hmf. Well, I guess Mizuki will be losing our bet, then...
KLOP
oh...
ANOTHER CUP OF TEA?
TOUCH
Ahem...
HELLO?
BRRRRR
BRRRRRR
!?
!
HEH
I THOUGHT SO.
!?
WH... WHAT ARE YOU...?
LOOM!

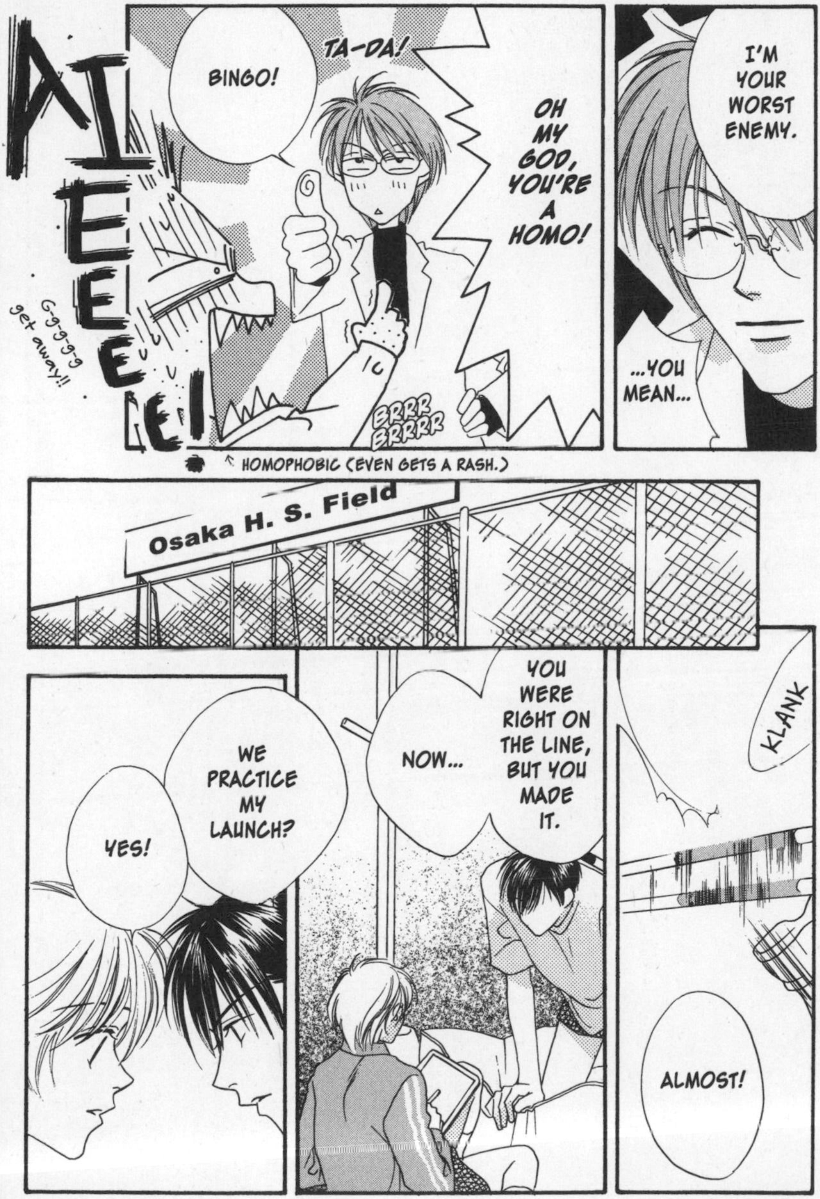
I'M YOUR WORST ENEMY.
...YOU MEAN...
OH MY GOD, YOU'RE A HOMO!
TA-DA!
BINGO!
AIEEEEE!
G-g-g-g-g get away!!
BRRR BRRRR
↑ HOMOPHOBIC (EVEN GETS A RASH.)
Osaka H. S. Field
KLANK
ALMOST!
YOU WERE RIGHT ON THE LINE, BUT YOU MADE IT.
NOW...
WE PRACTICE MY LAUNCH?
YES!

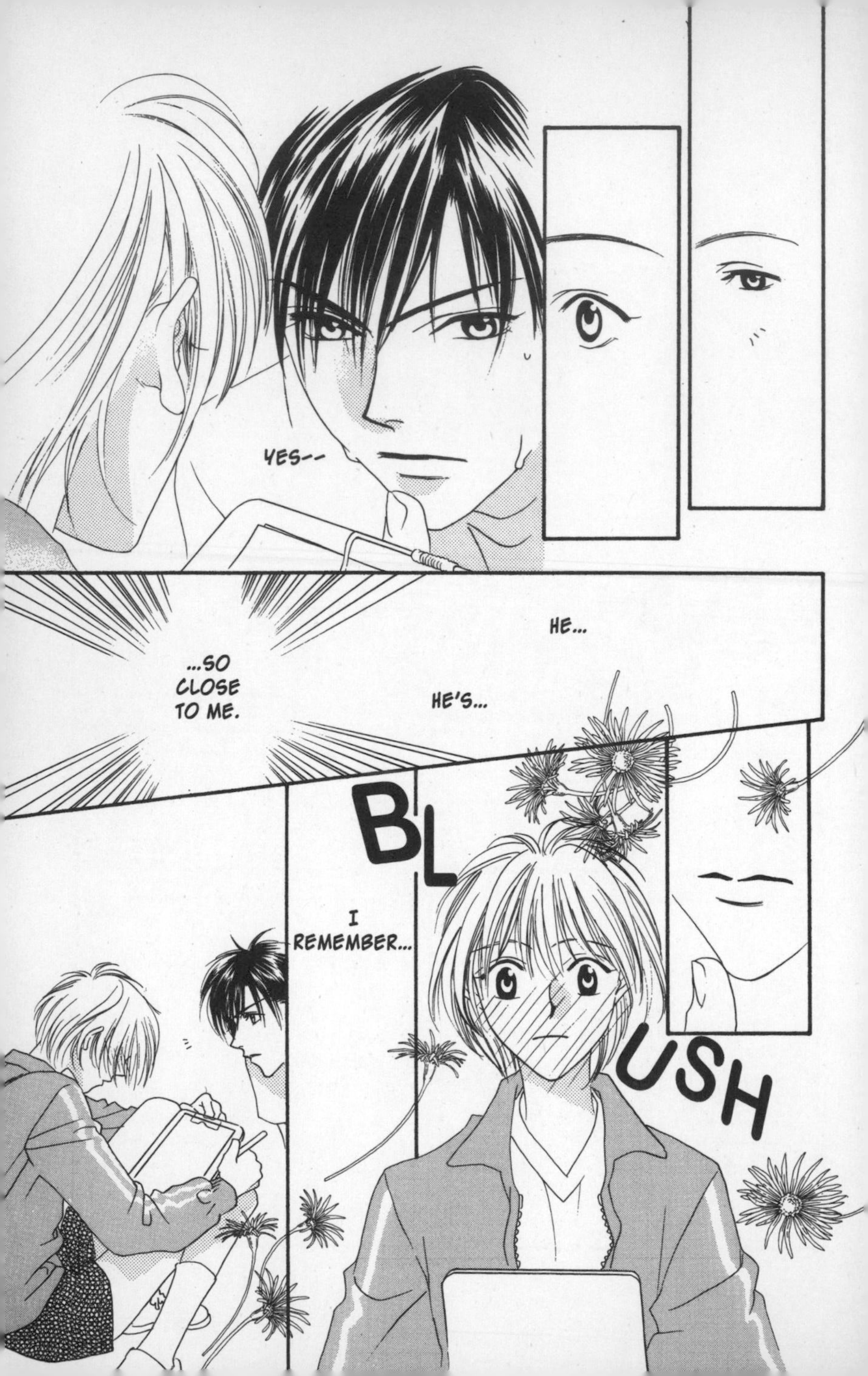
YES--
HE...
HE'S...
...SO CLOSE TO ME.
BLUSH
I REMEMBER...

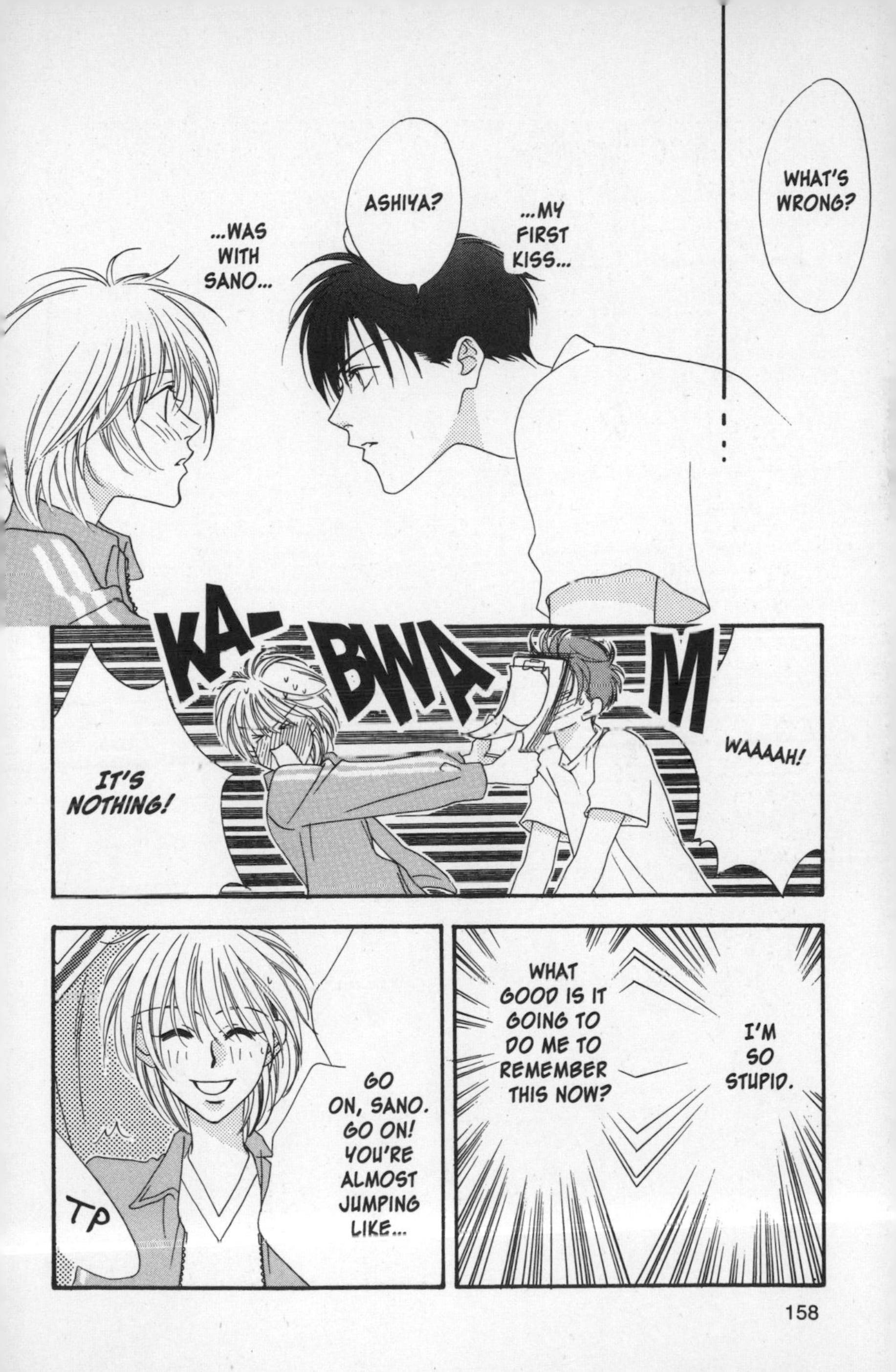
WHAT'S WRONG?
...MY FIRST KISS...
ASHIYA?
...WAS WITH SANO...
WAAAAH!
KA-BWAM
IT'S NOTHING!
I'M SO STUPID.
WHAT GOOD IS IT GOING TO DO ME TO REMEMBER THIS NOW?
GO ON, SANO. GO ON! YOU'RE ALMOST JUMPING LIKE...
TP

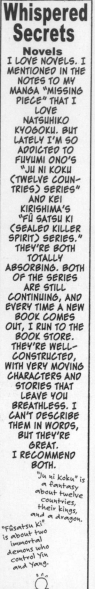

Whispered Secrets

Novels

I LOVE NOVELS. I MENTIONED IN THE NOTES TO MY MANGA "MISSING PIECE" THAT I LOVE NATSUHIKO KYOGOKU. BUT LATELY I'M SO ADDICTED TO FUYUMI ONO'S "JU NI KOKU (TWELVE COUNTRIES) SERIES" AND KEI KIRISHIMA'S "FŪ SATSU KI (SEALED KILLER SPIRIT) SERIES." THEY'RE BOTH TOTALLY ABSORBING. BOTH OF THE SERIES ARE STILL CONTINUING, AND EVERY TIME A NEW BOOK COMES OUT, I RUN TO THE BOOK STORE. THEY'RE WELL-CONSTRUCTED, WITH VERY MOVING CHARACTERS AND STORIES THAT LEAVE YOU BREATHLESS. I CAN'T DESCRIBE THEM IN WORDS, BUT THEY'RE GREAT. I RECOMMEND BOTH.

"Ju ni koku" is a fantasy about twelve countries, their kings, and a dragon.

"Fūsatsu ki" is about two immortal demons who control Yin and Yang.

BOTH ARE AVAILABLE ON CD.

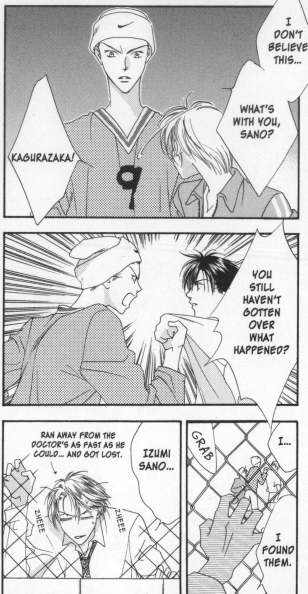

I DON'T BELIEVE THIS...

WHAT'S WITH YOU, SANO?

KAGURAZAKA!

YOU STILL HAVEN'T GOTTEN OVER WHAT HAPPENED?

RAN AWAY FROM THE DOCTOR'S AS FAST AS HE COULD... AND GOT LOST.

ZHEEE

ZHEEE

IZUMI SANO...

GRAB

I...

I FOUND THEM.

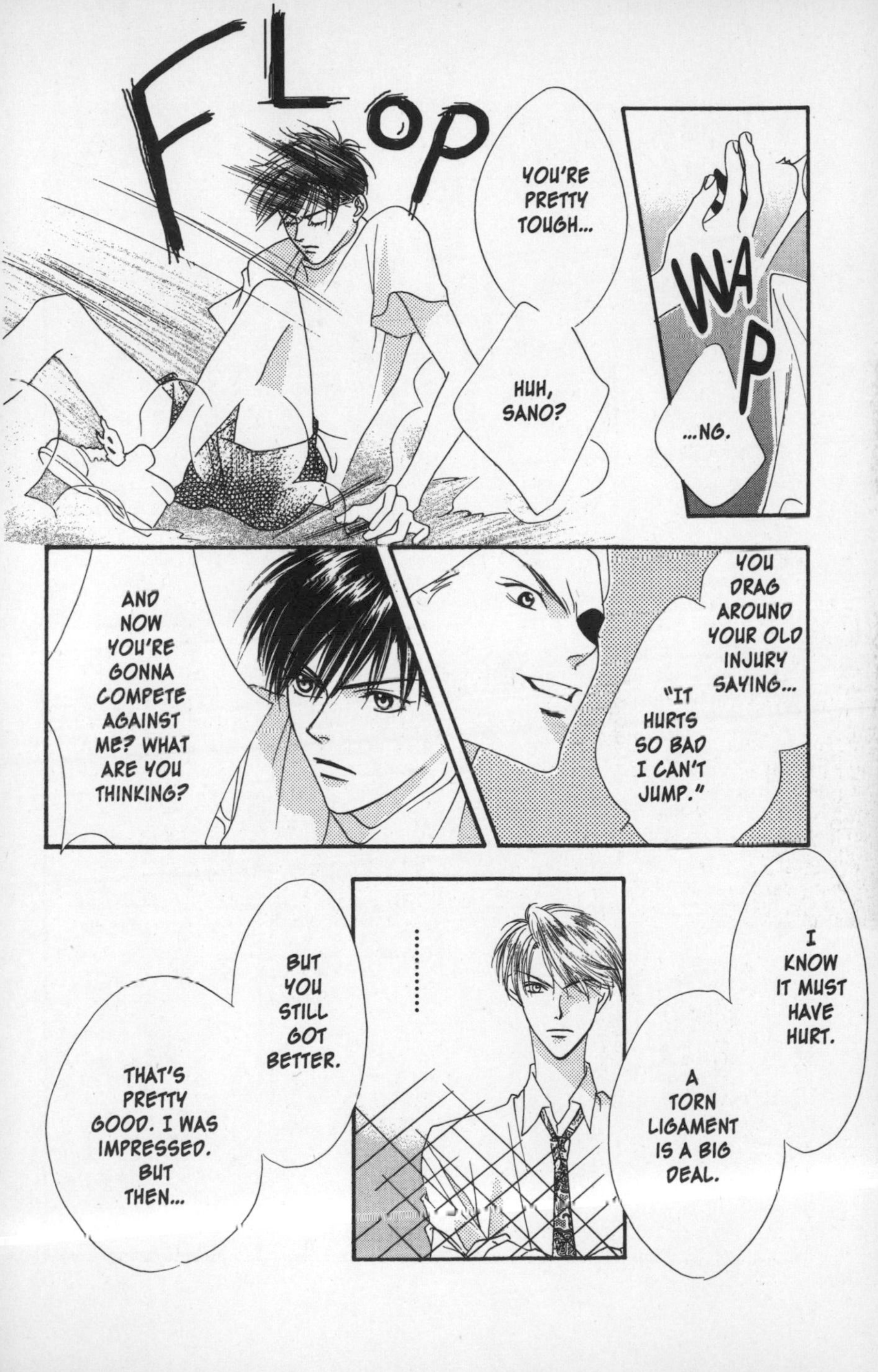
WAP
...NG.
YOU'RE PRETTY TOUGH...
FLOP
HUH, SANO?
YOU DRAG AROUND YOUR OLD INJURY SAYING...
"IT HURTS SO BAD I CAN'T JUMP."
AND NOW YOU'RE GONNA COMPETE AGAINST ME? WHAT ARE YOU THINKING?
I KNOW IT MUST HAVE HURT.
A TORN LIGAMENT IS A BIG DEAL.
......
BUT YOU STILL GOT BETTER.
THAT'S PRETTY GOOD. I WAS IMPRESSED. BUT THEN...

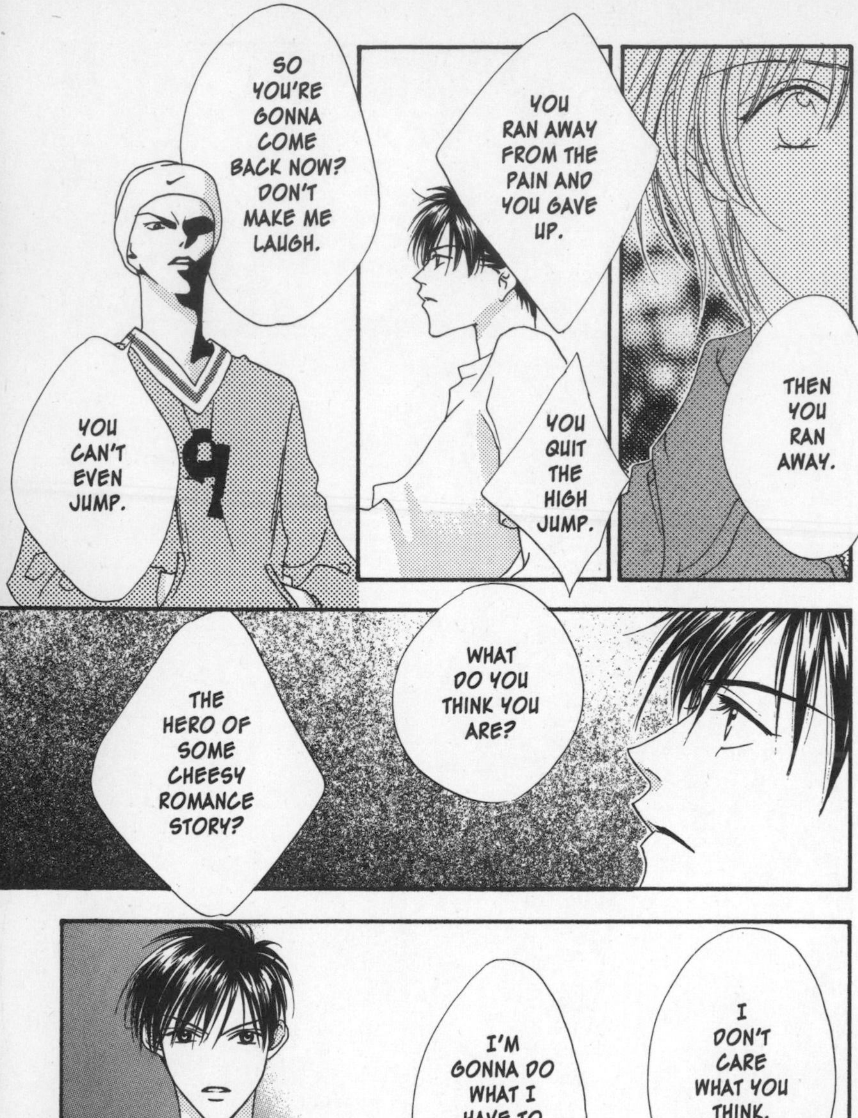
THEN YOU RAN AWAY.
YOU RAN AWAY FROM THE PAIN AND YOU GAVE UP.
YOU QUIT THE HIGH JUMP.
SO YOU'RE GONNA COME BACK NOW? DON'T MAKE ME LAUGH.
YOU CAN'T EVEN JUMP.
WHAT DO YOU THINK YOU ARE?
THE HERO OF SOME CHEESY ROMANCE STORY?
I DON'T CARE WHAT YOU THINK.
I'M GONNA DO WHAT I HAVE TO DO.

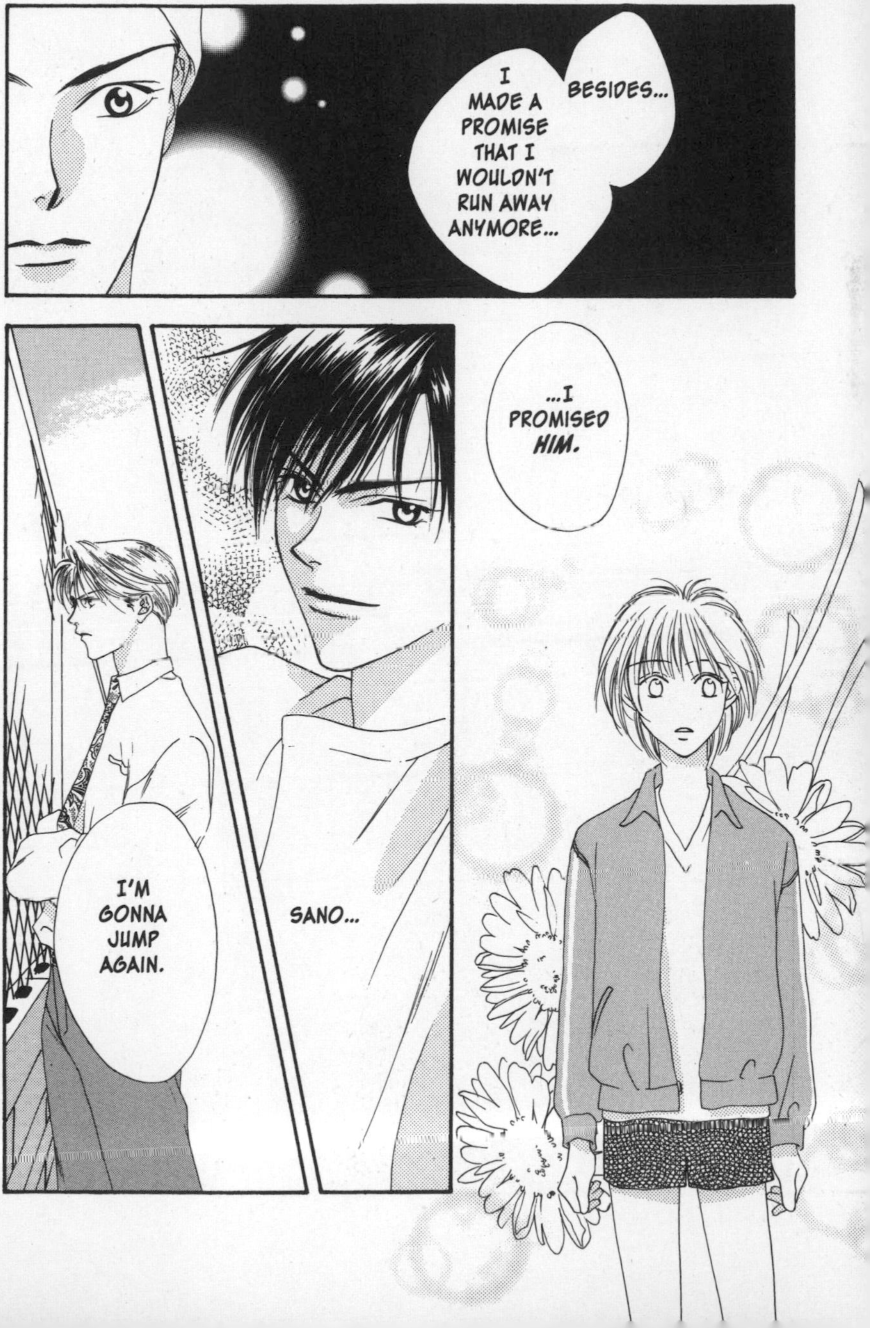
BESIDES...
I MADE A PROMISE THAT I WOULDN'T RUN AWAY ANYMORE...
...I PROMISED *HIM.*
SANO...
I'M GONNA JUMP AGAIN.

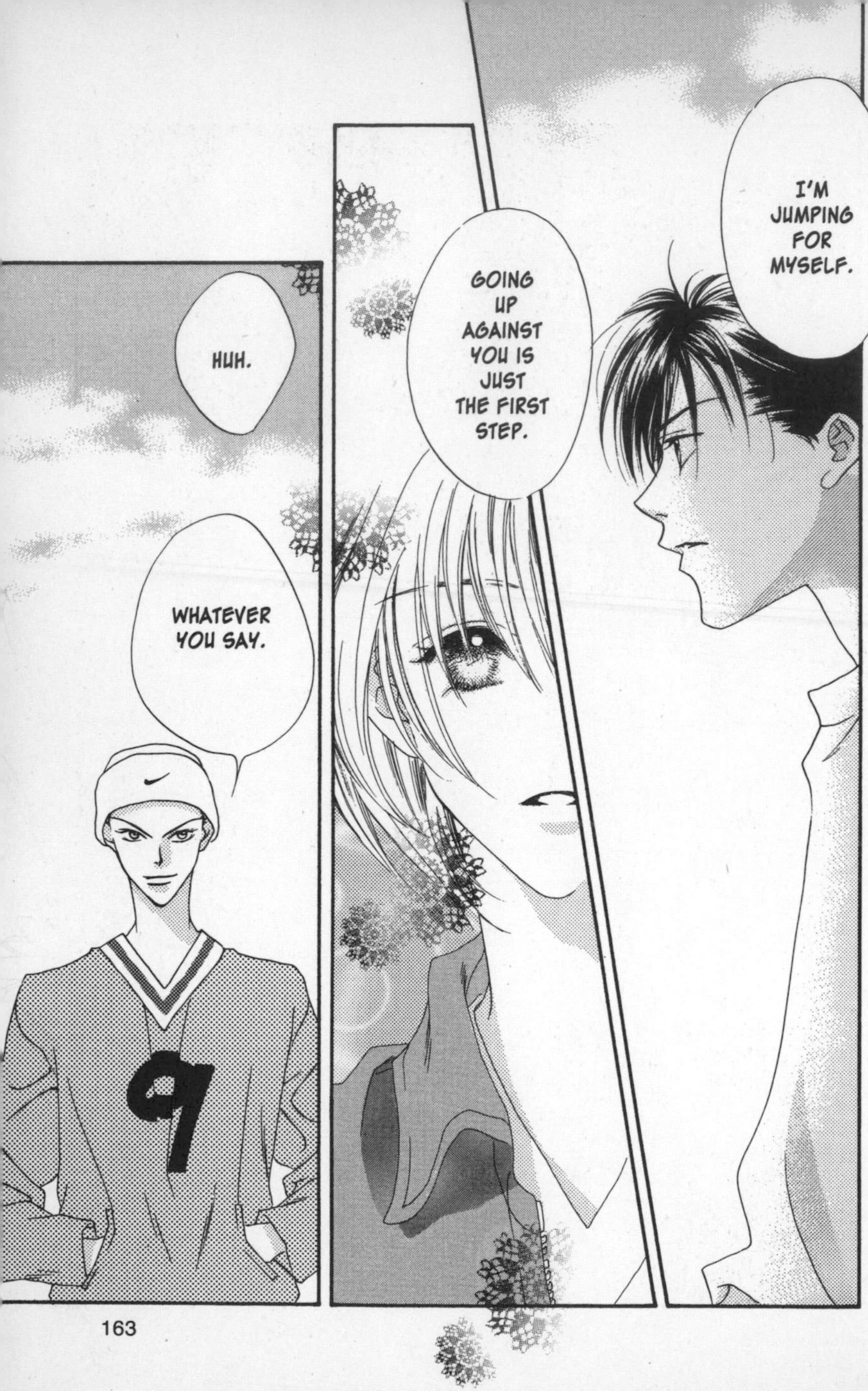
I'M JUMPING FOR MYSELF.
GOING UP AGAINST YOU IS JUST THE FIRST STEP.
HUH.
WHATEVER YOU SAY.

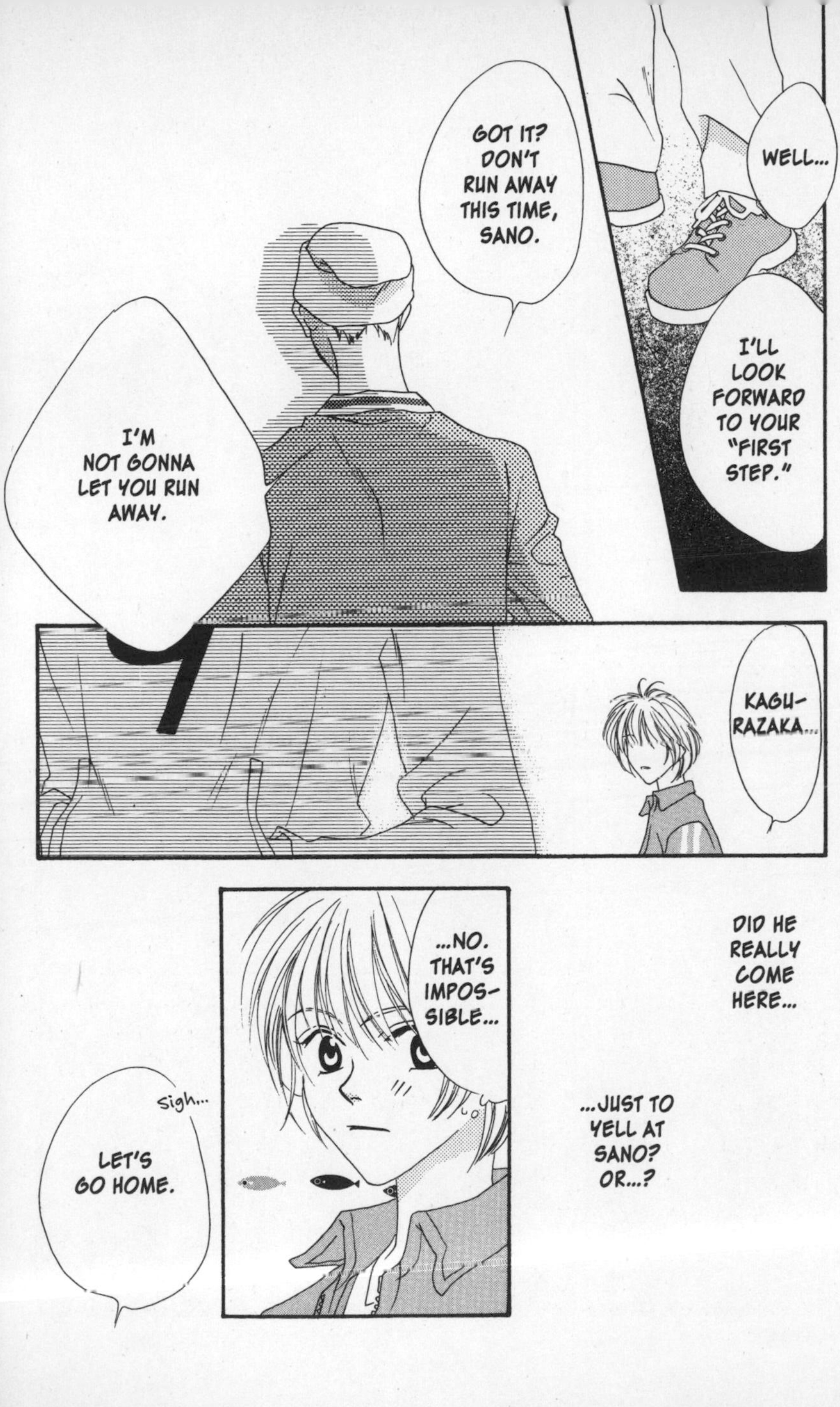
WELL...
I'LL LOOK FORWARD TO YOUR "FIRST STEP."
GOT IT? DON'T RUN AWAY THIS TIME, SANO.
I'M NOT GONNA LET YOU RUN AWAY.
KAGU-RAZAKA...
DID HE REALLY COME HERE...
...JUST TO YELL AT SANO? OR...?
...NO. THAT'S IMPOS-SIBLE...
Sigh...
LET'S GO HOME.

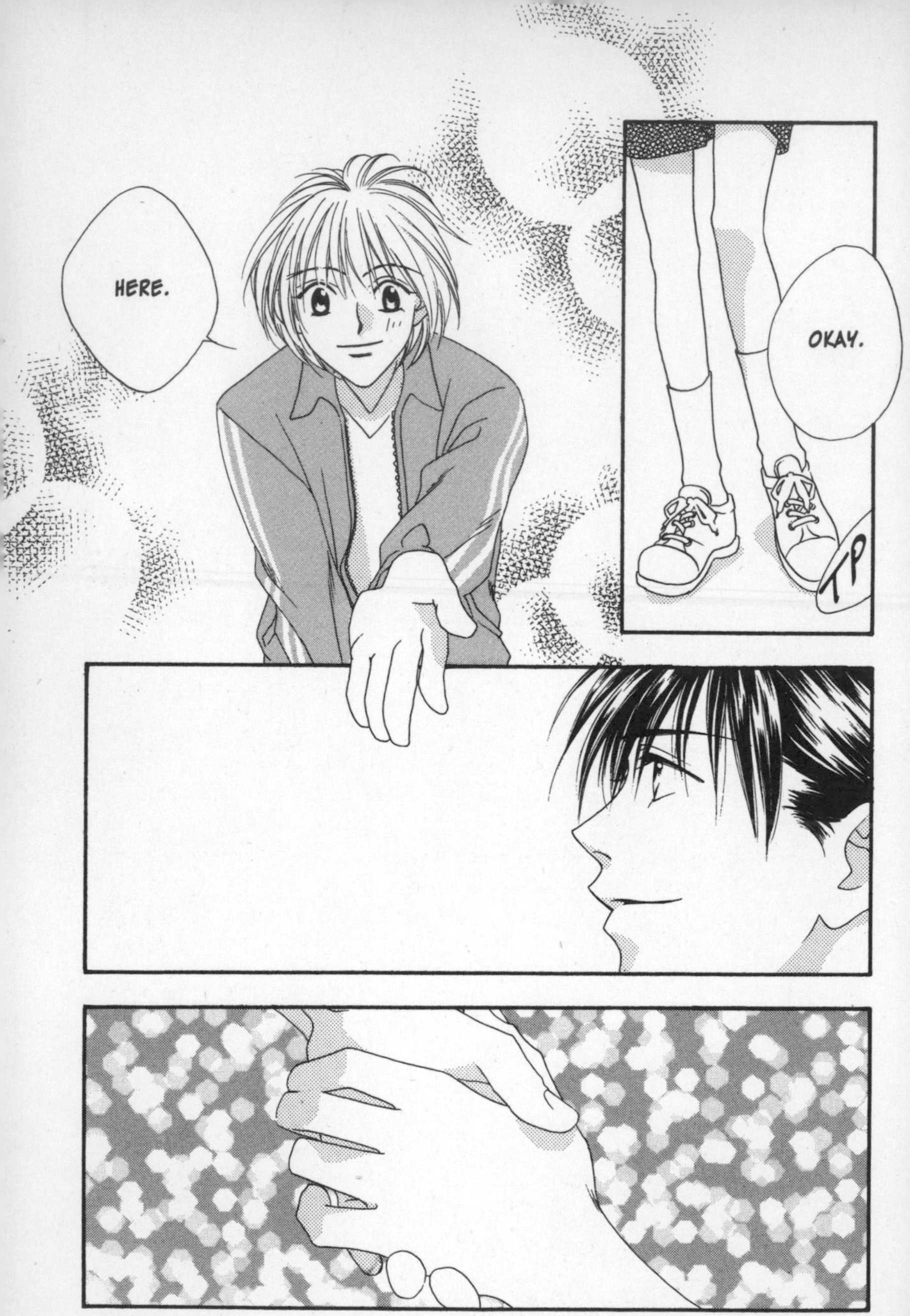
OKAY.
TP
HERE.

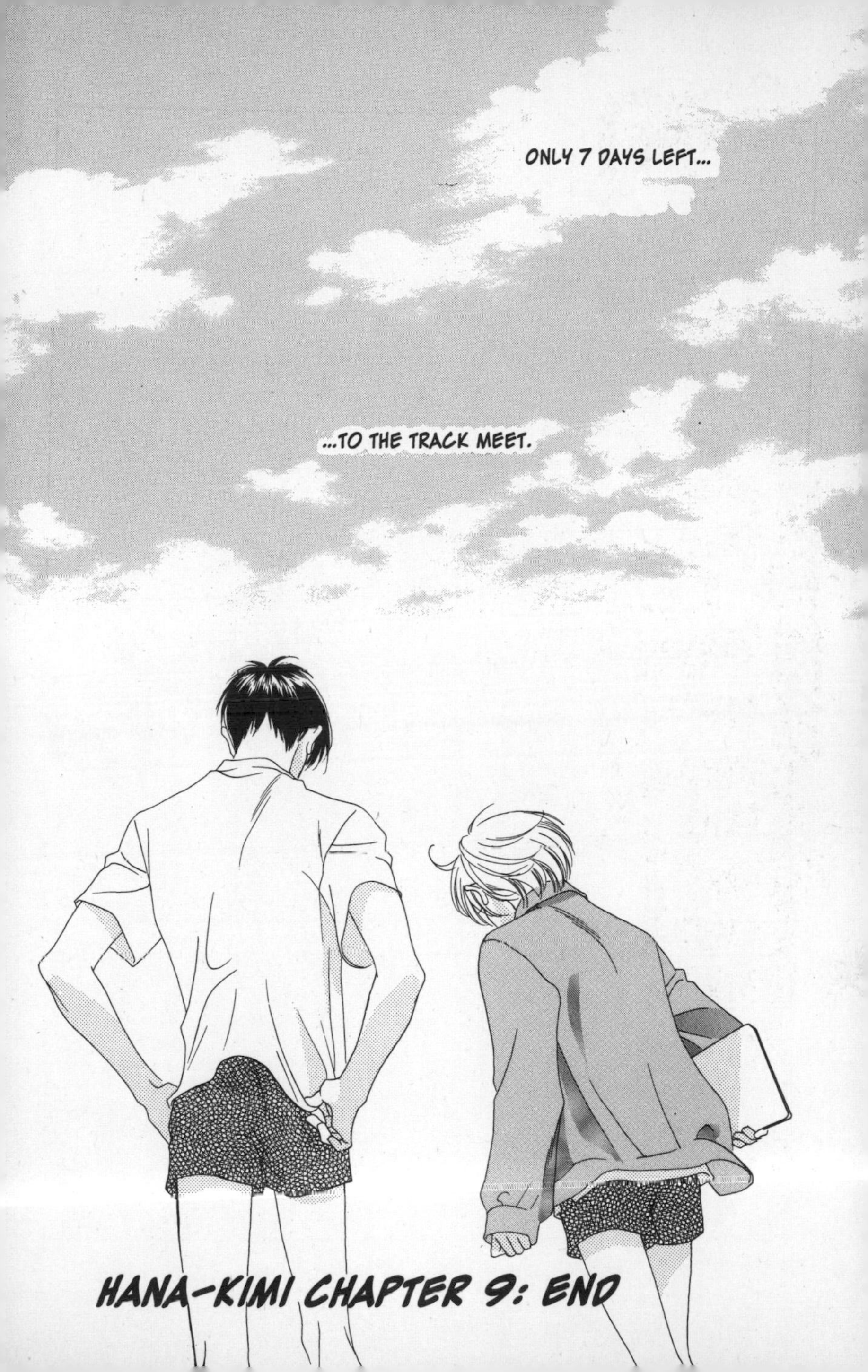
ONLY 7 DAYS LEFT...
...TO THE TRACK MEET.
HANA-KIMI CHAPTER 9: END

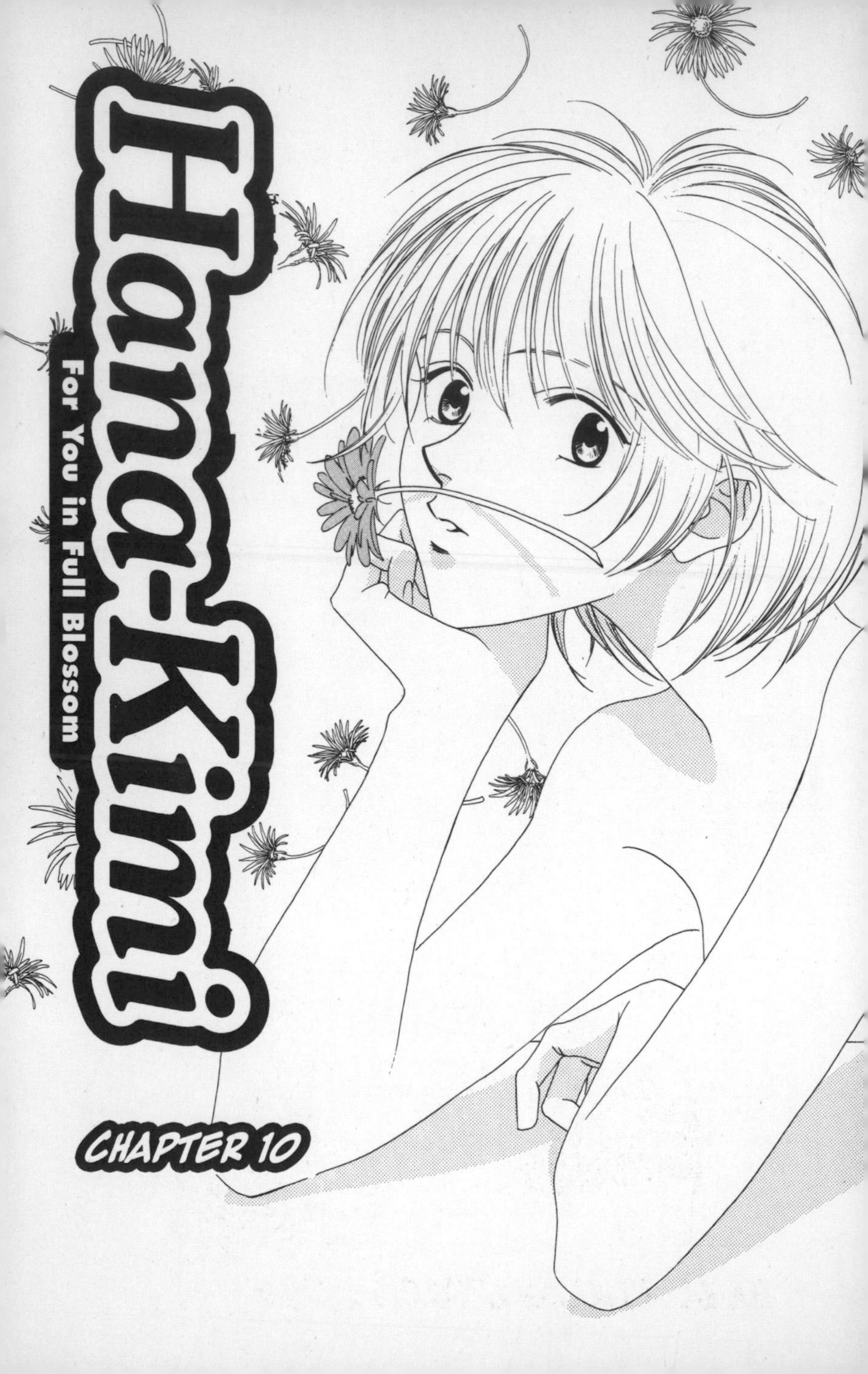
Hana-Kimi
For You in Full Blossom
CHAPTER 10

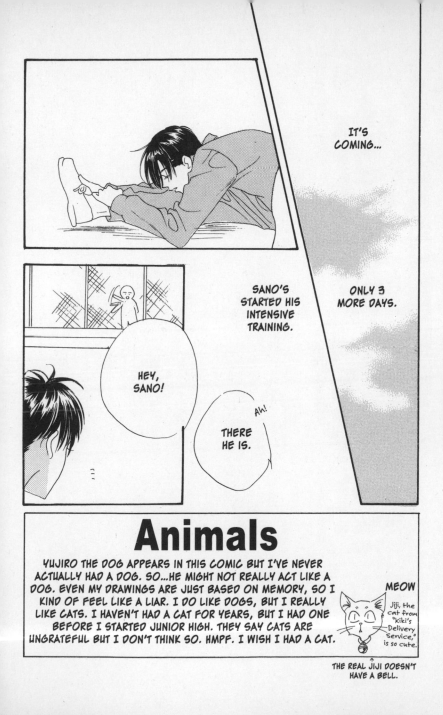

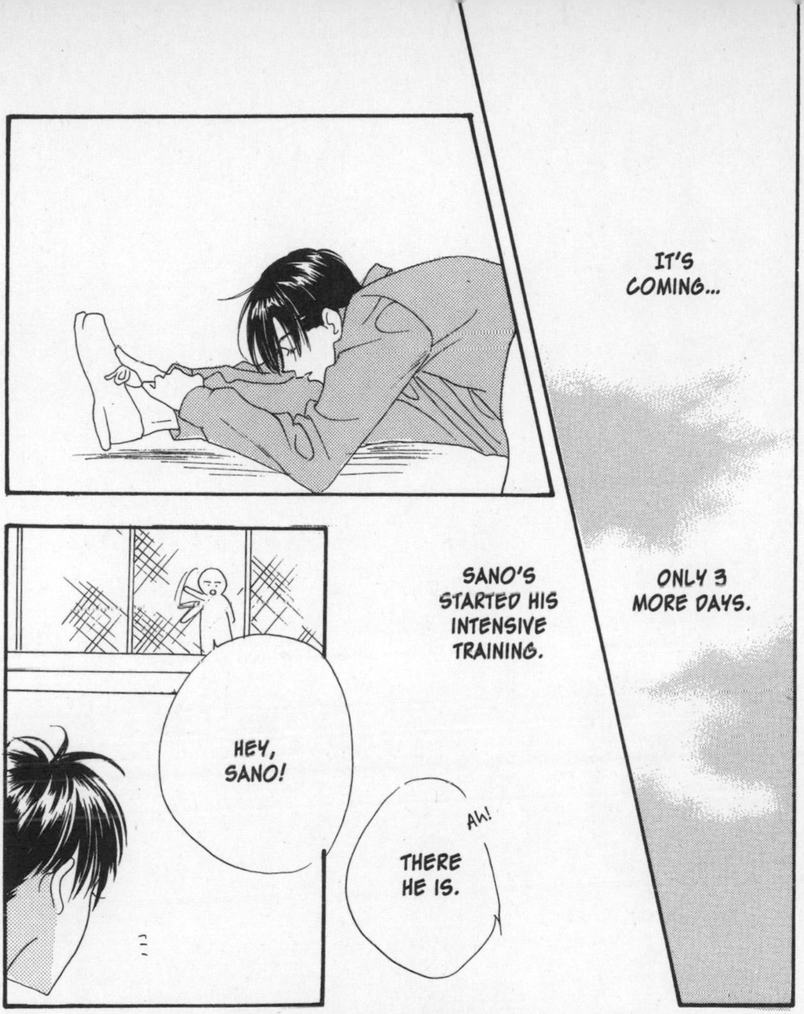
IT'S COMING...
ONLY 3 MORE DAYS.
SANO'S STARTED HIS INTENSIVE TRAINING.
Ah!
THERE HE IS.
HEY, SANO!

Animals

YUJIRO THE DOG APPEARS IN THIS COMIC BUT I'VE NEVER ACTUALLY HAD A DOG. SO...HE MIGHT NOT REALLY ACT LIKE A DOG. EVEN MY DRAWINGS ARE JUST BASED ON MEMORY, SO I KIND OF FEEL LIKE A LIAR. I DO LIKE DOGS, BUT I REALLY LIKE CATS. I HAVEN'T HAD A CAT FOR YEARS, BUT I HAD ONE BEFORE I STARTED JUNIOR HIGH. THEY SAY CATS ARE UNGRATEFUL BUT I DON'T THINK SO. HMPF. I WISH I HAD A CAT.

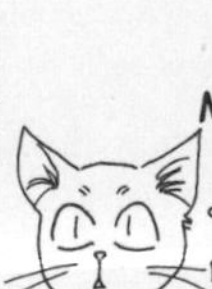
MEOW
Jiji, the cat from "Kiki's Delivery Service," is so cute.
THE REAL JIJI DOESN'T HAVE A BELL.

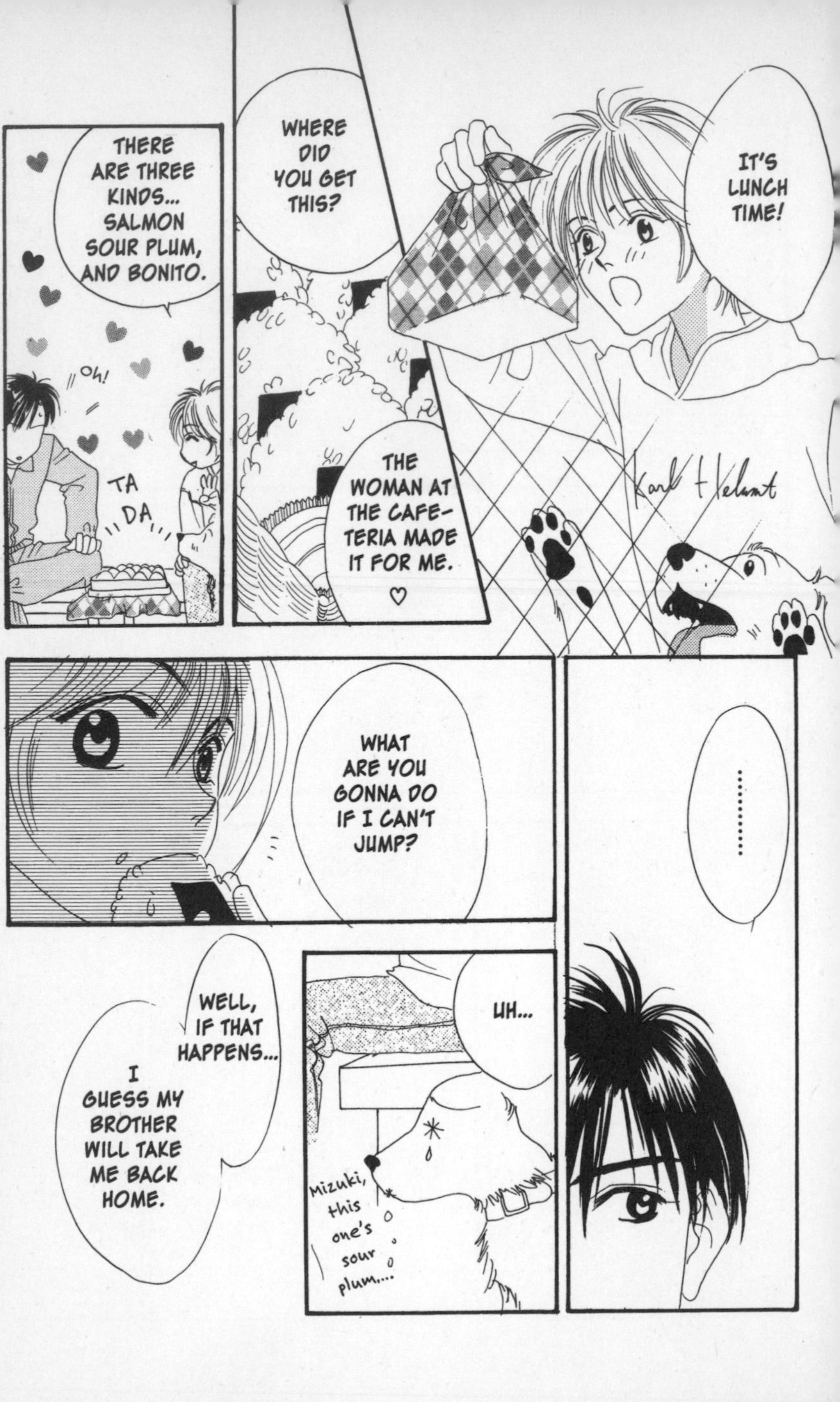
IT'S LUNCH TIME!
Karl + Helmut
WHERE DID YOU GET THIS?
THE WOMAN AT THE CAFETERIA MADE IT FOR ME. ♡
THERE ARE THREE KINDS... SALMON SOUR PLUM, AND BONITO.
Oh!
TA DA
....
WHAT ARE YOU GONNA DO IF I CAN'T JUMP?
UH...
Mizuki, this one's sour plum....
WELL, IF THAT HAPPENS...
I GUESS MY BROTHER WILL TAKE ME BACK HOME.

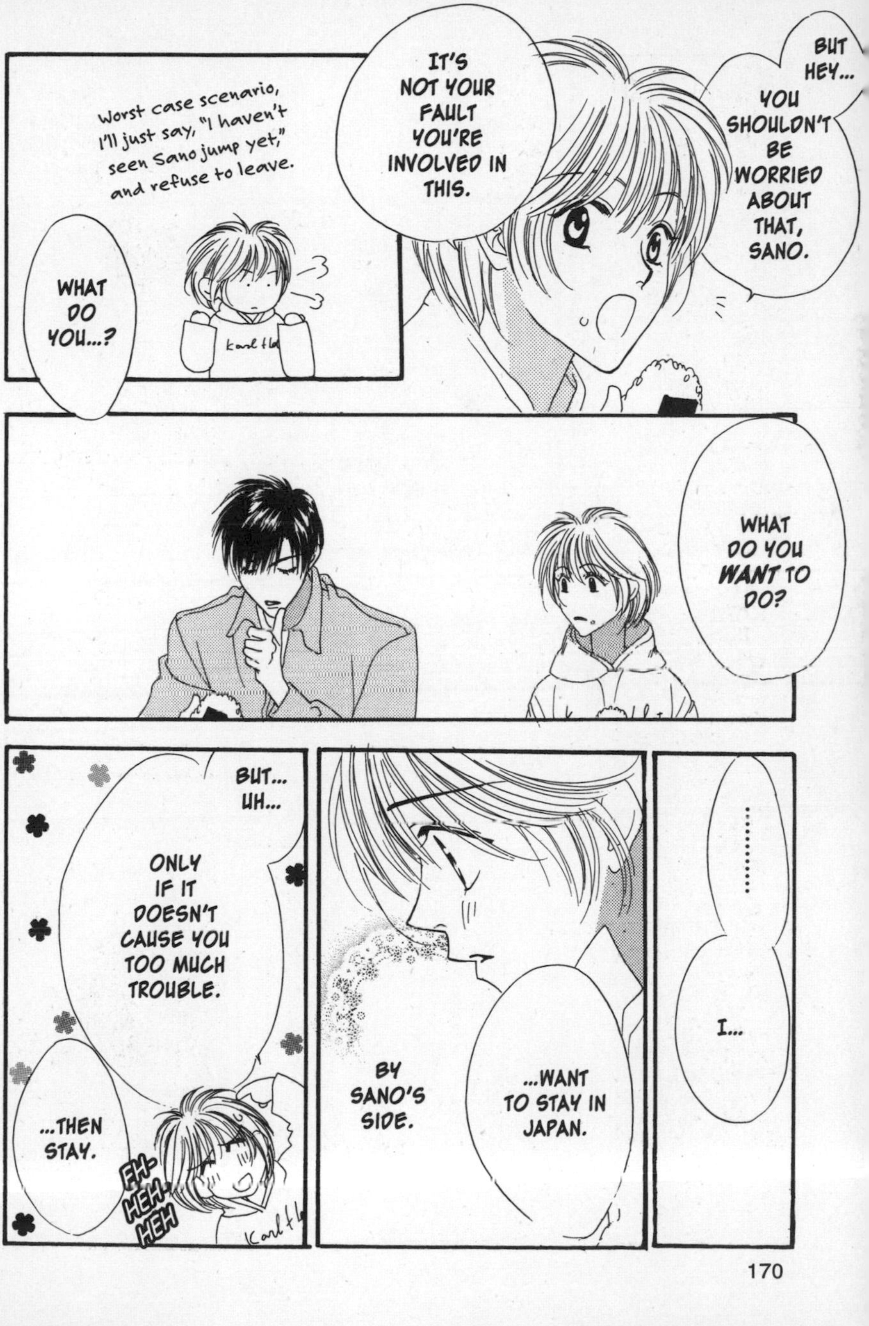
BUT HEY... YOU SHOULDN'T BE WORRIED ABOUT THAT, SANO.
IT'S NOT YOUR FAULT YOU'RE INVOLVED IN THIS.
Worst case scenario, I'll just say, "I haven't seen Sano jump yet," and refuse to leave.
WHAT DO YOU...?
WHAT DO YOU WANT TO DO?
......
I...
...WANT TO STAY IN JAPAN.
BY SANO'S SIDE.
BUT... UH...
ONLY IF IT DOESN'T CAUSE YOU TOO MUCH TROUBLE.
...THEN STAY.
FH-HEH-HEH

Whispered Secrets

Me and Hana-Kimi

NOW THAT I THINK ABOUT IT, THIS IS MY FIRST SERIES THAT'S GONE PAST 6 CHAPTERS. I'M USED TO DOING SELF-CONTAINED 4-CHAPTER MANGA, SO THIS WAS A LITTLE MUCH FOR ME AT FIRST...IT WAS A REAL ADVENTURE HAVING TO THINK OF THOSE TWO EXTRA CHAPTERS. BUT FINALLY I'VE GOTTEN THE HANG OF DRAWING THE CHARACTERS AND IT'S GETTING EASIER. IT'S FUN TO DRAW THEM (EVEN WHEN I ONLY HAVE THREE DAYS TO DO IT). AND IT'S STILL CONTINUING! I DON'T KNOW WHAT'S GOING TO HAPPEN NEXT, BUT I'M GOING TO WORK HARD TO MAKE THIS A GREAT MANGA. I'M HANGING IN THERE.

SEE you NEXT Book! ByE²

1997. 7. 7

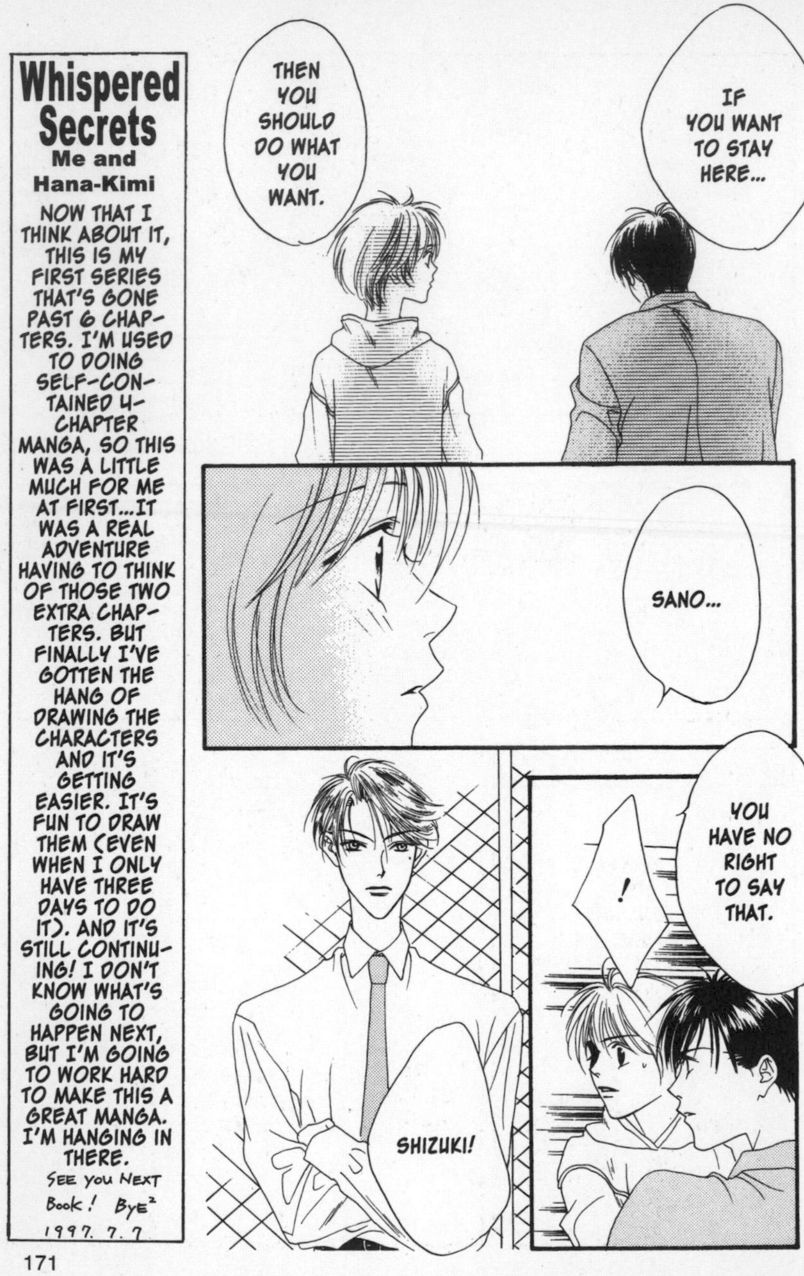
IF YOU WANT TO STAY HERE...
THEN YOU SHOULD DO WHAT YOU WANT.
SANO...
YOU HAVE NO RIGHT TO SAY THAT.
!
SHIZUKI!

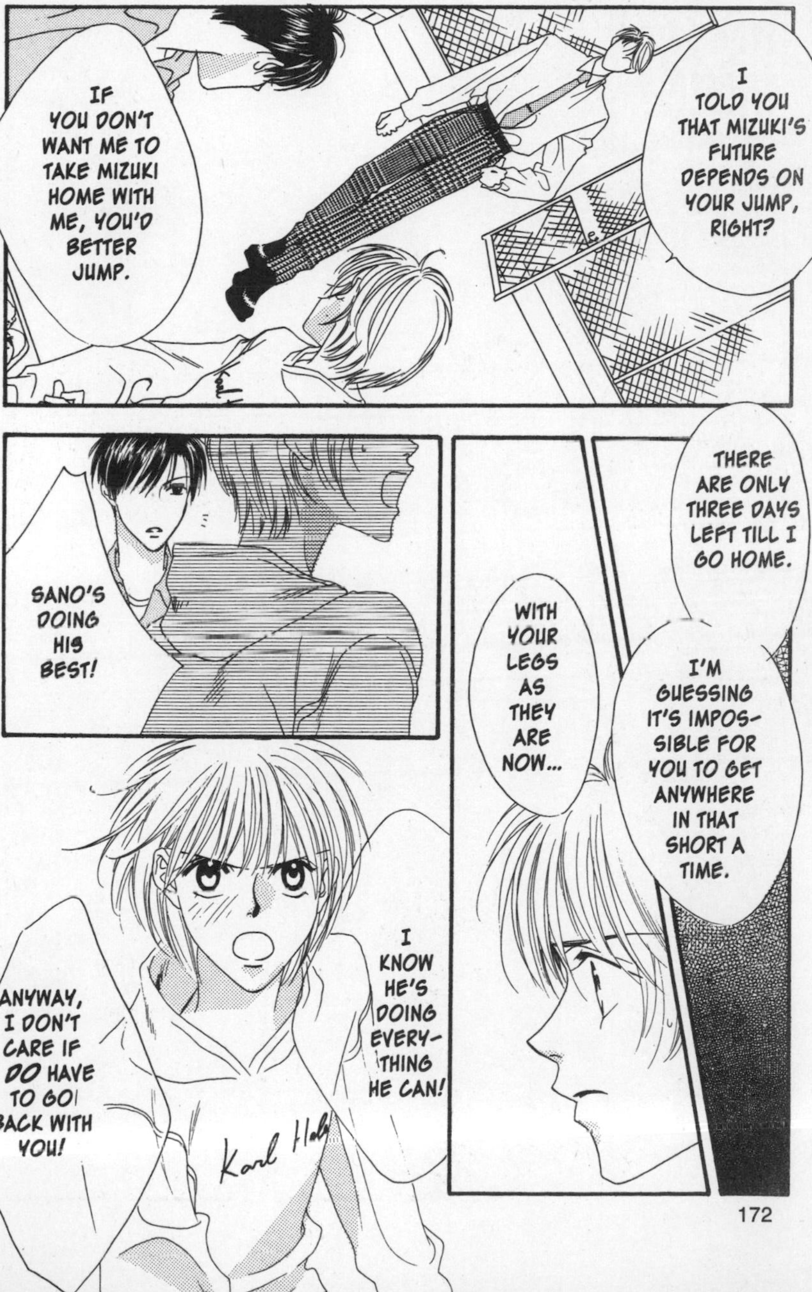
I TOLD YOU THAT MIZUKI'S FUTURE DEPENDS ON YOUR JUMP, RIGHT?
IF YOU DON'T WANT ME TO TAKE MIZUKI HOME WITH ME, YOU'D BETTER JUMP.
THERE ARE ONLY THREE DAYS LEFT TILL I GO HOME.
WITH YOUR LEGS AS THEY ARE NOW...
I'M GUESSING IT'S IMPOSSIBLE FOR YOU TO GET ANYWHERE IN THAT SHORT A TIME.
SANO'S DOING HIS BEST!
I KNOW HE'S DOING EVERY-THING HE CAN!
ANYWAY, I DON'T CARE IF I *DO* HAVE TO GO BACK WITH YOU!

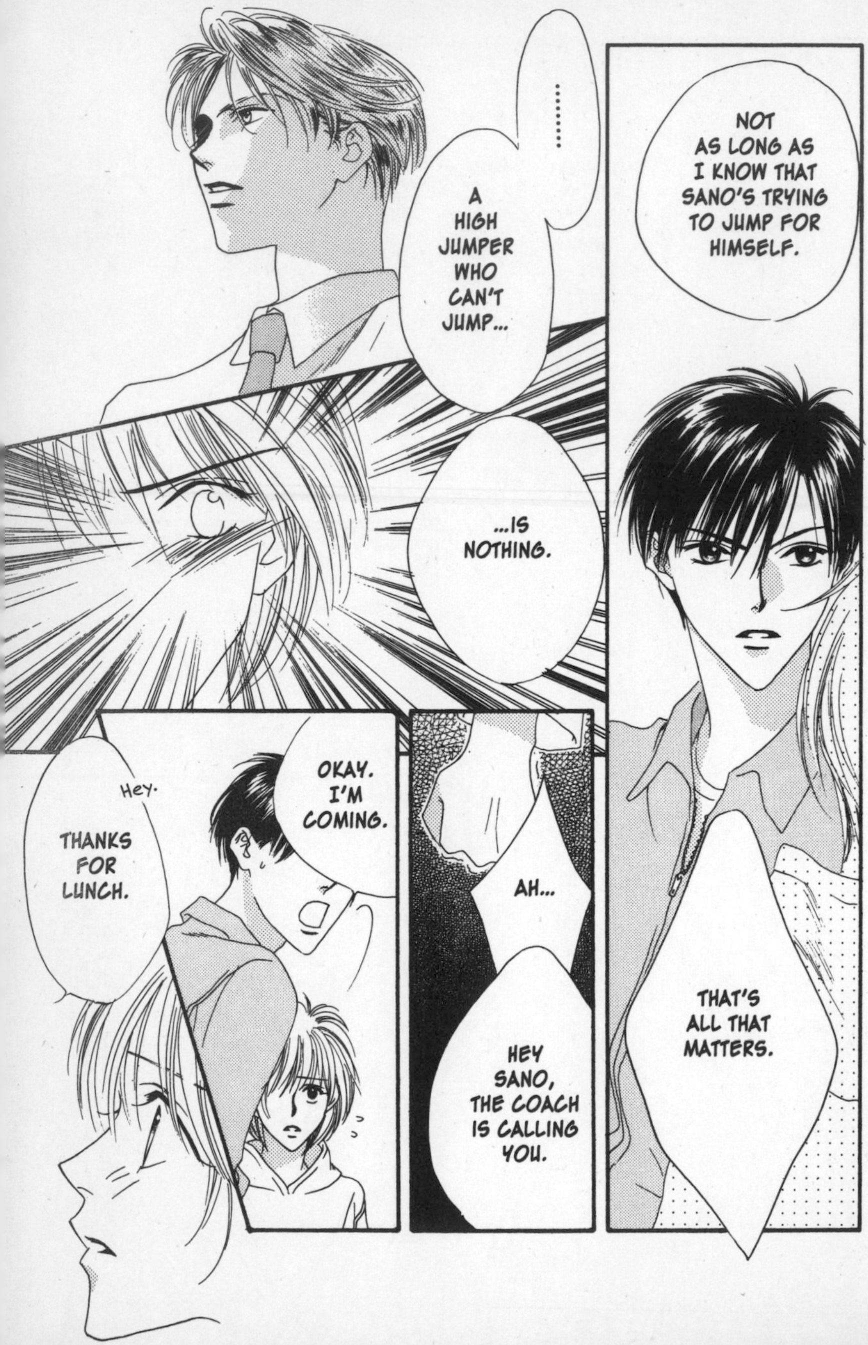
NOT AS LONG AS I KNOW THAT SANO'S TRYING TO JUMP FOR HIMSELF.
THAT'S ALL THAT MATTERS.
......
A HIGH JUMPER WHO CAN'T JUMP...
...IS NOTHING.
AH...
HEY SANO, THE COACH IS CALLING YOU.
OKAY. I'M COMING.
Hey.
THANKS FOR LUNCH.

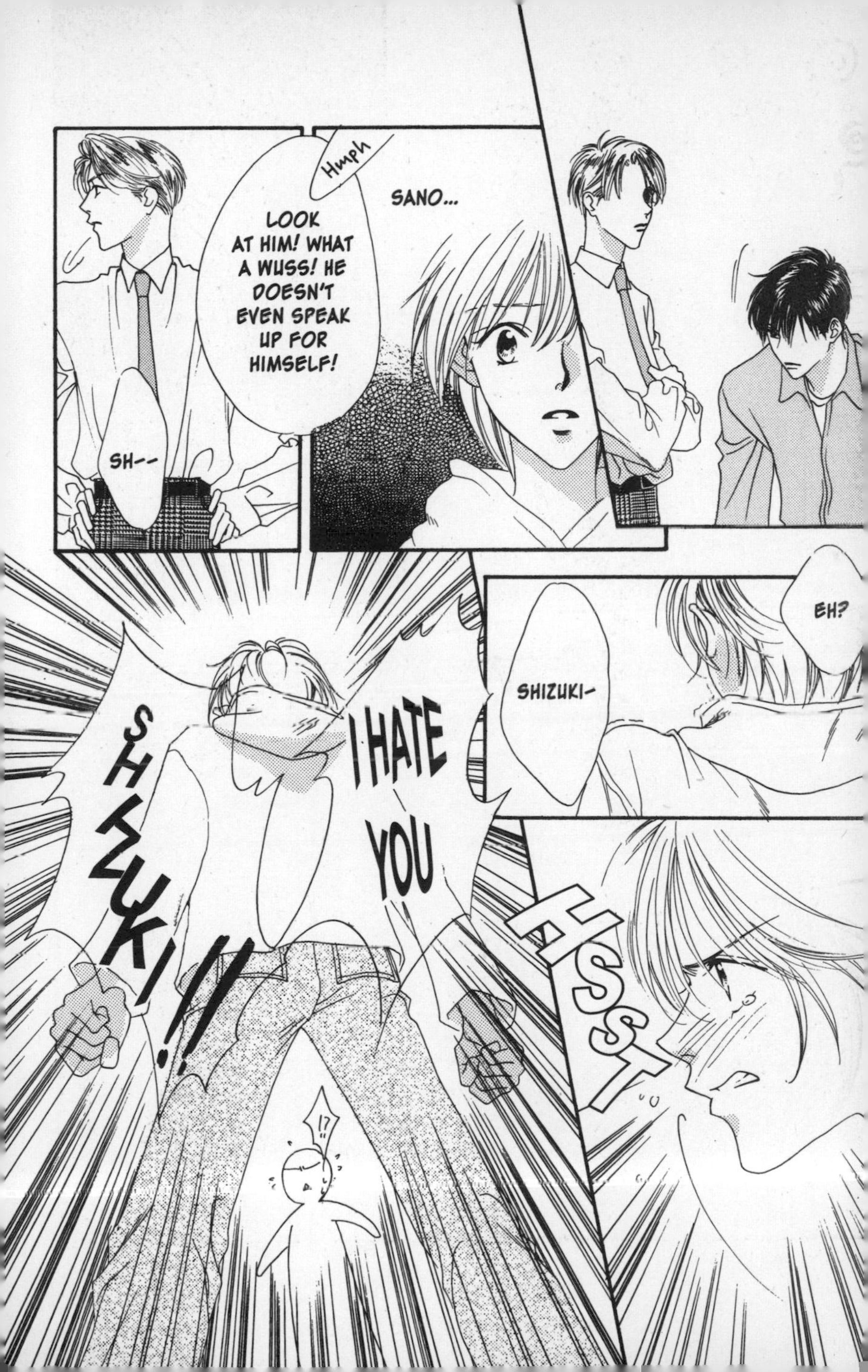
Hmph
SANO...
LOOK AT HIM! WHAT A WUSS! HE DOESN'T EVEN SPEAK UP FOR HIMSELF!
SH--
EH?
SHIZUKI-
HSST
I HATE YOU
SHIZUKI!!
!?

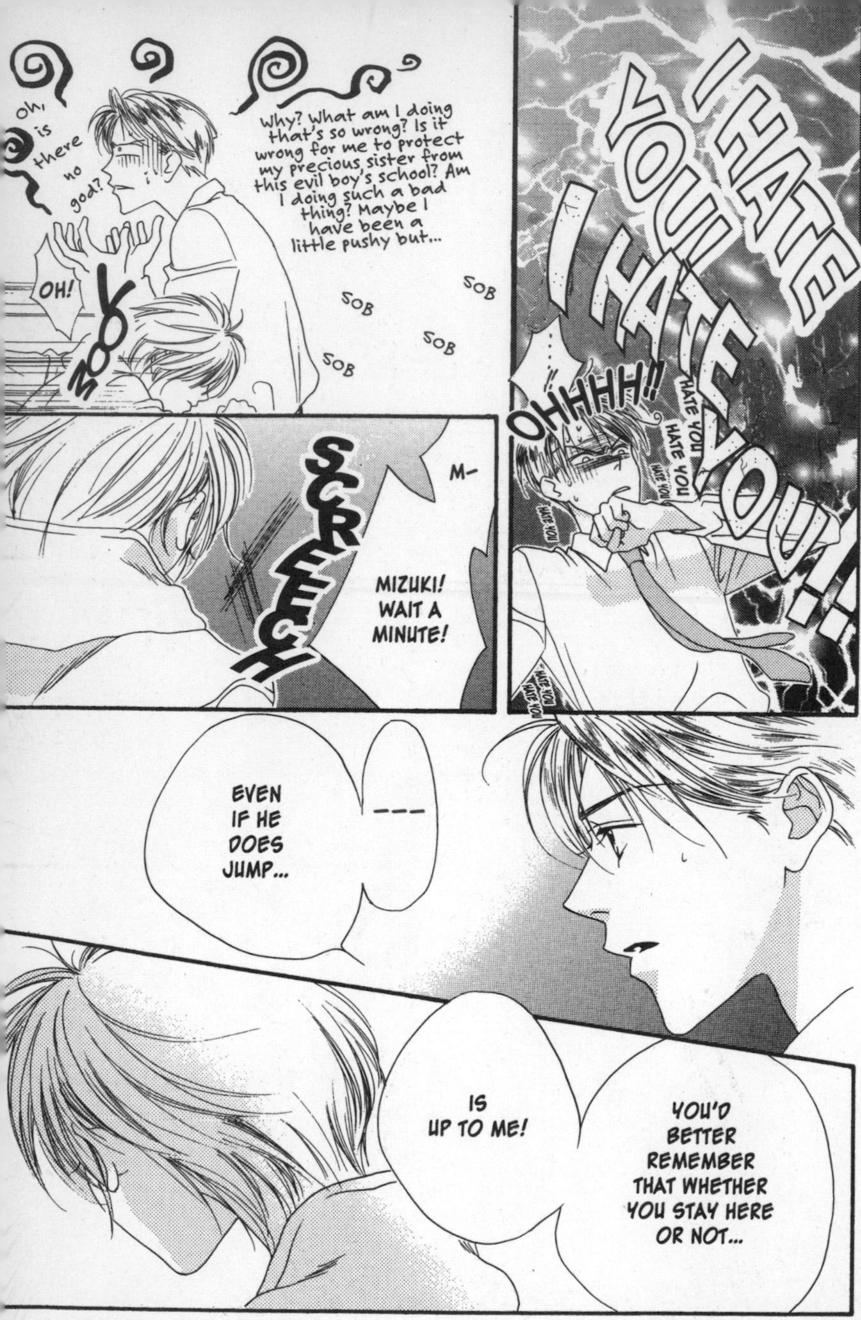
I HATE YOU!!
I HATE YOU!!
...
OHHHH!!
HATE YOU
HATE YOU
HATE YOU
HATE YOU
HATE YOU
HATE YOU
Why? What am I doing that's so wrong? Is it wrong for me to protect my precious sister from this evil boy's school? Am I doing such a bad thing? Maybe I have been a little pushy but...
oh, is there no god?
OH!
ZOOM
SOB
SOB
SOB
SOB
M-
SCREECH
MIZUKI! WAIT A MINUTE!

EVEN IF HE DOES JUMP...
YOU'D BETTER REMEMBER THAT WHETHER YOU STAY HERE OR NOT...
IS UP TO ME!

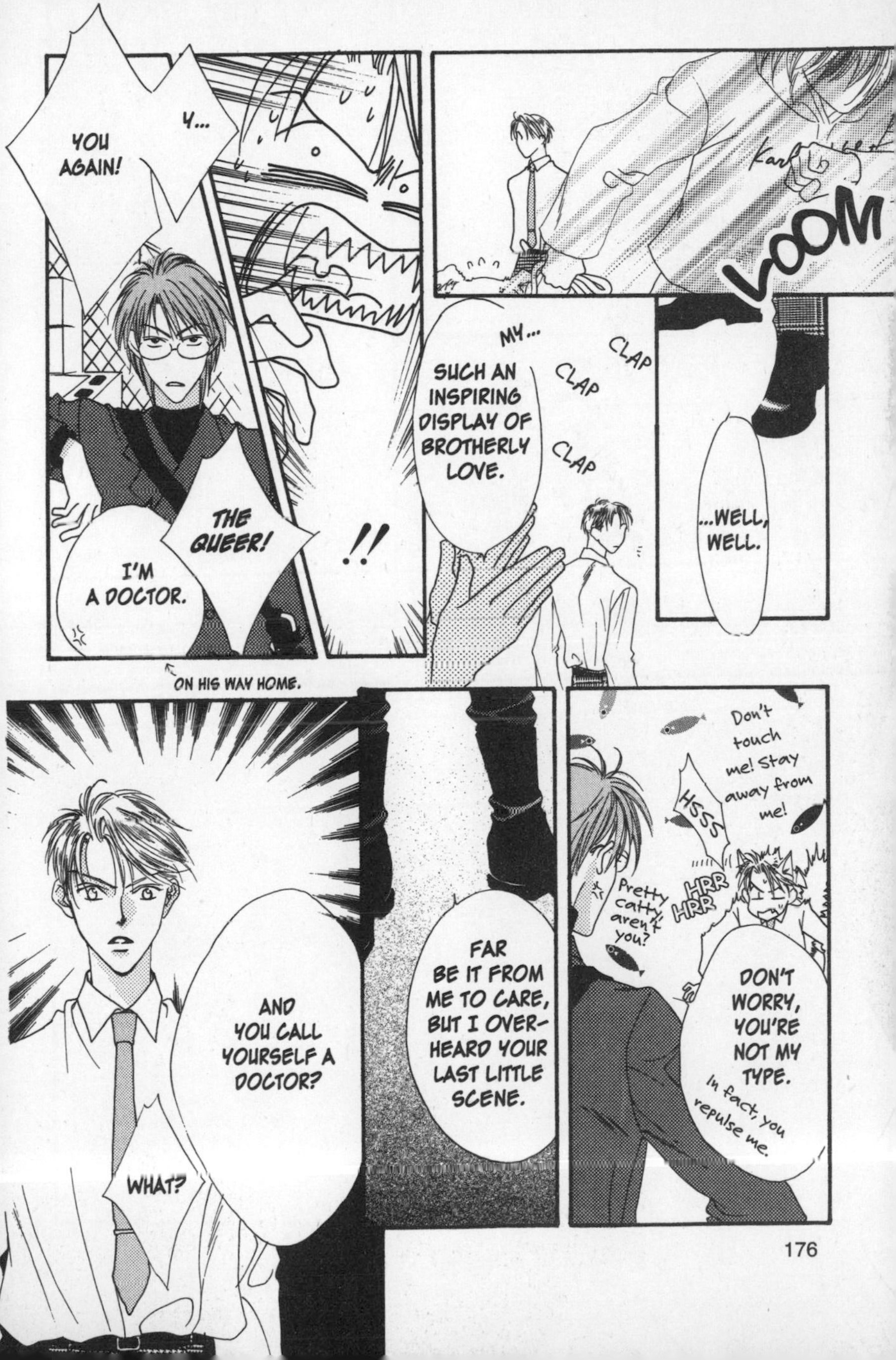
Karl
LOOM
...WELL, WELL.
CLAP
CLAP
CLAP
MY...
SUCH AN INSPIRING DISPLAY OF BROTHERLY LOVE.
!!
Y...
YOU AGAIN!
THE QUEER!
I'M A DOCTOR.
ON HIS WAY HOME.
Don't touch me! Stay away from me!
HSSS
HRR
HRR
Pretty catty aren't you?
DON'T WORRY, YOU'RE NOT MY TYPE.
In fact, you repulse me.
FAR BE IT FROM ME TO CARE, BUT I OVERHEARD YOUR LAST LITTLE SCENE.
AND YOU CALL YOURSELF A DOCTOR?
WHAT?

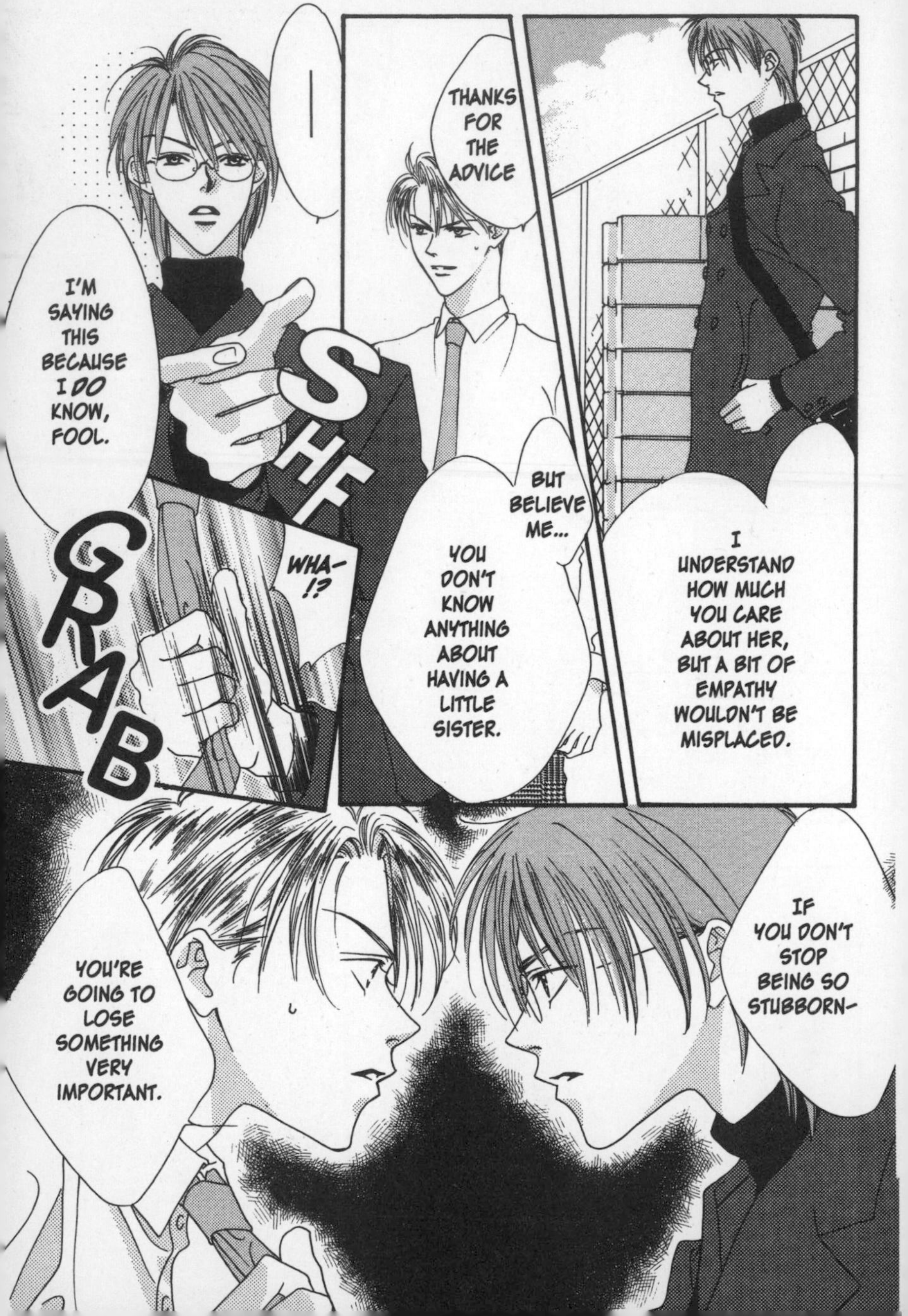
I UNDERSTAND HOW MUCH YOU CARE ABOUT HER, BUT A BIT OF EMPATHY WOULDN'T BE MISPLACED.
THANKS FOR THE ADVICE
BUT BELIEVE ME...
YOU DON'T KNOW ANYTHING ABOUT HAVING A LITTLE SISTER.
I'M SAYING THIS BECAUSE I *DO* KNOW, FOOL.
SHF
WHA-!?
GRAB
IF YOU DON'T STOP BEING SO STUBBORN-
YOU'RE GOING TO LOSE SOMETHING VERY IMPORTANT.

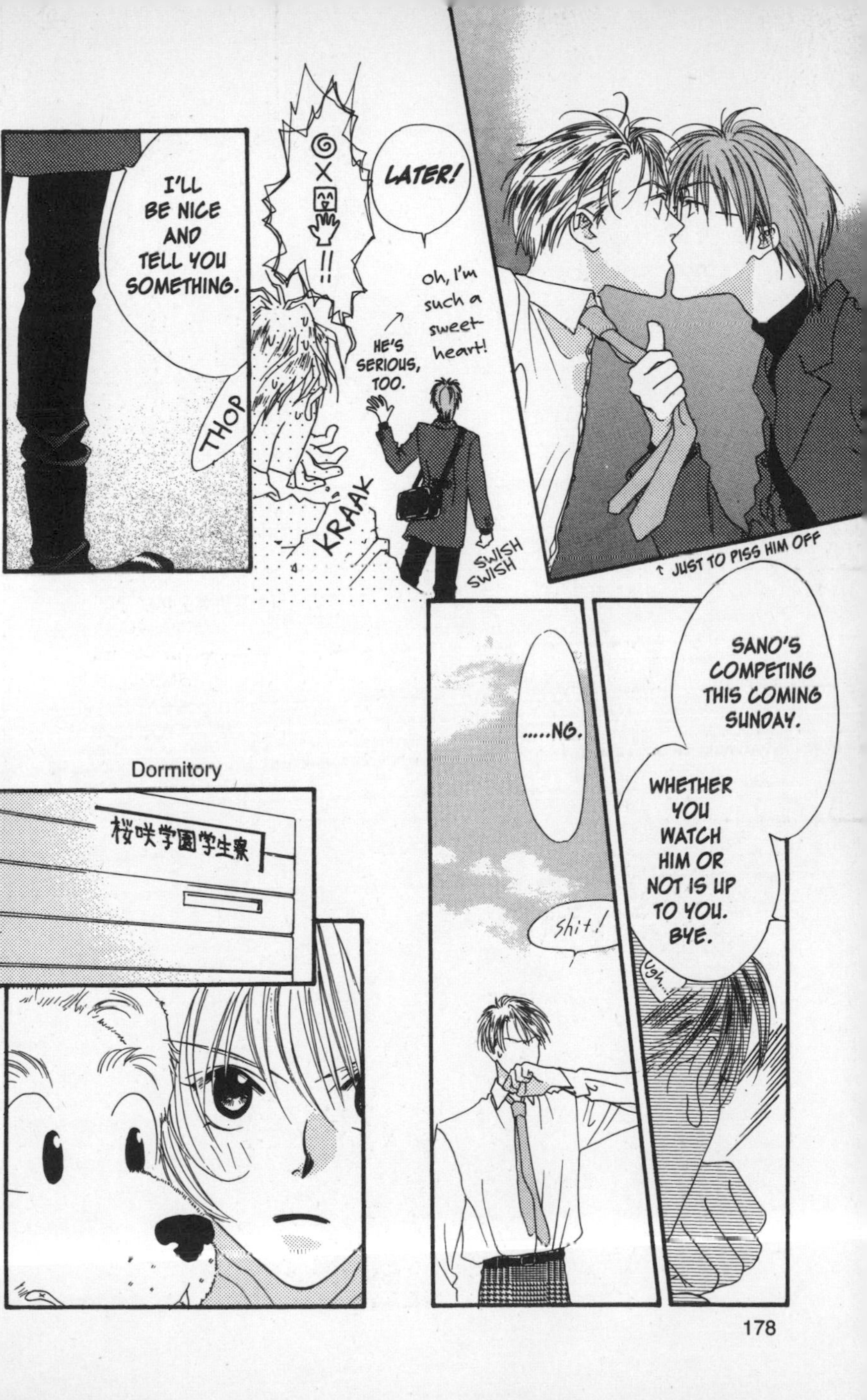
↑ JUST TO PISS HIM OFF
LATER!
Oh, I'm such a sweet heart!
HE'S SERIOUS, TOO.
!!
KRAAK
SWISH SWISH
I'LL BE NICE AND TELL YOU SOMETHING.
THOP
SANO'S COMPETING THIS COMING SUNDAY.
WHETHER YOU WATCH HIM OR NOT IS UP TO YOU. BYE.
Ugh...
.....NG.
Shit!
Dormitory
桜咲学園学生寮

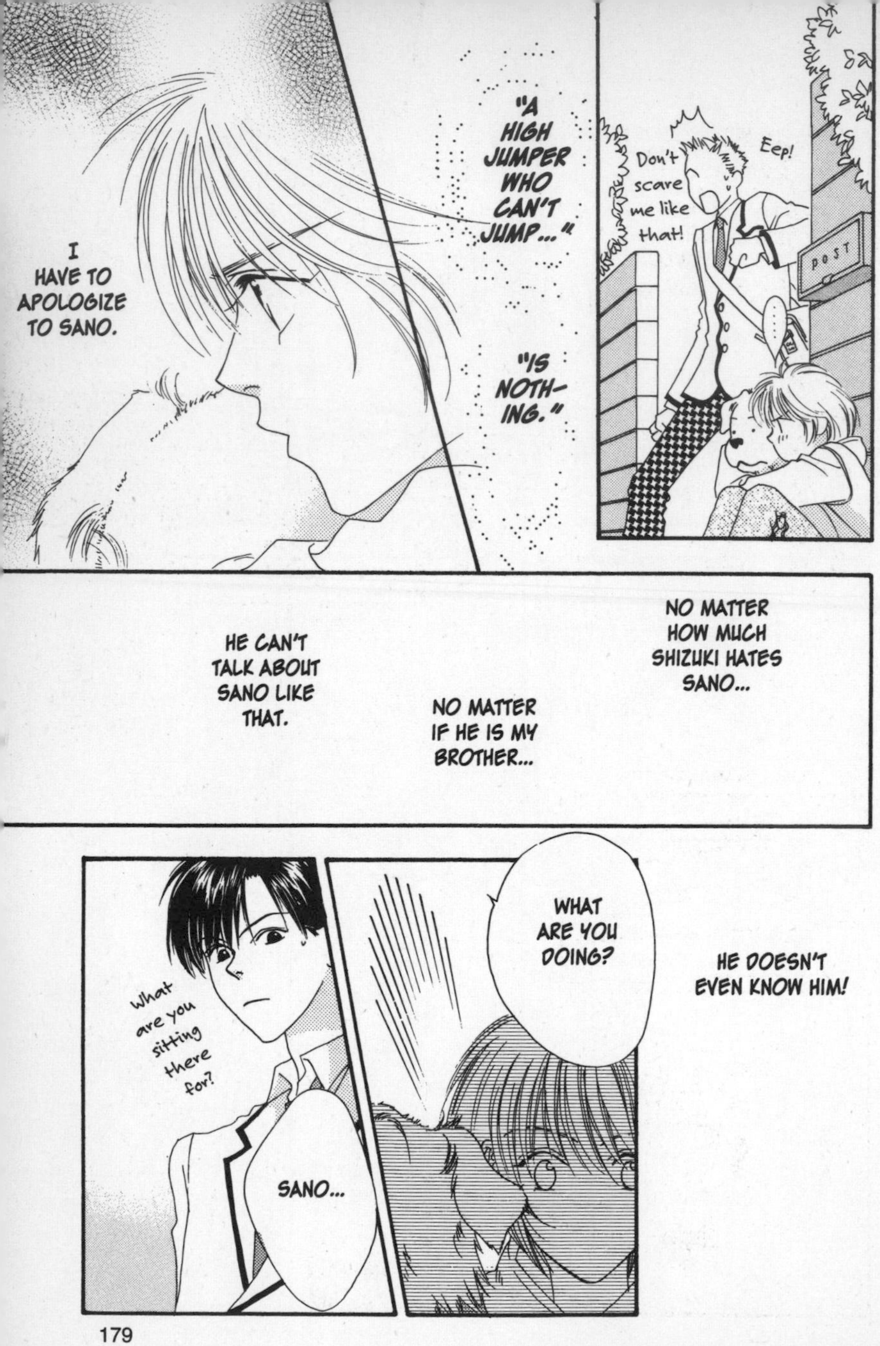
Eep!
Don't scare me like that!
"A HIGH JUMPER WHO CAN'T JUMP..."
"IS NOTHING."
I HAVE TO APOLOGIZE TO SANO.
NO MATTER HOW MUCH SHIZUKI HATES SANO...
NO MATTER IF HE IS MY BROTHER...
HE CAN'T TALK ABOUT SANO LIKE THAT.
HE DOESN'T EVEN KNOW HIM!
WHAT ARE YOU DOING?
what are you sitting there for?
SANO...

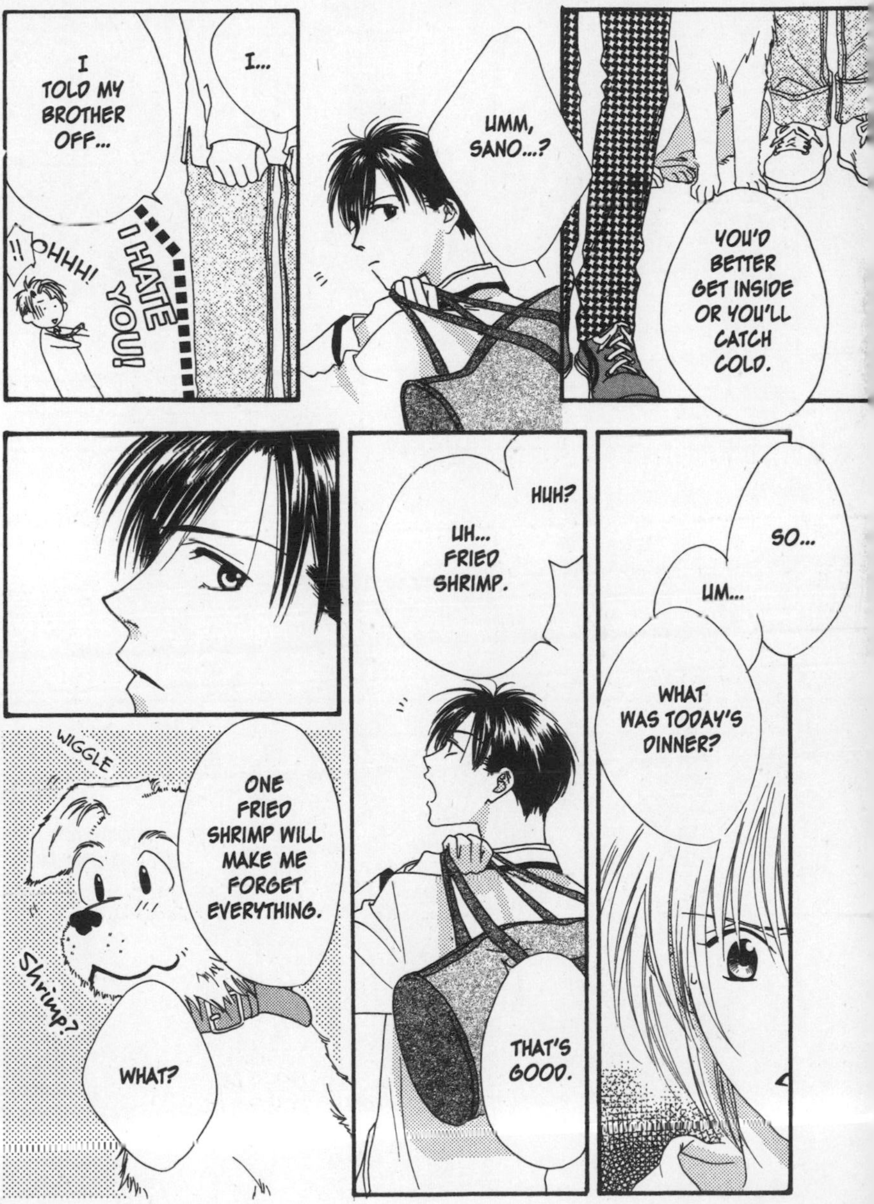
YOU'D BETTER GET INSIDE OR YOU'LL CATCH COLD.
UMM, SANO...?
I...
I TOLD MY BROTHER OFF...
I HATE YOU!
OHHH!!
SO...
UM...
WHAT WAS TODAY'S DINNER?
HUH?
UH... FRIED SHRIMP.
THAT'S GOOD.
ONE FRIED SHRIMP WILL MAKE ME FORGET EVERYTHING.
WIGGLE
Shrimp?
WHAT?

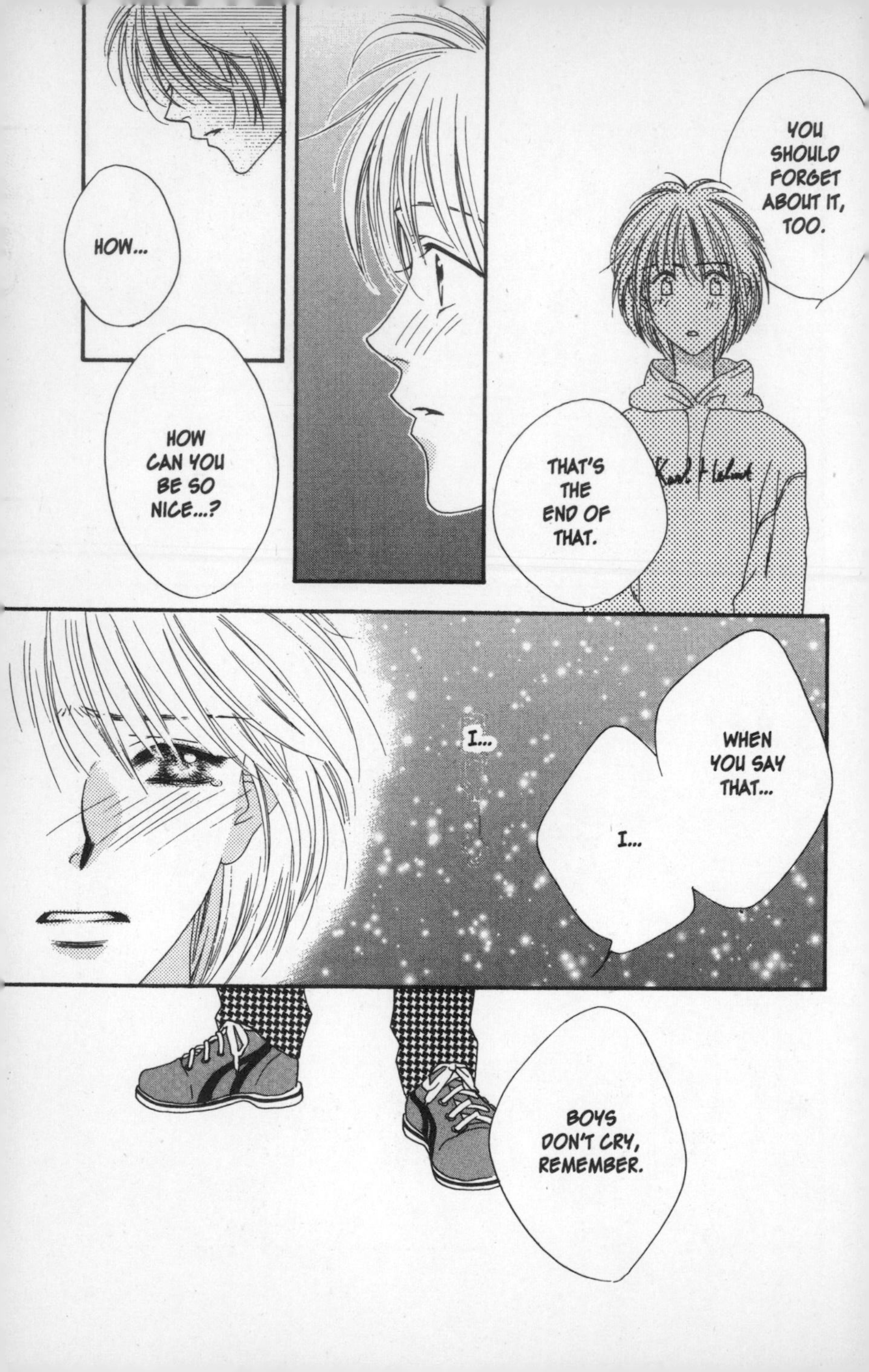
YOU SHOULD FORGET ABOUT IT, TOO.
THAT'S THE END OF THAT.
HOW...
HOW CAN YOU BE SO NICE...?
WHEN YOU SAY THAT...
I...
I...
BOYS DON'T CRY, REMEMBER.

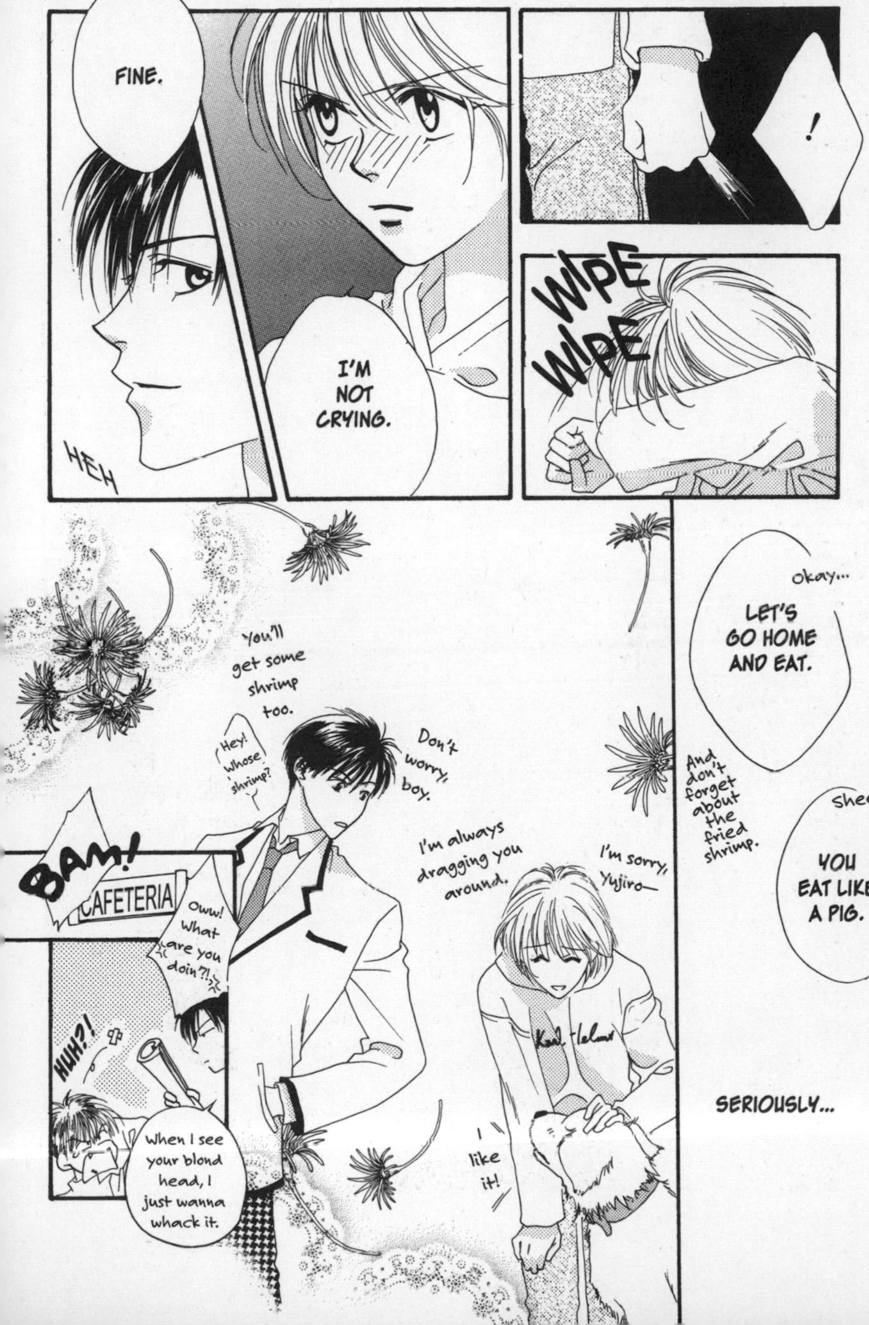
!
WIPE WIPE
I'M NOT CRYING.
FINE.
HEH
okay...
LET'S GO HOME AND EAT.
And don't forget about the fried shrimp.
Sheesh
YOU EAT LIKE A PIG.
SERIOUSLY...
I'm sorry, Yujiro—
I'm always dragging you around.
I like it!
Don't worry, boy.
You'll get some shrimp too.
Hey! Whose shrimp?
BAM!
CAFETERIA
Oww! What are you doin?!
HUH?!
When I see your blond head, I just wanna whack it.

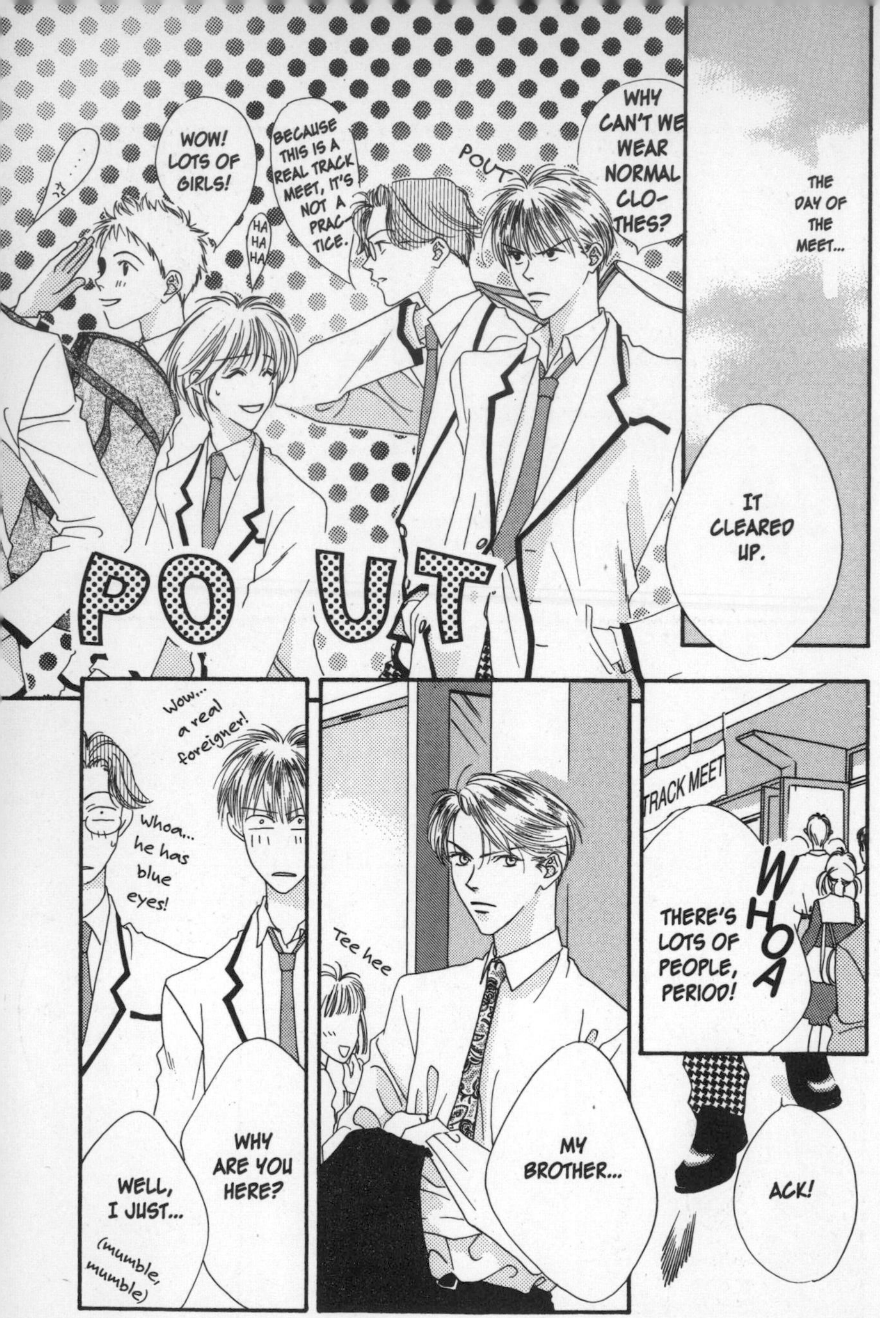
THE DAY OF THE MEET...
IT CLEARED UP.
WHY CAN'T WE WEAR NORMAL CLO-THES?
POUT
BECAUSE THIS IS A REAL TRACK MEET, IT'S NOT A PRAC-TICE.
HA HA HA
WOW! LOTS OF GIRLS!
POUT
TRACK MEET
WHOA
THERE'S LOTS OF PEOPLE, PERIOD!
ACK!
MY BROTHER...
Tee hee
Wow... a real foreigner!
Whoa... he has blue eyes!
WHY ARE YOU HERE?
WELL, I JUST...
(mumble, mumble)

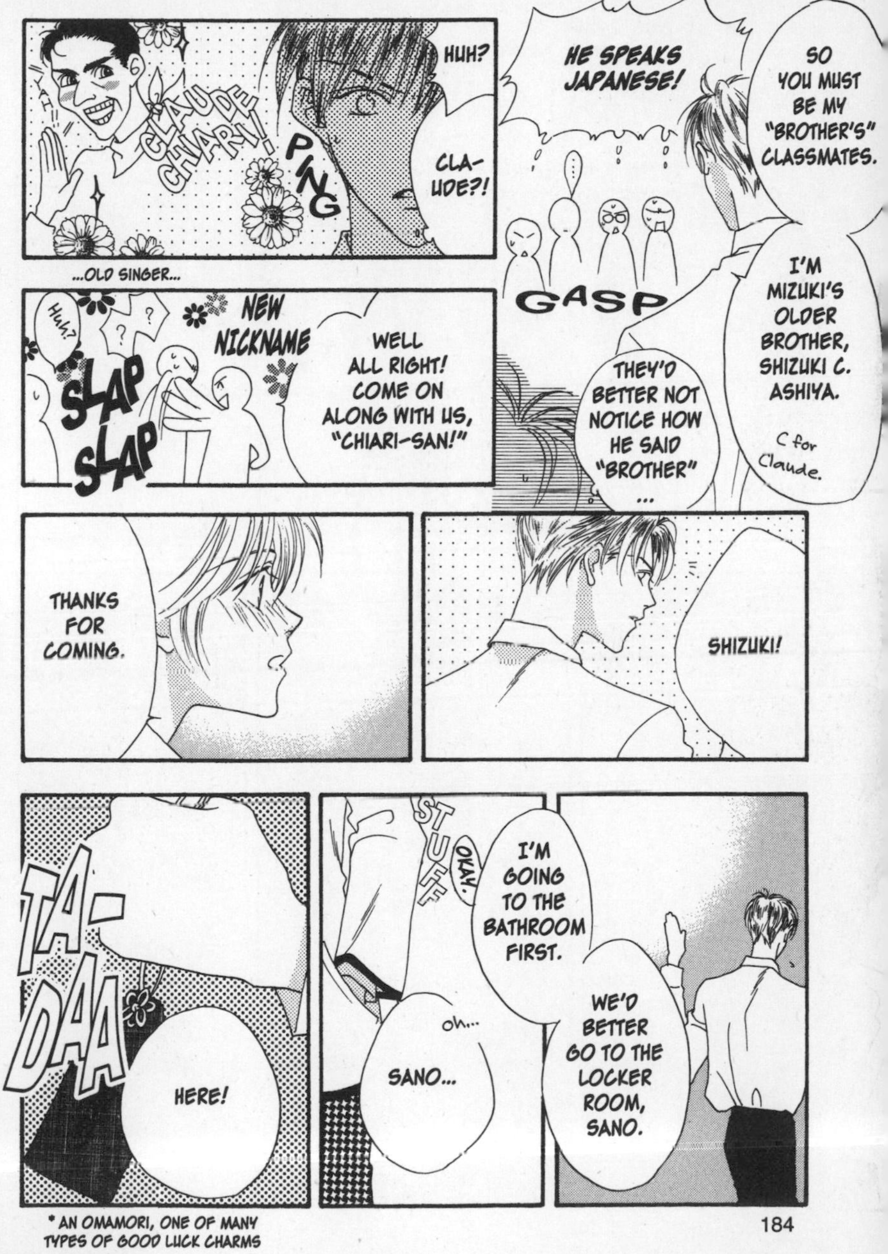
SO YOU MUST BE MY "BROTHER'S" CLASSMATES.
HE SPEAKS JAPANESE!
GASP
I'M MIZUKI'S OLDER BROTHER, SHIZUKI C. ASHIYA.
C for Claude.
THEY'D BETTER NOT NOTICE HOW HE SAID "BROTHER" ...
HUH?
CLAUDE?!
PING
CLAUDE CHIARI!
...OLD SINGER...
WELL ALL RIGHT! COME ON ALONG WITH US, "CHIARI-SAN!"
NEW NICKNAME
SLAP SLAP
Huh?
SHIZUKI!
THANKS FOR COMING.
I'M GOING TO THE BATHROOM FIRST.
WE'D BETTER GO TO THE LOCKER ROOM, SANO.
STUFF
OKAY.
oh...
SANO...
TA-DAA
HERE!

* AN OMAMORI, ONE OF MANY TYPES OF GOOD LUCK CHARMS

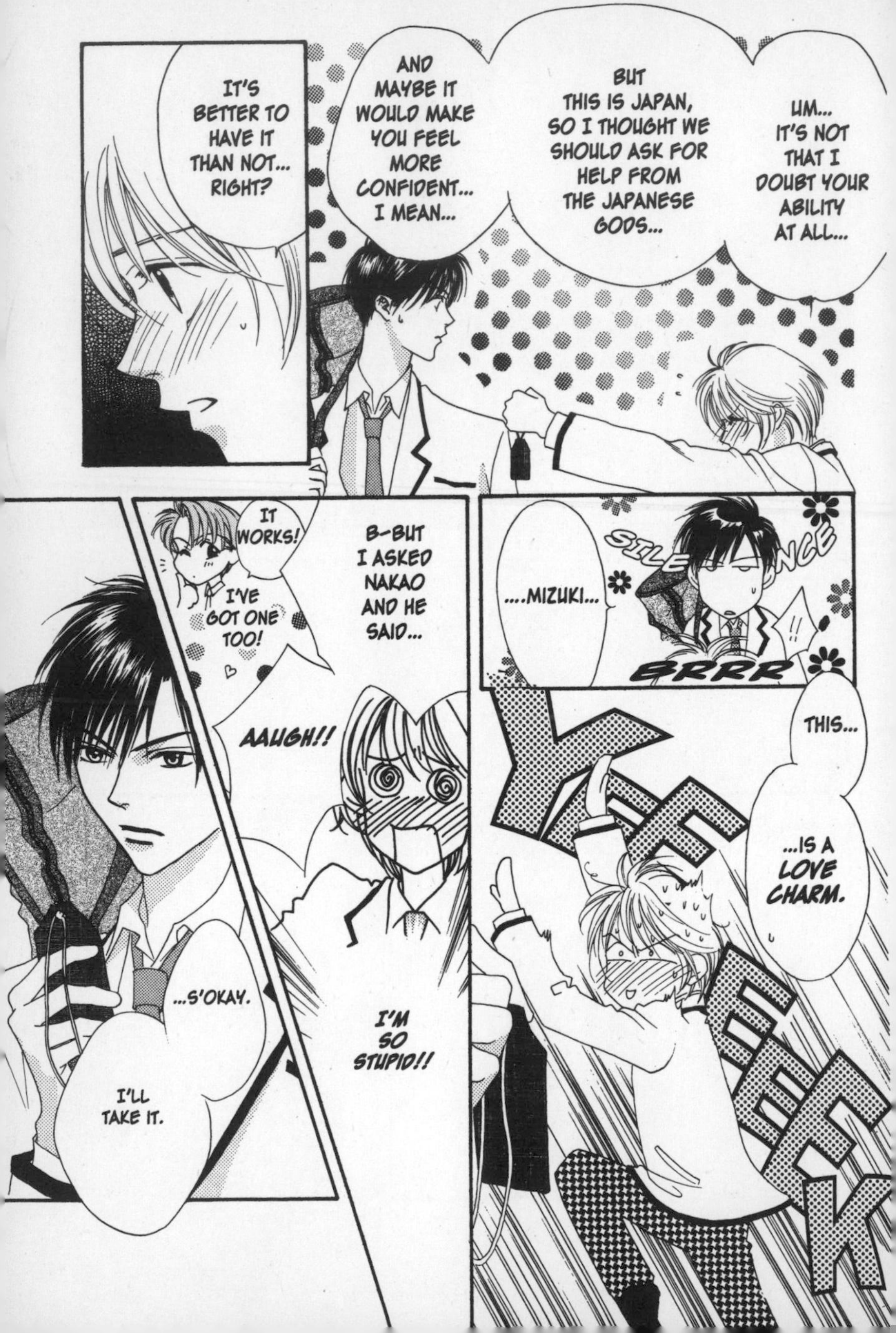
UM... IT'S NOT THAT I DOUBT YOUR ABILITY AT ALL...
BUT THIS IS JAPAN, SO I THOUGHT WE SHOULD ASK FOR HELP FROM THE JAPANESE GODS...
AND MAYBE IT WOULD MAKE YOU FEEL MORE CONFIDENT... I MEAN...
IT'S BETTER TO HAVE IT THAN NOT... RIGHT?
SILENCE
....MIZUKI...
!!
BRRRR
THIS...
...IS A LOVE CHARM.
B-BUT I ASKED NAKAO AND HE SAID...
IT WORKS!
I'VE GOT ONE TOO!
AAUGH!!
I'M SO STUPID!!
...S'OKAY.
I'LL TAKE IT.

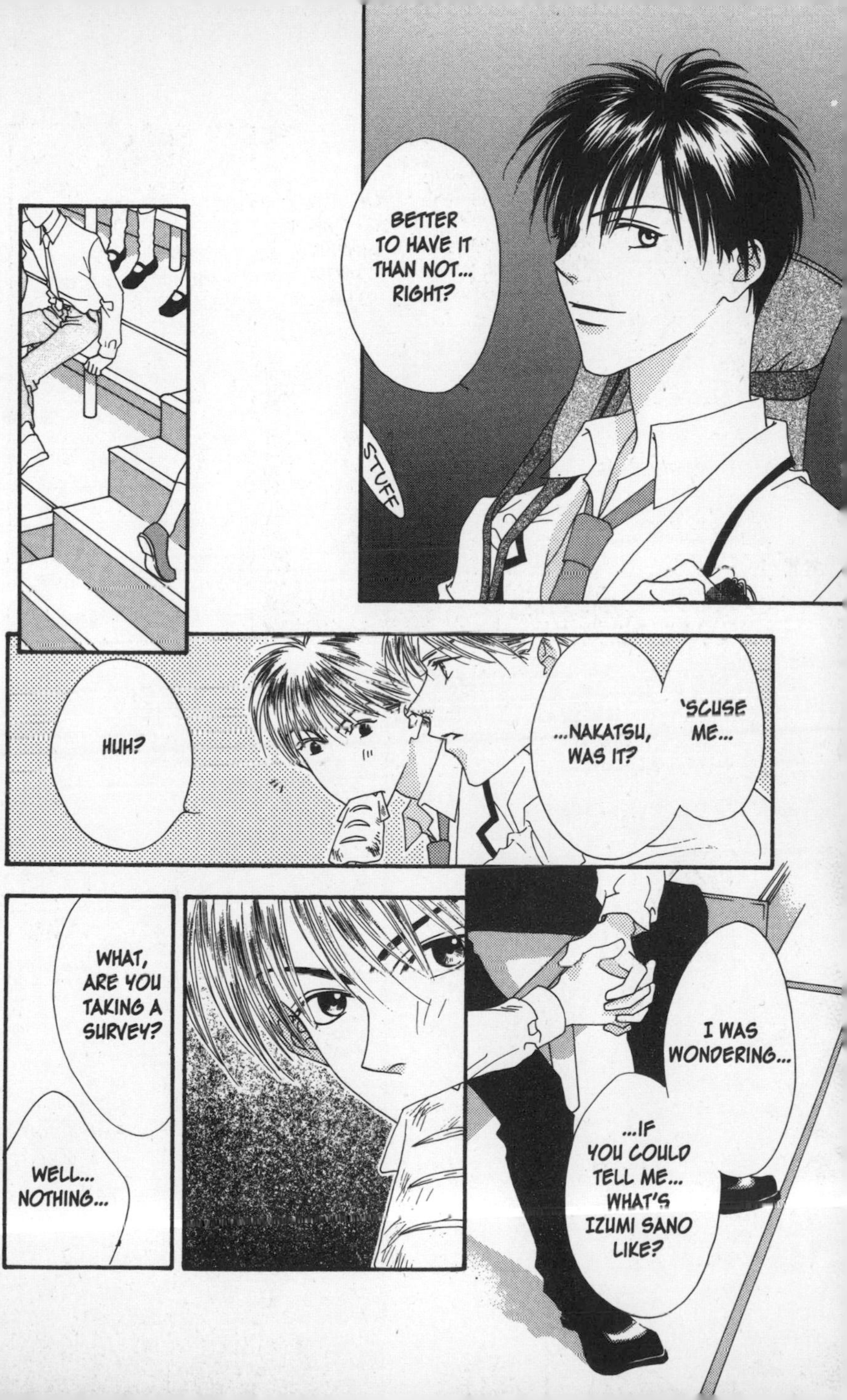
BETTER TO HAVE IT THAN NOT... RIGHT?
STUFF
'SCUSE ME...
...NAKATSU, WAS IT?
HUH?
I WAS WONDERING...
...IF YOU COULD TELL ME... WHAT'S IZUMI SANO LIKE?
WHAT, ARE YOU TAKING A SURVEY?
WELL... NOTHING...

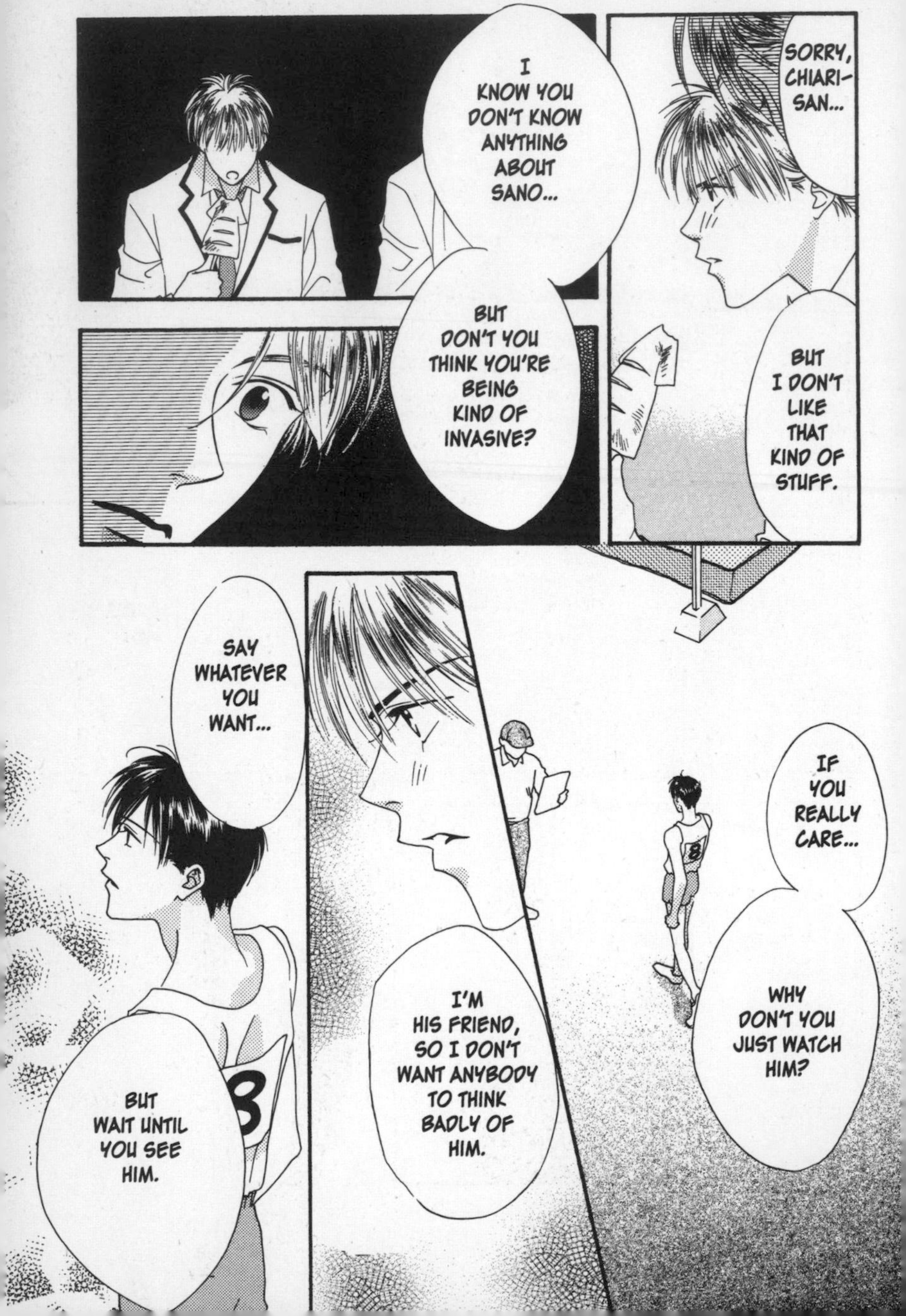
SORRY, CHIARI-SAN...
BUT I DON'T LIKE THAT KIND OF STUFF.
I KNOW YOU DON'T KNOW ANYTHING ABOUT SANO...
BUT DON'T YOU THINK YOU'RE BEING KIND OF INVASIVE?
IF YOU REALLY CARE...
WHY DON'T YOU JUST WATCH HIM?
I'M HIS FRIEND, SO I DON'T WANT ANYBODY TO THINK BADLY OF HIM.
SAY WHATEVER YOU WANT...
BUT WAIT UNTIL YOU SEE HIM.

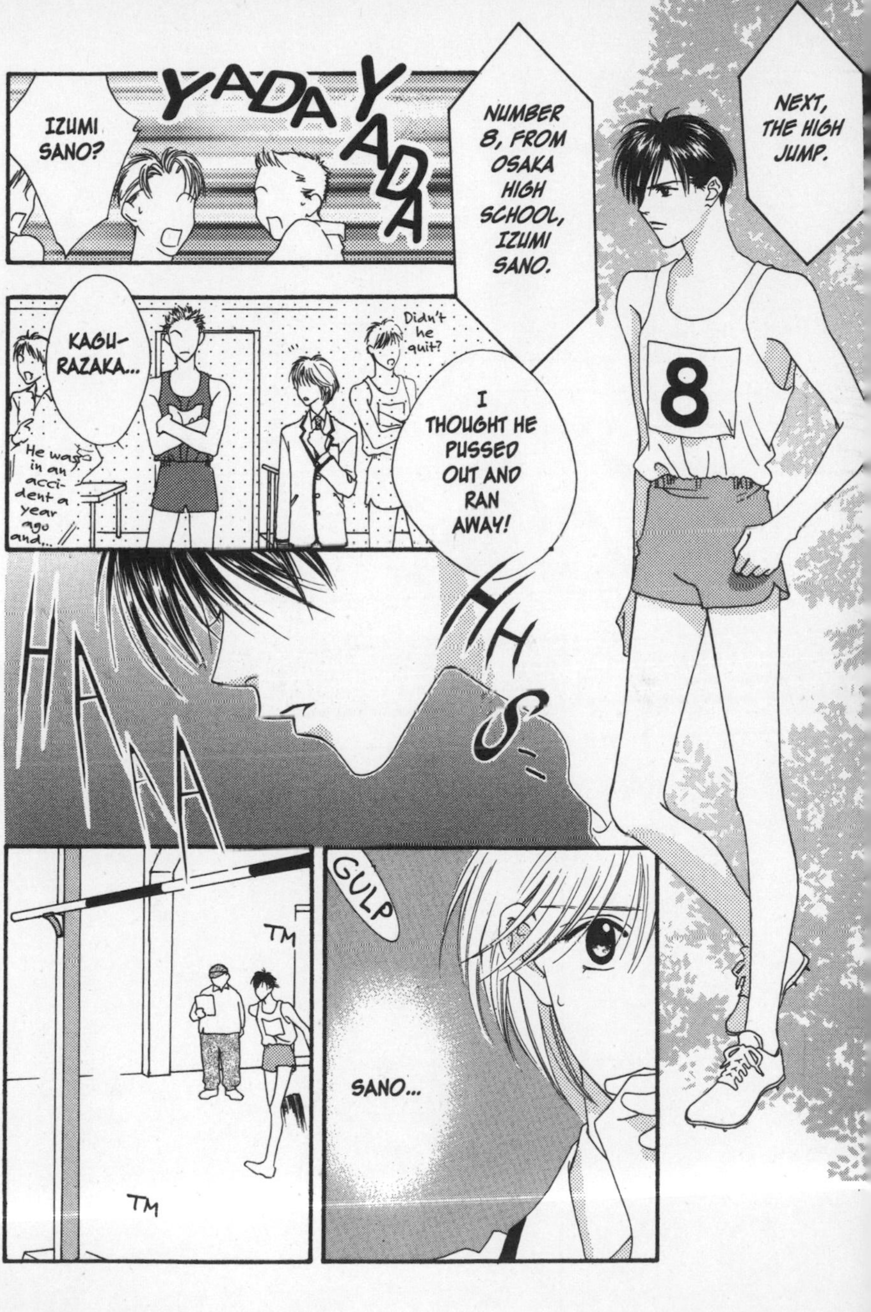
NEXT, THE HIGH JUMP.
NUMBER 8, FROM OSAKA HIGH SCHOOL, IZUMI SANO.
YADA YADA
IZUMI SANO?
I THOUGHT HE PUSSED OUT AND RAN AWAY!
Didn't he quit?
KAGU-RAZAKA...
He was in an acci-dent a year ago and...
HHS
HAAA
GULP
SANO...
TM
TM

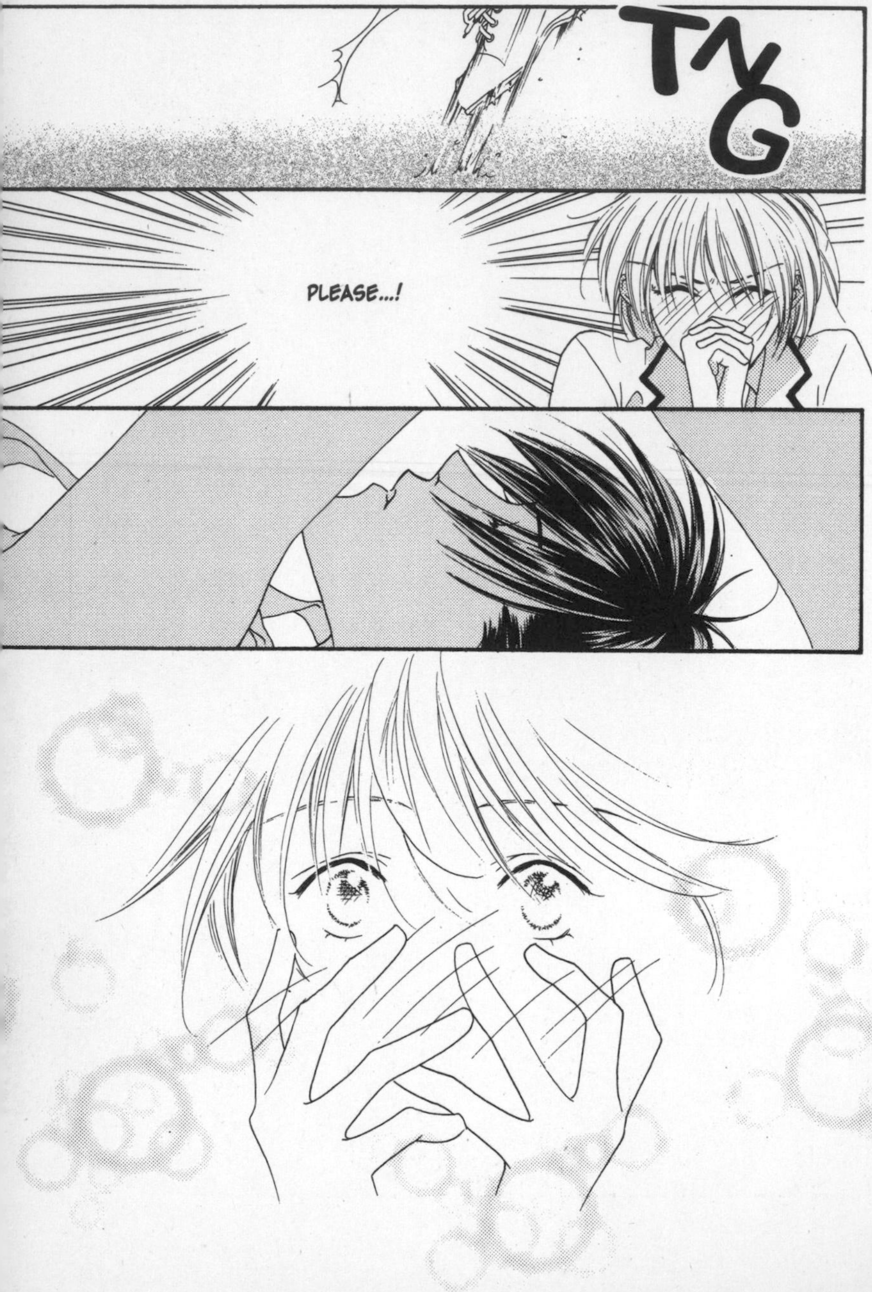
TING
PLEASE...!

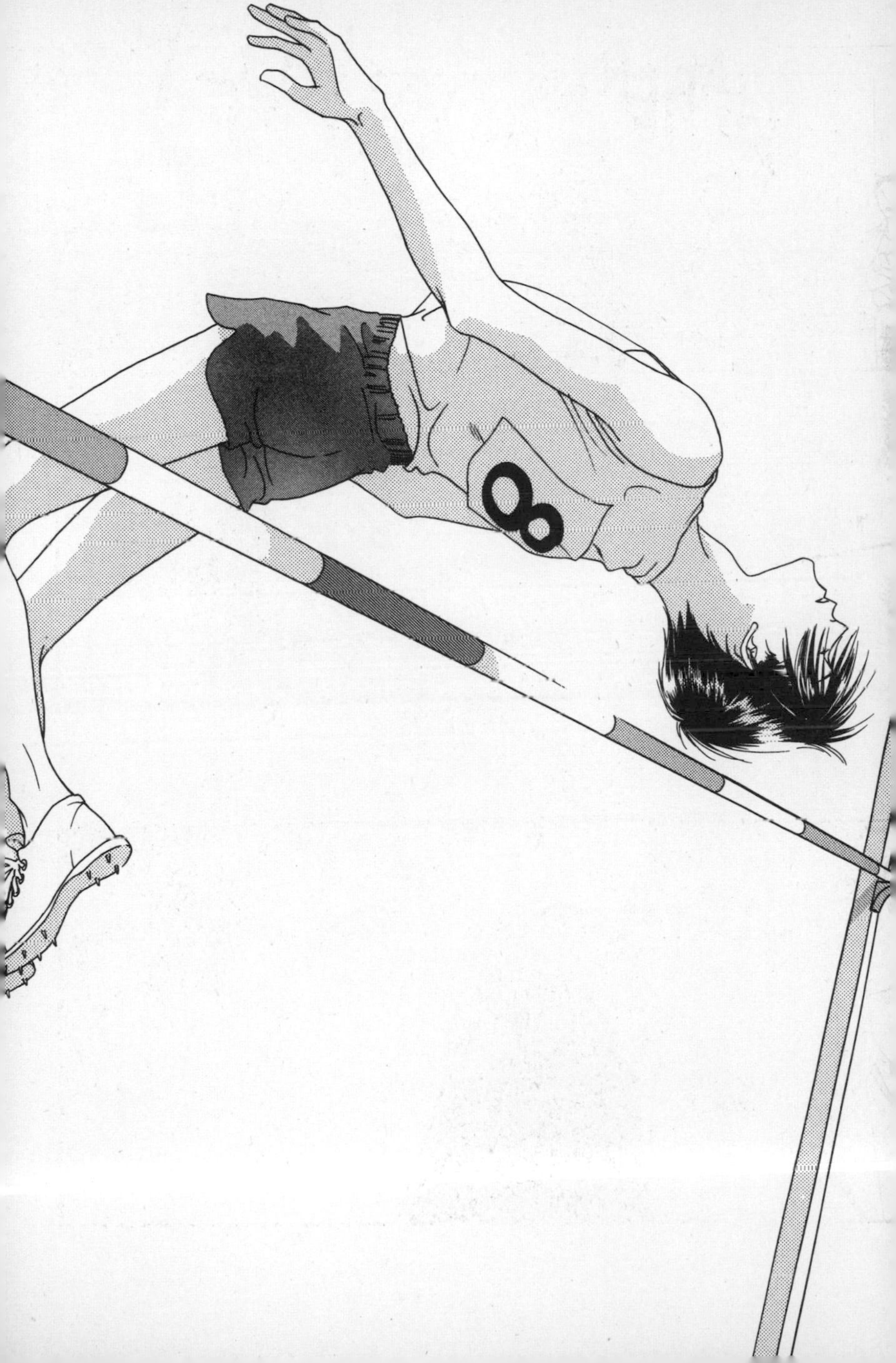
8

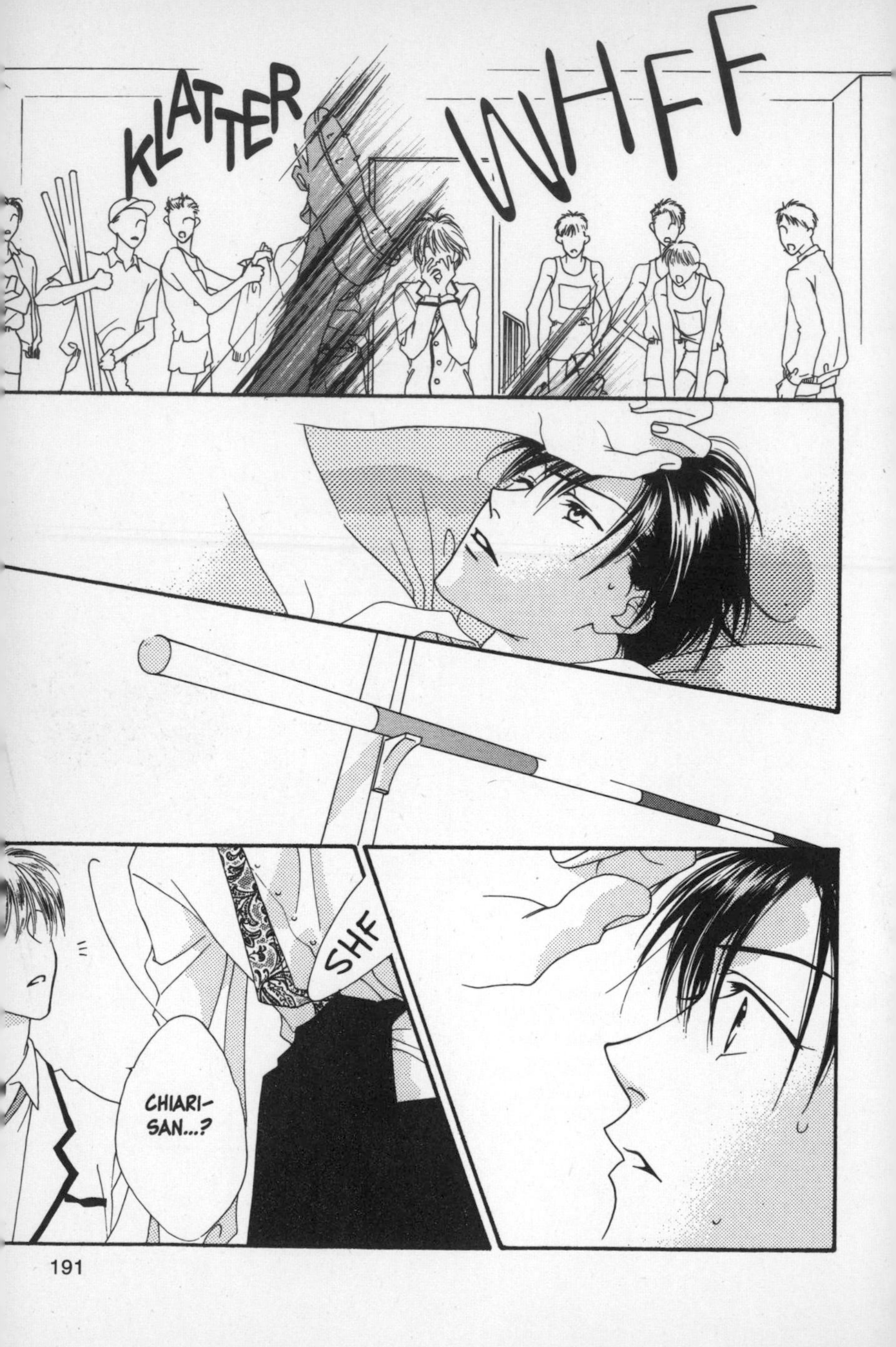
WHFF
KLATTER
SHF
CHIARI-SAN...?

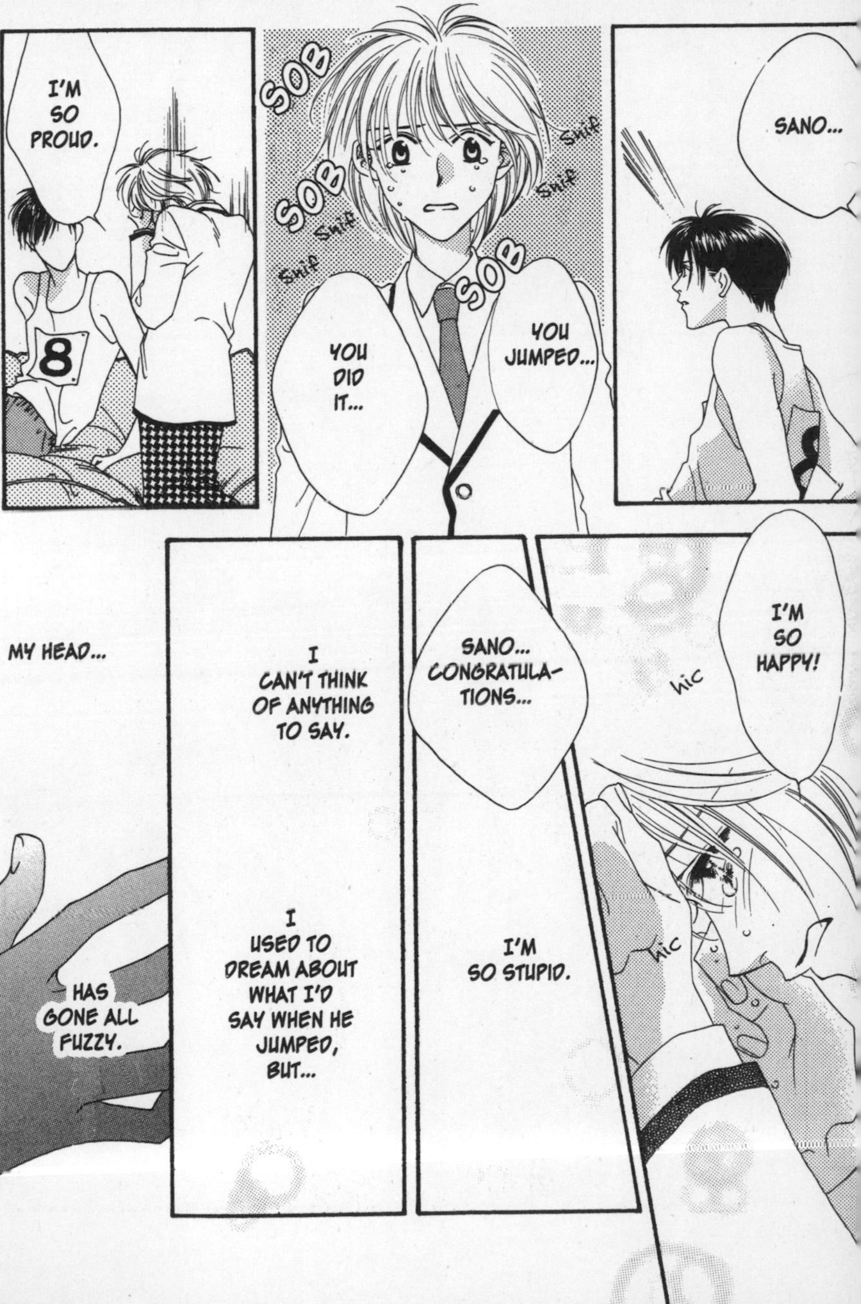
SANO...
SOB
SOB
SOB
Snif
Snif
Snif
Snif
YOU JUMPED...
YOU DID IT...
I'M SO PROUD.
I'M SO HAPPY!
hic
hic
SANO... CONGRATULA-TIONS...
I'M SO STUPID.
I CAN'T THINK OF ANYTHING TO SAY.
I USED TO DREAM ABOUT WHAT I'D SAY WHEN HE JUMPED, BUT...
MY HEAD...
HAS GONE ALL FUZZY.

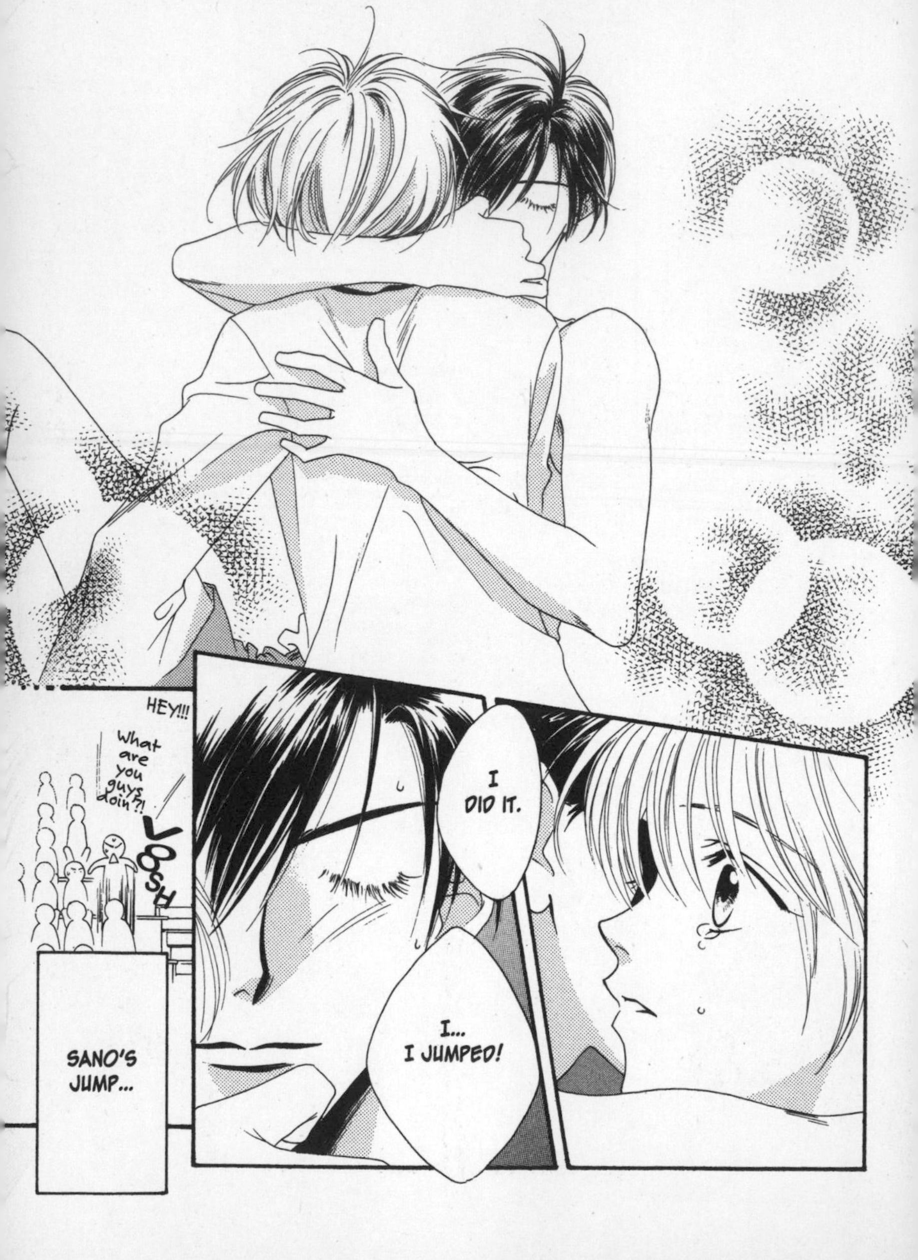
I DID IT.
I... I JUMPED!
HEY!!!
What are you guys doin'?!
VOOSH
SANO'S JUMP...

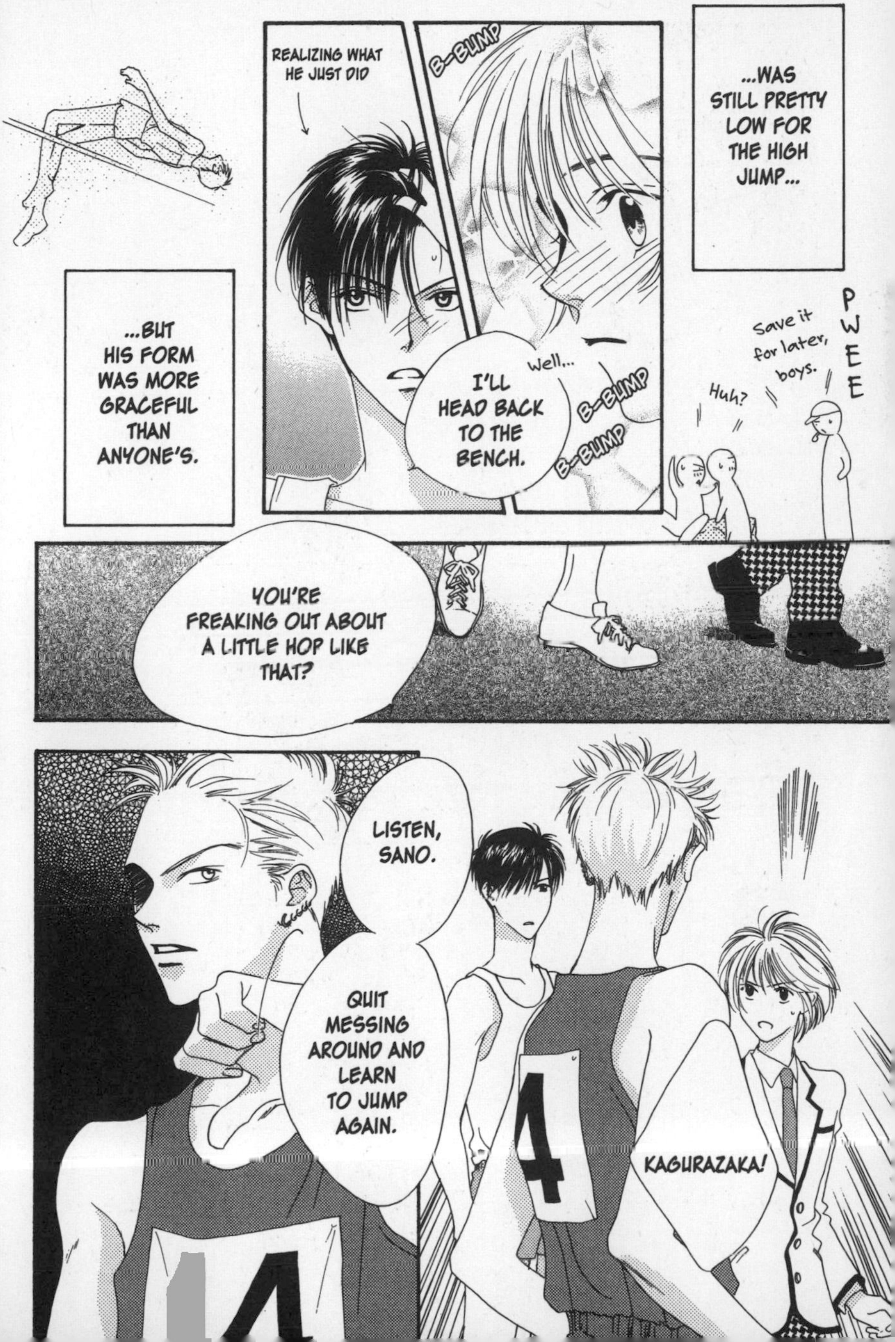

...WAS STILL PRETTY LOW FOR THE HIGH JUMP...
B-BUMP
Well...
B-BUMP
B-BUMP
I'LL HEAD BACK TO THE BENCH.
REALIZING WHAT HE JUST DID
...BUT HIS FORM WAS MORE GRACEFUL THAN ANYONE'S.
PWEE
Save it for later, boys.
Huh?
YOU'RE FREAKING OUT ABOUT A LITTLE HOP LIKE THAT?
KAGURAZAKA!
LISTEN, SANO.
QUIT MESSING AROUND AND LEARN TO JUMP AGAIN.

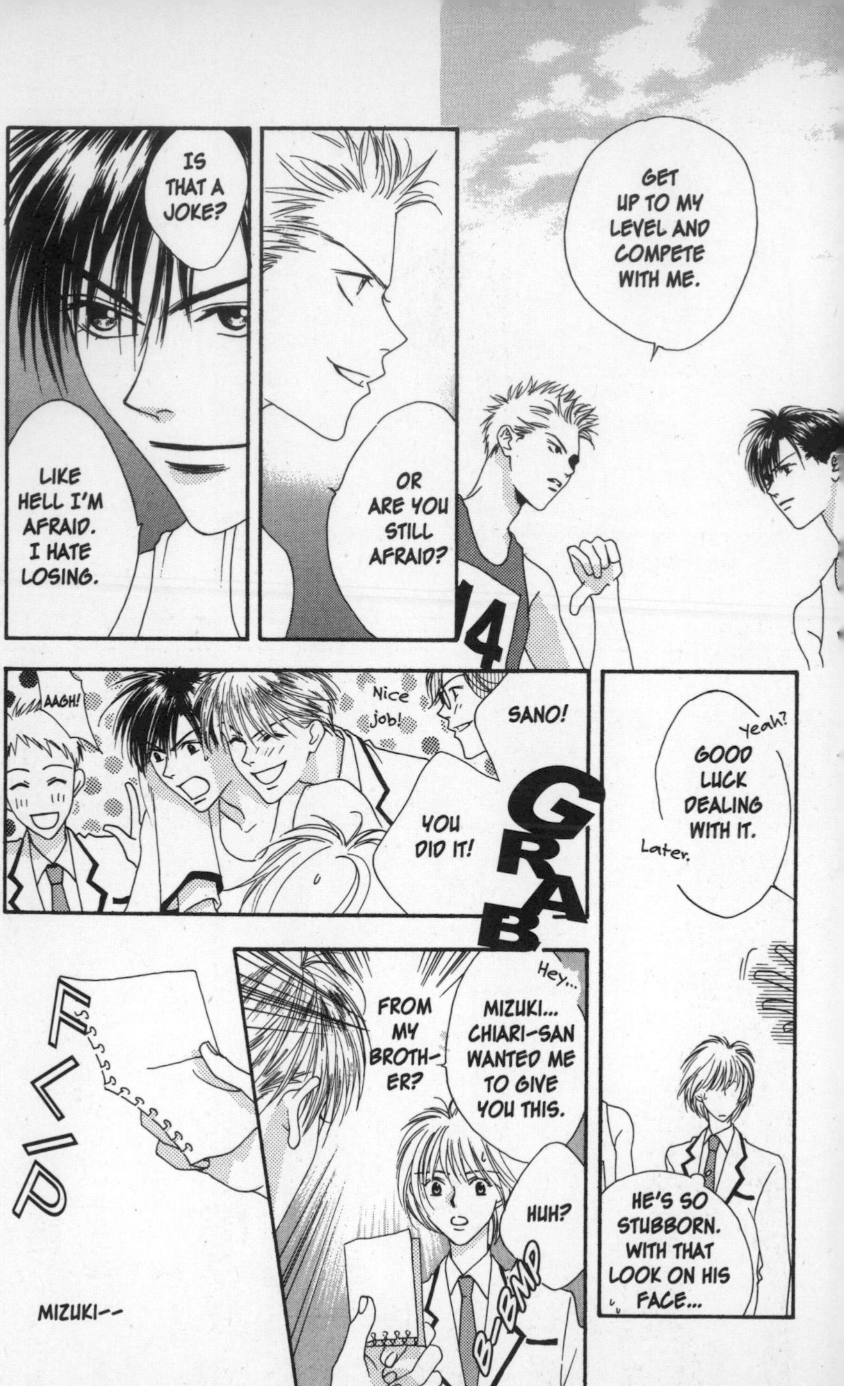
GET UP TO MY LEVEL AND COMPETE WITH ME.
OR ARE YOU STILL AFRAID?
IS THAT A JOKE?
LIKE HELL I'M AFRAID. I HATE LOSING.
Yeah?
GOOD LUCK DEALING WITH IT.
Later.
HE'S SO STUBBORN. WITH THAT LOOK ON HIS FACE...
SANO!
Nice job!
YOU DID IT!
AAGH!
GRAB
Hey...
MIZUKI... CHIARI-SAN WANTED ME TO GIVE YOU THIS.
FROM MY BROTHER?
HUH?
B-BMP
FLIP
MIZUKI--

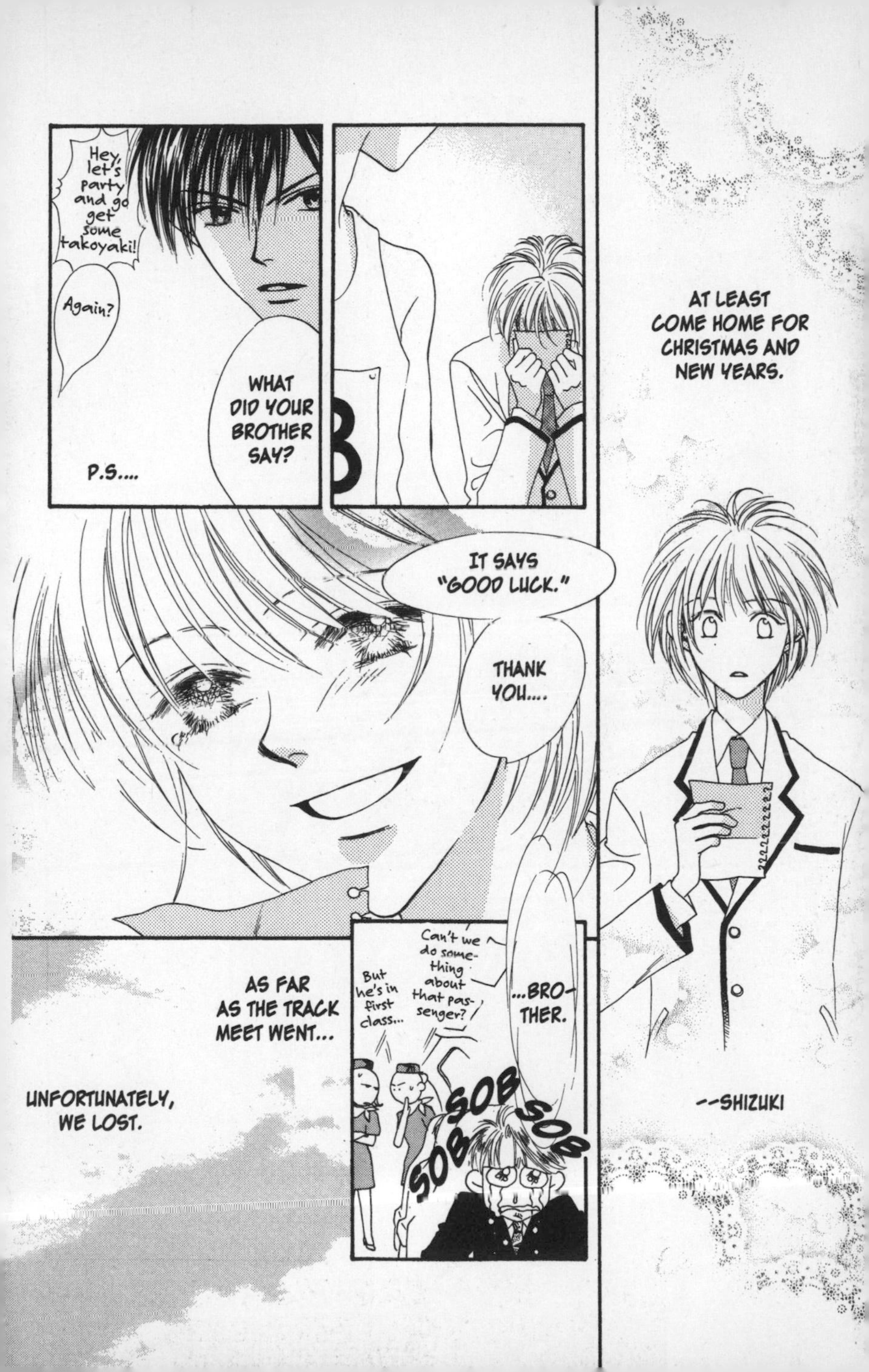
AT LEAST COME HOME FOR CHRISTMAS AND NEW YEARS.
--SHIZUKI
Hey, let's party and go get some takoyaki!
Again?
WHAT DID YOUR BROTHER SAY?
P.S....
IT SAYS "GOOD LUCK."
THANK YOU....
...BROTHER.
Can't we do something about that passenger?
But he's in first class...
SOB
SOB
SOB
AS FAR AS THE TRACK MEET WENT...
UNFORTUNATELY, WE LOST.

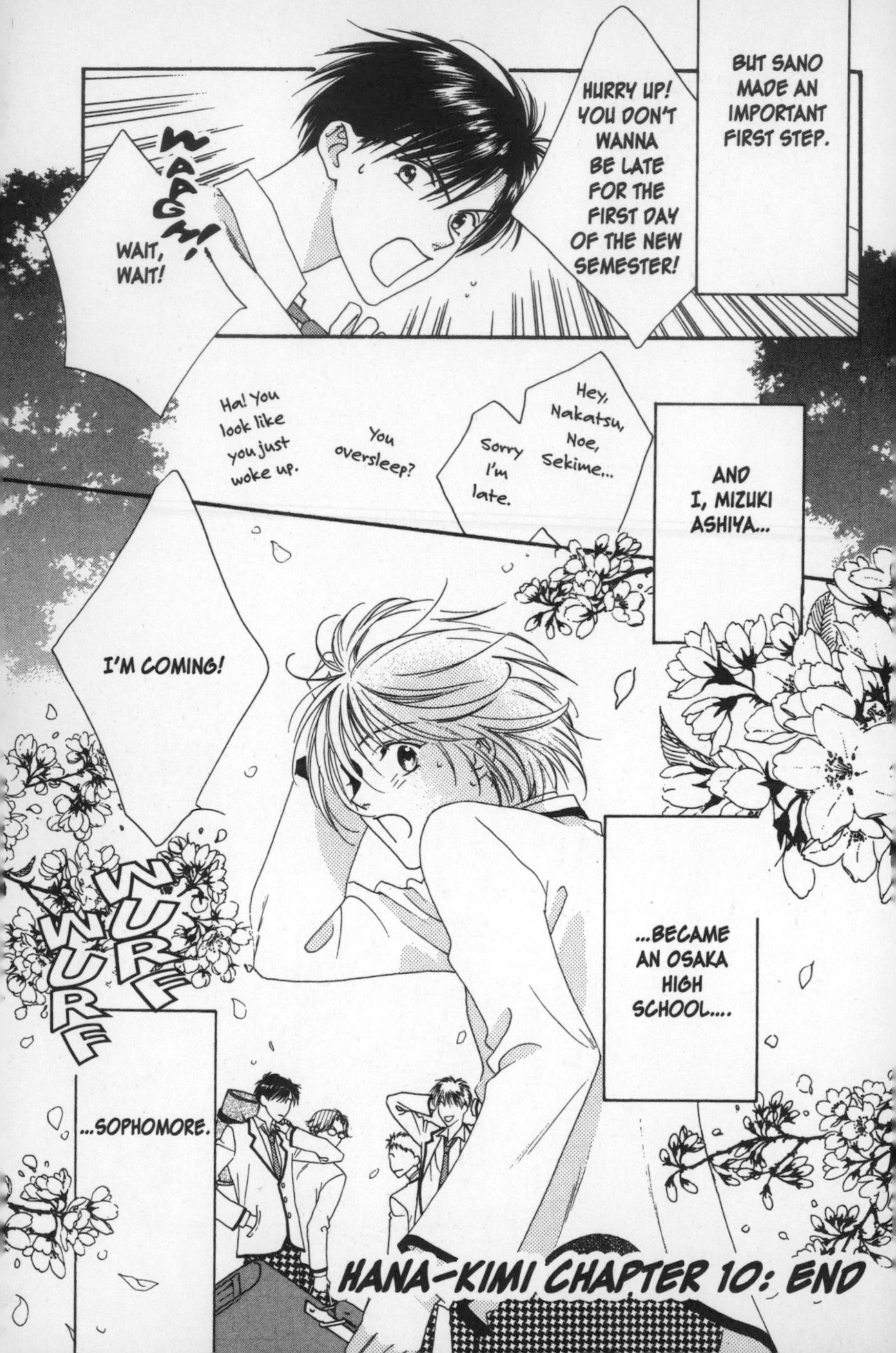
BUT SANO MADE AN IMPORTANT FIRST STEP.
HURRY UP! YOU DON'T WANNA BE LATE FOR THE FIRST DAY OF THE NEW SEMESTER!
WAAGH!
WAIT, WAIT!
AND I, MIZUKI ASHIYA...
Hey, Nakatsu, Noe, Sekime...
Sorry I'm late.
You oversleep?
Ha! You look like you just woke up.
I'M COMING!
...BECAME AN OSAKA HIGH SCHOOL....
WURF
WURF
...SOPHOMORE.
HANA-KIMI CHAPTER 10: END

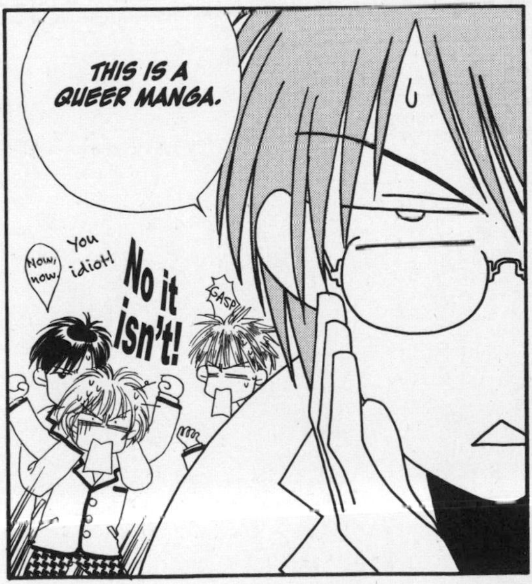
THIS IS A QUEER MANGA.
GASP
No it isn't!
You idiot!
Now, now.

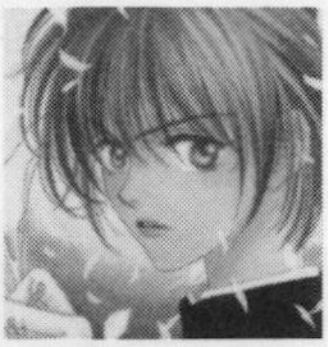

ABOUT THE AUTHOR

Hisaya Nakajo's manga series **Hanazakari no Kimitachi he** ("For You in Full Blossom", casually known as **Hana-Kimi**) has been a hit since it first appeared in 1997 in the shojo manga magazine **Hana to Yume** ("Flowers and Dreams"). In Japan, a **Hana-Kimi** art book and several "drama CDs" have been released. Her other manga series include **Missing Piece** (2 volumes) and **Yumemiru Happa** ("The Dreaming Leaf", 1 volume).

Hisaya Nakajo's website: **www.wild-vanilla.com**

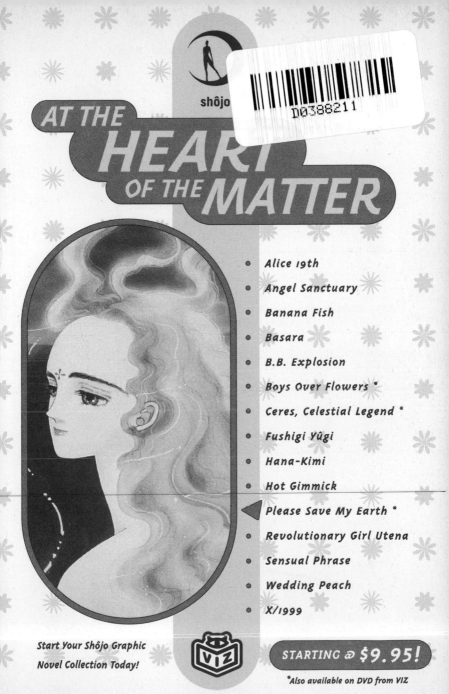